The Armies of A[ncient Persia]

From the founding of the Achaemenid State to the fall of the Sassanid Empire

By
Marek Adam Woźniak

The Armies of Ancient Persia: From the foundation of the Achaemenid State to the fall of the Sassanid Empire by Marek Adam Wozniak
Cover design by Jan Kostka
Inside Image by Dobroslaw Wierzbowski
Translated by Vincent W. Rospond

This edition published in 2019

Winged Hussar Publishing is an imprint of

                Pike and Powder Publishing Group LLC
17 Paddock Drive   1525 Hulse Rd, Unit 1
Lawrence, NJ 08648   Point Pleasant, NJ 08742

Copyright © Marel Adam Wozniak/ Winged Hussar Publishing, LLC
ISBN 978-1-945430-008-4
LCN 2019943225

Bibliographical References and Index
1. History. 2. Ancient. 3. Persia/Iran

Pike and Powder Publishing Group LLC All rights reserved
For more information on Pike and Powder Publishing Group, LLC,
visit us at www.PikeandPowder.com & www.wingedhussarpublishing.com

twitter: @pike_powder
facebook: @PikeandPowder

This book is sold subject to the condition that it shall not, by way of trade or otherwise, be lent, resold, hired out, or otherwise circulated without the publisher's prior consent in any form of binding or cover other than that in which it is published and without a similar condition, including this condition, being imposed on the subsequent purchaser.

The scanning, uploading, and distribution of this book via the Internet or via any other means without the permission of the publisher is illegal and punishable by law. Please purchase only authorized electronic editions, and do not participate in or encourage electronic piracy of copyrighted materials. Your support of the author's and publisher's rights is appreciated.

Dedicated to:

For Asia, becaue it is ...

The Armies of Ancient Persia

TABLE OF CONTENTS

Preface	3
Chapter I Achaemenid Empire and the Iranian Highland Kingdoms	24
Chapter II Arsacids - Kings from the steppe	123
Chapter III Sassanids - The Second Persian Empire	272
Appendices	330
Chronology	331
Glossary	337
Rulers of Persia	359
Bibliography	364

The Armies of Ancient Persia

PREFACE

Through several centuries of bloody conquests in Europe, Asia and Africa expertly trained legions of heavily armored infantry served as a key tool in implementing a policy of aggressive expansion. A young Roman Republic did not encounter worthy themselves opponents from the Cisalpine Celts, Italian Greeks, Carthaginians and finally powerful Macedonia - all fell successively under the blows of their swords. Only when Pompey and Lucullus expanded the range of power of the nascent empire to the tattered remnants of the once glorious Seleucid monarchy and invincible Roman infantry legions reached the Euphrates did Rome encountered strength, restrained their armies from marching east along the route of Alexander the Great for more than six centuries. The force that was occupying huge areas the current Iran, Turkmenistan and Iraq, the Parthian kingdom, and itd successors - the Persian Sassanid Empire. Thanks to the tremendous work of many generations of historians, we know a great deal about the organization and armament of the Roman legions as well as the previous conquerors of the east – the Macedonians, along with the principles that guided the strategy of their leaders. We still know very little about the armies of their principal antagonists, the Persian monarchies of the Achaemenid, Sassanid and Parthian Arscid Dynasty.

The earliest history of the south-western wing of the people known as "Indo-European" by linguists and historians "Indo-European" has long been shrouded in darkness. Archaeological research, however, coupled with new information acquired from ancient texts - mostly Assyrian and Babylonian has them arriving at the end of the second, at the beginning first millennium BCE from the Caucasus. These tribes that were already living in the steppes of present Ukraine and southern Russia began to gradually migrate through areas of present-day Armenia and Azerbaijan south along the coast of the Caspian Sea and the mighty Zagros Mountain range. Somewhere at the middle of the first millennium BCE, these warlike nomads were probably already divided on the historical predecessors of the Persians and Medes (Persians sometimes are considered a branch of the Medes) occupied the territory from the present province of Fars in Iran to the Iranian Kurdistan, the valleys of current Armenia, Georgia and Azerbaijan. Based on their tribal confederation they quickly grew into powerful military empires that in the course of history instrumentally contributed to great changes in the political landscape of the Ancient Near East.

The first empire was created by the Medes inhabiting the area around what is today Hamadan - ancient Ecbatana in the north-western Iran - in alliance the Chaldean Babylonia at the end of the seventh century BCE. This resulted in a series of bloody clashes that ended powerful and ancient empire of the Assyrians.[1] Aftr defeating the Lydians, the kingdom of the Medes under Cyrus the Great stretched his borders to the Halys River (today Kizylirmak) in Anatolia. Among the dozens of subject peoples themselves under these conquerors was the related tribe – the Persians.

The daughter of the Median ruler Astyages, married one of the most powerful of the Persian chiefs, Cambyses and from this relationship a son was born who would be one of the great victors in the history of the ancient world, know to history as the first Persian king - Cyrus the Great of the Achaemenid dynasty. According to the testimony of Herodotus - the first and most famous of the ancient Greek historians - his grandfather feared a prophesy that this child would usurp his power and wanted Cyrus killed. Instead he was hidden and raised by nomadic herders. The truth probably was a little less dramatic.

Perhaps the future ruler was not even a grandson of the king of the Medes and the kinship was implied after he gained power to legitimize his right to the throne, as well as having the blessings and divine mandate to rule - the so-called, "The Great". Around the year 553 BCE young Cyrus raised a rebellion against the authority of the Medes. After initial defeat, according to Herodotus, with the help Median nobles dissatisfied with the harsh way of governing by Astyages, and the Persian warriors of his own people, the two met in the great battles to defeat the Median royal army. Cyrus was finally able to defeat the royal army when some of the nobles defected. Astyages was defeated and sent into exile, where he stayed until his death (Herodotus, Bk. I, 130). In 550 BCE Cyrus' victorious troops marched to Ecbatana.

After this great victory he did not stop but continued to conquer territory. He had no problems taking Elam, followed around 548 BCE by capturing Hyrcania. His next prey was Armenia; in 547 BCE he took Lydia in Asia Minor after a short campaign, and in 539 BCE Babylon becoming the most powerful monarch to rule the ancient East. In the 529 BCE he

---
[1]K.Farokh, *Shadows In The Desert: Ancient Persia at War,* London 2007, p. 25.

attacked the Massagetae – nomadic warriors living in the steppes of Central Asia. Cyrus underestimated his opponent and the terrible battle that followed ended the massacre of his army as well as Cyrus being killed. More than likely his body was desecrated as the Massagetae were related to the Scythians who took the heads of the enemy. His body was eventually interned in a modest tomb complex at Pasargadae one of the capitals of the Achaemenid Empire. The tomb believed to be Cyrus' is still standing today.

Herodotus says the successor and ruler who continued the policy of the first king of the Persians was his son, Cambyses, who is often depicted as cruel. Under his command a mighty Persian army attack and conquered Egypt in 525 BCE. After a rather long struggle the invading forces made the once glorious empire of the Pharaohs into another satrapy - the largest province of the Achaemenid state. This Satrap was extremely rich, but also extremely rebellious. To allegedly prevent the newly conquered territories from rebelling, Cambyses allegedly not only committed atrocities, but also a blasphemy against religion and the temples of the gods. After completing the pacification of the newly acquired territory, the Great King decided to continue expansion. He sent his troops to conquer Ethiopia, but returned with nothing, decimated by the terrible conditions in the southern desert. He sent forces, out of Thebes northwest to command the oasis of Siwa which the locals considered the most holy oracle of Amon, but none supposedly returned. This supposedly dampened the enthusiasm of the Achaemenid and contributed to his madness.

Most likely the news about failures on campaign, and perhaps the long absence of a ruler and his army in Persia contributed to a rebellion in 522 BCE within the Persian heartlands led by Cambyses' brother named Bardija (or Tanooxares), who was proclaimed the king. No one knew, however, except for the mad Cambyses, his trusted envoy, and perhaps some courtiers, that the true Bardija was treacherously murdered on the orders of Cambyses at the beginning of the war with Egypt. Problems begin to arise out of the history of this tale. Herodotus seems to base his history regarding the murder Bardija on the official version circulated by the late King of Kings Darius, who as a participant in the so-called, "Conspiracy against Gaumāta" - which is very likely used to justify their usurpation. This is the tale placed on the famous relief carving near the present-day village Behistun upon orders of Darius along the ancient road from Babylon to Ecbatana. As represented, Bardija was Median Magus, which is probably Aryan priest – named Gaumāta. It has been proposed, however, that Bardija was actually the true brother of the King, and the whole story of his murder and usurpation had become a cover for the treacherous plot against him and the new, policy by Darius relegating the Medes to a secondary position. After the victory of the conspirators, it became the official version of the story.

> *"Betrayal is not conducive to happiness because it, favors those who will betray it."*

Cambyses did not return and suppress the rebellion himself. On the way back to Persia, he cut his thigh on a dagger that every mighty Persian wore tucked into the front of his belt while mounting his horse. Daggers like these are visible today on the so-called "relief of dignitaries" in Persepolis. In one version of the tale about this incident his scabbard was torn, he scratched himself and either did not know or did nothing about it. In the hot climates of Egypt and Palestine infection kills quickly. On his deathbed he supposedly had the most powerful nobles pledge to put down the rebellion and kill Bardija. They succeeded and as it happens Darius, was a highranking member of the king's bodyguard. The Magus was stabbed to death in his palace or fortress at Nisa in Media.

By the end of 522 BCE only one of the conspirators could claim the throne of the King of Kings, which is Darius. He created a pedigree, where he was not as one of Cambyses guard, but descendant of the Achaemenid family. So, is one of the greatest Achaemenid rulers a usurper? We might not ever know, but he was worthy successor of Cyrus. He spent the next year brutally suppressing a series of rebellions against his rule by the satraps of the Achaemenid nation. In one month of fighting he supposedly killed more than fifty-five thousand rebels. After dealing with uprisings Darius proceeded on a series of strong campaigns for further conquests. He expanded the borders of the state by attacking the Scythians called, "Saka Tigraauda," or "Sakae in the north-pointed caps" on the eastern borders of the empire and the Thracians on the borders of north-western. He only suffered defeat in 512 BCE during a trip to the area north-west Scythians, where nomads lived with their family across a boundless steppe where he could not come to grips with the enemy.

In 517 BCE the Persian armies occupied Egypt again after it succeeded in becoming independent for a short time, sometimes causing trouble for the invaders. Between 500 and 493 BCE he bloodily suppressed a huge uprising of Ionian Greeks in Asia Minor and Cyprus. In revenge for aid provided to insurgents with a few ships, Darius treated this as Cassus Belli, the army of Darius invaded the Greek mainland after previously occupying the Aegean islands. The first punitive expedition against the Greeks commenced in the year 492 BCE under the command of Mardonius from Asia Minor to the north-west and marched into Thrace. During one of the stops, he was attacked by Thracians. The Persians defeated them in a heavy, bloody battle before subduing them. Rather than continuing the march back to Asia, the whole Persian Army continued with the sole aim of conquering the Thracian lands in preparation for the invasion of mainland Greece.[2] The famous expedition started, however, against the Greek city-state of Athens in 490 BCE, was originally commanded by Datys and Artaphernes. First, the Persians occupied Euboea - an island off the coast of Attica, burning most of the local towns as well as Eretria, then landed on the seaside plain near the village of Marathon.

The Athenian army blocked the path of the Persians here. At this great battle approximately eleven thousand Athenian hoplites and Plataeans faced roughly fifteen thousand invading infantry who were deprived of cavalry support through a tactical error. After a failed Persian attempt to take the Athenians by surprise attack the Persian were outflanked. Realizing their peril, they turned and retreated.

Ten years later they returned, led by the King of Kings Xerxes, successor and son of the late Darius the Great in 486 BCE. The Achaemenid army included all the guard units, which only took part in the field under the command of the Great King. They continued by land from the north by the Balkan peninsula supported by a coastal fleet. The heroic resistance by the Greeks under the command of Leonidas consisting of three hundred Spartans and one thousand Plataeans died a heroes' death worthy of a Spartan before being swept away. Athens was eventually occupied and burned. Greeks subsequently won a naval battle at Salamis against the Royal Fleet in 480 BCE. The Greek morale, however, was not very high as the enemy still ravaged country. Then came news that Xerxes had to return to Babylon, to put down a rebellion. It is more likely, however, that the Persians had supply issues for such a large body of troops in the hilly Greek countryside. Faced with potential food shortages and the onset of winter they withdrew to their own territory with the intention of returning in the spring. The king took most of the best units back to Asia in 479 BCE, leaving Mardonius in command of a diminished force of only one thousand heavily armed Persian infantry forming his bodyguard, and the rest consisted of unarmoured archers and light troops on duty in Achaemenidian garrisons of occupation. He was also unsure about the loyalty of the veteran cavalry of the Thessalonian and Macedonian allies His other cavalry probably amounted to only a few thousand. It seems that Mardonius was planning to protect majority of the withdrawing forces, and as far as possible to maintain the main army during the wintering until the forces in Asia Minor returned. The Greeks, however, forced him to accept battle and defeated the Persians at Plataea in 479 BCE, where Mardonius was killed. The rest of the fleet and the remnants of his troops

---

[2] A. Kravchuk, *Marathon*, Warsaw 1989, p.167

were cut down at the subsequent battle of Mycale. The Greeks then tried to take the war to enemy territory. Several expeditions were sent to the Greeks of Asia Minor. After some initial successes in battle, the Satraps of the empire managed to fend them off. Even though Sparta and Athens provided a great deal of assistance to the rebellions these areas it did not help, and eventually the armies of the new king, Artaxerxes III Ochus gradually edged them out and destroyed the insurgent army.

One instance of Greek intervention in the Achaemenid Empire, however, was part of the collective memory of the Hellenes and the Persians. Ironically, this expedition was led by a Persian, Brother of the Great King Artaxerxes II - known as Cyrus the Younger. In 401/400 BCE using twelve thousand Greek mercenaries he tried to gain the throne. But, his forces were defeated at the battle of Cunaxa, a village in the middle of Mesopotamia, where Cyrus was killed. After their commanders were killed through treachery, the Greeks fought across hundreds of kilometers of Persian territory and lands of hostile tribes, until they reached the southern coast of the Black Sea and from there were able to return to Greece by ships. Their retreat is described by Xenophon is known in history as the "Ten Thousand". They went farther into the depths of the Achaemenid Empire, then anyone under arms until the time of Alexander III, called "the Great".

In the year 334 BCE with an army of slightly more than forty thousand men, the young monarch entered the continent as part of a contingent sent by Philip II - father of Alexander - to Asia Minor to seek military glory, booty and prey. In May of that year, the Macedonians defeated in the Persian Satraps at the battle of Granicus on the river, south of the Hellespont - today's Sea of Marmara. Later, in the year 333 BCE at Issus and again in 331 BCE at Gaugamela, Alexander defeated Imperial Persian forces led by the Great King Darius III. They marched east to India without suffering a major defeat, opening up those areas to Greek culture and the Greeks themselves to entirely new worlds.

With the death of Darius III, the Achaemenid Empire collapsed and passed into the hands of Alexander, who did not enjoy this achievement for too long. In 323 BCE he died under mysterious circumstances in Babylon, and the "Spear Won" state was torn by wars of succession waged by the generals of his army. Their reign began with descendants of Seleucus called Nicator in Asia, Antipater in Greece, Antigonus the One-Eyed in Asia Minor, while in Egypt it was Ptolemy Lagidy.

The Persian monarchy was reborn, however, faster than any of the Greek conquerors could have imagined, although it had not come from Persians, but a foreigner, Scythian in origin of the people and his dynasty. The new masters of Asia traced their origins to the military chieftains of the Parni, nomads inhabiting the steppe areas east of the Caspian Sea in the third century BCE. Somewhere around 239 BCE after the disastrous war between the Seleucids and the Ptolemy's, one of the provincial Satraps named Andragoras rebelled against the Seleucids, further disrupting the region and eventually falling to a confederation of Dahae tribes that included the Parni, who flooded into the north-eastern section of the Empire known as Parthia.

The leader of the Parni would later be known as Arsaces I of Persia. According to Strabo, however, he was not even a Parn ((Strab.XI.9, 3), but came from an area in northern Aparnian near the Bactrian border. There is disagreement on his origins, but the Parni seem to have been pushed west after their defeat by Diodotus in Bactria. Having killed Andragoras in battle, the Parni under Arsaces took over the province. Ruled by the ambitious leaders of the Arsacid dynasty, they quickly assumed the titles of Great King and King of Kings. This caused problems for the Seleucids however, even as they expanded their rule into nearby Hyrkania. This is bececause: I. the Seleucids army was not as powerful as it once was and, II. If attacked, the Parni would retreat into the steppes as nomads did and no one was brave enough to go after them.

During his eastern expedition of 209 BCE, Antiochus III managed to bring Parthia back under control when Arsaces II sued for peace as a vassal of the Seleucids, however, the Arsacids soon reasserted their independence. After the death of Antiochus III, Antiochus IV was distracted by other areas of his empire with more important things than half-nomad herdsman in remote border of his Empire. This was also the last chance he probably had to pacify these young, aggressive steppe warriors. Between 170 – 140 BCE Mithridates I created a strong foundation for the Parthians, conquering Media, Persia, Elymais, Characene and Mesopotamia.

Mithridates entered Bactria, which was also under attack in the northeast by the Yue-or, but the Parni were not as strong this area as they were in other locals like Farsa. When the Syrian Seleucid King Demetrius II tried to recapture territory lost to the Parthians such as Elymasi, and Persia, the powerful Greco-Bactrian state offered to help him. Despite this, Demetrius was defeated, but treated with honor because he was still politically useful. He was sent to Hyrkanian under guard and given a daughter of the Parthian king as his wife.

Another of Seleucid interventionists – Antiochus VII Sidetes failed much worse at trying to contain the Parthians. After some initial successes and victories by his well-trained Hellenistic style army in 129 BCE, the newly conquered territories erupted in rebellion under the supervision of Parthian supporters. At the same time Antiochus was forced to face a large Parnian-Parthian army in the field. In the ensuing battle, Antiochus was killed and thousands of his soldiers were forced to fight for the Parthian king against the invading Saka.

The Parthian king Phraates II, sent his opponent's body back to Antioch with full honors, then focused on the Saka, who began invading the former Seleucid territories with their steppe cousins and destroyed the kingdom, sacking the cities of Merv, Hekatompylos and Egbatane. They may have intended to attack the Parthian Kingdom next, reinforced by their cousins, the Yuezhi. They supposedly burnt old Nisa, the first capital of the Parthian state. When King Phrates II attempted to push back the Saka, many of the former Seleucid troops refused to fight against them and the King was killed in a great battle with the invaders around 124/123 BCE. His successor, Artaban II also died combatting the Saka leaving the country in a perilous position.

Finally, the ascension of another Arsacid, Mithridates II, brought a worthy candidate to the throne. He quickly put down a revolt of the Babylonian Governor and recaptured Oxus. The Yue's in Bactrian settlements posed a constant threat to the eastern and north-eastern borders of the Parthian Monarchy. The Seleucids, meanwhile, became embroiled in conflict with the growing strength of Rome, men vying for the throne and rebellions of conquered peoples (i.e. The Jewish Provinces). All this brought on increasingly severe economic difficulties which eventually led to their fall in 64 BCE as the sad remnants of the land was occupied by legions of Gnaeus Pompey who invaded Syria after his victory over King Mithridates III of Armenia.

Though the Arsacid Empire was torn by deadly invasions of the steppe people and rebellions, it was still a powerful force; powerful enough to return Mithridates III to the Armenian throne (58-55 BCE). This strength was quickly tested when one of the triumvirs, Marcus Licinius Crassus with more than thirty thousand soldiers attempted to conquer Northern Mesopotamia in 53 BCE. However, Crassus made a big mistake by ignoring the advice of his Armenian allies and was betrayed by his guides. He was encouraged to deploy near the village of Carrhae (Harran), on a desolate desert plain, surrounded by ten thousand Parthian cavalry under the nobleman Surena, of which ninety percent of this force were lightly armed horse archers. For nearly two days the Romans remained under a constant hail of arrows. Cut off from water sources and the impossibility of withdrawal, hundreds of legionnaires died a horrible death. Crassus' son, Publius, died after his men were cutoff, while the general himself was murdered during surrender negotiations. This painful lesson dampened the Roman appetite of conquest in the east for twenty years.

The Armies of Ancient Persia

In 51 BCE however, the Parthians decided for a "follow-up blow" hitting Syria and almost reaching Jerusalem. Despite initial successes, they were not accustomed to fighting on battlefields unfavorable to cavalry. In 40 BCE, without good infantry support the Parthian forces were trapped by Roman soldiers and beaten, resulting in the death of their commander Pacorus, the son of King Orodesa II.

The continuation of the "struggles of giants" was picked up by the triumvirs. In 36 BCE Marcus Antonius, learning from the terrible example of Crassus, used that knowledge to move through the mountains of Armenia attacking the Arsacidian state from the northwest through Media at Atropantene, around today's Iranian Kurdistan. This expedition, however, did not end much better than Crassus. Though going an easier route through mountain passes, camps with ballistae were subject to ambushes and his forces were defeated near Fraaspa. Deprived of conquering this fortress, they were surrounded by units of Parthian cavalry. In this position, the Roman forces were cut off from supplies from Roman depots. With nothing else coming through, they faced the necessity to retreat. Attacked from all sides, the invaders began melting away at an alarming rate. The remaining troops suffered from hunger in the wastes of the mountain passes. The next expedition in 34 BCE bore no greater fruit and Antonius abandoned hope of expanding the borders at the expense of the Arsacidian monarchy. For a long time after this there was peace between both sides.

The embers of war then burned constantly in Armenia. As a result of Parthian intervention and uprisings in the first century AD the local Prince Rhadamistas was replaced by Tiridates, the brother of the Parthian King Vologeses. What is not understandable is how this appealed to the Romans, but in the 50's and 60's AD there were a series of bloody wars under the command of the outstanding Roman general, Gnaeus Corbulo. The Parthians faced many natural disasters, but also suppressed simultaneous rebellions in their lands, defeated a great invasion of the Kushan's, who reached Hyrcania and finally displaced Nero's legions from Armenia. Tiridates not only maintained the throne but was able to get confirmation of his authority by the Roman Emperor in exchange for a public homage. The entrance of the eastern monarch into Rome in 66 A.D. was one of the most splendid spectacles the city had ever seen.

Following the end of the "Parthian Wars" relations between the Arsacidian and Roman Empires quieted down. Both empires were busy cleaning up their affairs durimh this period. The Romans were forced to cruelly suppress the Jewish uprising known as, "the first Jewish War". The Arsacids fought subsequent attempts to usurp the throne by other members of the family as well as invasions from the steppe people.

The Armies of Ancient Persia

The two giants, "took to battle" again at the start of the second century AD. The reason again centered on non-approved modifications to the Armenian throne. The Parthian placed the reigning prince Ashkhadar, on the throne without consulting Rome, only to replace him with his brother Partamasir. For the Emperor Trajan, however, with the end of the "Dacian Wars" in 104 A.D., this was a "Cassus Belli".

There were several reasons prompting the Romans for direct intervention in Armenia and Mesopotamia. First, in 106 AD, they annexed a weakened Nabatean state. Officially its Arab kings remained neutral or sometimes allied with Rome. Unofficially it was known that the Parthians maintained a close relationship with the kingdoms of the Arab Gulf Coast along with the Persians and Arabs of Mesopotamia. This led the Parthians to be concerned about the proximity of a powerful neighbor who had already subjugated the client kings of the east, the ruler of the Nabateans and massacred the Jews. The Parthians decided it was necessary to make these borders safer for them, or at least enable them to check Roman advance from the eastern provinces. It was also possible that with a camel corps with Arab guides they could strike at Palestine, not from the north, but from the desert. Trajan could not afford to leave an unprotected flank during an expedition deep into enemy territory.

After taking over Nabatea and their capital at Petra in 114 AD, the Romans first struck Armenia, and later headed for Mesopotamia. Their success was incredible, overcoming many brave soldiers of the client kingdoms which the Arsacid kingdom could not effectively resist. The Parthians tried to mobilize their client states, but all the vassals possessed different degrees of independence - most were more occupied with internal strife than beating off the invasion.

In 116 AD Trajan gained control of all Armenia and northern Mesopotamia, until the Roman legions reached the coast of the Persian Gulf. Then, however, the situation turned around. As a result of activity by Parthian agents, Jewish zealots in Alexandria and on Cyrus exploded in uprisings against Rome. Additionally, a large number of Parthian forces attacked northern Mesopotamia. The Romans began to feel the effects of terrible climate, lack of food and equipment combined with increased harassment in guerilla actions. In 117 AD Trajan decided to withdraw troops from the conquered territories.

The successor of Trajan, Hadrian, made no attempt to follow in the footsteps of its predecessor. He had bigger issues, dealing with constant Jewish rebellions. Rome did not abandoned plans, however, for the conquest of the crumbling Parthian kingdom. In 163 AD, the Legions of Lucius Verus moved in the footsteps of Trajan. In 114 the Arsacid could not put up an effective resistance. Many cities of key strategic and economic importance (i.e. Dura-Europa) fell. Even today, around the ancient walls of Hatry in northern Mesopotamia the earthworks dug by the Romans as a position for siege machines are still visible.

When the capital of the Arsacid, Ctesiphon fell, the situation seemed tragic for the Parthians. The invaders did not know that pestilence reigned in those areas of Parthia. When the legionaries began to die by the thousands, their terrified commanders gave the worst possible orders and deciding to pull back. The retreating units dragged the invisible death to their own country. The terrible epidemic killed tens of thousands of people including the Emperor himself. For a long time, the Romans were terribly afraid of crossing the Persian border again. They overcame this fear at the end of the second century, invading again and causing great political trouble for their neighbor. This expedition did not meet with great success either and then the border remained static for some time.

The beginning of the third century AD brought great trouble to Rome and huge changes to Persia. Arsacid dynasty was dying, torn apart by terrible battles and constant clashes with other principalities in the kingdom. The situation resembled the worst of the "War of the Diadochi", the "Warring States Period" in China and "Sengoku" in medieval Japan.

At the beginning of the third century AD, in the cradle of Persian state at Parsi, a local prince, Papak, defeated rivals and declared himself king, completely disregarding the sovereignty of the Arsacid kings. His son Ardashir did not stop with the achievements of his father and followed up with conquests of neighboring principalities. He continued onward and through military intervention took the throne from Shahanshah Artabanus V on 28 April 224 AD near the village of Hormozdgān in a battle between the two rulers. Artaban was defeated and killed, and his head was exposed to public view in the temple of the goddess Anahity in Perepolis. After the victory, Ardashir gradually completed the conquest of most of the former Arsacid state. His victories created such an impression that offers of friendship came from deputies of the powerful Kushan Empire in Bactria.

From the beginning of its history the Sassanids attitude were much more nationalistically than their predecessors. They appealed to the Achemenidian tradition, and as the "True Farsi's" of Persia, sincerely intending to return the boundaries of the ancient empire of Darius the Great. The Persians initiated the war with the Romans, but this was viewed as part of the continued quarreling with the Parthians. In 233 AD Ardashir defeated the great army of Alexander Severus at Ctesiphon. This campaign started off well enough for the Romans by forcing the enemy to retreat and occupying Hatra; but that was only at the beginning of the campaign.

After the death of Ardashir, his son Shapur enthusiastically moved forward with his father's plans. In 244 AD, using the confusion of the eastern provinces, the Romans under the Emperor Gordian, invaded the Persian Empire, occupying most of northern Mesopotamia and coming close to the vicinity of the Sassanid capital. The decisive battle took place at Misiche near Ctesiphon where the Romans suffered a rout and the Emperor Gordian III was killed. The remnants of his troops were barely able to retreat to Syria. The successor to the fallen ruler was the newly appointed Emperor called Philip the Arab. Finding himself in a difficult situation, he was forced to sign a humiliating peace, agreeing among other things to pay the Persians five hundred thousand gold denars as a penalty as well as withholding support for the Armenian Arsacids against the Sasanids.

Approximately 256 AD Shapur initiated an attack on the Roman frontier. First, he attacked Mesopotamia, later Syria as well as a large part of Asia Minor. The Persian Army captured and burned remaining Roman outposts including Dura-Europos, proceeding as far as Antioch – the former capital of the Seleucid kingdom. In the year 258 AD around Edessa, Shapur blocked the way of a seventy-thousand man Roman Army under the command of the Emperor Valerian. In a hard-fought battle, the Romans were routed, and the Emperor was captured. Valerian was sent into captivity where there is some debate on what happened to him. Roman soldiers captured at Edessa were sent as prisoners to Gundishapur where they built bridges and helped with the construction of the new city of Biszapur. After their great victory, the Persian Army they entered Cappadocia burning and pillaging. The remnants of the Roman troops retreated suffering heavy losses. Was it not for an unexpected attack of Arabs, probably on camels by the ruler of Palmyra, Odaenathus, returning the borders of Persia to the time of Darius would have been quite real.

The Palmyrians together with thousands of warriors along with their allies from the Arab tribes, marched out from the northeast desert striking the Persian supply routes and later attacked Shapur's army returning from Anatolia. The Persian forces pulled from all corners of the empire was ill-prepared for defending against guerilla warfare, withdrew to central Mesopotamia giving back most of territorial gains. The anemic Romans, with much to gain from Oaenathus, gave him no support and were not able to capture the bordering areas of their powerful neighbor. After stabilizing the situation on the western borders of the empire the Persian army moved east. The once mighty state of Kushan was destroyed without any major problems. Part was incorporated into the Sassanid Empire while the other lands and established the so-called invaders established a Kushano-Sassanid state with a ruler coming from the Sassanid dynasty.

After the significant conquests on the eastern borders of the state, Shapur, many years older, decided to move into the area around the Caucasus. The motivation for this action was the unrest caused by the assassination of the King of Armenia. The Persians settled this by placing Hormizd, the son of the King of Kings. He was from Iran and part of the Sassanid royal family as well as the throne of Lazyki (part of today's western-Georgia).

After the death of Shapur I (the Great) in 272 AD the intensity of the battles was significantly reduced. The interest in expanding Persia's borders was weakened by new religious influences, particularly the development of orthodox Zoroastrianism. The most important figure of this period was the all-powerful priest Kartir – a figure resembling the ability to intrigue like Cardinal Richelieu. Thanks to Kartir, after the death of Shapur, he promoted Hormizd I to ascend the throne, not his brothers Narse or Bahram. Raids on the eastern provinces of the Roman Empire did not stop completely however. The Roman border force made it difficult for the Persians to maintain the status quo. Over time the struggle started to favor the Romans. They were able to push the Persians in northern Mesopotamia to the Tigris and further their interest in Armenia.

The succeeding rulers of Shah did not have the abilities of Ardashir or Shapur and were not able to master the situation. The important and most powerful feudal clans weakened the power of the King of Kings. There were numerous attempts at usurpation, as well as constant invasions from the implacable enemy of the Persians – Rome. In this momentary weakness the enemy saw the chance to recover lost land and revenue from the time of Shapur. Finally, Shah Bahram II was able to repel the invasion of the Roman Emperor Carus, who managed to sack Ctesiphon, put down a revolt by his cousin Hormizd who occupied the throne of Kushan. Another Sassanid rule, Hormizd II, Narseh's son, finally won the throne by force, resisting attempts to usurp the throne by Prince Papak and these were not exceptions to the problems they faced. In 309 A.D. the King of Kings was given to the under-age Shapur II, also known as "The Great". Thanks to the support of the clergy and the goodwill of the regents he was able to live to the age of majority which was no mean feat in the Sassanid Court. After taking power he re-established the power of the Shah. In 345-348 A.D. in the example of his namesake led campaigns in Northern Mesopotamia but not significantly change the status quo. This invasion, however, was to be a harbinger of a bad future for the eastern provinces of the Roman Empire.

The Armies of Ancient Persia

After the end of the war with the Romans, the young Shapur II sent a punitive expedition against the Arabs and in 357 A.D. he defeated the eastern nomad Hionita (Scythian Massagetae). These brave warriors could not overcome the Persian forces and they ceased ravaging the border of the Sassanid Kingdom. Eventually, they agreed to become vassals of the Persians and provide military support.

In 359 A.D. Shapur launched another great expedition against the Romans in Mesopotamia and Syria. The military superiority of the Persians was so overwhelming that their opponents did not risk fighting in the open field and retreated, using scorched earth tactics. Shapur's army took many cities whose populations were slaughtered or sent back to Persia. During this expedition the King of Kings army contained a large contingent of Hun cavalry.

After a series of terrible and bloody battles the Romans managed to oust the Persians from the occupied territories, but they did not recover all of them. In 363 A.D. the Emperor Julian organized a punitive expedition which entered deep into enemy territory in the course of his campaigns against the Persians. Shapur's armies were still very powerful and stopped the invaders around Ctesiphon. The Emperor died during the battle, possibly killed by one of his soldiers. The remainder of the Roman Army was constantly harassed by guerilla activities and barely reached the borders of the empire. On top of this defeat, the Persians negotiated a treaty with the new Emperor Jovian that gave the Persians control of Armenia. The forts and fortifications of the western border on the edge of desert were also strengthened. At this time, Shapur II hired mercenaries from the Lakhmid tribe to protect Sassanid's Mesopotamia against raids from desert nomads and the pro-Roman Ghassanids.

After the death of Shapur II the situation on the border between the two empires calmed down as the Persians experienced internal contention for the throne. The border town of Nisibis passed back and forth during this period.

The Byzantine historian Procopius claimed that the border fighting lost momentum because the border lands had been terribly destroyed. The Byzantines under Theodosius II celebrated a victory over the Sassanid Bahram V in Armenia, however, this was not significant since after this defeat the Persians could still easily resist an invasion by the Hephtalites (White Huns) and proved they were still strong enough that in 451 A.D. Shah Yazdegerd II invaded Armenia. It was not however, the powerful empire of Shapur II.

The successor of Yazdegerd II was Peroz, who was forced to deal with a huge invasion to the northeast borders by the Hephtalites. The Shah met the dangerous invaders on the battlefield at Herat in 484 A.D.

and was killed along with most of his army. His successor, Peroz Balaz found himself in a difficult situation and was forced to pay tribute to the Hephtalites. The Persians had been committed to support the nobility of Armenia, this support was not maintained, however, and after four years the king was overthrone in a court coup.

The next Shah of note was Kavadh, who had to deal with nobles who were becoming too independent and forced him to seek refuge with the Hephtalites. The two years of the reign of the usurper Djamasp were marked by the rise in popularity of the Mazdak rebellion. Then, Kavadh returned at the head of Hephtalite troops. He sought to limit the powers of the nobility who forced his exile and winning the support of the rebels was able to regain control to the country. This success did not mean this was the end of succession conflicts.

Out of the chaos of this situation came one of the most famous Sassanid rulers - Khosrow I (Chosroes or Anushiruwan). He finally crushed the Mazdak, conducted military reforms aimed at reducing the importance of powerful feudal families and subject lower nobility from private armies not under the control of the Shah and his commanders. He adapted his army to fight the highly mobile troops of the nomadic tribal people because he was tired of the Hephtalites from ravaging the eastern areas of the country.

In 540 A.D. during a war against the Byzantines, Khosrow I captured Antioch and significant parts of Syria. His armies withdrew only after receiving significant contributions of gold and tribute from cities in exchange for breaking the sieges and leaving. Emboldened by these victories the Persians also took Lazica (the western part of Georgia), that the Byzantines had regained after fifteen years of war, receiving additional payments in gold. On the eastern border Khosrow formed an alliance with the Turks and then went on to destroy the Hephtalite state. Unfortunately, the Turks turned out to be just as bad neighbors. Approximately 570 A.D. the Persians succeeded in occupying Yeman and thus took control of the so-called, "Trail of Incense".

Despite the many wars he fought, Khosrow did not stop his efforts to secure and stabilize the state's borders. He extended a line of fortifications along the borders of the steppe people: i.e. a powerful defensive line on the pass between Derbent on the eastern end of the Caucasus Mountains and the Black Sea coast. Around this time the King of Kings returned to the old habit of the Achaemenid to stop leading cavalry charges in person and commanding the army from specifically located positions in the hills.

The successor of Khosrow was clever and talented, but his talents were no match for the great reformer. The huge and powerful former empire began to crumble fast. Rebellions, usurpations and continuous war with the Byzantines sometimes led to the depletion of the state's resources. At this time, attacks by the Turks began to intensify. One such invasion was successfully repulsed by the Persian general of Parthian origin, Bahram Czobin, of the famous Mihran clan. He was a powerful commander who was victorious in Armenia and the Byzantine border. He almost took the throne from one of the great Shah's, Khosrow II "The Victorious". Khosrow recovered his throne in 591 AD, but only with the support of the Byzantines and Armenians. Bahram was defeated only after a long and exhausting war in conjunction with the Turks. Most likely he was murdered by agents of "The Victorious".

Khosrow II maintained peaceful relations with the Byzantines while the Emperor Maurice ruled. When he was murdered in 602 AD Khosrow marched with a huge army to the borders of the Roman Empire, announcing that he intended to avenge him and his five sons. He divided his army into two columns which marked its trail with devastation and graves. The army quickly captured Dara and Edessa.

The Persian first column moved through Asia Minor towards the Byzantine capital at Constantinople. The second followed south through Syria and Palestine to Egypt, burning and murdering civilians. The Persian Army also attacked Cyprus and occupied Rhodes. In 619 A.D. Alexandra fell. In 626 A.D. the Persian armies stood under the walls of Constantinople and it seemed that the young Khosrow would accomplish something his ancestors sought, creating a monarchy that srteched from Asia Minor in the north to Yemen and southern ends of the Hijaz in the Arabian Peninsula, from Egypt in the west to India in the east – even larger in size than the Empire of the legendary Darius the Great.

At this point, the Byzantines decided to take a mad step but showed a brilliant future. Leaving regents in the city they loaded as many soldiers as they could into ships and sent them to Lazik in the Causcasus. From there, the seventy-thousand man army under the command of the Emperor Heraclius was preparing for a decisive attack on northern Mesopotamia and Armenia. At the same time the Byzantines moved through the northern passes of the Caucasus' passes at Hazara. As a result of these actions the Persians fighting in Asia Minor and the Levant were threatened to be cut off. Khosrow pulled up the siege of Constantinople and returning all the troops in Anatolia back to Mesopotamia. After several tense years, the Byzantines launched a decisive offensive occupying north-eastern Mesopotamia and entering the Medes homeland. The Byzantine Army seized and burned the most sacred of Persian temples, the Great Royal Fire Temple at Sziz, Takht-e-Soleiman and others in Ctesiphon. In November 628 A.D., Khosrow II was assassinated by a group

Battle shown on a golden comb from the mound at Soloch

of noble conspirators' intent on making peace with the Byzantines. His successor Kavadh II, "Siroe", immediately asked the Emperor Heraclius for peace and returned the relic of the True Cross to Jerusalem.

The death of Khosrow effectively meant the end of the power of the Sassanids. Relentless struggles for the throne broke the power of the nation and the prestige of the kingship. This is best evidenced by the fact that when the daughter of Chosroes and regent, Boran, died in 632 A.D. and Yazdegerd III ascended the throne, twelves Shahanshahs had ruled in the last four years. The Persians were so caught up in their internal struggles that they did not recognize the new power growing to their south on the Arabian Peninsula. When they finally turned their attention to that direction the enemy was standing at their borders.

The Persians initially experienced varying degrees of success against the Moslem forces. As early as 610 A.D. the Persians repelled an Arab invasion at the battle of Dhu-Qar. In 633 A.D., however, the situation of the Sassanid's was much worse. They were weakened by many years of war against the Byzantine Empire and internal strife. A huge army of Caliph Khalid ibn al-Walid took Hira and used it as a great base to stage further invasions. The Arabs occupied Ctesiphon as early as 638 A.D., but the devastating defeats at the battles of Qadisiya Ram Hormuz and Nehawend incurred by the Perian army sealed the fate of the empire of the last of the Sassanids. Yazdegard III, first hid in a mountain fortress and later moved to Bactria. He reportedly sought help from the Emperor of China, but he was murdered in exile around the area of Merv.

So here is briefly presented more than 1,100 years of the history of the ancient empire of Persia. Of course, this a just a kind of introduction, and this description is far from detailed. Many details of the history of ancient Persia is still an object of inquiries and disputes of researchers and parties of this study are not the place for broadcasting issues which for years have puzzled most distinguished specialists.

Thanks to the records of historians from Rome, Greece and Arabia an overview of the history of Persia is quite well known, although there are of course periods with more detail and others almost completely unknown. Research on specific issues from Iranian antiquity, especially in regard to military science and the tactics of the Persian and Parthian armies are not as well studied. Of the different studies the level of research and number of monuments from the different eras of Persian statehood varies. There are not a great deal of studies concerning the military arts of the Achemenidians concerning arrowheads, armor plates and other remains of weapons discovered during the American excavations at Persepolis.[3] Significant findings also came from the research of Deve Hüyük in Syria, at Pasargadae in the Iranian Province of Fars and many other small sites. The most interesting archeological remains of weapons come from the late-Parthian and Sassanid periods in the form of arrows, horse armor, armored corpses of warriors and weapons from the excavations of M. Rostovceva in Dura-Europos, a Greco-Roman city on the Euphrates. One can find information on this in the six-volume book on the subject.[4]

One can also find monuments of this type in the first capital of the Parthian Empire (now Old Nisa, near Ashgabat in Turkmenistan) in the form of remains of armor, arrows and arrowheads.[5] The Sassanid era is somewhat poorer in terms of artifacts though there are superb examples of swords, helmets and staves of arrows supplemented with numerous iconographic presentations and descriptions. Unfortunately, in order to find substantial material regarding the military science of ancient Iran it is necessary to use other sources by analogy on the equipment and field strategies used by Iran in their many conflicts against the Steppe tribes. The leading role in this field that are easily available for Polish historians are from the Soviet Union and Russia, of which many are from the Central Asian republics of the former USSR, complemented by increasingly excellent publications in English and German. Looking over the articles resulting from the last one hundred years of archaeological excavations with commentary by ancient historians (sometimes only available in small fragments) we have obtained a great deal of interesting details in order to form a general image of the tactics and armament proper of all Iranian speaking people. Over the course of hundreds of years of warfare, the

---

[3] E. Schmidt, Persepolis, vol. 2, Chicago 1953
[4] М. И. Ростовцев, *The excavations at Dura-Europos conducted by Yale University and the French Academy of inscriptions and Letters, Preliminary Report of Sixth Season of Work*, New Haven 1936.
[5] Г. А. Пугаченкова, О панцырном вооружени парфянского и бактрийского воинства, VDI.2,1966, pp. 27-43.

Iranian military system greatly influenced the growth of armored cavalry supported by light infantry archers.

General information on manufacturing technology and the use of ancient weapons can come from experiments and reconstruction from archeology. This field is used on a large scale for weapon technology but is undervalued by researchers. They are often used for organizing all kinds of events, popularizing for scientific research. This has helped popularize field archeology, which requires not only great knowledge, but also long hours of training, a great a deal of practice, often physical. By engaging in these experiments, you can obtain useful data on how to weigh melee weapons, and thus indirectly the ways to use it. Important information can be developed on bows such as tension and arcs of fire as well as shot penetration, armor and manner of fighting. Information can also be discovered by comparing their representation of iconographic techniques for using weapons as described in medieval military treatises. Sometimes these invoke old traditions which best describe the struggles of steppe people known from ethnological studies and whose way of life was substancially conditioned by the climate and terrain as well as types of weapons used. These factors have not changed for thousands of years.

Broader query in written sources and in special cases results in a different type of archeology (battlefield archeology not pracriced in Poland) to support research of tactical solutions – tactics of individual people and armies finding similar ways to obtain technical solutions. In the same way that better weapons displace worse, more effective organization and manner of fighting displaces less effective ones or causes modifications. The comparable importance of the developing tactics of each army is influenced by the tactics of their potential enemies based on local conditions and climate that the fights were supposed to take place. Besides historians interested in military matters (which in Poland mainly deal with recent history) hardly anyone deals with investigations on a grand scale.

At its core this work is based on various sources to create an overall picture of functioning armies of the individual Persian monarchies, their organization, the types of weapons used and techniques they used those weapons. It also hopes to explain how methods of steppe warfare were transformed until it became familiar to Greco-Roman sources and examines how the various military eras in the history of ancient Persia continued the methods of fighting and armaments of the Iranian speaking people of the great steppe. Additionally, we examine the factors and trends in the military science of Asia could affect how they were perceived. Due to the nature of this goal, this work will not only look at Persia, but also the neighboring peoples. On this basis one can draw reasonable conclusions on the development of military science of those times. Clearly such research must extend to a significant segment of the history of Iran and Asia since the establishment of the monarchy of Cyrus the Great, through invasions of steppe nomads, the war with Greece and Macedonia, the appearance of the Dahae and the control of the great empire of the Arsacids until the fall of the last of the Persian monarchies – the Sassanid kingdom. Such a long view permits us to observe what is most important – as military contact between belligerents continue, sooner or later forces sides to mix their technical solutions and manner of combat which leads to the creation of achievements which are not only military, but the culture of both antagonists. This truth applies equally to fights on the borderlands of Persia, China, Rome as well as the war in Vietnam.

    The present work does not exhaust even part of the issues on the subject, but aims to gather a handful of facts already known on the subject, which are currently not very popular studies in Poland in this course of study, placing several questions and theories which might only be the beginning of new research and discussions. Polish works on archeology and history of the Iranians, (led by researchers from Gdańsk under the leadership of Prof. N. Sekunda, Toruń Prof. Mielczarek as well as UJ Prof Dąbrową) are now under development, especially in comparison to the mature research institutes of archeology in Western Europe, the U.S. and Russia, but perhaps in a few years this field of military history expertise will reach the level of European studies, which at this moment is envious.

Chapter I
The Achaemenid Empire and the Iranian Mountain Kingdom

When the dust of the Battle of Marathon subsided, and defeated the Persian invaders retreated to the shore of the Aegean Sea, the Greeks knew it was time to abandon their current way of thinking about the lands of the east. It ceased to be the lands of myths, the source of curiosities and unusual goods. Eastern armies had begun to seriously threaten the Hellas, which willy-nilly was forced to cease their local disputes and wars, to oppose the huge power which had grown up not so long ago in the immediate vicinity. The source of these concerns was a shadow that first slowly covered the land of the Ionians and Aeolians, later the Aegean Islands, then Thrace, Macedonia and some of the states – cities on the Greek mainland, was the largest empire of the contemporary world – with less than one hundred years of history, the Achaemenid monarchy. At the end of the VI and beginning of the V centuries BCE under the reign of the King of Kings[1] Darius called, "The Great" it reached its maximum range. The powerful descendants of Achaemenes stretched from the mountainous areas of Macedonia and Thrace to the humid and stuffy Delta lands of the Indus. From the steppes of the east coast of Lake Aral over the huge river called Jaxartes by the Hellenes (known to us as the Syr Darya) to the deserts of southern Egypt in the area lying in the trough of the great Nile island of Elephantine.

    The lord of this vast space reigned over countless tribes and nations humbly paying taxes, submitting tribute and in many cases just waiting to jump at their master's throat. They did this repeatedly, and perfectly in the familiar atmosphere and the area of ancestral lands which was the best ally of rebels, equally murderous as the most determined armies. Reaching the heavens of perennial snow covered foggy peaks, or rot breathing marshes full of snakes and mosquitos, the land gave shelter for many years to rebels and semi-independent tribes against Ach-

---
[1]Shahanshahs

aemenid authority. In the VI century BCE the Chinese leader and expert in the art of war, General Sun-Tsu wrote, *"Know the enemy well and know yourself as well, and in a hundred battles you will experience no defeat... Recognize the conditions in the area and the weather, then your victory will be total."* (Sun-Tsu, The Art of War, III, 31, X, 26) Let us, however, in place of the Ancient Greeks learn about the enemy and his country.

Darius called himself, "The Great", (per Darajavahuš) in his inscription on the rock at Behistun, located on the orad from Babylon to Ecbatana which lists twenty-three provinces in the Empire, known by the names of the administrators of the Satrapies.[2] At the time this inscription was created, the Persians had not yet reached area of Europe, the Indus Valley and the Aralian steppe that the great King Darius conquered in the course of its ongoing thirty-six year (from 522 to 486 BCE) reign. If you analyze the properties of each province and group them by their main morphological features – by climate, they would look like this:

1. Desert lands, semi-desert and steppe – about as equal to or slightly flat surface without a large number of water obstacles, enabling easy maneuverability of light and armored cavalry combined with compact ranks of infantry. It was an excellent place to wage large and regular battles with fields in the region of Cunaxa. It was inhabited by highly mobile and warlike tribes of nomads who had perfected the art of guerilla fighting: Saudis, Assyrians, Babylonians, Scythians, Parthians, Arians, Khwarezms, Sattagydians, Arachosians, Makans, Drangians Sogdians.
2. Mountainous lands or heavily rocky – substantially limiting the ability to use of cavalry, especially in a massive or dispersed large units, that is full of places suitable for guerrilla warfare. They imply the use of small, mobile, largely independently operating light cavalry and infantry units, composed of men familiar with the area. Perfectly suitable for organizing all kinds of ambushes, even with small forces. Contains harsh mountain climate; Persia, Armenia, Media, Ionia, Macedonia, Thrace, Phrygia, Cappadocia, Bactria.
3. Lands with a variety of features - beds cut from great rivers with numerous marshes and swamps, full of islands and reeds. Such areas gave shelter to many fugitives, rebels and, the like high mountain tribes blind to anyone's sovereignty. Extremely difficult or even impossible to master in the long run. Needing long, extensive large-scale pacification campaigns from time-to-time using boats and military engineering; Egypt (especially in the Delta),

---
[2] J. Lendring, The behistun inscription, www.livius.org/be-bm/behistun/behistun01.html.

southern areas of Babylonia, Elam, India (Hindu) Gandara.

4. Island areas - during hostilities they require efficient war fleets, vulnerable to enemy attacks from the sea, possible to maintain by preserving the superiority and domination of their fleet over their harbors. Easy to cut-off and blockade: Aegean islands, Cyprus

All these lands were ruled by the Persians at the end of the reign of Darius I, within eighty years of the V Century BCE when he was busy suppressing rebellious subjects and the Greek counter-offensive had not yet begun. At that moment the Empire seemed stable. His was the greatest empire of the contemporary world; essentially nomads from the VII – VI centuries BCE, they started to settle areas, but kept their own military tradition as well as influenced by the military achievements of their neighboring countries with whom they clashed before the creation of a powerful state, or invading the borders to become the object of attack – for example Assyria (or Elam).[3] They next took large portions of the Iranian Plateau and incorporating many aspects of the Mesopotamian military, especially field training, organization and the use of infantry. Massed use of spear-armed cavalry archers which the Persians were famous for when they appeared in Iran were probably first used by the Medes (influenced by steppe nomads like the Cimmerians and Scythians) and later the Persians. Units of this type first appeared around VIII century BCE. They had appeared in the armies of other countries i.e. Assyria (perhaps ever since Aššurnasirapli II and Shalmaneser III, which were depicted on the bronze plates at the gate of Imgur-Enlil or Balawrat), but they seemed to reflect more of the style of fighting chariots.[4] "True" horse archery and heavily armored cavalry only appear in Assyria at the time of Sargon and they were most likely from the people of the Iranian plateau's response to the use of such units by the Cimmerian Scythians and the Medes.[5]

1. The Army of the Achaemenid Empire

From the beginning the main source of power for the large Persian Monarchy was the army. It followed on from the best features of a long series of military commanders deep in the history of ancient Mesopotamia and Iran. The synergy in the organization of its various formations was a precise instrument of war hundreds of years before the time of Epaminon-

---

[3] G. Roux, *Mezopotamia*, trans. B. Kowalska, J. Kozłowska, Warszawa 1998, p. 250.
[4] G. Roux, op. cit. pp. 249-250.
[5] R. E. Dupy, T. N. Dupy, *Historia wojskowości, Starożytność-Średniowiecze*, trans.. M. Urbański, Warszawa 1999, pp. 7, 12.

das and Philip of Macedon operating under the principals later described as "combined arms". The synergy often demonstrated it effectiveness in battle and even when it was finally defeated in battles with the Greeks and Macedonians it could still inspire the conquerors to its great value to creating the modern type of army linking the qualities of Oriental and Hellenistic art of war.

    The Achaemenid Empire built their military art from the long and rich military history of the people of Mesopotamia – half-savage, nomadic steppe tribes. Who do you suppose the Assyrians and Babylonians owed their methodical, precise formations and the specific use of various infantry units? The eternal eastern armies found out long ago, ways to solve the problems besetting the huge, multinational armies of Cyrus the great, Cambyses and Darius I. Centuries earlier they united and exploited the benefits of a mixture of different armaments and the military tradition of other nations. From childhood, the nomads became accustomed to the use of weapons as a model for intimidation with cavalry to conduct battles in the conditions of the endless space of the Asian steppes and deserts. The effectiveness of this military tradition is best demonstrated by the fact even a force as technically and tactically advanced war machine as the Greek-Macedonian Army recognized the mastery of weapons and tactics used by the nomadic people of the great steppe from the first clashes Alexander's army had with the troops at Spitamenes. After the Achaemenids were conquered the steppe tactics were coordinated with the splendid Greek infantry.

Cavalry. The use of this type unit did not have a long tradition in Iran, but it was of great importance. The mass use of cavalry by the Persians was probably learned (as evidenced by a twisted and often misunderstood passage in the "Cyropedii" of Xenophon) in the days of Cyrus I from the neighboring Medes. This was reflected for a long time by the high position Medes as commanders of cavalry. Their proficiency in riding and especially archery was owed, according to Herodotus, from the nomads of the great steppe, especially the Scythians. Since the creation of the Empire of the Medes, cavalry was created from units of Iranian shock troops, in a similar way that the Macedonian Companions would strike as armored cavalry or later heavily armored cavalry of Arsacid's Parthian and Sassanid Persians. We know very little today about their structure and tactics, having only glimpses of references in the surviving works of Herodotus, Xenophon, Diodorus, Justin or Arrian. The closest comparisons were similar formations of mounted units of other Iranian-speaking nomads. These people were recruited into the army of the Great King, fighting with their own weapons and contingents in their own national style. These were mainly known as eastern Scythian cavalry, also known as Sakae in the west, which with the Persians clashed during the famous expedition of Darius in their lands. The analogy of Scythians is applicable for the early period of development of Achaemenid cavalry when these formations were more like skirmishers in that they represent a similar way of fighting, weapons and effectiveness. The Persians lost a great battle with the Massagetae somewhere on the northern plains when Cyrus the Great was killed. A brief description by Herodotus gives some interesting details:

> *"Tomyris (...) gathered all its power and offered him battle. I consider this battle the deadliest of all, that the barbarians had fought this far, and learns that such was its course. They moved forward shooting each other from a distance with arrows, then, when they ran out of arrows they collided with lances and knives in a clash. They have kept fighting for a long-time in a square and neither side would give way in the end, however, the Massagetae gained the advantage. The greater part of the Persian army had been killed, and so was Cyrus."*
> (Herodotus. I, 213)

Although the description does not mention any serious tactical maneuvers during these clashes, on this basis we can derive some assumptions as to the formations adopted for battle by the Iranian armies of this period. It clearly shows in a battle of nomads there was initial an archery contest and then a frontal clash with melee weapons. Both parties adopted the same tactics and it is likely to conclude that their armies did not differ much in both terms of tactics and weaponry. This is corroborated to some extent by archeological finds. Most of the forces of the Scythian-Massagetae was comprised of cavalry on the steppes because infantry was recruited from agricultural communities settled on small areas of cultivated lands or living in the mountains which were the lowest and poorest class of the population. While units made up of farmers, though sometimes quite numerous were not very mobile and usually poorly equipped and trained. They were only used in general inter-tribal battles or if necessary, to repel invasions from the outside. Their diminished value in combat in conjunction with difficulties in movement meant that they were no used in long trips for plunder. Though one can assume that an army like the Massagetae also used infantry untis in the battles with Cyrus, they were not a key combat formation. For this reason, the infantry was probably omitted from all descriptions and consequently know nothing about them.

The Armies of Ancient Persia

In Cyrus' army the number of armored cavalrymen in relation to the number of light cavalry was slim since there was no mention of any significant numbers of Persian heavy cavalry. The Persian sagas loved any cavalry maneuvers which influenced the outcome of battle for their heroic overtones. They would be part of the narrative that Herodotus would later use. This is not surprising, that even in the late Achaemenid the super-heavy armored cavalry was mainly recruited from the nomadic and semi-nomadic peoples inhabiting the north-eastern provinces of the empire and the great steppe areas adjacent to the borders. Another type of the heavily armored cavalry was characteristically only raised in service in Asia Minor and the Persian themselves generally only had average armor on their cavalry.

From excavations in Scythian territories we know that in this period and even a long while after, resources for metal were poor and metal armor was expensive. It was primarily used by chiefs and high-ranking warriors, often supplemented by cheaper armor from organic (mostly bone and boiled leather) materials. In return for the expenditure incurred for such armor, they gave the owners short reflexive bows with long range, but not greater penetration power. They had few heavily armored warrriors to oppose heavily armed warriors with light troops or other less armored cavalry. The Massagetae chieftain and aristocratic warriors, were the best armed to distinguish themselves from their vassals. Herodotus shows the Massagetae were protected exclusively in metal armor, but he may have heard that these tribes lived near the western Scythians, who were well-known to the Greeks and were used as the fashion basis of their western relatives. The western Scythians wore metal armor modelled on those worn by Middle Eastern and Hellenic neighbors of Scythia which were confirmed by archeological excavations were much more popular than in Sakae.[6] According to him:

"The Massagetae wear the same clothes and lead the same lifestyle as the Scythians, fighting both as infantry and cavalry (they practice both kinds of warfare) as archers and spearman, but also carry bronze axes. They adorn their heads, belts and straps with gold. They adorn their horses in the same manner with bronze plates on their chests and bridles while belts and harnesses are adorned with gold." (Herodotus, I, 215)

The earliest image of certainty we have of the Persian Army come from the time of the Greek-Persian Wars, about a half century later than the reign of Cyrus II. We were left with a description of the line of march of Xerxes armies leaving Hellas. The depiction of the whole army suggests

---

[6] E.V.Černenko, *Voennoe delo Skifov,* Nikolaev 1997, p. 5.

that it could have come from an eyewitness to the march of the royal army, despite the fact that it comes after the date of Herodotus birth.[7]

Of the ten thousand guard cavalry, there were two thousand elite horse guards separate from the rest (the ethnically Persian cavalry amounted to approximately thirty thousand men). Unfortunately, there is no mention of their weapons which suggests that the cavalrymen, like the foot guards differed only in the degree of their ornamentation. This would be supported later in Xenophon (Anabasis, I, 8). Herodotus claims that all the cavalry wore Persian scale armor: "The cavalry (...) The Persians (...) they were armed in the same manner of the infantry, but some of them had helmets forged from brass or iron." (Herodotus, I, 811).

All adult Persians from noble families were ordered by the King of Kings to take part in the muster.[8] He tried to create a real warrior class of armored cavalry as existed in India such as the Kshatriya. The infantry was gathered from young men capable of bearing arms from Assyria and Babylonia who wore special accoutrements.[9] Regardless of the social class of the Persian cavalry, the lack of helmets on the part of the riders does not equate to the extremely high price to make (although it was cast or forged from a single piece of bronze or iron, which required great craftsmanship), but rather a personal preference of the warrior, or simply that they did not wear them during the march. Because of the dust kicked up by a column, troops covered their heads with a tiara and turban as the most practical way of protecting them against the sun and the dust. This habit is borne out in surviving depictions such as the Kinch Grave in Lefkada, Macedonia, showing a Companion Cavalryman from Alexander the Great.[10] Such a helmet depicted was then a hat strengthened in a similar manner to the "Kuban" helmets were strengthened by the Scythian bahlyk.[11]

The armor of commanders were made from the highest quality scale armor with gold ornamentation. The most famous example of this was Masistius, commander of the cavalry during Xerxes Greek campaign. Three such plates were found during excavations of an area called, "The Treasury" at Persepolis.[12] Much of the armor seems to have been colored, dyed or worn with embroidered caftans. Herodotus describes this

---

[7]E. Wipszycka (ed.), *Vademecum Historyka Starożytnej Grecji i Rzymu*, Warszawa 2001, p.71.
[8]Е. В. Черненко, *Скифо-персидская война*, Киев 1984, op.cit., p. 34
[9]D. Head, *The Achemenid Persian Army*, Kingswood Grove 1992, p. 13
[10]M. J. Olbrycht, *Aleksander Wielki i świat irański*, Rzeszów 2004, Tab. 2.14.
[11]Bahlyk is a traditional Circassian, Turkic and Cossack cone-shaped headdress hood, usually of leather, felt or wool, an ancient round topped felt bonnet with lappets for wrapping around the neck.
[12]Е. В. Черненко, op. cit., p. 22.

in the death of Masistius, "When Masistios fell the Athenians rushed him. They grabbed his horse as well as him as he tried to defend himself. They killed him, although at first, they could stab him because he was armored. The commander had golden armor covered with scales, on top of which he wore a purple coat. As long as they struck the armor, they could not accomplish anything..." (Herodotus, IX, 22). We do not know if all the Persian cavalry wore caftans. Their uniforms were probably made like the Scythians, scale armor on leather underlay. Bronze and iron armor plates were discovered that date from this period, among others in the Temple of Apis at Memphis and at Dur-Sharrukin (Khorsabad).[13] As evidenced by the finds at Persepolis, the scales were in rows that overlapped each other so that the upper scale covered the lower, overlapping each other and on the sides which protected them from penetration, especially from the side. In the V century BCE written sources (Diod. XIV, 22.6) provide evidence that some cavalrymen (usually the wealthiest) wore solid bronze Greek breastplates.

If the armor for the cavalry was similar to those worn by the infantry, they could also have short shoulder pieces, permanently attached or as often the case of Scythian armor separately attached on the edges. We don't know exactly how long this armor was. One can conclude that like the Scythians (Hulajgorod, Staršaja Mogiła) they were not too long.[14] The armor could go no farther than the hip to the groin without hindering mounting a horse. The armor itself as evidenced by discoveries in Derveni (presently in northern Greece) from Tomb B dating back to the IV century BCE[15] that sometimes a solid collar that protected the throat supplemented the scale armor. The use of such collars was recommended by Xenophon (Hipparchicus, Ch 12). In the days of Darius and Xerxes, it does not seem as if any leg protection was used, or at least there is no mention of them in written sources or archaeological evidence. They appear later, however, as part of the armaments mentioned by Xenophon who described a select squad of armored horsemen in the guard of Cyrus the Younger boiling in armor at the battle of Cunaxa against the army of Araxerxes II: *"All those except Cyrus were encased in armor, helmets and faulds"*(Anabasis, Ch 1.8).[16] Clearly there is emphasis on the distinction of faulds from proper armor, which forces us to reject the theory that it was part of a mid-length scale jerkin as was prevalent in VII century BCE Sogdian armor or Sakae armor in the IV century BCE shown in relief on a terracotta jug of Khumbuz Tepe. Considering that this type armor was

---

[13]Е. В. Черненко, op. cit, p. 24.
[14]Е. В. Черненко, op. cit, p. 38.
[15]M. J. Olbrycht, *Aleksander Wielk,* Tab. 2.20
[16]Pieces of plate armor worn below the breastplate

Relief of Darius I from Bisotun with the presentation of the defeated rebels to the Achemenid ruler inthe beginning of his reign (according to L. Vanden Berghe, Reliefs rupestre de l'Iran ancien, Tab. 6)

Macedonian cavalryman attacking a Persian infantryman. The so-called. "Kinch's Tomb" - Lefkadia. (according to M. J. Olbrycht, Alexander the Great and the Iranian world, *Tab. 2.14)*

Armor scales uncovered in the so-called "Treasury" in Persepolis (according to E. Schmidt, Persepolis)

Scythian armor from Hulajgoród and Starej Magiła (a), reconstruction of the appearance of armored Scythian horsemen (b). (according to E. B. Черненко, Скифо-персидская война, fig.20, J. K. Kozłowski, Historical encyclopedia the world, fig.392)

The Armies of Ancient Persia

An armored catraphract from Anatolia, Relief from Yenicekőy IV w. BCE (according to D. Head, The Achaemenid Persian Army, *fig.25a)*

A greave protecting the leg of the heavy Achemenid cavalryman of the 4th century BCE, painting with Karaburun tumulus II, Elmalii (according to D. Head, The Achaemenid Persian Army, *fig.43 a)*

A heavy achemenid cavalryman from Anatolia. Notice the coverings protecting legs. Payavy sarcophagus around 375-350 BCE, (according to D. Head, The Achaemenid Persian Army, *fig.43c)*

The Armies of Ancient Persia

Plate armor depicted on surface terracotta pot from Humbuz-Tepe (Chorezm). (according to J. Harmatta, History of civilizations of Central Asia, fig.56)

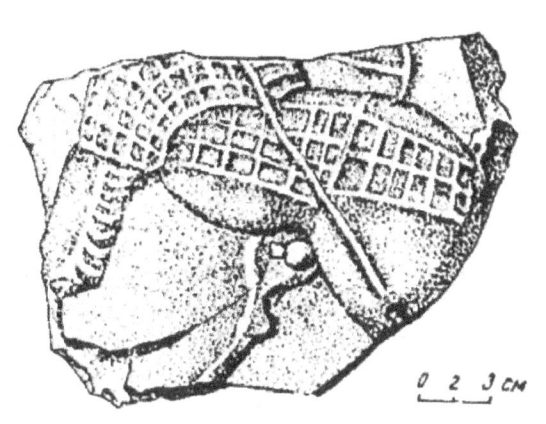

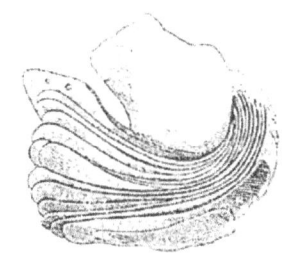

Part of the armored collar and manic from Czirik-Rabat (according to M. J. Olbrycht, Alexander the Great and the world of Iran, Fig.1a and 1b, p.145)

Scythian armor with shields and shoulder armor - Gladkovščina (according to J. K. Kozłowski ed. Encyclopedia historical world, fig.56)

Armored collar from grave No. 2 from Derveni (according to M. J. Olbrycht, Alexander the Great and the Iranian world, Tab.2.20.)

not known in Mesopotamia and in Greece was only used by the infantry where it went out of style somewhere at the end of the VI century BCE[17], it was possibly the source of inspiration from the local traditions of Asia Minor or the Scythian steppes where faulds were in use in the V century BCE. They were a separate part of the armor from the cuirass ((Ždanovo, Aleksandrovka, Gladkovščina).[18] Faulds were made of scales or long metal slats, sewn onto a leather base and fastened to the thigh with separate belts. They protected the leg from the hip to the knee and sometimes such as those from the mound at Novoj Ryžanovce. It is reasonable to assume that this type of armor was referred to by Xenophon in his writing.

Findings from Asia Minor, i.e. the relief from Yeniceköj, the painting at Karaburun in Elmali (tomb of barrow II), the image from seals of the Achaemenid period allows us to recreate the leg coverings composed of laminated metal or leather armor covering down to the ankle[19] which protects the rider and the horse's side as well according to Von Gall.[20] Based on reliefs this protection could be wrapped around the front of the saddle. These theories would be backed up by notations in Xenophon regarding the use of cuirasses of Cyrus' army. However, the total absence of images and descriptions from other parts of the Achaemenid Empire, points instead to local variations such Lydian military traditions. Keep in mind that at the time of Cyrus, Lydia was home to excellent heavy cavalry. Armor did not guarantee absolute protection against all types of weapons. The Persians, like the Scythians originally used it as protect against arrows and sword cuts, but was not proof against thrusting spears, which moreover heavier armor did not stop as evidenced by cases of knights killed or wounded by spear points used with the additional force of momentum of mass cavalry provides a blow to the rider (Xenophon, Anabasis, Bk1, ch 8).

Finally, in V and early IV centuries BCE the old Persian army reached its apogee, through increased and frequent clashes with the Hellenes and the influence of Greek armaments. Gradually, the army moved away from the old metal scaled armor, replacing it with linothorax – many layers of linen glued together, sometimes with metal bands or scale armor around the waist and/or the shoulders. This was lightweight and strong, perfect for use by cavalry and subject to development for different use by the hoplites, then for armored cavalry. A painted stone sarcophagus discovered at Çan (Turkey) that dates from the early IV century BCE

---

[17] S. Żygulski jr., *Broń starożytna Grecja, Rzym, Galia, Germania*, Warszawa 1998, p. 33.
[18] J. K. Kozłowski (ed.), *Encyklopedia historyczna świata*, Kraków 1999, p. 222.
[19] D. Head, op. cit, p. 39, Fig. 43a,c,d.
[20] H. Von Gall, *Reiterkampfbild in der iranischen und iranisch beeinflussten kunst partischer und sasanidischer zeit*, Berlin 1992.

shows a rider whose armor looks like it could be linothorax, but different in some respects. First, there is a large plate protecting the neck, otherwise it is typical of linothorax with a backplate, however, much smaller. The hoplite is exposed to blows in the front and back requiring a strong shield. A horseman dressed in similar outfit, is protected from heavy swords using a slashing motion, familiar to all cavalry when an attacked passes his opponent at the gallop. When the attacker has passed there is less of a chance of parrying the blade forcing cavalry to duel by striking with his slashing sword, the handle facing upwards and attacking the face and chest with the point. The Achaemenid sword was used for the execution of "the flat cut", which could take of a man's head from his neck with one blow. A second difference from the traditional linothorax and arms of a cavalryman on the sarcophagus was the inclusion of large shoulder straps. Though the relief on the sarcophagus does not allow us to exactly evaluate the image, it shows significantly extended flaps forming what are typically shoulder straps of a linothorax. They protect the arms and collarbone (as well as the upper arm) from vertical blade cuts in a similar manner as Celtic chain mail shoulder piece. They are also thicker and more resistant than shoulder pieces of typical Hellenic armor. These shoulder pieces had to be divided in strips to provide mobility of the arms. The artist of the images however does not provide sufficient details. The image looks similar to "feathers" or pteruges, perhaps make a symbolic reference. In order to show the shape of the acinaces[21] on the thigh rather than suspended on the belt.

The magnificent sarcophagus at Çan presents strong links to the stylized art of the period, while the realistic view of the Achaemenid military in Anatolia are confirmed at the discoveries from the Temple of Poseidon that existed on the Isthmus of Corinth in Greece. Among the votive offerings donated to the Gods discovered there was a flat, unusual type of helmet almost identical to one worn by the rider shown in the hunting relief on the Çan sarcophagus.

The trend toward Hellenization of armor in the Achaemenid Army in the IV century BCE is reinforced in the so-called, "Alexander Mosaic" discovered in the House of the Faun in Pompeii, thought to be a copy of a Hellenistic painting. The Persian horse guard of Darius III is portrayed dressed in linothorax flap-type armor. Although they are not as utilitarian as the armor on the Çan sarcophagus, they are the second proof that the Persians had their own type of armor. The issue is complicated, however, as even in the V century BCE the Persian infantry used armor made of lightweight material, like the Hellenistic style. Most likely, both types

---

[21] A short sword or dagger used by the Persians, Medes, Scythians and later the Greeks.

of linothorax - Greek and Persian were copied from Egypt, though they developed separately over time from the battles between Persia and the city states of Hellas while retaining many distinct characteristics. The armor features many Persian characteristics i.e. lack of flaps, high, stiff collar and quilting.

The benefits of the Hellenic military were shown stronger in those areas of the Empire that lived closer to Hellas. This is most noticeable in the developments in the western province of the Achaemenid Empire. In the eastern areas, i.e. in Central Asia, we find extremely few traces of them. A ceramic dish originating from Humbuz-Tepe shows a warrior from the period analogous to the time of the Anatolian sarcophagus. Fragments of armor visible on the surviving part of the dish are diametrically opposed to each other. It shows long, knee-length skirts of heavy plate armor in the old style. Within the armor were sewn metal plates or perhaps hardened leather superb at protecting the wearer from a long sword or axe, developed from "armored coats" of the Sakae warriors which were visible two hundred years later from the vessel at Humbuz-Tepe and the bone plaque of Orlat.

The remnants of a metal jerkin with an attached metal collar dating back to the IV century BCE was found in a burial tomb at Czirik Rabat in Khwarazid.[22] If the dating is correct it would also show a type of segmented shoulder protection, which was a primitive prototype, or perhaps the equivalent known and commonly used during the Achaemenid period and certainly has Hellenistic lamellar armor covering the arms and legs of the armored horseman. A jerkin such as this was used in the Successor Armies in conjunction with horse armor, borrowing equipment from the Iranian heavy cavalry of the central Asian peoples. Xenophon mentions this type of armor worn by the drivers of Persian combat vehicles (chariots). In his day, however, jerkins of this type were made of hardened leather.

As for helmets, there are two types that have been generally attributed to Persian cavalryman. Both are very similar, having a graduated cone shape.[23] One was found in Olympia, in the treasury of the temple, with the inscription: *"Zeus the Athenians, who took him from the Medes"*.[24] A second was found in at Memphis in Egypt.

While there might be questions about the helmet from Memphis, there is little doubt about the second one from Olympia, supposedly cap-

---

[22] М. В. Горельик, *Сакийский доспех*, в Б. Б. Бернгард, Г. М. Льевин, (ед.), Центральная Азия Новые памятники писсменности и исскуства, Сборик статей, Москва 1987, с. 118.
[23] S. Żygulski, op.cit., pp. 59, 60.
[24] Е. В. Черненко, op.cit., p. 21

The Armies of Ancient Persia

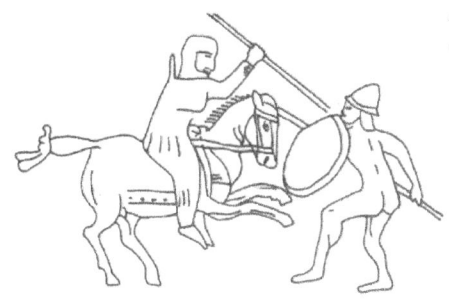

Achaemenid armored cavalry against a Greek soldier from a cameo at Bolsena

An Achaemenid cavalryman in Hellenic armor on a stamp from the Hermitag

Armor of a heavy cavalryman from the late era of the Achaemenid - from the stone sarcophagus of the prince Çan - Anatolia

Scythian or Persian helmet submitted as a votive offering in the temple of Poseidon in Greece

Scene of hunting from the "prince" sarcophagus from Çan-Anatolia

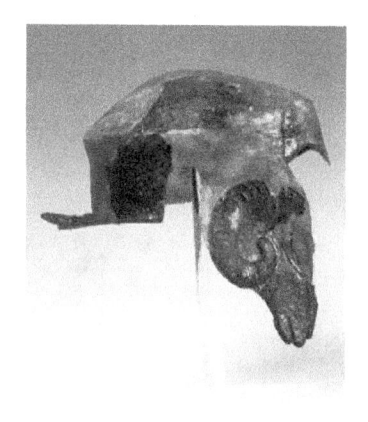

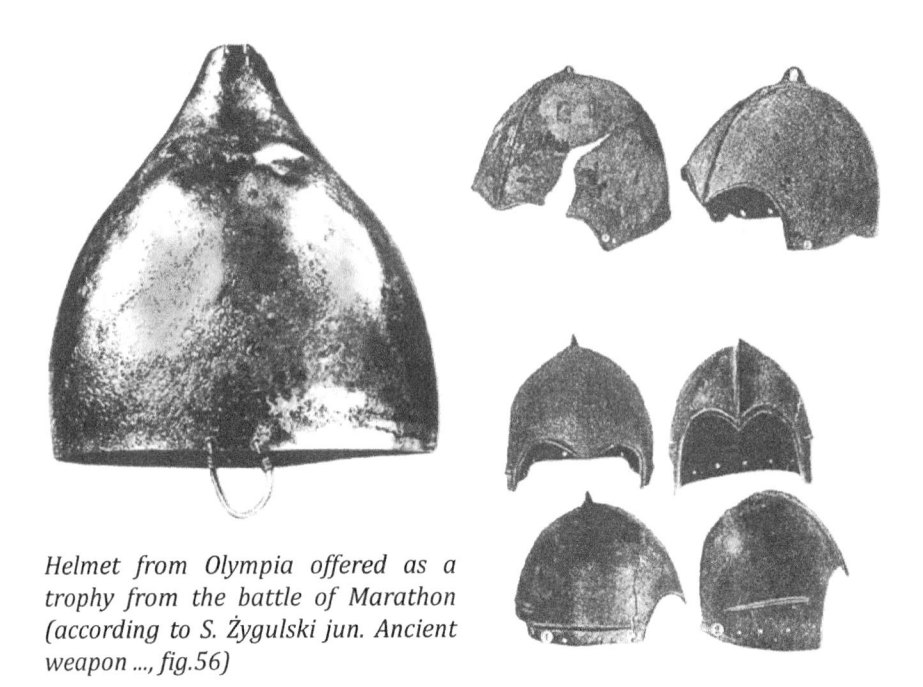

The Armies of Ancient Persia

Helmet from Olympia offered as a trophy from the battle of Marathon (according to S. Żygulski jun. Ancient weapon ..., fig.56)

Kuban helmets (from the basin of the Kuban river) (according to E. B. Черненко, Скфф досnex, fig.4.44)

Persian helmet from Memphis (according to S. Żygulski, Broń ancient ..., fig.57)

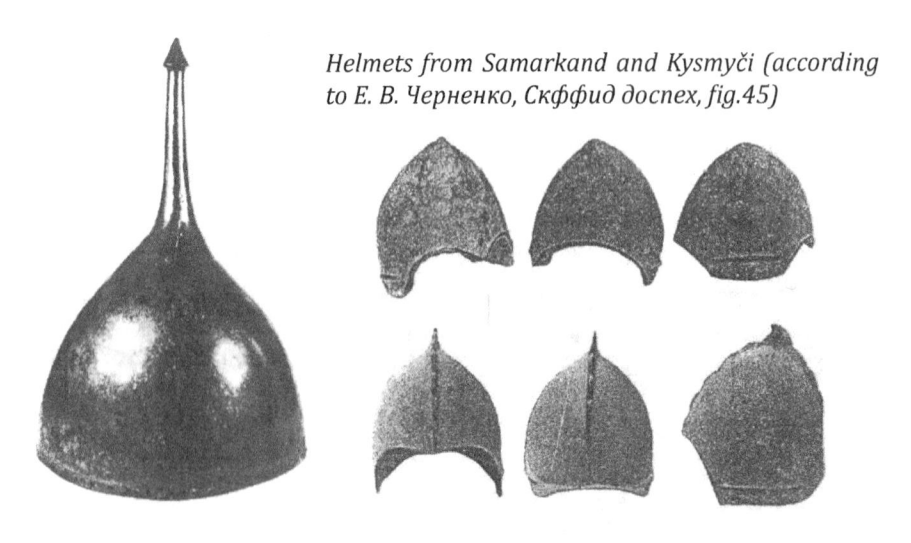

Helmets from Samarkand and Kysmyči (according to E. B. Черненко, Скффид досnex, fig.45)

tured by the Greeks at the battle of Marathon. Before the battle the cavalry division was stationed in the Persian camp. The night preceding the battle they were going to be loaded onto ships to be sent to the Faleron, for a quick strike against the city whose gates would be opened by prosperous minded citizens.[25] In his description, Herodotus has no mention of how the cavalry was used. He writes with confidence about the Sakae fighting in the wedge formation (Herodotus, Bk VI, ch 113), but remembering that the Sakae, like the western Scythians occasionally had infantry units, it could be assumed that on the day of Marathon they did not fight as cavalry. Even if the Sakae did go as cavalry, they probably did not wear conical helmets as the warriors prefer "Kuban" style headgear.[26] One captured at the Temple of Zeus, might be attributed to an infantryman, a soldier of one of the national quotas, composed of various Persian subjects. Perhaps it was Armenian, Syrian or Mesopotamian, where this type of helmet had been used for centuries. The same can be inferred for the second copy. Perhaps it comes from a garrison of the Achaemenid, these were composed of mercenaries, in addition an almost identical helmet of an unknown date almost certainly from the Achaemenid period comes from Asia Minor.[27]

An interesting hypothesis put forward by M. B. Gorelik concerning Iranian helmet types, mainly known from excavations which date from approximately VII century BCE at Kuban tomb mounds and later finds (about V-IV centuries BCE) in and around Samarkand and Kysmyči, near Dzhambul (Taraz) in the Talas River valley.[28] This type differs from the Scythian helmets from the areas of the northern and western Black Sea. These are derived from types common in Greece, usually direct copies of Greek origin. There are also probably helmets of local design of beaten metal scales (Gladkovščina). Based on findings from Sfid-Rud (IX – VIII century BCE), Gorelik believes it shows a warrior from the treasure of Amu Darya (Oxus treasure), or a seal of the Achaemenid Persian period, showing that the Sakae or Scythian adopted this type of helmet from the Persians and Medes. This theory is rejected by E.V. Černienko.[29] It is important, however, to pay attention to several issues. First, the helmet discovered at Sefid-Rud is the Mesopotamian or Chaldean object of local production, neither original, Chaldean or Mesopotamian models indicate that is likely of "Aryan" origin. In the VIII century BCE, the ancestors of the Persians and Medes were already mentioned in the Assyrian chron-

---

[25] A. Krawczuk, *Maraton*, Warszawa 1989. pp. 184-185.
[26] Е. В. Черненко, *Скифский доспех*, Киев 1968, p. 77.
[27] http://www.artigua.com/store/artemisgallery/items/181773artigua.html.
[28] Е. В. Черненко, loc. cit.
[29] Е. В. Черненко, *Скифо-персидская война*, Киев 1984, pp. 17-18.

The Armies of Ancient Persia

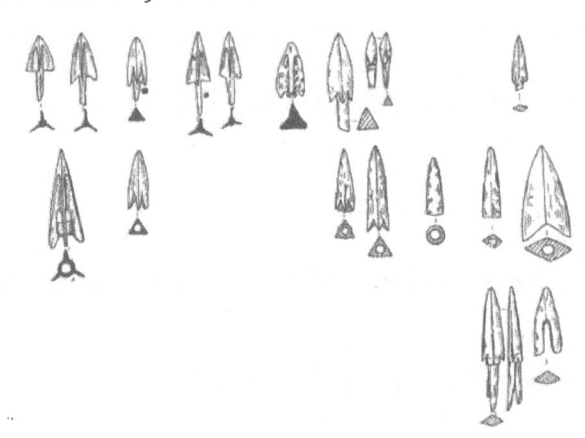

Arrowheads from locations at Chem and Chayyrakan (top)

Gorytos of the Achemenid soldier, probably a cavalryman rider (according to R. Ghirschman, Perse.Proto-Iraniens, Medes, Achaemenides.) (left)

Arrowheads from Persepolis (a) and from the Marathon battlefield (b) compared for comparison with scythe shots western (c) and eastern from Tuwa (d) (according to Е. В. Черненко, Скифо-персидская война, Fig. 7, 22, and В.А. Семенов, Суглуг-хем и айыракан: могильники скифского времини ..., tab104.) (left)

Different types of scythe-shot arrowheads equipped with bushings (according to J. Chochorowski, Koczownicy Ukraine, fig. 9, 34) (right)

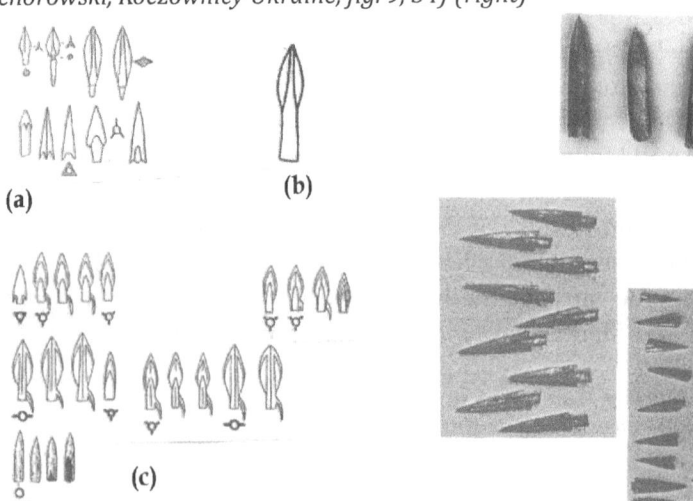

(a)

(b)

(c)

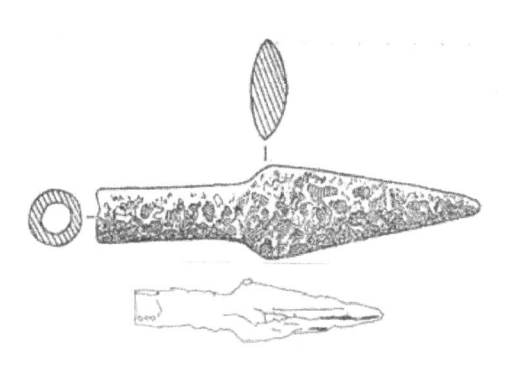

The head of the Persian spear discovered in Persepolis (according to E. Schmidt, Persepolis, vol. 2, pl. 76.)

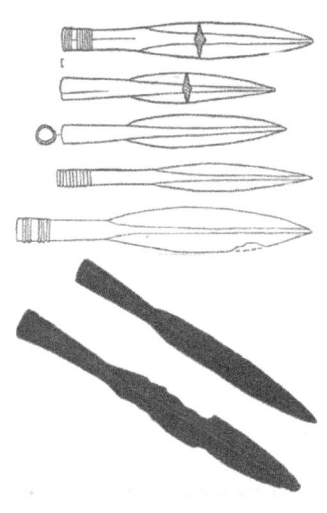

Scythe spear tips. Repjachovata Mogila. Cross-sections (a), originals (b). (according to Е. В. Черненко, Скифо-персидская война, fig.23, J. Chochorowski, Ukraine's nomads, fig.10)

Persian spear heads of the royal guards are almost identical, with a tip discovered in Persepolis. (by R. Ghirschman, Perse. Protocol Iraniens, Medes, Achemenides, fig.217)

icles in the areas of Armenia and Media. The existence of this type of head covering was common in the lands of the western Scythians, can be explained by the good practice of trade between the Steppe peoples and Achaemenid Persians. The age of the helmet, however, may indicate that this exchange existed since the pre-Achaemenid or even the pre-Median times. Incidentally, headgear of this type were so popular among the Sakae, that they were used with minor alterations up to the II-I century BCE as evidenced by the representations on the bone badge of Orlat.[30]

The helmet was composed of a bell-shaped casting to fit on the skull, with the tip equipped with a ring to attach a plume, or the tip will bend slightly forward to imitate the peaked cap of the nomads. On the bottom edge was a row of holes for mounting, which according to some scholars were for leather cheek straps or neck-piece. More likely, however, the helmet was a "Kuban" type which was strengthened at the most vulnerable point to protect blows to the head with a thick leather cowl that the nomadic people of the Great Steppe used to wear. Their design, for instance, is similar to the traditional thick caps worn by the Kazakhz today, an ancestor of the "deerstalker".

At the moment we have very few references to the use of Persian and Median cavalry shields. The hoplon[31] shield was used by the troops of Darius III at the battle of Issus. This type of shield was also found among the horsemen's equipment at Gadal-Iama described on a plate uncovered in Babylon. He was supposedly armed with two iron tipped spears, an iron club, 120 arrows, wearing iron armor, a bronze shield and helmet. Both examples are, exceptions, however that prove the rule. It can be inferred that as was the case later of the Macedonian Companions, because of sufficient armor, the use of the shield was limited to those most exposed in combat like those in the front line, while the rest of the cavalry lacked them.[32] This was only true for armored cavalry units. Sakae and Scythian light cavalry archers used a light, round or square; wicker or cane shield (such as those found at Pazyryk tomb mounds) in conjunction with the armored cavalry. For archers, they accounted for the only available substitute for armor. A warrior that needed both hands free while shooting could have the shield mounted on his forearms, shoulder or back by straps or belts. Shields, mounted in the last instance, were used by the western-Scythians were metal plates that covered the upper back and arms against not only head shots, but weapon blows fighting during a melee.

---

[30] К. Абдулаев, *Nomadism in Central Asia*, A. Invernizzi (ed.), In the Land of Gryphons, Papers on Central Asian Archeology in Antiqity, p. 159.
[31] Aspis
[32] N.G.L.Hammond, op.cit.,pp. 125, 379 (ed. 1992).

The Armies of Ancient Persia

Since the formation of armored cavalry (mainly in Central Asia, but also in Asia Minor), the valuable horses like the riders were usually supplied with protection. The horses had their heads covered with a headstall and scale metal aprons, probably to protect the breast to the legs, and sometimes even the sides of the animal. This type armor might have been inherited from the steppe peoples, because according to Herodotus, this type of saddle cloth was known and used by the Massagetae at the time of their clashes with the troops of Cyrus II the Great (Herodotus, Bk 1, Ch 215). His description is confirmed by the representation on the Humbuz-Tepe plate.

The primary weapon of the Persian and Media armored cavalry was the Iranian bow and spear. Bows are prevalent on many reliefs at the royal complex of Persepolis which was known as the Scythian type. This was characterized by a small length (70-100 cm), composite construction on the interior of horn and segmented construction on the outside.[33] This means the core was composed of wood (as the so called Scythian type discovered at Barrow of the Three Brothers at Kerch in the Crimea, made from several layers of wood)[34] covered with horn at the corners and sinews with the bowstring making it take the shape of a "C" or as a circle to give power to the archer. The archer would string the bow before battle because do to the shape of the bow it was difficult to do in the saddle. The shape of the bows in the reliefs show they were severely bent when it is strung the potential energy stored in the bowstring was significant.

A recursive bow is a bow with limbs that curve away from the archer when unstrung. A recursive bow stores more energy and delivers energy more efficiently than the equivalent straight-limbed bow, giving a greater amount of energy and speed to the arrow. A recursive bow is shorter than the simple straight limb bow for a given arrow energy and this form was often preferred by archers in environments where long weapons could be cumbersome, such as in shrubs and forest terrain, or while on horseback)

The primary method of storing and transporting bows by cavalrymen was the use of a so-called, gorytos[35], which was widely used among the Iranian speaking peoples. It had compartments sewn on to the quiver to form of pocket dividers lengthwise. The case was then covered by a flap to protect the bow and the strings which would have been sensitive to weather conditions and protection against moisture.

---

[33] А. М. Хазанов, Очерки военного дела Сарматов, Москба 1971, pp. 29-30.
[34] M. Mielczarek, *The Army of the Bosphoran Kingdom*, Łódź 1999, p. 49.
[35] A bowcase for short recurve or Scythian bows

The Armies of Ancient Persia

In contrast to Scythian gorytos, however, Achaemenid cavalry quivers had flaps mounted as if from the side, which hid the top, and covered the pocket. For archers, the gorytos was worn in Persian fashion, horizontally with the quiver facing back. The gorytos was worn on the left side attached to the belt via a special hook. Wearing the gorytos horizontally seemed a slightly bizarre, but completely effective way to draw a shot from the quiver. While shooting, the gorytos with the exposed flap should move with the hips slightly back and standing (or sitting in the saddle) as arrows were removed by the right hand reaching straight back from the quiver and placing them on the string. Such a system would make shooting quicker.

Examples belonging to wealthier owners were probably decorated in a similar fashion to the Scythians, with studs or precious metals. Quivers belonging to the rank and file seem to have been decorated with bone or embroidery.[36] Interestingly, on the reliefs at Persepolis, there are several warriors with just such cases on their belts that were considered part of the Median infantry guards. However, since the Medes did not serve in the royal guard and the short bows in the Achaemenid gorytos are of a type worn by the "dignitaries" on the relief dressed in the "Persian" style, this theory is called into question. If you look at the descriptions contained in the "Acts" by Herodotus, who says the Median dress [37]or leather pants, shoes and jackets with long sleeves were worn by both nations which should be interpreted as utilitarian riding outfits. Herodotus describes the marching columns of Persian Infantry and Immortals, going from Sardis to Greece, clearly says that they included long quivers and much long than cavalry bows (Herodotus, Bk VII, Ch 61) which would exclude the shorter cavalry bows worn in a gorytos. Lowly Median Kardakes (who could not have used this weapon) and were not allowed in the vicinity of the king, whereas the protection of the king rested with the Persian guards, so between the guard on the reliefs Persepolis it can be inferred that this was a scene of real-life events in the palace.

From works about the Medes from Arrian we know that armored cavalry troops at the Battle of Gaugamela, and perhaps other battles were placed between the infantry formations (influenced by the less mobile heavily armored infantry) (Arrian. *Anabasis*, Bk III, Ch 11), they would have the ability to fire on par with the infantry. They looked for the most effective way to destroy the front ranks of the enemy formations.

Arrows shot from their bows were of typical Scythian length, approximately 60-70 cm[38], made of wood or cane. When the latter is used,

---

[36]В. Черненко, op.cit., p. 42.
[37]A. T. Olmstead, *Dzieje Imperium Perskiego*, ed. K. Wolicki, Warszawa 1974, p. 232.
[38]Е. В. Черненко, op.cit., p. 26

they sometimes insert hard wood in the center. Arrowheads are sometimes discovered preserved with these inserts according to a publication of findings at Persepolis by E. Schmidt.[39]

In the "treasure" room at Parsi (Persepolis) and Pasargadae[40] arrows were discovered made of bronze with two and three-cornered leaves, some typical of Scythians, while another larger shaped point was for longer, heavier shot. It seems that arrowheads and funnels were fixed with pins pushed directly into the shaft of the cane. One example of a Persian arrow found on the battlefield of Marathon[41] has a long, flat leaf shaped arrowhead equal to the length of the funnel.

From finds in Central Asia, Iran and the lands occupied by the Scythians are shafts with a pin that is more characteristic of eastern territories, roughly east of the Caspian Sea, and those with funnels from the western lands, although there are numerous exceptions on both sides. This may be associated more with the absence of bamboo or tough Asian cane, using western woods for bows and more frequently inserts. The shaft with the funnel were included the entire length of the arrow in which a pin is pushed. Arrowhead with the shaft covering the outside is much stronger than one where the arrowhead is just pushed into the wood. This is particularly true for the short arrows used by Scythian horsemen – the use of a pin holding the head in would destroy the thin shaft whose diameter generally did not exceed 7 mm.

Another of the main weapons for Persian cavalry was the spear. Its use is confirmed by numerous references in the works of ancient historians (Diodorus, Herodotus, Arrian, et. Al.). Xenophon for example writes, "Cyrus jumped down from the chariot, put on his armor, mounted his horse and took a spear in his hand." (Xenophon, *Anabasis*, Bk I, Ch 8). It was probably the same type of spear carried by the Immortals, since Herodotus claimed the cavalry was armed in the same manner of the infantry. The length of the weapon was about two-meters long with a diamond or leaf shaped blade with either a short or long funnel depending on the design and made of iron, with balance achieved through a decorative element on the other end of the shaft. The spear did not seem to have a second point at this time, since its use was only adopted after years against Greeks. Unfortunately, we do not have too many complete examples of these weapons from archeological finds. Our best example is a spearhead discovered in Persepolis, although we can not one hundred percent be certain that it is Persian.[42] Identical ones can be seen on the

---
[39] E. Schmidt, op.cit.,p. 99.
[40] P. Stronach, Pasargadae: *A report on the Excavations Conducted by the British Institute of Persian Studies from 1961 to 1963*, Oxford 1978, p. 218.
[41] Е. В. Черненко, loc.cit.
[42] Е. В. Черненко, op.cit., p. 28.

reliefs depicting soldiers on the wall in the Hall of a Hundred Columns. They independently confirm the words of Herodotus that the infantry and cavalry were both armed in the same manner.

The spear was used in a thrusting manner against the other cavalry, but also against the enemy on infantry. "Cyrus was surrounded by (...) his entourage, it surrounded him, did not pause for a moment and with a cry, 'I see the man' he ran towards him striking him in the breast and wounding him through his armor, which the doctor Ctesias said he was able to survive. When the blow was finally given it struck him under the eye." (Xenophon, *Anabasis*, Bk I, Ch 8).

Based on this information, it is clear that the spear was mainly used in close quarters to penetrate the armor. If you failed to pierce the armor on the pushback, the cavalry practiced racing in to thrust at the face and throat. Such a blow killed Cyrus the Younger and Xerxes cavalry commander Masistius. This technique was not unknown to the enemies of the Persians and themselves. This is the way Alexander the Great's soldiers attacked the Persians as described by Arrian, "When Alexander's cavalry and himself (...) attacked in waves and struck the Persians in the face with their spears, so that when the compact Macedonian phalanx, bristling with spears stormed the line, Darius became frightened. The whole horror of the situation played out in front of him, which caused him to run." (Arrian, Bk III, Ch 14). Persians spears would be of similar length or shorter, to those used by the Scythians, whose heavy javelins were known from finds in aristocratic burial mounds (i.e. the Repiachowata Grave).[43] Some relief sculptures of the Achaemenid period show Persian horsemen with two identical spears. On this basis one can conclude that one spear was thrown on direct collision with the enemy, while the other was used in combat.

Influenced by the battles with the Greeks, attempts were made to lengthen the spear that the cavalry used for close combat. References to such reforms appear In the texts referring to, "the long spears." The last such reference took place during the reign of Alexander the Great, when the best cavalry (probably Guards) were equipped with weapons similar to the Macedonian Xyston.[44] These experiments, however, were only carried out on a small scale and did not produce the desired effects. It was only after the fall of the Achaemenid state that the long spears became a staple of the Iranian cavalry equipment, as evidence by the representations of the period, such as the outside of the ceramic dish of the IV-III century BCE at the Koi Krylgan Kala site in Chorasma.

---

[43] Е. В. Черненко, op. cit., p. 44.
[44] M. Mielczarek, *Cataphracti and Clibanari Studies on the Heavy Armoured Cavalry of the Ancient World*, Łódź 1993, p. 48.

The Armies of Ancient Persia

The sword was also used in melees, albeit less than the spear. Perhaps the most famous example is the Persian sword hanging on the belt of one of Darius' courtiers standing behind the king and the heir in the audience scene carved on the central panel of the eastern staircase of the Apadana in Persepolis. The sword of the man identified by some as Aspatines[45] is a type used by all Iranian speaking people. On other versions of the Persepolis relief, there are plainer versions of the weapon worn by representatives of many other nations, not only Persians. Herodotus calls this type of weapon "acinaces" (or akinakes), *"After prayers, Xerxes threw a bowl into the Hellespont, as well as a golden krater and a Persian sword called acinaces."* (Herodotus, Bk VIII, Ch 54).

The sword had a flattened, oval head, Median and Sakae versions had two antithetically set animal heads and geometrical motifs decorating the handle. The guard was square to the handle with the top edge showing two crescent-shaped notches, while the lower edge was convex. The cross guard of most Persian acinaces were tailored to be hidden in the sheath so that they appeared seamless. Some swords, however, only had a thin cross-guard at the base of the handle that was still flared. A wooden scabbard of this period was discovered in Egypt and housed at the British Museum. It is similar to the Achaemenids in shape, but smooth and without ornamentation, it is similar to a sword found in Kuban and an unusual specimen at Čertomlyk.[46]

The scabbard was made of leather, wood and precious metals and bone, sculpted and appointed with gold foil and at the bottom was a bulbous extension decorated with carved and highly stylized representation of strangely arched lions, goats, etc. This particular acinaces scabbard shows a "Median" costume in relief depicting an audience covers the base of the hilt with two antithetically set figures of winged griffins standing on their hind legs and on the scabbard is a second set of goat's hooves. At the end of the scabbard is an extension for greater comfort to balance out the weight of the metal, bronze or like the Scythians, gold braided which was attached to a strap and was strapped to the thigh.

Swords were worn on the right side, strapped to the waist with a special strap mounted to extend the length of the scabbard. The weapon was hung so that the handle faced away so it could be drawn out the shortest length and most of the Scythian swords varied in length between 30-40 to 60 cm long.

Representations of acinaces, except for small details and ornamentation, are identical to those of the Persepolis reliefs that can be seen on scenes in the treasury at Amu Darya (Oxus Treasury) and the rhyton

---
[45]Е. В. Черненко, op. cit., p. 29.
[46]Е. В. Черненко, op. cit. pp. 48-49.

Dariusz I and his son Xerxes surrounded by courtiers and guards - the royal auditorium - Persepolis (a), a sword hanging at the belt of a royal courtier - perhaps Aspatines (b) (according to R. Ghirschman, Perse. Proto-Iraniens, Medes, Achemenides, fig.255,205)

The Armies of Ancient Persia

The hilt and sheath of the VIth-century sword probably from Čertomłyku - the scabbard and the lower part of the handguard are a modification from the 4th century BC (according to Gold der Skythen, fig.s.105

A Saka with a hilt of two animal heads facing opposite directions- A gold plate from the treasure of Oxus (treasureJammu-daryjskiego). (according to Father Daler, PowersŚwiat, fig. P. 186)

The ends (caps) of the akinakes sword sheaths from reliefs in Persepolis. (according to R. Ghirschman, Perse. Proto-Iraniens, Medes, Achemenides, 28,27,288, according to Е. В. Черненко, Скифо-персидская война, fig.17)

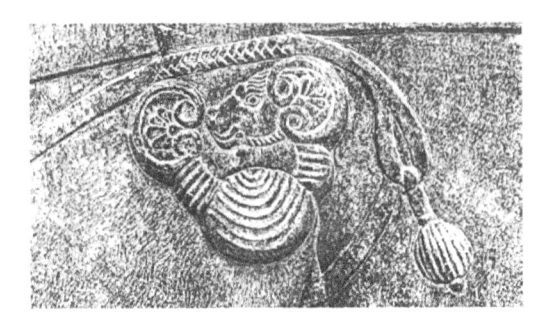

The warrior's sword is identified with Aspathines at Persepolis (according to R. Ghirschman, Perse. Proto-Iraniens, Medes, Achemenides, fig.289)

The Armies of Ancient Persia

Golden akinakes scabbard of Achemenid type from the treasury at Oxus (the Ammu-Darian treasure). Find (a), reconstruction (b) (according to R. Ghirschman, Perse. Proto-Iraniens, Medes, Achemenides, fig.118, according to Е. В. Черненко, Скифо-персидская война, fig.18a)

A stone akinakes scabbard decorated with images of a lion and a deer - Taht-e Sangin. (according to Е. В. Черненко, Скифо-персидская война, fig.18)

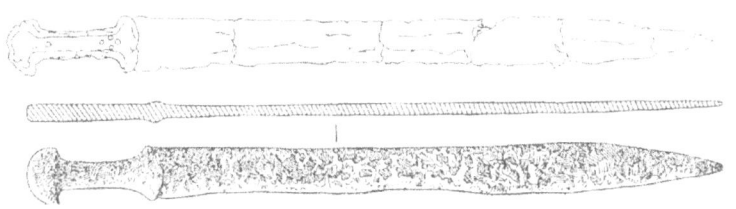

The blade and the handle of the long sword from Persepolis. (according to Е. В. Черненко, Скiffer-персидская война, fig.7)

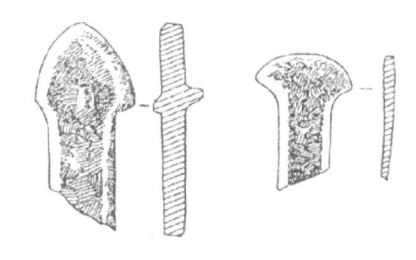

Pommel of swords or daggers with parts handles - Persepolis (according to Е. В. Черненко, Скфор- персидская война, fig.7)

- 53 -

of Erebuni.[47] As mentioned, in the Treasury and as found at Takhti-Sangrin there are two examples of preserved sheathed swords in the similar style of Achaemenid tradition. They were beautifully made, especially the later which had an ivory handle (26.7 cm long) without a cutout to hide the hilt. It is adorned with an image of a lion standing on its hind legs, holding a disproportionately small stag with a weapon suspended at its belt. The bottom plate shows a stylized image of a goat.[48] As far as can be estimated the acinaces including the handle amounted to 45 cm.

Swords of this kind, similar to a gladius seem to have been worn by all warriors. Herodotus does not really state the cavalry wore any other kind. Excavations conducted in the steppes, however, have shown that a long sword was used to fight from horseback by armored horsemen, though this is not an invention of the Iranian-speaking people of earlier times. S.A. Skory gives twenty-four examples of Scythian copies of this weapon in his work, having a length exceeding 70 cm, while one example from Izjumovki in the Crimean measures 110 cm.[49] So, is this the weapon the Persians knew? It turns out that it is, "yes". It is different, it is true, from the shape of Scythian swords, but its use was the same. A weapon with a similar blade was discovered in Persepolis with a bare handle and hilt made of iron slightly more than 80cm long.[50] It had a mushroom shaped head and the handle was probably covered with some organic material – wood, horn, etc., which unfortunately has not survived. It was riveted to the tang, which was visible from the holes. The heavy sword had a lenticular shaped cross-section, and, on the blade, the sharp edge expands slightly, which moves the center of gravity forward to increase the cutting force. The size of the guard, without metal acted as a counterweight to the blade, leading towards the assumption that is was made for chopping and only partially for thrusting which did not make it suitable for fencing. Due to its length and the comparison to the Scythian copies, it should be recognized as a cavalry weapon. This finding is supported from a description by Arrian: *"At the moment Roisaxes rode up to Alexander, he hit him in the head with a sword, but it only broke off a piece of the helmet, absorbed the strength of the blow(...)Spitridates came with his sword (...) from behind, but Cleitus, the son of Dropidas came to his aid and slashed them with his sword"* (Arrian. *Anabasis* Alexander. vol I, Ch 15). There are two fragments of sword hilts from Persepolis that are similar to the descriptions above indicating that they were somewhat common. E. V. Černienko believes that swords with long-handles are visible behind

---

[47] A conical container used for drinking fluid or pouring fluid in a ceremony
[48] Е. В. Черненко, op. cit., p. 33.
[49] С. А. Скоры, *Скіфскі довгі мечі*, *Археологія* 1980, 37, pp. 24-25.
[50] Е. В. Черненко, op.cit., p. 33.

the line of dignitaries immortalized in the relief from the platform on the Apadana of Darius.[51] Although there is a great resemblance to the Scythian swords, i.e. they are shown wearing two swords, the short one was worn on the right side, while the long one was worn on the left under the gorytos, although many reject this thesis by Černienki. First, on the relief showing the dignitaries you cannot see the bottom of the scabbard, which at that length would have been visible under the quiver. Secondly, the short acinaces was considered a decoration, considered a weapon to be worn on parade in the palace, a symbol of the professional warrior belonging to this class. It was worn like a small sword on a nobleman's coat, while the long sword was a fighting weapon that was not worn at a costume gala. The dignitaries can clearly be seen with the handle of the short, wide daggers stuck in their belts as a symbol of their status and the shape harkening back to a defensive weapon. The short dagger may have constituted a set with the sword like the katana and wakizashi in medieval Japanso so that both were worn on military campaigns. It was a dagger tucked into his belt that Cambyses hurt himself while getting onto a horse.

Another weapon that was used in hand-to-hand combat which was very effective in penetrating armor, was the horseman's pick-axe. This was probably used by different units in different nations. The most famous example is a copy held by the courtier in the "Median" outfit on the relief. Even if it is not Aspatines, he probably belongs to the group of the king's "relatives" or "friends" and they represent the top commanders in the infantry as well as the most important armored cavalry commanders. The courtier carefully holds the horseman's pick-axe in his right hand with an elongated forked head. The lower part of the axe is wrapped for a better grip, while judging the proportion of the axe to the shaft the total length is estimated at 70cm.[52] This allowed the user to deliver the force of the blow so strong that is was possible to puncture a helmet or light armor. Two slightly different versions of this weapon have been discovered: one was famously found from the Achaemenid era at Deve Hüyük and the other in the throne room at Persepolis.[53] The first one was like the usual Scythian pick-axe with a long slightly curved beak, while the second has a pointed spearhead without a shaft cast from bronze. The beak is diamond shaped and slightly forked at the hammer-end. Under the beak is it was decorated in a distinctly stylized head of an eagle.

Part of the construction is a slightly wedge-shaped cross-section, which adds strength to the shaft and allows better protection to the

---

[51] loc. cit.
[52] Е. В. Черненко, op.cit., p. 28.
[53] loc. cit..

Dignitaries - maybe so-called "Royal relatives". Relief from the apadana platform of Dariusz I- Persepolis. (according to R. Ghirschman, Perse. Proto-Iraniens, Medes, Achemenides, fig.235)

The Armies of Ancient Persia

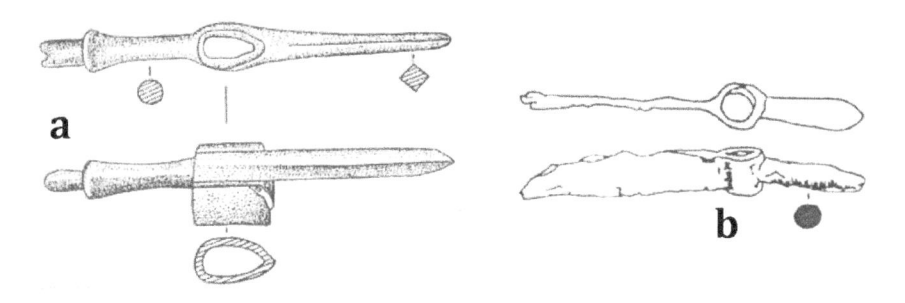

An iron nadziak discovered in Persepolis (a) and Deve Hüyük (b) (according to E. B. Черненко, Скіffer-персидская война, Fig. 7 and M. J. Olbrycht, Alexander the Great and the Iranian world, fig.2.9,)

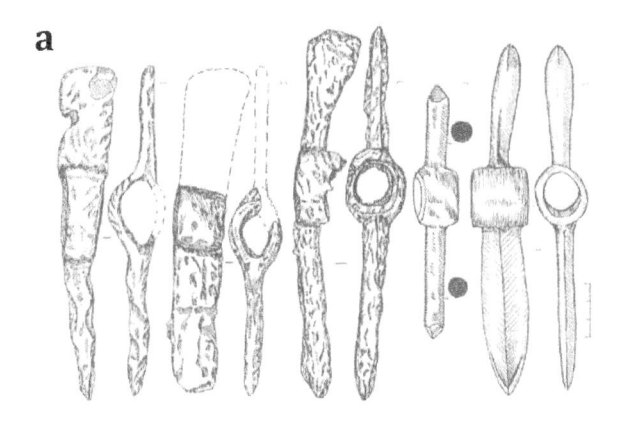

An iron nadziak from East-Scythian (a) cemeteries of Sugług-Chem I and II (b) bulldog with a cushion decorated with the image of a panther. Bezirk k. Krasnojarska.(according to A. Семенов, Суглуг-хем и Хайыракан: могильники скифского времини ..., tab.107 and Gold der Skythen, fig.s.222)

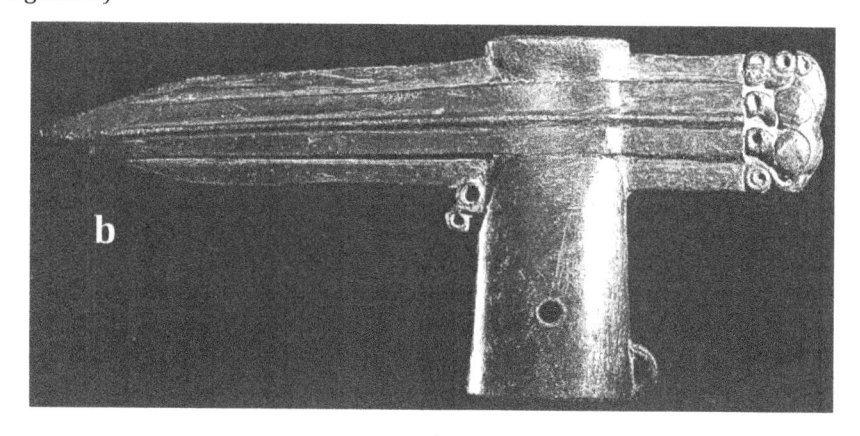

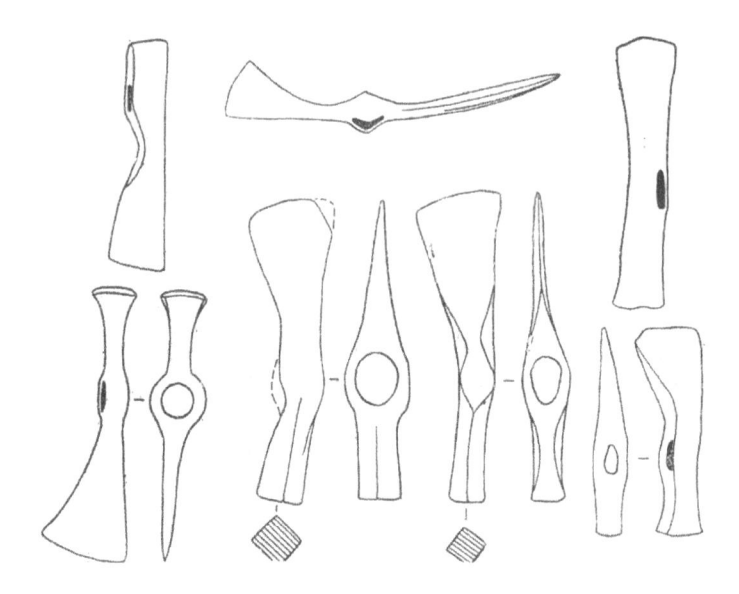

Iron Scythian battle axes. (according to E. B. Черненко, Скіffer-персидская война, fig.23)

The 'prancing' steed Alexander the Great - bas-relief from the so-called Alexander's sarcophagus which in reality belonged to the ruler of Sidon - Abdalonymus or the Satrap of Celesyria Laomedon (according to N. G. L. Hammond, Ancient Macedonia, fig.9)

horseman's grip while they are delivering the blow. These types of weapon were also used on the steppes. Examples of these pick-axes have been found in Scythian burial mounds with metal blades where the hammer head is represented as a stylized figure of an animal. More often copies are found where the hammerhead incorporates a small axe blade. These are similar to what are known as "ice axes". The steppe people also had heavy double-bladed axes mounted on long handles called the *Sagaris*. Herodotus describes these types of weapons belonging to the Massagetae, while Iranian and Scythian soldiers are depicted equipped with such axes in illustrations adorning Greek ceramic vessels.

At this point we conclude our description of Achaemenid heavy cavalry. Unfortunately, because of the scarcity of archaeological data and iconography it cannot be more complete. Having the descriptions of ancient historians, we can add a few words on the strategy and use of cavalry.

Achaemenid Cavalry Tactics. The core cavalry units in the early days of the Achaemenid State were the Medes and Persians. The highest nobles (and therefore the richest) generally fought in the front ranks in support of their own lightly armed cavalry, in collaboration with a large variety of infantry units. During the reign of Xerxes, the Persians created a cavalry bodyguard for the king, and somewhat earlier during the time of his father Darius the dependent nations provided excellent heavy armored cavalry added to the famous cavalry nations from in Central Asia – such as the Sakae, Massagetae and Bactrians. From the eastern provinces large contingents of light cavalry were gathered to support the heavy cavalry (Arrian. *Anabasis of Alexander*, Bk III, Ch 13), especially horse archers and spearmen. From written sources, it is apparent that over time the Persians and Medes developed an elite troop of cavalry he called, "Medium Troops" who perfected tactics for close cooperation between cavalry and reformed armored infantry.

The commander of great large armies, or all troops of a large area e.g. Asia Minor (as in Cyrus the Younger) was known as "Kara". Below it in the hierarchy was the commander of the cavalry (Asapatiš – equerry) and infantry. Below them were probably brigade commanders. A Persian commander exercised control over the quotas supplied by each of the sovereign nations. These were mostly part of the royal family supported by highly respected local chiefs. The Achaemenid Army was organized on the decimal system so that there were commanders of ten thousand (Bajvarapatiš), one thousand (Hazarapatiš), a hundred (Satapatiš) and ten soldiers (Datapatiš). In the days of Xerxes, the army was divided into six brigades commanded by Mardonius, son of Gobryas, Tritantaechmes son of Artabanus, Smerdomenes son of Otanes, Masistes son of Darius and Atossa, Gergis son of Ariazos and Megabozos son of Zopyrosus.[54] Based on this one can conclude that the command system was pyramid shaped (Herodotus. Bk VII, Ch 81).

The elite squadron of cavalry in the time of the first Achaemenid probably similar to the typical formation Scythian, which moved in the attack wedge-shaped with the commander leading the whole unit. The size of the squadron was probably approximately 500 riders, although two squadrons numbering 1,000 cavalry are frequently mentioned.[55] It is believed that the native Persian cavalry numbered about thirty-thousand riders.[56] There is an indication of using Scythian style combat tactics in campaigns along the northern shores of the Black Sea - against the Macedonian satrap Zopyrion in the time of Alexander the Great in the Battle of the River as well as the time of the succession wars over the Bosphorian Kingdom.[57] Over time, perhaps before Darius I and Xerxes the main formation was built around armored infantry trained and equipped from Mesopotamian (somewhat similar the Assyrian) with the impact force of cavalry focusing mainly on the wings. The most powerful cavalry units were of the Asiatic type. Part of the cavalry squadrons were set alternating with the first-line infantry, so that if they broke and retreated the other units could counter-attack the enemy army. The king was always located in the center of the lines of shielded infantry and Guards cavalry units (two units of a thousand horsemen and a thousand infantry called, "Household." On the basis of references to weapons used by Iranian troops during the Achaemenid period and iconographic representations, we can assume, that in the initial phase of the battle, Iranian cavalry moved in front or between the lines to launch a massive fire of archery. We known that almost all Achaemenid cavalry were equipped with bows, and the range of those bows used by the horse archers exceeded the range of the infantry bows. This is what some authors to recognize about the unusual formation adopted by Arsites' troops during the battle of the Granicus, ie charing into the first line with the infantry, while the cavalry on the river bank showered arrows in expectation of the enemy attacking[58] - in light of information about military tactics of the Iranian peoples this would be something completely normal. At Granicus, or Issus it was not necessary for Persians to contact the enemy to wipe them out in combat. Their cavalry had less men in the attack formations than

---

[54] A.T.Olmstead, op.cit, p.232.
[55] N. Sekunda, *The Persian Army 560-330 BC.*, London 1992. p. 57.
[56] Op.cit, pp. 55-56.
[57] M. Mielczarek, op.cit, pp. 60-64.
[58] P. Green, *Aleksander Wielki*, tłum. A. Konarek, Warszawa 1978. p. 438.

the later armored clibanariów, or a banner of medieval knights and used the momentum of attack.

Battle in general was a different matter, after firing a shower of arrows they quickly attacked the enemy infantry or moved behind them in a cavalry maneuver. Immediately after the initial barrage the cavalry would charge into contact with the enemy using melee weapons or spears. The commander took a position in the front rank (on the wings), or between the ranks of armored infantry and heavy cavalry, initially moving to attack a positon in the center of the lines. As a result, intentionally or not, the delay allowed the squadron to attack in a wedge, moving slowly so that the infantry could keep with the cavalry and then tear into a charge in a cohesive formation. In this way, the Persian army attacked in a tooth shaped formation with the wedge of cavalry charging the enemy battle line. In an attack such as this you had to be very close and then charge over a short distance. Because the use of this tactic forced the armored infantry to stay close together this was a more effective formation to attack at close range using missile fire.

In many places Herodotus also points out (Herodotus Bk IX, Ch 20, Bk IX, Ch 22) that Achaemenid cavalry always charged in squads formed into wedges. These statements seem to be confirmed by descriptions contained in the *"Anabasis of Alexander"* by Arrian for example, *"(Alexander) seeing that Mirthridates, son-in-law of Darius, charging forward on horseback at the head of his cavalry in a wedge formation, quickly cut in front of his horse and hit Mithridates in the face with his spear, knocking him from his horse."* (Arrian, *Anabasis of Alexander*, Bk I, Ch 15). Herodotus' description also clearly shows that a direct attack was not about throwing a javelin: *"When the Greeks advanced, he sent Mardonius entire cavalry command after them, instructing Mastisius of the great importance to Persia (...) as horsemen rode up to the Greeks and attacked them by squads, challenging them to fight and calling them women."* (Herodotus, Bk IX, Ch 21). He then charged, riding at the head of his command, alone or with others as was later the case with the Macedonian Companions.[59] In conjunction with this idea is a description of special training of horse, probably the most valuable mounts who were specially taught to strike out with their hooves against soldiers forming the front rank in order to break their formation, *"Artybios (the head of Persian cavalry for Cyrus) learned to leap against formed soldiers. Standing on stout legs and snapping against all they approach. When Artybios was on horseback he attacked Onesilus (the ruler of Salamis on Cyprus) and as trained, his retainer struck at the advancing Artybios, but when the horse threw his feet on the shield of Onesilus it struck such an imposing blow that it knocked him off*

---
[59] N.G.L. Hammond, op.cit., p. 108.

his feet." (Herodotus, Bk V, Ch 111). This system of training horses was specified during the reign of Alexander the Great and was even known in Greece. The "Alexander Sarcophagus" belonging to the King of Sidon - Abalonymus or Alexander's General, Laomedon, shows the Macedonian ruler in relief in this position. (There are different opinions on who this represents).

Although the general obligation to serve in the royal army weighed heavily on all adult Persian upper classes, refusal to participate during the military expeditions was punishable by death (Herodotus, Bk VII, Ch 39). There was a level of hierarchy that even the less well-off would not serve at light cavalry. This is a topic that historians do not dwell on since the Persians were called the subjects of the "King of Kings" without reference to ethnic distinctions. The only clear distinctions mentioned separating Persian troops are, "Immortals", and regular armored infantry recruited for war. They were probably recruited from military colonists, coming from the lower classes. (Herodotus, Bk VII, Ch 85).

Based on the list of nations and allies described by the Greeks sources from the great battles, the Persians brought javelin-armed light cavalry provided by various nations such as the Sakae, Dahae or the Sagartians as support for the Persian armored cavalry as necessary (Herodotus, Bk VII, Ch 85). They "plied" missiles and arrows against the Greeks at Plataea, using this as one of several techniques for conducting an attack. The first part of "Skirmishing" in many parts of the world is based in the use of cavalry in loose formation attacking towards the enemy, then curving away from them (usually towards the right) and throwing javelins into the enemy ranks or shooting their bows before the enemy could react, and making room for the next group to follow them up. (Tacitus. Ger. Bk VI). This style of fighting guaranteed the relative safety of unarmored riders, while at the same time providing the maximum effectiveness for the horse javelins.

The steppe people, unlike the Persians, avoided rolling battles, applying another technique called, "the Scythian Wheel" or later "the Parthian Circle". In this tactic, the attacker is drawn into an ambush by a small group of riders that act as a "decoy" only to have the enemy find themselves surrounded by a ring of mounted archers who provided a continuous barrage of arrows for many hours. But, if the enemy attacked, trying to break from the encircling enemy archers, were attacked on the flank or rear by Scythian armored troops waiting in reserve. Alexander only encountered this method of fighting in the north-eastern areas of the Achaemenid Empire. It was used, for example, by the Sakae battling against the Macedonians at the Jaksartes River in 329 BCE. In these lands the principals of guerilla warfare practiced by these nomads greatly increased the casualties incurred by the Greek-Macedonian army that was used primarily for regular battles. While the Macedonians were enamored with great battles and heroic duels, the Persians sought a more pragmatic use of land as free nomads led by a local nobleman Spitamenes, used these old tactic for two years, fighting successfully against a dangerous invader.

Both formations of Asian cavalry – heavy lancers and light horse archers could be used by separately, i.e. during partisan-reconnaissance operations, and in close cooperation within a massive formation, was proceeded by "carpet" fire by batches of archers such as at Granicus or Gaugamela. The close quarter melee was fought with spears, swords, axes and horsemen's pick-axes. It was similar the style of cavalry fighting of the Scythians, Sassanids and the Samurai of the feudal period of war in Japan (XV – XVII centuries). When the heavy cavalry met resistance on impact they could circle back to their previous positions and attack again if necessary, act independently or in cooperation with the infantry, serving a similar role to the Scythian light cavalry support.

To summarize, based on descriptions and reconstruction of weaponry, the Achaemenid heavy cavalry was preceded by a quick barrage of archery, a massive attack in wedge formation, in the case of the eastern armies their formationn was independent of the infantry, armored cavalry wedges on the wings and rear of the bow armed cavalry. The attack was directed on the wings (though sometimes on the center) of the enemy formation, trying to deliver a crushing blow. At the same time, the Achaemenid heavy infantry would break through the center of the enemy formation causing them to escape or the death of the enemy commander leading to a rout.

This tactical system was rooted in the military traditions of the Iranian nomads, perfectly suited to the conditions of endless steppes, convenient for maneuvering cavalry in battle. The Asian provinces of the Persian Empire and the later Seleucid state continued this after the Greek victories. More than that, the success of the cavalry formations led to the introduction of new units to the Hellenistic armies such as armored cavalry called "Catraphracts" changed the tactical nature of the Seleucids troops.

INFANTRY. The second of the basic pillars of the Achaemenid army were the infantry. While the nomads lived a pastoral life between the mountains in the summer and lowlands in the winter (an example of which are still in Iran today) the wealthiest formed the cavalry, but the majority of the troops were composed of infantry. In the main Achaemenid army, the infantry had a high combat value, high morale, well-armed and equipped

– which included heavy armor – composed mostly of Persians and Medes, but also included Kissja (Elamites) and Hyrkana (Herodotus, Bk VII, Chapters 61-63). Peoples from other areas formed light troops; mainly infantry, archers, slingers, etc. Persian infantry units were recruited mostly from the lower strata of society, except for perhaps the King's Bodyguard, who were armed in whole or in part by the king as in Assyria, which explains the uniform clothing, weapons and equipment.

During times of war, equipment was issued to soldiers from the arsenals located in the cities as focal points of the troops. It is possible that the royal guard arsenal this was part of the so-called, "Treasury" located on the site of royal Persepolis. At that location we find tips arrows, spears, armor plates it would be equivalent to the Assyrian fort Shalmaneser in Kalchu.[60] In this way, heavily armored infantry troops were organized and well equipped, most probably due to the frequent wars. Great expeditions trained the core formation of combat troops of the King of Kings. Based on their resilience, heavy and light cavalry, could also withdraw under their protection to prepared for a re-attack.

The most elite unit of the entire formation created were the so-called "Immortals" (the Greek AΘANTOÏ - athanatoi). This name was first mentioned by Herodotus to whom they appear alternatively with the description "Myriad Persians". According to Herodotus, both in terms of the custom of supplementing the number men in the unit to the constant value just ten thousand soldiers. "After the soldiers came forward the best were selected from the myriad of Persians. They were the best infantry (...) they were called "Immortal" for the following reason: whenever they lost one of their number whether through death or illness, another man was chosen, and they were never more or less than ten thousand." (Heroditus. Bk VII, Chpt 83) Infantry from the "Immortal" units are mentioned in the "Cyropedia" of Xenophon, which identified the personal palace guard of the King of Kings, who are also represented on the reliefs of Persepolis.[61] A careful analysis of these reliefs leads, however, to conclude that the issue is much more complex. The Achaemenid portrayal of soldiers based on their armament can be divided into several groups. The first group of warriors were armed with spears and bows with long quivers thrown across their backs, dressed in long palatial flowing robes (according to Von Galla they were called Kapyris, and borrowed it from the Elamites, but in reality, most likely national Persian dress). Alternatively, other figures are in Median costumes wearing boots and trousers that are tied at the bottom and knee-length, belted jackets. They have short bows and arrows worn in a bowcase characteristic of the steppe

---

[60] J. Laesse, *Ludy Asyrii*, editor. G. Krasicka-Meuszyńska, a. l. a. p.162.
[61] A.T.Olmstead, op.cit., p. 231.

horsemen and Iranians. This dress, as previously noted, according to Herodotus and various iconography are typical as "field uniforms" for the primary Achaemenian Army units.

Precisely because of this combination of clothing and weapons (short reflexive bows due to their size and combat potential of the period are considered typical for cavalry) you can see them in the different formations of Persian warriors such as aristocratic armored cavalry. From written sources it appears that there were no Mede guards among the Immortals. Images shown on reliefs in the palace shows soldiers in the ranks can be seen today, show the guard outfits, not as a nationality, as after all they were all Persian, but portrays their military bearing. If so, the men in the flowing, Persian costumes and based on the detailed descriptions of the weapons in the "History" of Herodotus can be identified as infantry, their comrades must belong to cavalry units, even in the palace with their distinct weapons, were more comfortable for riding, and by that constitute the distinguishing outfits of their formation.

As mentioned in Herodotus, they were known as "Immortals" of ten thousand, in battle their squads alternated with armored infantry. Descriptions of these formations frequently occur in the "Expedition of Alexander" by Arrian (Arrian, Bk III, Chapter 11). Perhaps because of this battle formation, on the reliefs, they occupy with the other infantry on the lower levels of scenery decorating the gate of the "Hall of a Hundred Columns" because the soldiers in these formations mimicked what appeared at the palace ceremonies standing side-by-side.

The second group of soldiers in flowing robes are also armed with spears, bows and long quivers, but are presented alone, on foot without a mounted equivalent. Included in this group are the most famous of all the soldiers from among the base reliefs of glacé bricks at the palace of Darius I at Susa. A similar representation is shown on the carved steps of the staircase at Apadana in Persepolis.

The third group consists of soldiers only equipped with spears and classical shields, similar to the archaic Greek shields called, "Boeotian". They are dressed in long, flowing robes, falling into folds at the feet. Their representations on the reliefs are found in the center of the eastern ramps of stairs at Apandan in Persepolis.

The fourth group shows images of guardsmen not wearing bows or quivers, but only armed with spears. They are always represented as being near the rulers – both in front and behind, with representations of the courtiers and king shown in the scene of the audiences granted by Xerxes that were placed in the reliefs at the entrance of "the Hall of One Hundred columns". They wear long, flowing, gala robes of the Persian infantry.

The Armies of Ancient Persia

The fifth group consists of soldiers without shields, but equipped with spears wearing long flowing infantry robes, but with their hair encircled by woven hairbands. According to Strabo, such bands were only worn by soldiers of plebian origin who were recruited into the Immortals, but not directly part of the Royal Guard. The relief shows them on the right side of the stairs.

It has been proposed that the first group of soldiers in the reliefs show the basic units of the infantry and cavalry guards on foot in front of Xerxes column marching off from Sardis, the second group only shows the infantry guards of the King of Kings, forming the first of two regiments of infantry guards, the first group of soldiers, the so called, "Basilikoi Toxotai" (Royal Guardsmen). According to Heracleides of Kyme, the guards were recruited from among the Immortals,[62] however, since the Melophoroi (apple bearers) were recruited from the highest nobility (as stated in Herodotus Bk VII, chp 40-41) and on that basis they are known by the name Melophoroi) of select veteran "Immortals"- seasoned professionals. They were just Toxotai, "Immortal" ... "selected from the rest of the Persians..." and most likely soldiers from amongst the landed class. The third group are identified as the most elite regiment of guards, the Melophoroi Argyraspides (Μελοφόροι Αργυράσπιδες) along with the elite heavy cavalry. The fourth group – the elites of the elites of the King's personal bodyguard are referred to as simply, Melophoroi.

Their function as palace guards is especially indicated by their lack of bows – they were completely armed with hand weapons since their location was always near the king's rooms or his actual person. Herodotus mentions that the "Immortals" and Cardaces had bows but does not mention them as "guards". The lack of these weapons may be completely justified for tactical reasons since positioning the guards away from the front lines makes this weapon superfluous.

If Herodotus's version of the so-called "Conspiracy against Gaumata" and especially the fighting in the Magician's Palace is true, it would explain their use as some of the dramatic moments that would have been etched into the memory of the young Darius to affect the equipment he established for his bodyguard. Two guards were attacked by the conspirators in the private chambers. One probably took a bow off the wall, while the second got a spear. Due to the swiftness of the attack, the bow was useless. The second, fighting with a spear wounded two of the attackers (Herodotus, Bk II, Chpt 78). That's how easy it was for the conspirators to get in front of the most powerful royal mage, and events in the palace clearly convinced the future King of Kings of the necessity of

---

[62]Herakleides z Kyme in. *Die Fragmente der griechischen Historiker*, F. Jacoby (ed.) Berlin 1923. p. 689.

establishing an elite guard unit which used bows on the battlefield, but in the audience halls, however, they are not so effective.

References to the palace guards run through the works of other historians. They can be found in Xenophon (Xenophon, Cyropaedia Bk 8, Ch. 3), Quintus Curtius Rufus (Historia, Bk 3.3 Ch 15), Plutarch and Arrian, who also mention the Melophoroi of Darius III (i.e. Apple Bearers, named for the spear-butt shaped like an apple) (Arrian, W.A. Bk III, Ch 11. The longest and most intriguing passage we find on it, however, as we have been told by Herodotus, describing the march of Xerxes army from Sardis write, "Whereas half his army went through the space without seeing the king. In front of him came a thousand riders selected from all the Persians as well as another thousand lancers chosen from the populace with spears to the ground (...) acting like spearmen, while the bravest and noblest of the Persians of the thousands held their spears in the same way as the thousand riders chosen from the Persians." (Herodotus, Bk VII, Ch 40-41). Evidently, we are dealing with the guard again, even in the column marching as close as possible to the ruler. These units functioned like the more numerous Macedonian Guard counter-parts of archer guards – the so-called basilikoi hypaspistai, melophoroi - basilica doryphora and somatophylakes, just as the Immortals were the equivalent hypaspist guards. The rest of the infantry corresponded to the phalanx. It is interesting to what extent the Macedonians drew inspiration to create such units from their neighbors and nobles?

The famous "Immortals" are not shown until the fifth group on the reliefs of soldiers, portrayed from the scene of the audience, the guardsmen are probably standing apart from the podium of Apadana Darius. On the reliefs of the walls of Darius' palace we see soldiers in flowing costumes, with only spears and armbands, wider than the bands on the other "Immortals". These are probably the Melophoroi Guards, but with weapons and uniforms from the time of the Great King.

Within the elite branch of Melophoroi two groups of soldiers can be primarily separated based on their position within the so-called portal, "Hall of the Hundred Columns" built by Xerses. Archers and Melophoroi are lined up facing one direction with a line running vertically through the decorations. A special characteristic of Near-Eastern art and easily seen in the reliefs produced by the state of New Assyrian palaces in Nineveh, approaching all the soldiers seen as lined up on both sides of the court leading to the audience room, shown with a high waist. Two units of Melophoroi occupy the top row with soldiers standing on attention on both sides of the hall entrance (perhaps the portico of the Apadana), other guards on the long side of the courtyard north of the Hall itself – the so-called "Unfinished Gates" up to the very entrance of the "Hall of the

Infantry royal guards (perhaps regular "immortals") – Darius' Persepolis platform (according to R. Ghirschman, Persia, Proto-Iranians, Medes, Achemenides, fig.218)

Achemenid dignitaries in "median robes" - Persepolis (according to R. Ghirschman, Persia. Proto-Iranians, Medes, Achemenides, fig. 209)

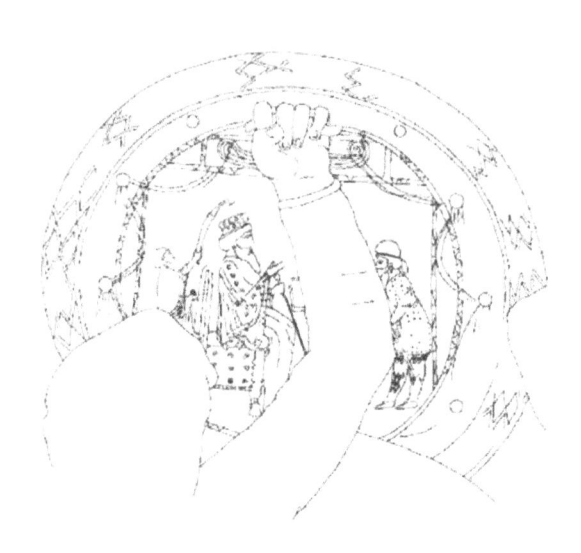

Presentation of the royal audience on the inside heavy shield of the Persian soldier as shown in the battle scene on "Alexander's sarcophagus" (according to S. Paspalas, On Persian-Type furniture ..., fig.9)

Hundred Columns."

The Melophoroi are separated with two solider on each side of the doorway only equipped with spears (additionally one of the guardsmen equipped in a similar manner is located on each side of the stage in the audience room inside the hall), and three of the spear wielding soldiers are carrying what looks like a Boeotian style shield. Those standing closer to the rulers in the same hall belong to the more elite of the guards than those with shields. These suppositions seem to be confirmed by the descriptions of the late court and guard of Alexander the Great, who followed the guard organization used by the Achaemenid. During official audiences, in addition to the traditional Macedonian guard, there were also two units of Iranian guards called, "Melophoroi" corresponding to the more prestigious noble Achaemenid guard and "Toxotai" corresponding to guard units shown on reliefs, equipped with boxes. (Diodorus, Bk 18, Chp 27,1).

In addition to the infantry guard, the ruler was protected by another group of trusted confidants. On the Persepolis reliefs this group is shown in a very prominent position depicted in long flowing robes decorative robes, heavy gold necklaces or torques and bracelets or knee length long coats belted at the waist. Each of these is reminiscent of those later worn by Turkish nomads. In each place on the platform the courtier is holding a lotus in his hand. These so-called, "dignitaries" are dressed in costumes different from the Guards. Their attire is not really a uniform, but as the attire of courtiers, delegates and Satraps shown in the so-called "Sacrificers Platform" relief of nationalities from the Apadana Darius. From the writings of ancient historians we know that many of the royal "relatives", "friends" and "table companions" (because such official titles were borne by the most eminent Achaemenid courtiers and advisers).[63] It was the origin of the highborn noble families of the Medes and other Iranian peoples.

Service at the King's table was considered the greatest possible honor, only accessible to the most noble. The position of the high dignitaries with their wealth of ornaments, take on an almost nonchalant pose which in showed they were ashamed to face the King of Kings on a daily basis. The most important and noblest of them even had the privilege of sitting with ruler at the same table, though not face-to-face because they were separated from the king by a veil.

Although the "dignitaries" wear different outfits, all historical texts indicate that they served as armored cavalry at the side of the ruler which created not only a kind of guard, but also a staff. Member of the "dignitaries" (including those in Persian robes) in cavalry units would be

---
[63] A.T. Olmstead, op.cit., pp. 87-88.

provided with a short reflexive bow in a gorytos strapped to their belt (often considered a typical Median weapon).

Because of their wealth, the best equipped were considered the bravest and most faithful "Friends," "Relatives" and "Companions Table" they fought in the direct defense the rulers. This fact is confirmed by historians, citing in many places, of course, on the occasion of the fighting, in which a person attending to the Great King, the names his finest adjutant. Even Xenophon noted the benefit of what can happen even when a true a true prince claims the throne, "When panic arose causing them to scatter, Cyrus road away with only a small retinue of six riders, the so-called Table Companions". (Xenophon, *Anabasis* Bk I chp 8).

In conclusion: the Achaemenid Persian Median infantry can be separated into different groups from the armored infantry. The first was composed, in the words of Herodotus, of Persians of the personal guard of the King composed of the best two-thousand men, selected as the Father of History claims – one thousand from the highest nobility (divided into spearman and shield bearers) , and one of one thousand archers and spearmen (toxotai-takabara) (Herodotus, Bk VII, chs 40-41) as in the criteria of the Argeada Macedonian recruiting: military experience, courage, growth, strength and blind loyalty to the ruler.[64] According to Arrian, the guards were positioned in front of the King of Kings in battle to protect him. According to Diodorus and Kurtius, his bodyguard fought heroically in defense of the ruler at Issus and Gaugamela allowing him to escape twice.

The second group created was "the Immortals" – a ten-thousand-man professional corps of archer-spearman acting as the core of the infantry anchoring the center line in front of the infantry and cavalry Royal Guard. At the time of Xerxes expedition into Greece, command of the assembled unit was held by Hydarnes son of Hydarnes (Herodotus, Bk VII, Ch 82).

The third group was composed equally of Persians, Medes, Cissians and Hyrkanians, completing the organization of spear armed infantry. They took up positions on the flanks of the "Immortals". Sometimes, according to ancient historians such as Arrian they were placed at equal intervals with the armored cavalry. The control of the infantry at the time of Xerxes was under the command of Otanes, father of Amestris, wife of the king, Tigranes of the Achaemenid family over the Medes (Herodotus Bk VII, ch 61-62), Anaphes the son of Otanes over the Cissians, and Megapanos over the Hyrkanians (Herodotus Bk VII, Ch 62-63). These soldiers were probably called Carcadaces.

---

[64] N.G.L.Hammond, op.cit., p. 138.

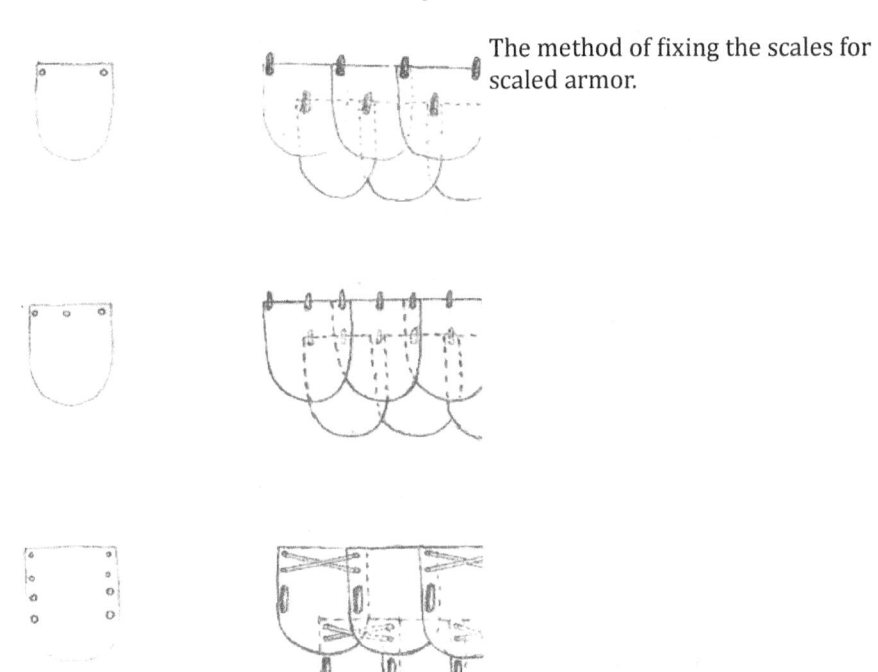

The method of fixing the scales for scaled armor.

Servants carrying goods for preparationone of the royal meals - he calls attention to the characteristic pointy hat called tiara. - Persepolis. (according to O Dalera ed. *Powers of the World*, fig. P. 227)

The Armies of Ancient Persia

Royal guards equipped only with spears and "beotian" shields (according to O. Dalera ed. *Powers of the World*, fig.s.227) (above)

Royal guards with a large reed shield (spara-gerron) - Persepolis (according to R. Ghirschman, Perse. Proto-Iraniens, Medes, Achemenides, fig.242) (below)

The Armies of Ancient Persia

E. V. Černienko notes that Herodotus states the obligation of military service at the time of the expeditions and general mobilization was heavily on the ethnic Persians. However, it is uncertain whether these were mainly peasants, or only those from the higher social strata. One could suppose that the people who served in the infantry could not afford to buy and maintain a horse as well as equipping himself. As in Assyria, they were armed by the king. This applies not only to the "Immortals" who were professional soldiers from the upper class and social status as well as the means – they had their concubines, separate food supplies, etc. (Herodotus, Bk VII, Ch 83).

Judging by the uniformity of all the Persian heavy infantry formations, weapons and equipment as described in Herodotus' "Acts", it not only shows the appearance of Otanes soldiers in detail, but clearly shows all the Persian and Median infantry were armed and dressed alike: "Medes went to war armed in the same way, {as the Persians}. It was indeed a Median outfit, not Persian" (Herodotus, Bk VII, Ch62).

The "Immortal" soldiers and the guards stood out, from the richness of their garments, ornaments and weapons. *"Those Persians ["Immortal"] were distinguished by their rich costumes, and they were the considered the bravest. The armament they were given [describing the Persian contingent] were gilded"* (Herodotus, Bk VII, Ch 83). For protection, mainly against enemy arrows, they wore heavy, most likely sleeveless scaly armor: *"On their head they wore a soft, felt hat called a tiara, on his body was a speckled jacket with sleeves (...) which had steel scales that looked like fish scales, while on their legs they wore trousers."* (Herodotus, Bk VII, Ch 61).[65]

These uniforms were seen by witnesses during the march of the Persian Army from Sardis according to Herodotus. The clothing was richly decorated in patterned designs, much like those worn in the late-18th century under the armor in which the sleeves were exposed. Some soldiers wore no armor and on-lookers might not have been able to tell which of the infantry units didn't have scale armor. Only the richest soldiers could afford this type armor, though the guards might have had theirs decorated with precious metals. Later, they were lightly armored, but painted in different colors. In the eight chapter of the first book of *"The Anabasis"* Xenophon describes part of the army of Artaxerxes II at Cunaxa against Cyrus the Younger: *"Enemy cavalry in white armor were on the left wing under the command of Tyssafernes"* (Xenophon, Anabasis, Bk 1, Ch 8). White was worn by all the rebel soldiers of Artaxerxes II might be due to his religious, Zoroastrian leanings. In this religion, white meant purity of intention and the fight for righteousness.

---
[65] Herodoti, *Historiae*, editio tertia, v. I/II, Oxonii, 1943.

The Armies of Ancient Persia

Based on numerous iconographic representations it appears that this armor did have metal sleeves. The length of the garment to protect the infantry was a little shorter than those used by the cavalry, while still protecting the groin, which was considered vulnerable. The armor strip protecting the waist or hips down incorporated strips of skin or cloth like pteruges on the Greek linothorax. In earlier times this part of the armor might be solid. Shell armor of that length and design later appear in Parthian and Sassanid forces.

The suits were made of metal – iron, bronze plates or scale with flat or round lower edges, hence that passage about the fish's appearance. Along the top edge two, three or four holes were made depending on the method of attaching the plate to the backing. A few examples of this type scale armor come from the "treasury" in Persepolis, Pasargades, Chorsabad and the Apis Temple in Memphis.[66] The scales belonging to the guard troops were especially small, measuring approximately 2 x 2 cm.

The method of constructing is essentially the same as the well-preserved examples of scale armor found in the barrows of the Scythian aristocracy (at Staršaj Mogiła, Nova Ryžanovka, Aksjutintsy, etc.). They are placed in such a way in each horizontal row covered the left side of the one next to it. In this construction, a jab from a spear on the right, or unshielded side, from slipping between the scales. Laces protected the lower edges of the top row of scales, some of which were purposely bent.

From the end of the fifth/beginning of the sixth century BCE, the Greek linothorax of glued layers of canvas were quite common. They were much lighter than the traditional scale armor, while providing good protection from blows. By the time the armies of Alexander the Great and the Achaemenids collided with each other in a great war, their heavy infantry troops were uniformly armored. Only the guard units had metal armor.

The Persian infantry rarely wore helmets, replacing them with what Herodotus called, "tiaras". As seen in the Persian reliefs they wore a kind of soft, pointy hat with elongated, "cheeks" which were used in a similar manner to the Arabian kufiyah. They wrap them around the neck as is evident in many reliefs for example, protecting against the sun and sand, excellent for checking the effects of sandstorm conditions or dust clouds caused by the trampling of a column of thousands of soldiers.

At the end of the Achaemenid era (late 4th Century BCE) as evidenced by numerous iconography, i.e. on the "Alexander Sarcophagus" or the mosaic in the "House of the Faun" in Pompeii, the infantry had adopted helmets and the cavalry, the Mede tiaras. Several seals from Persepo-

---
[66]Е. В. Черненко, op.cit., p. 22.

The Armies of Ancient Persia

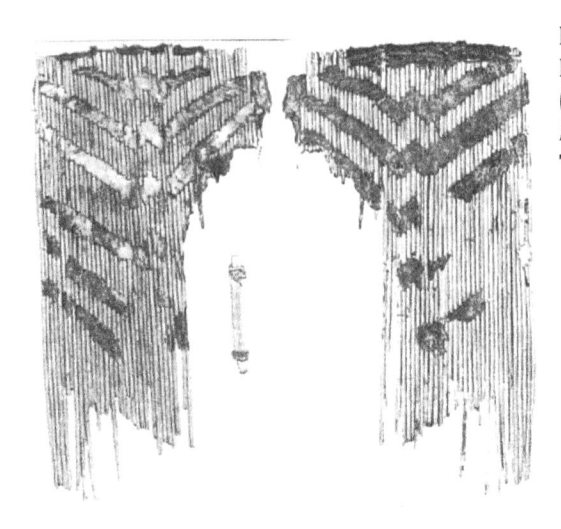

Large, reed shield from Dura-Europos - the Partian period. (according to M. Ростовцев, *Preliminary report* ... Vol. 5. Tab.26

Persian infantryman protected by a cane spara, kylix Brygos (according to D. Head, The Achaemenid Persian Army, fig. 9b)

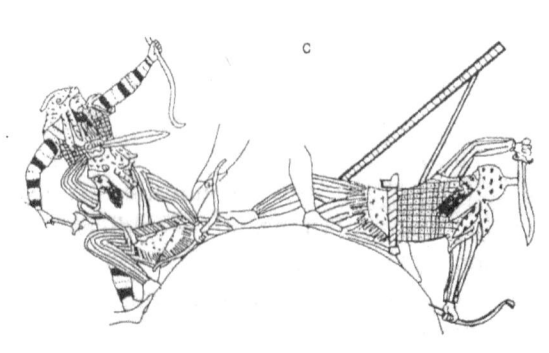

Persian infantryman defending himself from behind the spara shield barrier. Kylix brygos (by D. Head, The Achaemenid Persian Army, fig.9c)

lis show infantry wearing helmets that might be "Kuban", which could be associated with the desire to strengthen the headgear. It would appear that this was restricted to the most elite guard troops.

They did not seem to wear armor besides the scale jerkin. Soldiers wore pants, which were also probably colored, but it is unclear whether they are canvas or leather cavalry pants (Herodotus, Bk I, Ch 71), reaching just over the ankle, with laced shoes, such as those clearly visible on the brick frieze at the palace of Darius at Susa. The shield completed the integral protection and equipment of the soldiers. The Persians used three main kinds: The main infantry type was called the, "Pelt", which was made of wicker, small, round and the outer surface covered with rawhide. This did not have any metal fittings. Shields of this type are shown on the "Alexander Sarcophagus ". The Persian Pelt was probably about 60-70 cm in diameter, with the portion cut-out crescent shaped like the Thracian Pelt, only smaller. These devices were used by many of the Cardaces but were also popular with the soldiers of many nations subject to the Persians so as Thracians and Scythians.

Guard units from the time of Xerxes had shields that were much larger and stronger, ellipsoidal shield. Judging from proportion of the shield to the soldier (based on the upper row of the relief in the portal room in the hundred columns), the dimensions of the shield were about 1 to 1.2 meters in length to about 60 cm wide. This shield is oval with elliptical cutouts on the sides. This design is made of wood, with the exterior covered with one or more layers of hide.[67] As we know from ethnographic observations, the skin covering the shield in many places of the world was left raw, drying in the sun and to give it hardness, it was roasted over a fire. This gave it great strength and greater resistance to weather conditions. To cover the shield and use for armor, the best leather comes from the back of cattle where it is thickest.[68] The guard's shields were stripped of the bristles, which in the rain is easily penetrated by moisture.

This shield, very light and perfectly strong, lent itself to maneuver in combat, and its design had lower strength and resistance compared to the bronze shield of the covered hoplon when they were encountered in a clash of arms. The shield was held in the hand by cross straps which extended from the arms and the hand in the center protected by a metal boss. This example comes from the treasury of Oxus where a similar boss was covered with silver and gold - most likely the boss of the royal guard's shield, hence their name Argyraspides (Silver Shields) men-

---

[67] Е. В. Черненко, op.cit, p. 22.
[68] J. Cooles, *Archeologia doświadczalna*, tłum. M. Mickiewicz, Warszawa 1977. p. 202.

The Armies of Ancient Persia

The spear fitting of the Achaemenid cavalry spear (the so-called pom) Deve Hűyűk

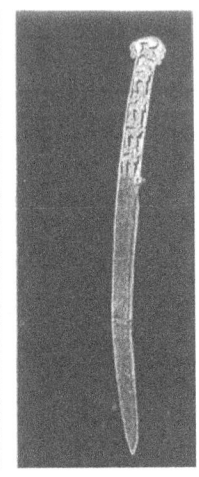

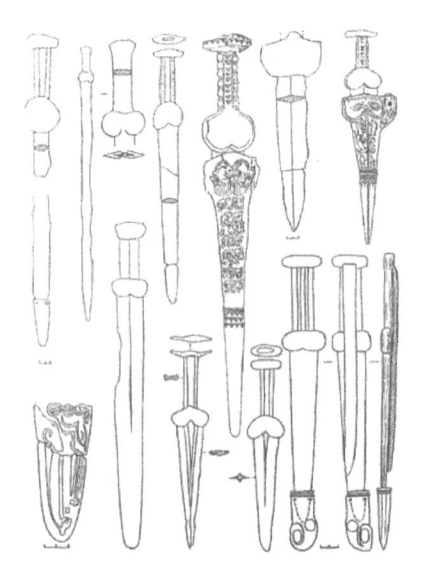

(Left and above) Different types of blades and hilts for Scythian acinaces - from the Western Scythian territories (a), acinaces and knifes from Minusińska basin (b) (by Е. В. Черненко, *Скифо-ерсидская война*, 24 is).

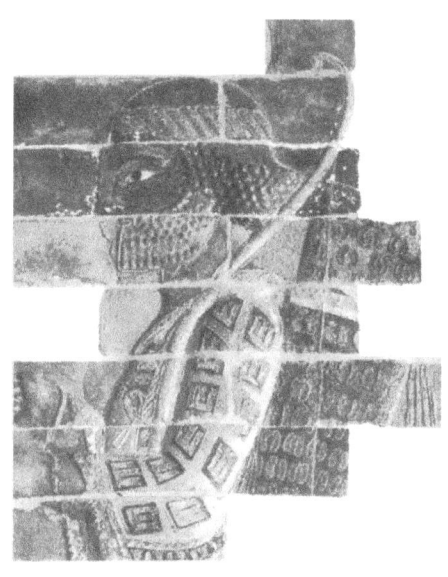

Neck of a long, reflective infantry bow from the archers' weapons of the royal guard - a frieze of glazed bricks from Dariusz's palace and in Susa. (according to O. Dalera ed., *Powers of the World*, fig.195.196)

Spear thrust "from below" in execution Greek hoplity - painting on a vase black and white figure. (A.J. Holaday, *Hoplites and Heroes* ...)

The Armies of Ancient Persia

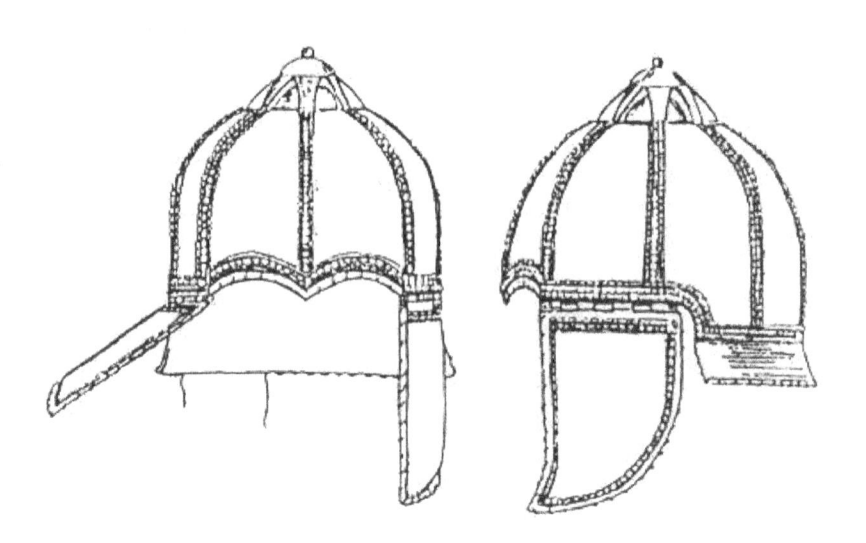

A Lydian helmet discovered in the ruins of a house from the end of the 6th century BCE in Sardes (according to D. Head, *The Achaemenid Persian Army*, fig.42)

Lydian chariot Terracotta warriors with Sardes. End of VIth Century BCE (according to D. Head, *The Achaemenid Persian Army*, fig.41c)

Scythian helmets from north and northeast Thrace (left) helmet from the Detroit Institute collections of Arts (below) image from the helmet of Agighiol, V century BC

Persian infantry from the times of Dariusz III on the hunt, equipped as in the battle with the aspis shield. (according to R. Ghirschman, *Persia. Proto-Iranians, Medes, Achemenides*, fig.447)

Two reliefs from the "Nereid monument of Xanthos in Lycia - an archer as used in the Achaemenid army supporting the Lycian hoplites (according to M. J. Olbrycht, *Alexander the Great and the Iranian World*, Tab.2.10 and 2.11.)

tioned by Iamblichus.[69] Such a shield was lightweight, flexible, resistant to arrows and sword cuts, while less so from the spear as the way the Greek hoplon was used. The closest analogy was probably the method of fighting with the archaic "Boeotian" shield and fighting technique using a spear and a large leather shield used successfully up to the nineteenth century during the Zulu warriors with the English. This type of fighting does not allow for passive moves, which would expose the shield to puncture, but used it in a way to deflect the thrusting spear of an opponent in such a way that the tip slipped from the surface of the leather covering without causing harm. The sword stroke was defended in the same way using the metal boss. This method of fighting required great skill and could only be gained through long exercises. Considering, however, the number of wars, and the rebels of conquered people the Persian warriors fought required a high level of training as were professional warriors.

Influenced by their wars with the Greeks between the V-IV centuries BCE, the Boeotian style shields were eventually replaced by the by shields typically used by hoplites in the more compact formations. The use of the hoplon by Persian infantry can be verified by depictions on the so-called, "Alexander Sarcophagus". Considering, that by this time the use of linothorax Greek style armor had spread to the cavalry and infantry, along with long spears, Persian units of this period began to resemble their Greek foes more and more.

The reliefs of Persepolis from the time of Darius I as well as descriptions of Herodotus show a different type of protection, very large cane shields called "spara" or "gerron" in Greek. They were made by weaving thick, fresh cane reeds. These shields were probably similar to those found in a Scythian barrow measuring approximately 1.4m high and .5m wide. These remains are similar to much later versions of Parthian shields found at Dura-Europos. This type shield was probably used by soldiers fighting in the front line called, "Sparabara". Most likely one thousand of the "Immortals" were officers placed at the head of every ten-man column were just the Sparabara, hence the lack of archers on reliefs. In the time of Darius, the shield bearer regiment also used spara shields. It was Xerxes who brought in the Boeotian style shields. During the later Achaemenid period both these types were replaced by the hoplon or apis. It appears that during the reign of Artaxerxes II, Xenophon still saw shield bearers with spara at Cunaxa.

According to Herodotus, these protective covers were used to make barriers in the front line of the infantry, especially in use for front line light troops, to protect them against arrows and projectiles, and mak-

---
[69]M.J.Olbrycht, *Aleksander Wielki i świat irański*, Rzeszów 2004, p. 149., Jamblichi Babyloniacorum reliqiae, (ed.) E.Habrich, Lipsiae, 1960, fragm. 1.

ing it difficult for enemy infantry to attack them. Numerous examples of Greek painted ceramics such as Kylix, "Oxford" and "Bassegio" confirm that they were held up by stick supports.[70] Shields like this were also sometimes tied together for protection when establishing military camps in the field. Herodotus described the fight for such a barrier at the Temple of Demeter at Plataea: *"The Persians bound shields into a wall letting loose with a large number of arrows, so that the Spartans found themselves in a difficult position (...), first the Tegeans (...) moved on the barbarians and then the Spartans, after Pausanias successfully scarified. When they finally came out successfully, they decided the time had come and moved against them. The Persians abandoned their bows as the battle raged against the shield walls. When this collapsed fierce fighting broke out near the temple itself."* (Herodotus, Bk IX, Ch 61-62). Spara Shield were also used during the Battle of Mykale (Herodotus, Bk IX, Ch 12).

Tall reed shields are also known from the Persepolis reliefs, where they are shown carried by soldiers in the palace dressed in long flowing robes, which is unusual since they did not typically wear these robes in the field. Perhaps they were used by the royal guard on official occasions when he was going around in public areas where he could be attacked, for example, by an archer. It is however, an untestable theory.

The primary offensive weapon of the Persian infantryman was a spear. There are many known iconographic representations of these weapons at Persepolis, Bisutun, Suza, etc. Its length can be estimated in comparison to the soldiers depicted next to it as approximately 1.7 to 2 meters long. Herodotus describes the Persians using short spears (Herodotus, Bk VII, ch 61) as compared to the size of the Greek hoplite spears which were 2.5-3 meters long. The spear point was leaf shaped, as shown on the brick friezes at Suza (most likely these belong to the older types used in the time of Darius!), or diamond shaped (the newer type from the time of Xerxes) from the reliefs at Persepolis and were made of iron.

Those spears depicted at Susa have a particularly long throat to protect the point from being cut off. A second type of blade was discovered in the so-called, "Treasury" at Persepolis.[71] This was 20 cm in length, and the leaf is lenticular in its cross-section with the sleeve one-half the length. This is basically identical to the examples shown in relief on the inner surface of the gate in the "room of a hundred columns".

The weight of the spear tip was counter-balanced by placing a weight on the opposite end. These were decorative (counter-balance) which for the elite regiments were represented as golden apples for the

---

[70] D. Head, op.cit., p.23.
[71] Е. В. Черненко, op.cit., p 28.

elite guard regiments, golden pomegranates got the officers of "Immortal" guard regiments and silver for the soldiers. "A thousand of them (the Immortals), had spears with a gold pomegranate butt spikes, while around them were nine thousand soldiers using silver pomegranates. Golden Pomegranates, and golden apples are shown pointing to the ground behind Xerxes. (Herodotus, Bk VII, Ch 41). This type of fitting has subsequently been found at Deve Hüyük.[72]

In combat the warrior held the spear in the middle of the shaft, limiting its effectiveness as only .85 – 1 m of the weapon was used in combat depending where you gripped it. This fact is highlighted by the fact that it was really used for short or medium distances. However, what was the advantage in a clash of hordes, was a shortcoming in confrontations with bristling ranks of long spears of the Greek hoplites. Battles with the Greeks therefore went better from the IV century BCE onward as the Achaemenid heavy infantry were equipped with the long hoplite spear.

In the second rank, swords were the most common weapon. Rank and file soldiers probably used a version of the "Immortal" acinaces which is commonly depicted in iconography. They are gorgeous and extremely decorative swords whose class and quality of work which emphasized the status of the owners.

A wonderful example of this weapon was found at Ecbatana. Although this is a ceremonial version entirely made of solid gold, its shape gives a good idea of how the best combat ones were used by the Iranian guards. It is a double-edged sword, with the blade slightly tapering toward the hilt. The hilt was made in the form of a lion's heads at the pommel and the crossguard had the heads of goats on the ends. The scabbard, however, has not survived but it should mimic the same shape as the acinaces.

A somewhat similar type of sword was discovered in the barrow at Čertomłyk with a handle that shows signs of modifications which are shaped with the heads of two sheep, with the style associated with different animals associated with areas of the Achaemenid Empire. The style dates from the late sixth or early fifth century BCE.[73] This weapon belonged to a cavalryman, as evidenced by holes in the pommel made for a strap so that they would not drop it in battle.

A well preserved, Achaemenid iron acinaces comes from the grave in the cemetery at Deve Hüyük.[74] Its hilt resembles the sword hilt at Črtomłyku, a flattened gold pommel and the pommel of the courtier standing behind the King and heir to the throne, Darius, on the relief of

---

[72] P.R.S. Moorey, *Cemetaries of the First Millenium BC at Deve Hüyük, near Carcemish*, Oxford 1980.
[73] Е. В. Черненко, op.cit., p. 49.
[74] N.Sekunda, *The Persian Army*, p. 20.

the audience all in the treasury at Persepolis.

The acinaces were short swords, not exceeding 60 cm in length, including those worn by the Persian foot except for the "Immortals" and can be seen to taper toward the point. The first rank was for stabbing and the second was for slashing.

In addition to the spear and shield, each of the infantry warriors was equipped, of course, with a bow and arrow. "Instead of large bows, they were small composite bows which were placed in bow-cases, another short spear as well as reed arrows" (Herodotus, Bk VII, Ch 61).

Infantry bows, although like the cavalry bows in design and shape, as well as being composite and reflexive, were probably a little longer. On the reliefs it seems the length of the bow was probably 1.3 – 1.5 m. These type bows allowed the possibility to use heavier arrows with more force behind it. On the upper part of the bow, the nock for setting the bowstring, was made of hardwood or bone and made to look like swans or gooseheads.

As shown in the scenes at Persepolis, or the glazed friezes of Suza, the infantry bow was worn slung, over the left shoulder. The absence of enclosed or protective cover made the weapon sensitive to moisture and atmospheric factors, which suggests it was coated to some sort of protective covering (in China and Japan, for example, they lacquered their bows).[75] This does not mean, of course, that during breaks between battles or campaigns, that the bow staff was not covered for protection, either wrapped in leather or clothe and the bowstring unstrung and stuck somewhere into the quiver. As the shape of the foot bows shows, these were simple bows, not made in the recursive style.

The arrows were about 90cm in length and kept in an ornamental quiver, with a functional outside flap. This quiver was colorfully decorated with strings attached at different lengths which are clearly visible on the Persepolis reliefs or the friezes of Susa. Shooting bows is much better when the string is quickly pulled out and re-strung, made easier by its quick application from the quiver. The long infantry quivers are shown worn over one shoulder, which made effective fire a little cumbersome. If it was worn that way, the quiver could easily fall off. It is more likely that the strap was worn at an angle across the shoulders from right to left, but this is not visible because it is covered by the large sleeves.

Arrows used by the infantry, as well as the shorter cavalry bows were made of bamboo-like reeds (cane?) and wood.[76] After the reed was freshly cut it was most likely straightened, dried and smoothed, then

---

[75]H. Onuma, D.i J. DeProspero, *Kyudo, Japońska sztuka łucznictwa*, tłum. W. Nowakowski,Bydgoszcz 2001. p. 42.

[76]Е. В. Черненко, *Скифские лучники*, Киев 1981, pp. 27-28.

trimmed to the correct size. The stalk was then introduced to a variety of substances to harden it. Three feathers for stability were added to the outside of the shaft end. According to experts, the feathers of birds of prey are the best, but when producing mass numbers of missiles, army units probably used cheaper species of birds.

Infantry missiles were probably the most numerous things founds in the "vault" at Persepolis. They were diamond and leaf-shaped with a reinforced rib. The arrowheads were usually affixed using a short stem. One long range missile found on the field at Marathon had a long throat and a leaf-shaped head.

Light Infantry - Satrap Contingents and Allied Nations. As discussed in the previous chapters assault weapons constituted the backbone of the Persian Empire army units. To complement this picture, before getting into a discussion of tactics used by the Persian infantry units, we should briefly look at the armament and equipment of those soldiers belonging to the Satraps of the enormous Achaemenid Empire. These units differ in combat value but were the largest contingent of combat troops in the Achaemenid force. The descriptions depicting the battles fought by the Persian Armies are usually general statements about the huge mass of light troops being used to in unspecified support of the assault troops. Sometimes, the heaviest of these units, mainly formed from the Asiatic satraps (especially in the V century BCE) even as secondary assault troops deserve mention.

The most complete description of these basic supporting heavy units of the mosaic of tribes and people are once again found in the "Acts" of Herodotus. Of course, this description comes from the reign of Xerxes, in the tactics and the types of light armament. Compared to elite units, these units would have been slow to change.

Analyzing the long and seemingly monotonous image of the marching Satrap contingents it seems that this huge and massed jumble of men would be impossible to reasonably and effectively command. While some of the contingent (i.e. the very colorful Ethiopian or Libyans) did not have much combat value and were probably included mainly as hostages or a show of obedience by the people of the Satrap to the reigning King of Kings, many of these individuals could be successfully divided between units of lightly armored support, heavy assault, infantry or cavalry. Based on their equipment the soldiers can be divided into three basic groups.

1. Heavily armored shock troops that fought either in the Hellenistic or Iranian style. Of course, in the later period (starting rough-

ly from the middle of the Vth century BCE), the impact of the former, especially in the western Satraps of the Empire was becoming more and more dominant. This does not mean total Hellenization of weapons and military tactics, i.e. Asian Minor Satrapy. "Nereid Monument" of Ksanthos, or sarcophagus of Çan indicate there was a combination of Oriental military traditions with strong Hellenistic influences.

2. Light infantry units supporting the front-line heavy. These troops not only had bows, but were also armed with melee weapons, which indicates the task of supporting heavy troops in the second phase of the fight.

3. Light Infantry troops only armed with close combat weapons used as cover and support for elite troops in the second phase of combat.

The first group includes most of the contingents from Asia Minor and the Greek Island – Lydians, Lycians as well as Egyptians. These nations provided excellent troops of great combat value (but as in the case of the Egyptians, not the most obedient to their Achaemenid masters. The Ionian Greeks used arms and equipment very similar to their European brethren. They carried heavy spears 2-3 m in length and usually the aspis shield. During the reign of Xerxes, they wore strong, forged bronze armor which was gradually replaced by lighter linothorax style armor from the Greek mainland. This type of armor worked well enough that, impressed by its use in the battles of the Greek and Persian wars, it was adopted as a whole or in part by the people neighboring the Greeks in the Balkans (Illyrians, Thracians and Macedonians), as well as in Asia Minor (Lycians and Carcians, even at the times of Xerxes, the Hellenic formations of the Great King's army from as early the mid-5th century BCE quickly used Hellenized equipment.). Images of Soldiers armed in the hoplite style against cavalry (probably Persian or enemy soldiers in the service of rebellious Satraps of the north-western border) are depicted in cameos of the Achaemenid period (they are even depicted on a Chalcedonian seal dated from the fourth century BCE at Panticapaeum in the Crimean, which came from Asia Minor).[77] Additionally, there is no monumental art of Asiatic troops fighting in the Greek way. The Nereid Monument of Xanthos clearly shows lines of hoplites dressed in linothorax armor with Corinthian, Attic or Thracian style helmets with xiphos (swords). A relief also honoring Pericles shows a soldier dressed in heavy armor with a long-sleeved, knee length tunic wearing a hoplite

---

[77] M.J. Olbrycht, op.cit, il.2.8.A

The Armies of Ancient Persia

helmet and aspis type shield.[78] A similar figure is shown on the Heroon at Trysy in the first half of the fourth century BCE.[79]

According to Herodotus, during the time of Xerxes' Greek expedition, the Ionic and Lydian units were armed and equipped in the Greek fashion, supported by lightly armed infantry units from Caria, Lycia and Pamphylians, equipped with bows, as well as swords, daggers, shields, leather, metals breastplates and greaves. The Egyptians were protected by scale armor made from strips of leather (as was done in southern-Europe using plates and leather straps), helmets with high wooden crests, armed with spears, axes, and the bent khopesh swords traditionally used in conjunction with the Ethiopian and Libyan armies. These were composed of soldiers who could fight as archers or light infantry swordsmen. Heavily armored auxiliary units of the Achaemenid also included a large contingent of Hellenic mercenaries, which increased over time. In general, it appears that the share of mercenary troops came from different nations, not only Greeks, in the Achaemenid army increased over time. Ionian and Aeolian mercenaries were already were already in the army during the reigns of Cyrus the Great and Cambyses (The Histories, 1,17,13,1,25). They were recruited from among the Chalybes, Taochi, Indians and Chaldeans and of course Jews, as we know from texts discovered in Egyptian Elephantine.

Units of well-trained Hellenic mercenaries were shown in use in descriptions of battles during Alexander the Great's eastern campaign as elite troops, interchangeable with the best assault units of the main battle line, or as an impact group such as the right wing at the battle of Cunaxa. Even at Cunaxa, however, Cyrus the Younger, as described in Xenophon's account used the Greeks to attack the central position of the King of Kings battle line. As is known, the portion of Artaxerxes sitting on the flank of Cyrus' army did not move for fear of being outflanked by enemy cavalry. During the time of Artaxerxes III and Darius III mercenary Greek hoplites and light infantry were employed to support the Persian Army operating in Egypt and Asia Minor.[80] The Greeks also accompanied Darius III at the time of his escape to Aria.

The second group of the Achaemenid's light infantry included soldiers mainly equipped with bows of different types (many made with composite wood, tendons and horn or long Asian types made of bamboo.), short spears, swords (often Iranian acinaces as seen on the Persepolis reliefs) or daggers. According to Herodotus, the troops fitting this type of description were mainly from the Iranian peoples (i.e. Bactrians,

---

[78]D. Head, op.cit, fig. 44 i.
[79]D. Head, op.cit, fig. 43 b.
[80]M.J.Olbrycht.op.cit, p.89.

Sakas, Arians, Caspians, Parishanians, etc.). Other excellent archers and warriors were the Armenians, Indians, Pakthians, Utio, Mykos, Kabali, Milyasians, Assyrians, Chaldeans, etc.

The third group includes contingents of people from Europe (Thracians) and Asia Minor (The Bithinyans resettled there by the Achaemenids such as Pisidians, Mizia, Alorian, Saspirians, Moschi, Tibareni, Macrones, Colchis, Paphlagonia, Matiene, Mossynoeci, Mara, etc.). All those soldiers were equipped with various types of bladed weapons, leather or woven wicker shields, spears, javelins and helmets of various material from leather to wooden.

The role of the massed light infantry within the tactical arms of the Achaemenid army is not known. From the descriptions of battles fought by the Persian armies during the years of the Achaemenid Empire, we believe that these units were most often placed behind the main battle line of assault troops, usually on the wings, behind the cavalry units to increase the length of the formation. Then they might secure their front lines in difficult terrain (as at Issus), or as a defensive line that combined cane reed barriers with rope known as spara (as in the battle of Plataea). The Light infantry was equipped with shields, spears and bows.

The light infantry was equipped with shields, spears and swords or daggers, providing excellent support for operating on the flanks with cavalry, especially the heavy cavalry. Because the overall tactics used by the Achaemenid infantry will be discussed a little later, it is still worth noting that most of the light troops fought in a dispersed formation so that the spear or shield and weapons such as the macharja or rhomphia (used for example by the Thracians) was not very practical to be used by heavily armored infantry in close formations.

In addition to bows and acinaces, soldiers from the eastern satrapies are shown in iconographic representations with axes commonly called "sagaris". This weapon most likely originated in the steppes where they are frequently found in graves along with various other types of axes. It was adopted early in history of Iran and Xenophon claimed it was also used in the hunting (Xenophon Bk 1 9,9). In this context, the sagaris was shown, for example, on the "sarcophagus of Alexander" or mosaics in the palace of Pella from the early Hellenistic period. Some of these infantry units (probably commanders) are shown wearing Kuban or conical helmets recruited from the eastern satrap units from Asia Minor or Mesopotamia.[81]

Herodotus describes (usually superficially and in generalities) the armaments, equipment and armor of the Achaemenid light infantry

---

[81] М.В.Горелик, *Зашчитное вооружеие Персов и Мидян ахеменидского времени* ВДИ 1982, 3, pp.90-105.

more because of their exotic nature, than what he perceives as their combat value. His writing dismisses them as a marching masses of barbarian warriors. Compared to the typical equipment of Greek hoplites, they are in lightweight or primitive equipment. After all it did not provide sufficient protection to effectively fight against their opponent. The lack of armor was especially emphasized by Hellenic historians. They were still accustomed to the sight of fully armed, powerful armored hoplites. None of them, however, thought that after the experience of the "Ten Thousand Expedition" and the Peloponnesian War, the military system of using combined arms, i.e. close cooperation of heavy infantry, cavalry and light infantry units on the battlefield was the future of Hellenic military.

The satrap contingents were most often led by a Satrap, who usually came from the royal family or the six privileged noble families. Larger units were commanded by Persians, but there were exceptions. Some of the tribes, especially the highlanders (i.e. Pisidian who frustrated Cyrus the Younger, as they did Alexander the Great) had the status of allies, fought under the leadership of their own chiefs and probably shared in the spoils of war. Similarly, this must have been similar for the hostile nomad tribes of the steppes, as well as the allied kingdoms of the Persians such as Caria, Lycia, the city-sates of Cyprus and temporarily, even Macedonia, Thessaly and various cities of northern Greece subject to the rule of Darius and Xerxes. They served as recruiting areas for royal army troops, especially cavalry. One such unit was commanded during Xerxes Greek campaign by Alexander I of Macedonia, the ancestor of Alexander the Great. It should be noted however, that during the "Peloponnesian War" and "Holy War" they were not famous for armored cavalry. These are the only instances where northern Greece and Thrace appear in this context. As for this later area, archaeological finds confirm the military influence of the Iranian speaking people (Persians or Scythians) on the armament of cavalry especially in the fifth and beginning of the fourth centuries BCE.

In regards of this, the brief description of the armament of the Achaemenid infantry is done. Of course, many of the issues raised here are constantly under discussion and each new discovery may significantly affect the generally accepted theories about the structure, weaponry and functionality of these units. To complement this image, we should now look at the infantry tactics of the Achaemenids.

Achaemenid Infantry Tactics. According to Herodotus, each of the Achaemenid heavily armed infantry (except of course those armed and fighting in the Greek style) was equipped with two sets of arms; spear, shield and a sword, as well as bows and arrows (Herodotus, Bk VII, Chp

61). Of course, using one set of arms excludes the use of the others. Warriors had to do so during battle, change or anticipate a change of equipment designed to keep fighting from a distance. But, what was the reason for such a maneuver?

It was probably the desire to avoid two major weaknesses of large archer formations. The first is their vulnerability to front assault by infantry with spear or metal arms. The second was the lack of protection to fire from enemy archers. Protection against enemy arrows was provided to the Achaemenid by excellent heavily armored infantry in metal armor which was later replaced in the most part by leather and textile armor (reinforced with metal or not). In the case of imminent contact with the enemy, the archers replaced their bows with spears and shields which over time became more like Greek hoplites and peltasts. This same action was followed after all the arrows in the quiver were shot. This maneuver of changing from fire to spear to meet the enemy attack was used by Persian infantry – i.e. the Cardaces during the Battle of Issus.[82] This system is reminiscent of the tactics used by Scythian and Persian cavalry.

Because of their spear length there could be no more than two ranks of men that could face attacking forces while they maintained a shield wall. The first row was high, often represented in Greek art as Persian reed spara. In addition to providing protection against enemy attacks which shielded the front, it also provided protection against direct fire from field pieces or of arrows. It was often used to protect infantry from missiles and was described as walls compiled as barriers and connected with ropes like a mobile fortress. The infantry was also protected by cavalry behind them, while on the flanks they placed light infantry without the need for additional protection from light-medium carcadaces infantry. They could support the battle with cavalry or by swarming them as was often the case with European armies. On the flanks, light infantry was next to the cavalry to protect the flanks of the heavy infantry.

The moment the enemy units hit the first line (the heaviest and armored) they were supported by two-three lines (lighter armed and probably in a loose formation armed like a peltast – a spearman called, "takabara") to form the so-called, "attack force" to maintain the cohesion of the whole formation. When archers fired arrows, all the heavy and light infantry joined in. The first line of infantry probably put their bows away, before any attack.

The most effective fire on an attacking opponent was the massed fire of archers. The shots had to be sent between and over the heads of the soldiers standing in front of them. The rest of the archers were con-

---
[82] N. G. L. Hammond, Geniusz Aleksandra Wielkiego, tłum. J. Lang, Poznań 2000, p. 97.

signed to the so-called, "winding" or "plunging-fire". We don't know how deep the Persian armored ranks were, but optimally it would have been approximately between 10-20 ranks deep (Herodotus and Xenophon in Cyropedia says the Achaemenid army used the decimal system). This formation provides adequate depth to "push," giving you the chance to stretch the line an appropriate distance (it was expected to be around one meter per soldiers) providing protection for the mostly unarmored archers. When the advancing enemy collided, the fight with the first rank of troops formed a tight, compact mass which became a target for the ranks of the Cardaces and subject national contingents to fire into the enemy. Using "plunging-fire", a skilled archer could easily loose 12-18 shots per minute, while the necessity of fighting against a well-trained Persian infantryman usually ended badly for soldiers that were lightly armored or without any at all as was the case with many warriors in the Ancient East. In the long run, it was only the heavy infantry, e.i. Greel Hoplites, which were able to hold on long enough to break through the heavy troops and attack the light troops set behind them.

    The first rank of the Persian infantry held their spears high over the right shoulder, or low at the elbow so as to strike from below. This method is a similar technique used by Zulu tribes who fought with their short 1-1.5 m broad headed spear and very long blade fighting behind a large shield - similar to the Roman gladius. The jab was made to see the opponent's reaction and reveal his intentions. This way of holding the spear and fighting with it was well-known in antiquity and was also used by some Greeks. It allowed for a quick jab and strong blow to main part of the opponent's body. The most practical way of doing this however, was an attack on the middle and lower part of the body, groin and thigh as these wounds were extremely dangerous because of the high probability to puncture vital organs or femoral artery. Support for the first rank was provided by the second rank, holding spears overhead in a similar way to the hoplites. The head and the throat of your opponent was probably exposed at first contact. The next rows were there to fill in the gaps caused by the wounds and deaths in the first ranks. The back ranks were still free to carry on firing over the heads of their comrades in front of them. With a pull in excess of 20 kg, launching bow shots at a distance of over one hundred meters is no problem. Armored cavalry - heavily armored Persians, Medes, Circassian and Hyrenian, as well as Ionic Greek and Hellenistic mercenaries formed up like this, acting as cover for much more numerous archers, infantry and light troops from subject nations which led to fire from outside the battle lines to protect the flank and unarmored troops – which under this tactical doctrine, did not need armor. Greek historians describe scores of unarmored Persians fleeing before hoplites, by which they mean that earlier in the battle the hoplites had to beat back and defeat the heavily armored Persian units. Often accounts ignore the fact that the elite units of bodyguards and immortals were often associated with the forces that could be called the "crown army" and were only set out under the direct control of the King of Kings. They were not in the many armies led by satraps, generals or minor pacification operations. Such an expedition led to the famous battle of Marathon where they were not present. Even under Mardonius at Plataea he no longer had armored infantry under his command, as most of the elite troops were taken by Xerxes either to winter quarters, or to suppress a rebellion in the important area of Babylon. The list of troops allegedly left behind for Mardonius corresponds perfectly to the order of battle of the heaviest units of the Persian armed forces, but even an inexperienced historian would be suspicious. Suspicious, in relation to Herodotus' account that the immortals would stay in Greece even though their commander Hydarnes returned with the king to Asia and they are not mentioned later in "Acts", so that Mardonius only had Cardaces as heavy infantry at Plataea, while the Medes were fighting later the same day at the Battle of Mykale, etc. In the balance of the land battles with the Greeks against the full power of the Achaemenid army (battles including the Ionian uprising, Thermopylae, Cunaxa campaign of Artaxerxes III, Ochos in Egypt, etc.) the story is not as rosy for the Greeks.

Sometimes, however, some Hellenic scholars show a more objective view of the fighting qualities of the Persian heavy infantry, *"Mardonius was fighting on a white steed and around him were one thousand of the best Persian soldiers who pressed their opponents to the utmost. When Mardonios was killed, the troops surrounding him, the largest part of the army fell back, at which point the the rest turned to escape and give way to the Lacedaemonians."*(Herodot.IX, 63.)

Please note that the reconstruction of the Persian army today is based on analysis battles carried out by ethno-archeological observations and descriptions of other people whose soldiers mainly used spears (i.e. Greeks), through experimental archeology. Outside of the one above which speaks indirectly on their use and Xenophon, we are lacking confirmation of how infantry formations functioned. There are other theories on their use however. First, the use of the infantry above is similar to those coming from the period when the Achaemenid Empire clashed with people on other battlefields (i.e. India). [83] Secondly, a description in Arrian concludes that it is highly fitting that Alexander organized his army along the Persian lines when he started his campaigns to Arabia. *"These troops were to be composed of (...) four distinguished Macedonians unit:*

---
[83] R.E.Dupy, T.N.Dupy, op.cit., p. 36.

three infantry, one command, in addition to twelve Persian units. All the Macedonians were armed with Macedonian weapons (shield and sarissa), the Persians and others were armed with bows." (Arrian, W.Ai., book VII, 22-23). It is logical that the Macedonians would be typically armed with their long sarissa, a shield, armor on their chest and left arm. The phalanx shields constituted better protection than the great sparas or later aspis, behind them were placed the archers and peltast-takabara. Macedonian veterans or those Iranians trained to fight in the Greco-Macedonian style, were organized into formation that were three to four lines deep. In the Macedonian army, the best paid lochagos – command of a lochosu (file)[84] took his position in the first row to maintain the proper alignment of the formation and the position of the front rank of spears in order to be supported by three ranks of similarly armed soldiers. The Takabara were armed with two heavy javelins, designed to throw one of them over the heads of the sarissa in the first row, while the second was to be used directly in the fight. The "composite" system under which the Persians troops operated has already been described by Xenophon. It is not necessary to explain that in 323 BCE, Alexander knew Persian fighting techniques and its effectiveness in challenging lightly armed enemy that the Macedonian troops would encounter in Arabia.

The third example of the way Achaemenid infantry functioned is their description on images from the so-called, "Nereid monument" from Ksanthos in Likii. These bas-reliefs are in the Greek style showing Hellenic hoplites going into battle armed in the traditional manner. They are most likely from the Ionian city states with archers in formation shooting the enemy between their armored comrades.[85] It is logical that such a system was taken by the Lycans from their Achaemenid military superiors and masters.

Taking all these observations into account, one can deduce that the tactics of the Persian infantry was a continuation of their military achievements of a from a century earlier. Earlier, the Assyrians, for example, were already aware of the need to shield archers and they applied the use of a large reed shield to this use while they practiced fighting styles with light and heavy formations in battle.

Knowing the history and level of advancement of the art of war in the pre-Achaemenid east should not surprise anyone that the tactics used by the Persian armies was largely a combination of the best solutions that existed earlier in the Mesopotamian and Iranian systems of fighting.

---

[84] According to Asklepodiotos 'Taktiki'
[85] M. J. Olbrycht, op.cit. Tab.2.10 i 2.11.

2. The Persian Army in Battle. Background on the Army with Examples of Historical Battles During the Achaemenid Era.

Having shown the operations of the major formations within the Persian Army, it is important to show their place and position within the entire order of battle for the King of Kings. We are in a far better position at this than when the discussion was the methods of fighting within the formations themselves. Greek historians have left us a lot, but unfortunately, very different accounts of battles in which at least one case shows an interesting battle in Mesopotamia at Cunaxa, where both armies were very much Persian.

Most of the best of them constitute a large battle fought by Persians and Macedonians during the Eastern campaign of Alexander the Great. Considering that Arrian wrote his work on the expedition based on the memoirs of Ptolemy's son Lagos, later King Ptolemy I, perhaps the "royal diary", which according to tradition supposedly described the day-by-day course of the expedition; might the details provided by him be reliable enough to be able to provide us with answers to the question: how did the ancient Persians fight?

The most available information for use in general research on the battles of the Achaemenid army provides descriptions of the battles at Cunaxa, Issus and Gaugamela. To some extent it might also be helpful to take a short look at Herodotus' account of the clash of Cyrus II, the Elder, with the Lydians of Croesus. Based on that account of Persian tactics, it might be possible to shed some light on the interesting and growing description of the Battle of Granicus, where the Asian satraps used an almost "textbook" version of a Persian army.

An analysis of several decisive battles should allow us to create a model with a "matrix" pattern that would be well known and was individually adapted by later Persian commanders to terrain, the forces available and how to fight the enemy. The case studies, with the exception of Granicus, was under the command of the King of Kings, which guaranteed that the best units were involved. The battles were planned with great effort, using the best troops, according to established battle tactics. Localized fighting was under the command of Satraps did not necessarily mean mercenaries were hired to deal with conditions. The battles examine are in chronological order.

The Armies of Ancient Persia

Sardis (547 BCE) was one of the first to be fought on the plains near Sardis by the new armies recently formed in the Achaemenid Empire under the command of Cyrus II, later called, "the Great" and the Lydian Army under Croesus. Herodotus describes it as, *"When Cyrus saw (...) Lydians set in battle formation, he feared their cavalry and he followed the advice of the Mede Harpagos. He gathered all the camels at the rear of the army, laden with supplies and baggage, ordering them to remove their burdens and put riders on them in uniforms; once properly armed they set the army in motion against Croesus, the camels went with the infantry and after them they placed the cavalry. (...) Camels (...) who were sent against the cavalry, but the horses feared the camels, tolerating neither their sight or smell when it hit their nostrils."* (Herodotus, Bk I, Ch 80). This quotation is significant is that it supposedly mentions cavalry combat tactics suggested by Cyrus' Median nobleman. According to Herodotus, the Medes had close contacts with the nomadic steppe people, who also wore pants and jackets which were perfect for riding and which the Persians adopted. The Medes were the best breeders of horses and riders, which the Persians probably learned from in ancient times.

It is extremely interesting that camel riders are mentioned. They were known to have been used by the Achaemenid army, but not in large quantities. This branch of troops is mentioned, i.e. in the description of Xerxes army (Herodotus, Bk II, Chpt 86) departing in the expedition against the Hellas. While they had Arabs in their ranks, they probably rode horses. They were not in the army of Cyrus II, since the Persian Empire only incorporated areas inhabited by the Bedouin Arabs after the conquest of Babylon in 539 BCE. Cyrus had to use Asian camels – the so-called, "Bactrians" which probably lived in much larger parts of Asia than it is today. They could be found in the north-eastern provinces of the Persian state of the day. Asian nomads often used them as pack animals, while in the Parthian and later, Islamic armies' long caravans of camels carried supplies such as food and weapons on their backs. No route was too difficult for these extremely tough animals. They could even carry water for the horses that were directly used in battle. Herodotus had, therefore, most likely, correctly argued that the animals were specifically used to carry supplies and equipment. Their formation, therefore, was created on the spot and not the product of a larger formation.

As for the course of the battle with the Lydian themselves, the description itself is very sparse. We have virtually no details on the specific actions of the combatants during the course of battle. We cannot even say what units of Persian infantry they were, whether they were organized in units along the lines of later times, such as, "Immortals" (though Xenophon says that Cyrus first raised these units). It I also interesting to note that Cyrus was supposedly afraid of the spear-borne cavalry that the Lydians had formed. They most likely fought as a heavy cavalry unit in a separate formation such as the later Thessalian or Macedonian cavalry. This seems to be supported by a large number of Anatolian art pieces from the Achaemenid period, showing cavalry duels using spears.[86] There is little proof of the nature of Cyrus II's fear of light cavalry. The collision of these type formations of armored cavalry probably resembled what happened the time the Persians charged the position of Alexander the Great's guard and Cyrus knew it.

Compared to the steppe nomads, the Mesopotamians and Elamite of Persia began to use infantry on a much larger scale. It is very likely, however, that the army of Cyrus II had not yet reached the efficiency, power and method of operations it was known for centuries later. Their proper creator was considered a reformer in other areas of life – Darius the Great.

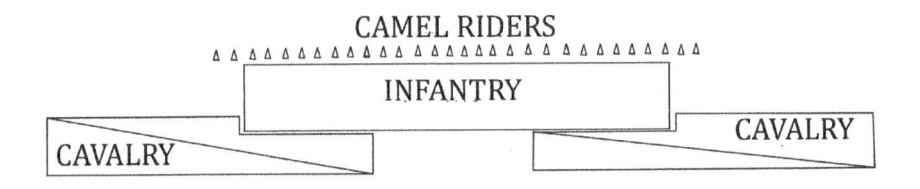

```
                    CAMEL RIDERS
          ▲ ▲ ▲▲ ▲ ▲▲ ▲▲▲▲▲ ▲ ▲▲▲▲▲ ▲ ▲ ▲ ▲▲▲▲▲ ▲ ▲▲
         ┌─────────────────────────────────────┐
         │              INFANTRY               │
┌────────┴────────┐                   ┌────────┴────────┐
│     CAVALRY     │                   │     CAVALRY     │
└─────────────────┘                   └─────────────────┘
```

Cunaxa (400 BCE.) Another well-known battle of great historical importance fought along the Euphrates River, not far from Babylon near the village of Cunaxa. It is probably one of the few occasions we have a first-hand account written by the person who saw it. Xenophon's part in the events and account has been accepted as highly credible. Unfortunately, with Xenophan as with any soldiers in battle except perhaps senior commanders, he could only describe the course of the fighting in the ranks and section where he was located. It is also true that he can discuss units that move away from his position, while he might know the units on the other side of the battle line, he would unfortunately not know their position. Therefore, he describes the enemy standing in this battle against the hired Greeks fighting in the rebel army on the side of Cyrus the Younger: "*As we approached there were bronze flashed as spears and ranks suddenly became visible. Riders in white armor were on the left wing of the enemy, led it was said, by Tyssafernesa. Adjacent this were units with woven shields; to their right were hoplites with wooden shields that reached their*

---
[86] B. Kaim, *Sztuka starożytnego Iranu*, Warszawa 1996. p. 165.

feet who apparently were Egyptians. In addition, there were horsemen and archers. They went on by nationality – every tribe of the people in the empire. A considerable distance in front of them drove chariots equipped with scythes." (Xenophon, *Anabasis*, Bk I, Chp 8).

In the picture that Xenophon paints, the left-wing of the troops under the King of Kings was organized as an armored cavalry bloc under the command of one of his most trusted Satraps – Tyssafernesa. He had designed this formation to launch a massive strike to protect the right flank of the hoplites and peltasts (i.e. spearmen and light spearmen) along with Paphlagonian cavalry. Such a charge would have blocked Cyrus from his best troops guarding the Euphrates, while fixed lines of Hellenic heavy mercenary infantry constituted a great threat to the left and center of the royal army. When the Greeks started their attack, however, something unexpected happened. All the Persians standing in front of the hoplites withdrew without a fight, which the Greeks pursued with joy. (Xenophon, *Anabasis*, Bk 1, Chp 8) Only the cavalry on flank of the left wing of the royal army made the charge without much resistance from the peltasts standing in front of them. The peltasts knew they could never stop this type of attack. The strange thing is that, according to Xenophon, as a result of the light armor of the peltasts no one died and on the contrary, they killed many armored horsemen. Even if the peltasts were veterans and tried to operate in a loose formation, the collision with a dense wedge of Iranian heavy cavalry would normally result in a massacre. The light troops probably retreated under the protection of the heavy hoplites on the right flank, guardng them from encirclement.

Although this seems possible (considering the relatively weak, morale of the non-elite Achaemenid units) as described by Xenophon, that the Persians were afraid of the approaching Greeks, so even in quick retreat they would be cautious. During this well-known Greco-Persian war, the famous royal infantrymen who fought against the heavily-armored hoplites so bravely were not merely "fancy barbarians". Describing the battle of Plataea, Herodotus admires their courage: *"When the shield-wall collapsed, there was a fierce battle near the temple of Demeter and the melee lasted for a long time, until the barbarian tried to grab the spears and were broken. The courage and the strength of the Persians yielded to the Hellenes..."* (Herodotus, Bk IX, Chp. 62). By the 4th century BCE Persian soldiers, through their long experience fighting in Asia Minor, knew the effectiveness of Hellenistic weapons where their courage in skirmishes with mercenary heavy infantry tested them to the extreme. This could have brought about cases of cowardice that could panic an entire wing of the royal army that made contact unlikely. If the consequences for failure had entailed punishment, it would have been terrible because Artaxerxes

The Armies of Ancient Persia

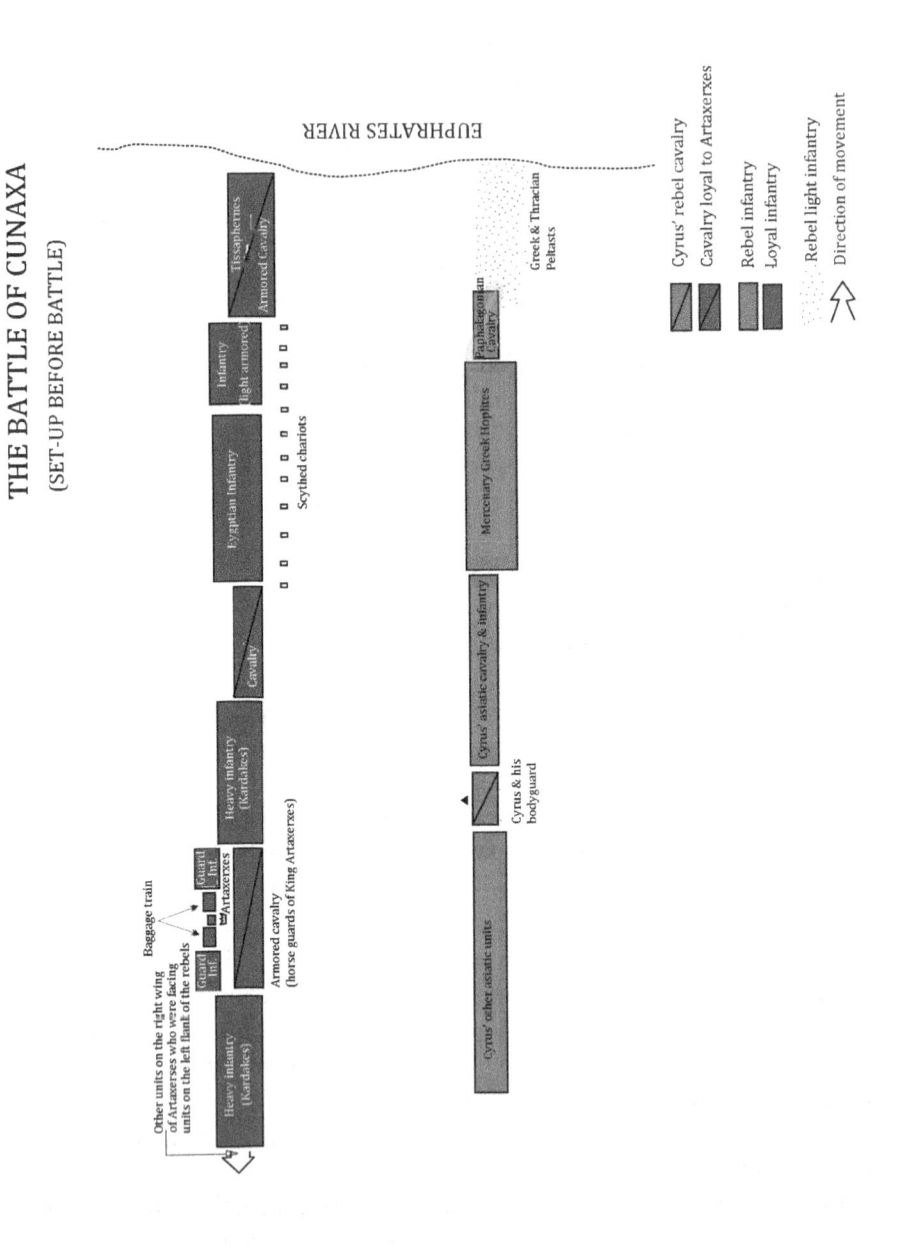

THE BATTLE OF CUNAXA
(SET-UP BEFORE BATTLE)

EUPHRATES RIVER

Tissaphernes Armored Cavalry

Infantry light armored

Egyptian Infantry

Scythed chariots

Cavalry

Heavy Infantry (Kardakes)

Guard Inf.
Artaxerxes
Guard Inf.

Baggage train

Armored cavalry (horse guards of King Artaxerxes)

Other units on the right wing of Artaxerxes who were facing units on the left flank of the rebels

Heavy Infantry (Kardakes)

Greek & Thracian Peltasts

Paphlagonian Cavalry

Mercenary Greek Hoplites

Cyrus' asiatic cavalry & infantry

Cyrus & his bodyguard

Cyrus' other asiatic units

Cyrus' rebel cavalry
Cavalry loyal to Artaxerxes
Rebel infantry
Loyal infantry
Rebel light infantry
Direction of movement

II was not known for mercy. Even a complete fool and a coward among the infantry would have been aware of that. Yet, even in the terrible fighting with the army of Alexander the Great seventy years later such things didn't happen.

Some broad propaganda even stated that the Greeks were uninjured, even though they were unarmored light troops. If the Persians fired a salvo from their "heavy" bows (or "light" and short for riders) specifically to start the battle, a lot of peltasts would have been killed or wounded. Finally, with a shout and attack the Persians attacked the hoplites without any attempt to make contact with the exception of the "blind" charge of Tyssafernesa, without a single salvo of arrows. Perhaps a few shots were fired, however, because Xenophon reported one (!) person was supposedly wounded (Xenophon, *Anabasis*, Bk I, Chapt 8). Perhaps in the face of such an odd number of instances, one might wonder if Xenophon is trying to hide something embarrassing?

Objectively speaking, despite what he might have thought about the "cowardly" army of Artaxerxes, if the royal army collided the Greek hoplites – well-armed and armored, veteran "Dogs of War" of the Peloponnesian War who lost their independence, the result of the clash would have been deadly. What's worse, after breaking the left flank of the King of King's forces they were sure they could hit them in the flank, or at the rear of the center, spreading out to pin them with the frontal attack of Cyrus' elite armored cavalry. They could only prevent this through a timely flanking maneuver of Tyssafernes cavalry division. He could not, however, stop the confusion. The Greeks retreat to the rear of Artaxerxes II's army would be equal to the king's defeat and the massacre of his troops. One could assume that the mercenaries had a little more skill in terms of maneuvering in battle than the citizen hoplites, for whom, anything outside of a straightforward attack would equate to a tactical miracle.

And what happened? The hoplites followed their escaping opponent but did not catch them. Since they could not catch them, they hit the center of the royal army as it fled without any losses, which at any moment could have turned on them, or hitting the rear of the king's units. The Greeks would attack when the enemy was between the hammer and an anvil, forcing them to fight on two fronts. Most likely, however, the Greeks are remembered for the chase and they did not even try to overwhelm them by a battle maneuver. Rushing ahead with abandon they left the rest of the battle to Cyrus and his men. It could be said they acted like schoolboys, not professionals. Sixty-two years later, in 338 BCE almost the same tactical error was made during the battle of Chaeronea that cost the Greeks not only defeat, but also their freedom. Then the skilled strat-

The Armies of Ancient Persia

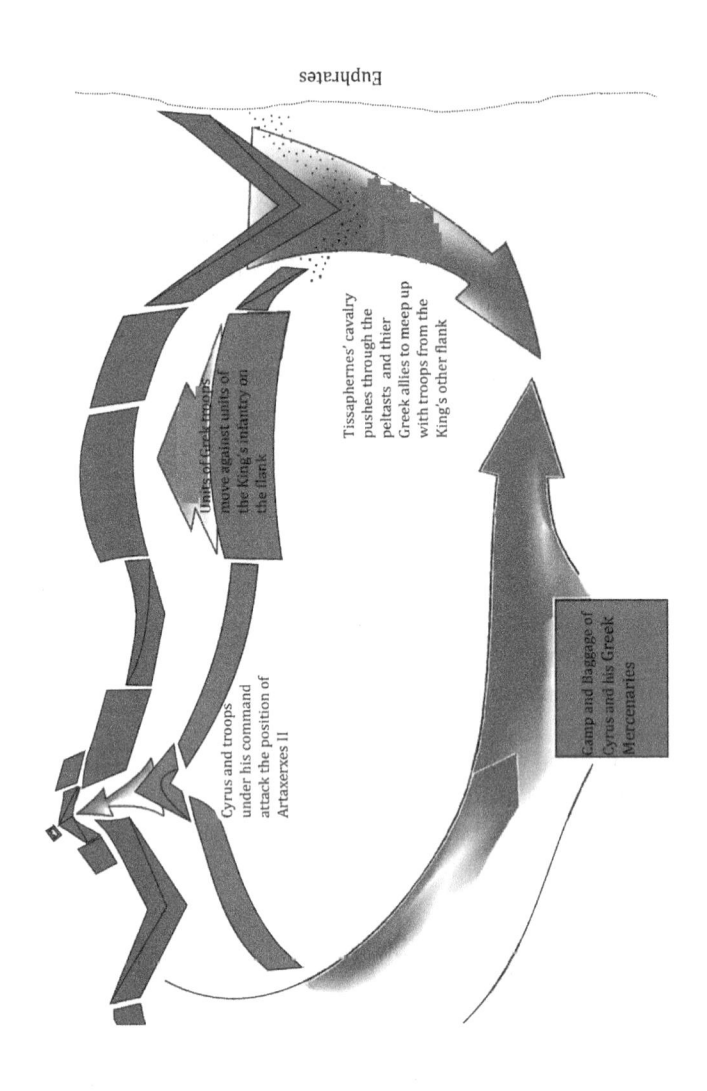

Euphrates

Tissaphernes' cavalry pushes through the peltasts and thier Greek allies to meep up with troops from the King's other flank

Units of Greek troops move against units of the King's infantry on the flank

Cyrus and troops under his command attack the position of Artaxerxes II

Camp and Baggage of Cyrus and his Greek Mercenaries

egist – Philip of Macedonia – by training his infantry guards, the so-called "hypastists" set on the right wing of the army to provoke a frenzied attack by the Athenians, thanks to which they overcame the Greeks and allowed the them to be encircled by the Companion Cavalry units under Alexander the Great.

According to Xenophon, during the Greek's attack on the center, the Great King's army attacked Cyrus' units on the right wing, extended far beyond flank before making a classic flanking maneuver to fall on the rear and Cyrus' camps to the rear of the Greeks. When they returned to the battlefield, believing they were the winner, they came face to face with a new battle against the troops of the King (Xenophon, *Anabasis*, Bk I, Chpt 10). While Artaxerxes was banging away on the right flank, the Persians on the left flank ran away from the enemy flanked by the Euphrates. The situation was tragic. The leader of the rebellion, Cyrus was killed, his camps with all food and supplies intended for the mercenaries were seized by the enemy. By then they knew they would not surrender even if they had to "sell their lives dearly", even though the Greeks had the option of surrendering to the Great King, as was appropriate and pass to his service because their employer was dead.

In the end as a result of mistakes made during the battle, only the "Ten Thousand' returned to Hellas because the Greek mercenaries repeatedly showd courage, military skill and excellent strategy. They used the latest tactical solutions created during the Peloponnesian Wars to protect themselves against attack. In addition to bold operations of light troops like those tried out during the withdrawal of Brasidas at Lyncus[87] or the Athenian battle with the Syracusians and Gylippus[88] in a four-sided battle formation (Xenophon, *Anabasis*, Bk III, Chap 2, Bk III, Chap 4). It should be noted however, that the Persians were not especially keen on chasing them. They never attacked with full force and the attacks they did make were only to keep the dangerous fugitives in place with one group under command of Tissaphernes and a subordinate. If they chose to present a full force for battle such as Artaxerxes and his staff which included people like the later famous soldier Megabyzos they might have been shown in a better light.

Back to the structure of the royal army; Arrian indicates it was common practice among Persian commanders that the right wing contained the heavy cavalry, where they could be intermixed with archers or treated as a standalone unit (Arrian, W.AI. Bk II, 8, Bk III, 11). Next to them were the soldiers with woven shields. From this, there are two

---
[87] G. Lach, *Sztuka wojenna starożytnej Grecji. Od zakończenia wojen perskich do wojny korynckiej*, Zabrze 2008, pp. 99-100.
[88] Op.cit., pp. 141-142.

possibilities: they were archers-heavy armored spearmen or light troops providing additional support for light cavalry archers in that these troop types were often used on the wings of Achaemenid formations. Placing these units in the first rank does not allow for attacks, as this position was usually composed of heavy infantry or ranks composed of *sparabara* in the front rank, followed by *takabara* and other archers. Examples of such infantry are the Cardaces at Issus and infantry with cavalry at Gaugamela.

Egyptian archers were equipped with woven shields which Xenophon recognized by their distinctive very tall, leather covered wooden shields (pavise). During most of the Achaemenid period, most of the soldiers from the Nile remain at the service of the Great King wearing leather scale or various types and they were primarily used as marines in Xerxes corps according to Herodotus (Herodotus, Bk VII, Ch 89). They were armed with curved swords, probably very similar to the old type khepesh (khopesh) and axes. Behind them "in row upon row stood horse archers". A similar tactic of combined arms was between heavily armored infantry and armored cavalry as described in Arrian's account of Gaugamela (Arrian, W. Al., Bk III, Ch 11). According to Xenophon in front of the Great King in the center of the army was a strong armored division, also probably working alone – without horse archers under the command of Artagersesa. Contributing to this formation could be the horse guards of Artaxerxes II, or additional heavy squadrons to reinforce the defense of the center. Ctesias indicates they were the later. Accordingly, it was supposedly made up of a unit from Cadusii (Cadusians).

Behind the infantry, the king was protected by a heavily armored squadron of cavalry composed of the so-called, "Companion's" (Household), one of who thrust the spear, "making a corpse of Cyrus" trying to kill ruler (Xenophon, Anabasis, Bk I, Ch 8). We don't know much about the other units forming on the right wing of the royal army except that the battle line extended beyond the left flank of Cyrus' troops. The rebels were taken in line fighting on the flank by a superior force with great fury and was thus defeated. Why didn't Cyrus try to use a different formation and start the battle under such unfavorable conditions? There is a puzzle about the "battlefield tactical errors" that cannot be fully explained. You wonder if Xenophon and his companions had indeed been so skillful on the battlefield that Artaxerxes II could have won something so important just by chance?

The Persian-Macedonian War. The battles already discussed, although they are extremely instructive examples of Achaemenid tactics, provide more questions than answers. So, it is time to take care of the three biggest battles in the history of the Achaemenid Empire. They are inextricably related, for tactical, logistical and historical reasons. They decided the fall of the great Persian monarchy and gave immortal fame to the winner – Alexander III, called the Great. The battles fought were these: Granicus, south of the Sea of Marmara, Issus in the northeast of the Mediterranean coast and ancient Gaugamela near Arbela (current Erbil). At Granicus, Macedonian troops clashed with the first line Persian defense, which were at time extremely powerful forces in the service of the Border Satraps.[89] At Issus, Great King tried to face the enemy invasion himself. He used units from the central and western provinces of his empire – mostly indigenous Persian-Median units of armored infantry and cavalry, as well as units of Greek mercenaries.[90] Gaugamela was the last of these "battles of nations" would be the most decisive clash. Crushed by the enemy forces hastened the fall of the Persian colossus. Darius III brought a huge mass of troops, this time mainly from the eastern provinces, as well as absorbing the survivors from the massacre at Issus.[91]

Issus was a battle of infantry, while at Gaugamela the decisive role was played by cavalry. Lessons learned from the clash with the royal army was used by both sides to prepare for the second. The action of these two battles should be analyzed together. But first, let's look at the battle fought by Alexander with the troops of Arsites and his allies on the river Granicus.

Granicus 334 BCE. In the spring of 334 BCE over forty thousand Macedonians[92] under the command of the 21-year old Alexander, the son of Philip II crossed the Hellespont into the vast area ruled by the Achaemenid Monarchy of the Great King Darius – the third ruler of his name – who made the biggest mistake of his life by ignoring these invaders. Darius exercised unquestioned power over these lands despite rebellions, bloody conspiracies and political murders in the last few years which incidentally Darius kept his power on the throne through his fantastic economic, financial and military abilities.[93] To the leaders of Parsa, Susa, Ecbatana, Babylon and thousands of other cities, with the riches and splendors of the western world, there was a time when one order was enough to crush these daredevils who crossed the border of his empire. But this was no longer that time.[94] There were many other "problems" on his mind, and a large part of his troops, for example, were just finishing

---
[89] P.Green, op.cit., pp. 164-166.
[90] N. G. L. Hammond, *Filip Macedoński*, tłum. J. Lang, Poznań 2002, pp. 94-98.
[91] P.Green, op.cit., pp. 262-267, N.G.L.Hammond, op.cit., pp. 111-115.
[92] P.Green, op.cit., pp. 149-150
[93] A.T. Olmstead, op.cit., pp. 453-454.
[94] A.T. Olmstead., op. cit. pp. 294-296.

The Armies of Ancient Persia

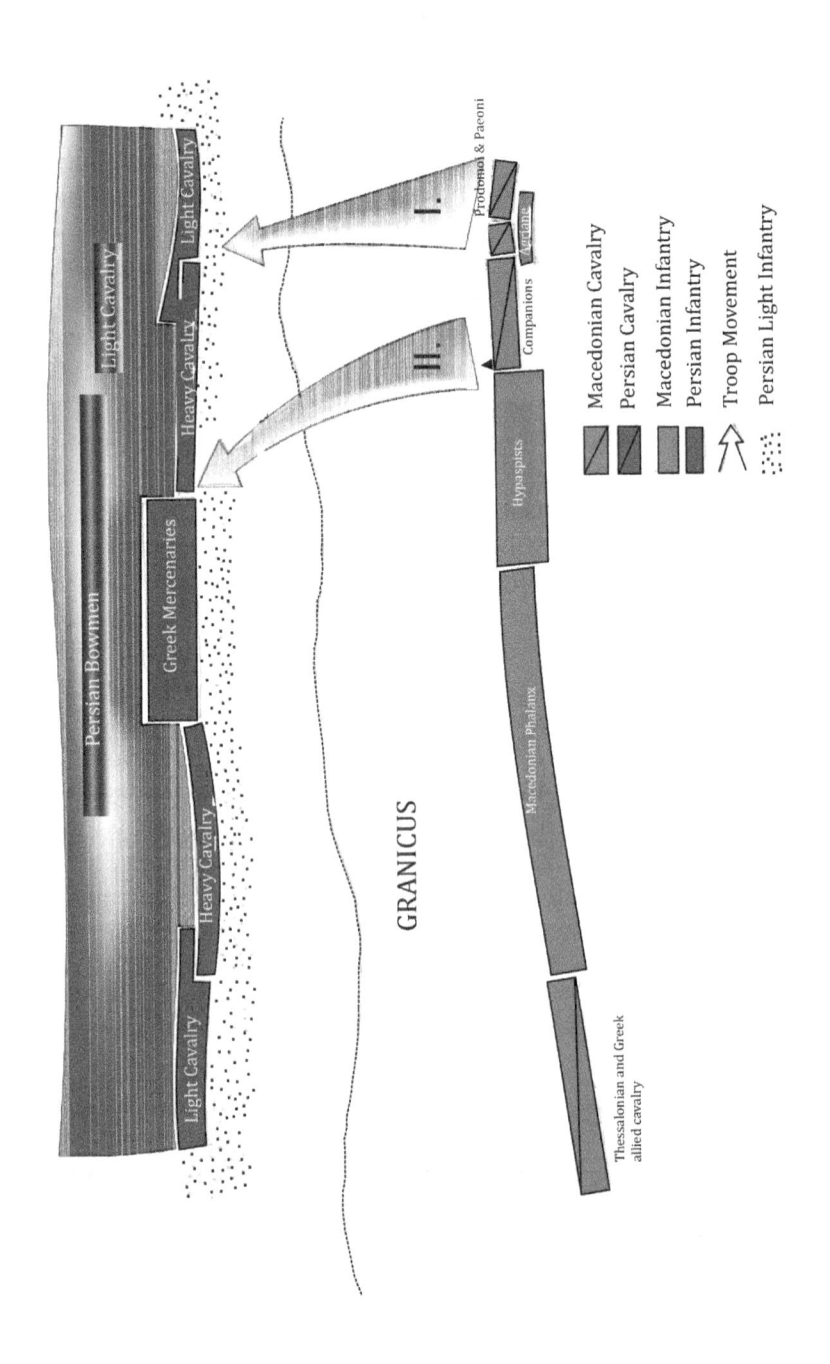

suppressing an uprising of the Egyptians.⁹⁵ The Great King did not see the need to send detachments of royal cavalry and infantry elite troops against these invaders. A force of more than one hundred thousand man "crown" army of Alexander encountered only hastily collected garrisons of the satrap of Asia Minor: Phrygia, Lydia, Ionia and Cilicia. Only the governors of these provinces, (in the military doctrine of the Persians, which constitutes the first line troops of defense), finally realized the seriousness of the situation. Despite all efforts, however, one summer day in 334 BCE their units occupied defensive positions on the eastern bank of the Granicus River, amounting to less than thirty-two thousand men, who were not as trained or numerous as the Macedonians.⁹⁶ The commanding officer – satrap of Phrygia on the Hellespont, Arsites, probably did not expect what he faced. The Persians waited anxiously for the enemy. Finally, about noon a dust cloud appeared on the western horizon as the "glow" of tens thousands of blades flashed. The enemy approached arrayed for battle.

Arsites deployed his troops in excellent defensive positions, just above the steep banks along the river. He used a typical Persian tactic of arraying his cavalry in the first and infantry in the second line.⁹⁷ In this position the Persian cavalry were not needed to perform charges, in the center (where the royal army always placed the elite guards and mercenaries) the heaviest infantry they possessed – Hellenic mercenary hoplites were placed.⁹⁸ The disposition of the Achaemenid army, as evidenced by such sources as Xenophon and Arrian, were already widely used and characteristic of them. The second line was traditionally light archers with infantry support. By staying there and doing nothing they retained their combat value. The initial tactics were conducted by "standing" fire, even in open battlefields, as did the cavalry which was a heavily armored archer-javelin-spearman. The Achaemenid cavalryman used the strength of the charge momentum in a small way because they used short spears, used in a similar manner to the kopia, underarm. At rest, the

---
⁹⁵P.Green, op.cit., p. 160.
⁹⁶P.Green, op.cit., p. 164.
⁹⁷N. G. L. Hammond, *Geniusz Aleksandra Wielkiego*, tłum. J. Lang, Poznań 2000, p. 77; P.Green, op.cit., pp. 437-451
⁹⁸On the basis of the arguments cited by P. Green, you can agree (maybe with not all his thesis) on inaccuracies and omissions in the relation of Arrian. The cause of these the ambiguity given by Mr. Green in his description of the battle of Granicus seems probable. It should be noted, however, that he was too quick to reject the relationship showing the cavalry in the first line. Maybe for Macedonian Companions (and I think not as much as thought up to now) this position would be a hindrance for cavalry, while the Achaemenids were for tactical reasons (initially firing their bows "standing up", not relying as much on the momentum of the charge, etc.) rather normal.

The Armies of Ancient Persia

absence of appropriate saddles and stirrups, even the Companion cavalry looked more like a type of equine phalanx, than a medieval knighthood.

In reference to the tactical changes in the use of existing units[99] it can be said that in the case of Persian cavalry, especially eastern units, e.i. Bactrian and Hyrcanian which was made up of armored and light cavalry – archer-javelins were set up on the riverbank, not up on the edge of the escarpment, but a few meters away. This would go against the technical rules for fighting from such positions, because it was the best place to attack the enemy when horses reached the top of the cliff. The defender avoids the necessity of moving up to attack the rider and mount before they reached level ground. In this method when it is also done in quantity provided the Persians a "breakthrough" with their mounts to support the impact. The hoplites were also able to support this attack by their pressure from the top of the slope while the hail of arrows from the archers continued to fall on them.

In battle formation on the edge of the banks, as already mentioned, allowed the Persians to set up in battle array in a regular deployment, which, depending on the opponent's moves allowed them to redeploy forces, i.e. as claimed by P. Green, in order to kill Alexander[100] or to reinforce the point of attack, when the enemy was still in the water as targets for javelin men and slingers of Arsites.[101] When an opponent approached and began to force the riverbank , they began to melee in the Greek manner – transitioning between lines (lohosami) of hoplites and columns of cavalry, the light troops retreating to the rear and leaving the job to the cavalry and heavy infantry.

As for the depth of formation for both the heavily armored cavalry and infantry in the front-line formations of the Persian army, it could not as previously stated, be too deep so as not to hamper the archers ability to fire or waste unnecessary non-combatant riders in back ranks. For technical reasons, cavalry advancing against the phalanx was difficult. Advancing alone the cavalry were vulnerable to stabbing at the horses which could frighten them and cause the whole formation to collapse. The depth of the units could not be too thin as to allow the enemy to punch through it with a large force. N.G.L Hammond indicates the depth of cavalry was sixteen ranks.[102] It seems, however, that this number is a little inflated, since such a unit would be unnecessarily powerful. Hammond calculated the depth of the formation guided by the data on Arsites' regiments and the depth of formation of Macedonian units, who during

---
[99]N.G.L.Hammond, op.cit., p. 78.
[100]P.Green, op.cit., pp. 166, 439.
[101]P.Green, op. cit., p. 439.
[102]N.G.L.Hammond, op.cit., p. 78.

The Armies of Ancient Persia

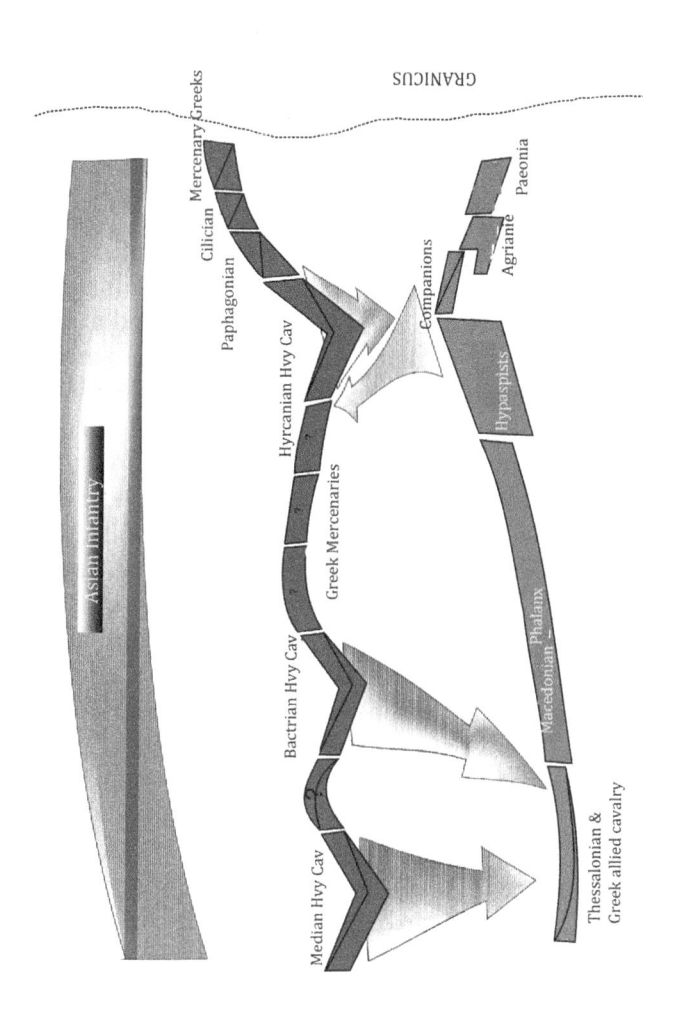

this period was an equal sized unit. Hoplites probably consisted of ranks eight to sixteen deep as practiced in Greece.

An attack on such a prepared group of troops positioned in such a wonderful defensive position even under the command of experienced Macedonian officers who gained their experience under the command of Philip II at first glance seemed like madness. Hence, with illusions of grandeur[103] Alexander was determined to do anything not to let the enemy escape. It was extremely important for propaganda purposes not to leave without a victory. But, also important was the vision of filling the temple from a cash rich expedition after borrowing money at an alarming rate.[104]

All the quirks and ambiguities in Arrian's description of the battle[105] seems to indicate that he is hiding some painful facts from the course of events. The first attack led by the young king with his characteristic heroic fantasy, the same afternoon he arrived at Grannicus. It was probably done in the typical style of the Macedonian army. The slight difference is it was probably not the first fight for the usual Agema[106] of Hypaspists and Companions, a squadron of Companions on the right wing supported by lightly armored cavalry (podromoi), Panonian cavalry and a unit of infantry, probably in light armor, to fight between the cavalry as was done by many people of Europe (Arrian. W.Al. Vol. I, ch 16). They attacked on the right flank in order to stretch the Persian line and weaken it where it was finally broken. This place was much closer to the center of the Persian line, at the point where the Macedonian units were grouped around the hypastasts and Companions. This is where Alexander himself led the attack. Despite this clever tactical move reminiscent of Philip II, an attack conducted under such unfavorable conditions, as claimed by P. Green (which was a good motivator) ended in a disaster.[107] It was probably then that 25 Companions and 9 infantrymen were killed, who according to Arrian, had died, "during the first charge "" (Arrian. W.Al. Bk I, Ch 16). As for the losses of an entire army in battle over difficult terrain, this number is odd. As a reward for their courage, the king placed posthumous statues of his armored companions in the Macedonian "Dion",[108] which he never did before or after. However, it should be noted here that such madness in the history of wars brought victory under very similar conditions in 363 AD. The Roman army cross the battlefield to attack the flank of a large Sassanid force and did so with great success. There the

---

[103] P.Green, op.cit., pp. 163-164.
[104] P.Green, op. cit. p. 163.
[105] P.Green, op. cit. pp. 437-451.
[106] A detachment of elite troops used in special purposes made up of Hypaspists.
[107] loc. cit..
[108] The great "sacred place" of the ancient Macedonians

river was much bigger and stronger, however; the Sassanid troops were missing support to counter such an attack. But nothing is certain.

After such a dramatic lesson Alexander did what he should have done from the beginning. Just like a few years later against the Indians at Hydaspes he crossed downstream at night so that in the morning he organized his troops in a line of battle on the so-called "Plains of Adrastus" in front of the Persians. Arsites and the other satraps moved quickly to act. They abandoned their original positions and set up the army perpendicular to the river. Cavalry was drawn up in the front line, while in the center of the formation they were supported by mercenary hoplites (perhaps they were an ad hoc unit of troops "from a variety of nations, numerous and very brave" of which were Sakae cavalry). Why did he change the order of battle that had worked so well the previous day? Arsites' units began to move slowly upon learning from the survivors of a small cavalry detachment, dispatched immediately after receiving information, about their opponent Alexander having crossed and drawing up his order of battle. They felt there was no need to move quickly because the Greek-Macedonian army sought a set-piece battle – after which everything began to move. A huge wedge of Companion cavalry and hypaspist infantry broke through the Persian lines at the point where the center was weakened from moving troops to the left flank, probably to oppose the strongest units centered on Alexander and his personal guards. It was a tough fight in which the young Macedonian king nearly lost his life from a Persian noble Rhoisakes with a heavy, long sword used by Achaemenid armored horsemen against his helmet. Alexander survived due to one of his guards, while the Persian units collapsed as a result of the simultaneous attacks of the Companion and Thessalian cavalry under Parmenion. In the center, the Hellenic mercenaries charged with their weapons as the cavalry on their flanks fled, dooming them as they fought dearly. Alexander remembered the great defeat the previous day he suffered from the Greeks. There was a terrible massacre where approximately three to four thousand Hellenes were killed. The rest – approximately two thousand, surrendered and as "traitors of the Hellenic Union" were fated to work in the terrible Macedonian mines. The Persian cavalry also suffered huge losses – about 2,500 killed as well as thousands in indigenous Iranians which included the son-in-law of King Mithridates.[109]

With the exception of the position of the Greek mercenaries in the line that Arsites' army adopted at Granicus this agrees with what we know about battle layout of the Achaemenid army. As usual (i.e. Cunaxa and Gaugamela) the cavalry was positioned in the front line. They used the traditional battle plan, rooted in the ancient Iranian tactics where the

---
[109] P. Green, op. cit., pp. 165-168.

steppe people initially attacked with arrows and then get into melee combat like Cyrus II's cavalry at the battle with the Massagetae. As expected in the course of that fight, you can find other characteristic features of Iranian tactics – wedge shaped formations of infantry and cavalry, as at Gaugamela and Cunaxa, shielding light archers by armored infantry and cavalry in the front ranks, as at Issus, continuous massive fire from the rear ranks in fights with the Persian front lines. All these elements are there, although we cannot ascertain strategic assumptions at the same time during other battles investigated.

Issus 333 BCE. The Persian troops were arrayed for battle in a way that suggested they were fighting a defensive battle, winning the attack "by way of contradiction".[110] Choosing the field for such a battle was most important. It was not enough that the Great King's army cut the supply lines of the Macedonians in addition to making it difficult for them to maneuver during the attack in their usual oblique pattern, right wing forward, as he did at Lake Lychnitis (Lake Sevan)[111], at Chaeronea[112] or at Granicus[113] attacking with armored Companions and Hypaspists. Then they had to attack over a thirty-meter-wide trough of steep stream, climb up a steep bank on which the enemy occupied the position and fight from this difficult position to break his line. Besides that, the whole way was covered with boulders and scattered rocks, which further impeded them.[114] The Persians occupied the whole length of the northern shore of the Pinaros River (Deli Çay River near Payas) and their deployment seems to resemble Arsites' position at Ganicus. The riverbed of antiquity seems to have run a further bit northward in its lower course[115] which meant that in order to crush the enemy all along the line, Alexander's army had to accept the protrusion of the left flank. In this alignment, if the Macedonians were defeated, this could easily have been driven into the water by a sweeping attack on the flank by the Persian armored cavalry. It should be noted that at that time, the shoreline was much closer to the hills than today. In the first part of the battle, the assault of the Achaemenid heavy cavalry could have screened a flank attack on Alexander's left wing while the other flank would have been pushed back to the sea by the heavy infantry, Hyrcanian and Median cavalry. By placing his cavalry anchored on

---
[110] N.G.L. Hammond, op.cit., pp. 96-97
[111] P.Green, op.cit., p. 34.
[112] N. G. L. Hammond, *Filip Macedoński*, tłum. J. Lang, Poznań 2002. pp. 200-203.
[113] P.Green, op.cit., p. 166-169.
[114] N. G. L. Hammond, *Alexander the Great: King Commander and the Statesman*, Park Ridge (NJ) 1980. p. 94-110.
[115] N.G.L.Hammond, *Geniusz Aleksandra Wiekiego*, p. 97.

The Armies of Ancient Persia

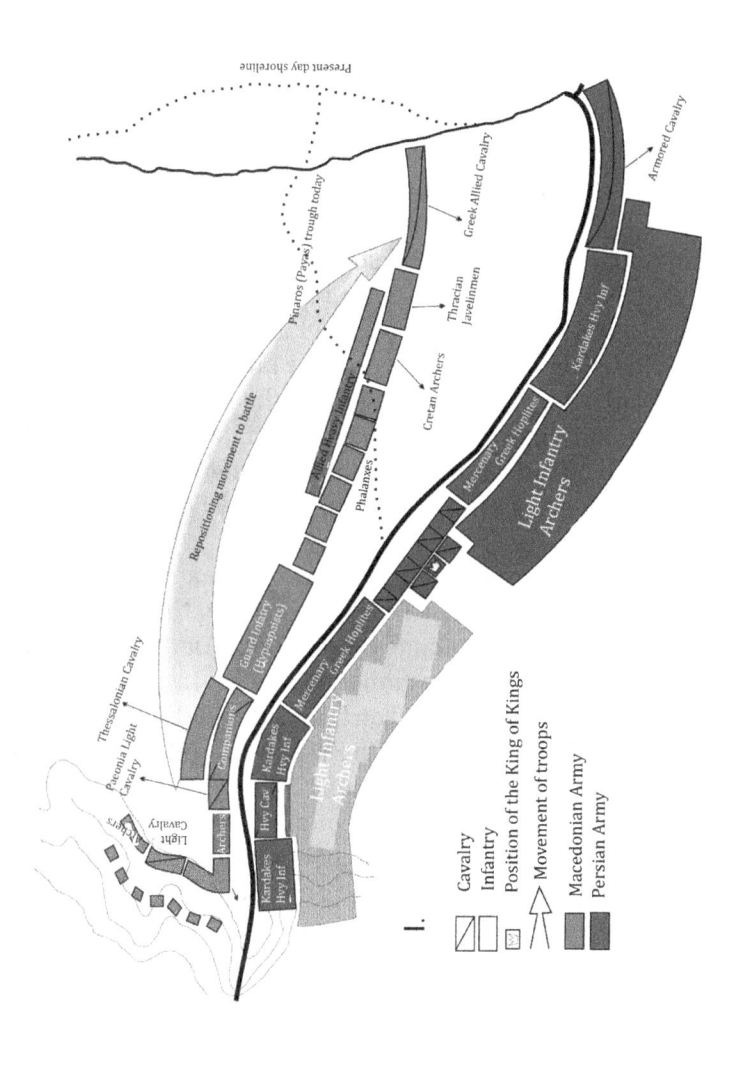

The Armies of Ancient Persia

the right wing, Darius may have wanted to neutralize the Macedonians with his cavalry. Alexander, however, did not use the Companions, calculating the if the Persians struck the Greeks and Thessalians would be strong enough to stop it.

Even if the plan to push the Macedonians was not feasible, as it happened the mass of Persian armored horsemen would probably crush and outflank the left flank of the Macedonian forces to attack the rear of the phalanxes.

The length of the Persian lines was about four kilometers long with the center held by the Great king along with the foot and horse guards. Arian syas the Greek mercenaries were lined up on either side with as many as 30,000 soliders (Arrian, W.AI., Bk I, Ch 8) but space was limited to accommodate such a mass of soldiers in 8 – 16 ranks, so that that the depth if not counting the huge 50-row block of Theban infantry, is typical for what was used in Greece, which means a unit of that size seems somewhat overstated. However, if the mercenaries were organized 24 or more ranks deep, it might be due to the fact that Darius was particularly keen on holding that position on the Pinaros and secure the line from being broken by the Macedonian infantry or going on the counter-attack in depth if the situation warranted. This would have created a frontage of about 1.2 to 2 km.

A large number of Cardaces (this formation as named for the first time shortly before 60's of the IVth century BCE among the forces of Autophradates fighting against the Datames (Kor. Nepos. Datam, Bk 8, Ch 2) although the Cardaces were also mentioned by Lucius (at the beginning of Darius I's reign) they were positioned on both sides of the mercenaries. According to Arrian (Arrian, W. AI, Bk II, Ch 8) there were 60,000 of them. This seems an exaggeration as well if we don't take the ranks beyond 20 men. Maybe these figures refer to the potential numbers of the Persian army and not the actual troops there? Who were these soldiers? Some scholars see them as light infantry troops[116], composed of the Carduchi, the ancestors of today's Kurds. It seems to deny that these units were in the main battle line with the Greek mercenaries. From this position, the Cardaces had to wrestle with the great Macedonian phalanx, and if they were lightly armored, they would be killed off quickly. The Persian commandeer was mostly likely perfectly aware of this. This view is shared by N.G. L. Hammond, who says the Cardaces troops were equipped in the same manner as hoplites, with long spears, heavy bronze aspides shields as well as bows.[117] Arrian says as well that the infantry were heavy: *"At first the heavy infantry unit of thirty thousand troops were setup in front of*

---
[116] P.Green, op.cit., p. 211.
[117] N.G.L.Hammond, op.cit., p. 97.

The Armies of Ancient Persia

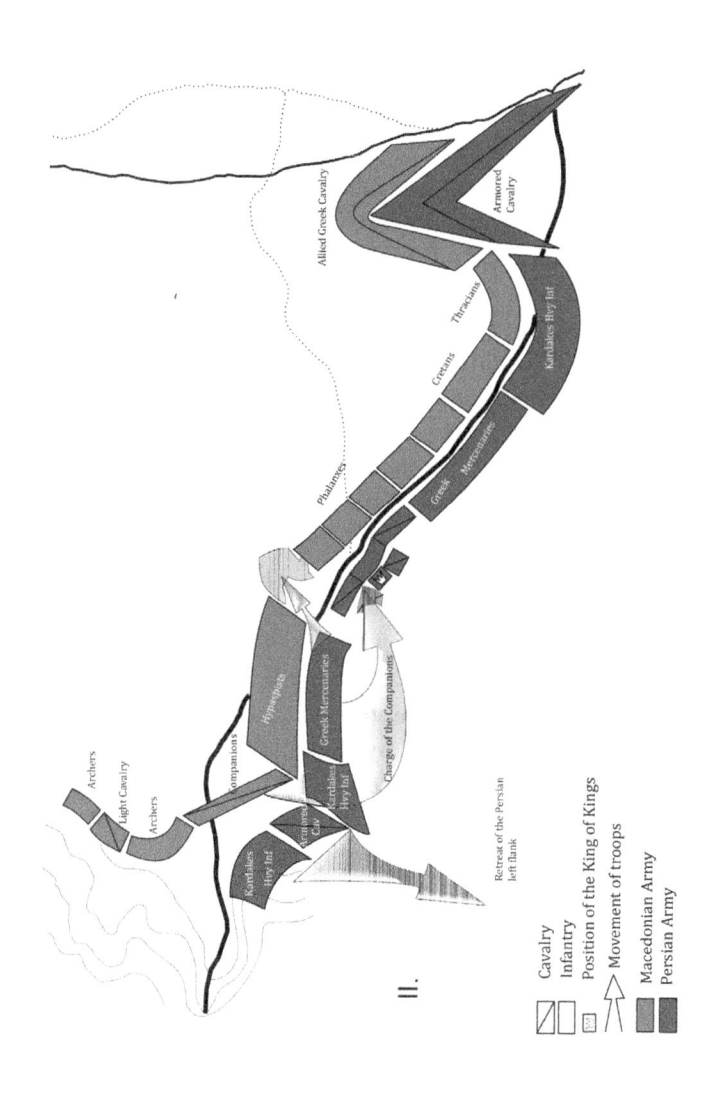

the Macedonian phalanx, so that on both wings were about sixty-thousand so-called Cardaces, also heavily armed" (Arrian, W. AI, Bk II, Ch 8).

This description of the formation is in line with the narrative of the Achaemenid army with the front rank – known from the time of Xerxes with Persian, Mede, Elamite and Hyrkana as armored infantry. It is logical that since the first time of the expeditions against Hellas to conquer the Greeks, influenced the adoption of heavier and better protection for the soldier's weapons and ways of fighting. It should also be remembered that all the names of the Persian armored infantry as given by Greek historians (mainly Herodotus) and used mostly as an anticdote of a unique custom – i.e. the habit of using a number as a constant value as was in the case of "Immortal (Herodotus, Bk VII, Ch 83)." None of the terms used by Herodotus are even Hellenized forms of the Persian name. If we assume that the Cardaces armored infantry is of the "Immortal" type, perhaps the Greeks of that period did not distinguish them from the "Immortals", while at Issus we are dealing with a situation in which they are typically in the center. This was composed of Greeks and Persians.

The rest of the Persian troops composing the second line, was most likely in accordance to the Achaemenid tactic composed of masses of light archers. This should also explain the huge number of shots fired in the first flight, which "collide in the air".[118]

At the edge of the Persian right flank was a mass of heavy Persian cavalry. The absence of cavalry, typically placed in front of the infantry testifies that the armored cavalry was moved to the right flank, all the Great King had at the moment. On the left wing, there was only one unit protecting the center of sixteen thousand. Mede heavy cavalry and Hyrkanian cavalry were opposed by Alexander's Companions.[119] Darius clearly understood that only armored cavalry could carry out an effective charge on the shore, push the enemy troops back or push his left flank back from the water and attack the phalanx from the rear. Incidentally, the Persians missed executing this by a hair when the Thessalonian cavalry commanded by Parmenion, was attacked on Alexander's left flank by the heavy cavalry and pushed away from the phalanxes. Thanks to great discipline and courage, the Thessalians managed to hold long enough for Alexander to break the line of Cardaces and hit the Great King. Darius managed to run away only because the fierce defense put up by his elite Guard infantry and cavalry. Once the army collapsed, the battleground that was an asset for the Achaemenid army had become a trap. The narrow mountain passes were immediately, "clogged with fleeing light-armored troops. Most of the Cardaces and mercenaries perished as they

---
[118]P. Green, op.cit., p. 212.
[119]D. Head, op.cit., p. 67.

were rolled up by the Companions and phalangites. Such huge losses might explain the small number of armored Persian infantry at Gaugamela. Those who survived had to go through hell to escape. The retreating heavy cavalry of the Great King trampled some of the fugitives while the Macedonians finished off the rest. Ptolemy later mentioned in his memoirs, all the dead bodies as proof of the difficulty of retreating through the mountain streams.[120]

The victory in this great battle was due to strong Macedonian discipline, the use of better and more modern weapons, but most importantly the ability to concentrate a strong coordinated attack of heavy cavalry and guard hypastasts on one point, which the Persians, despite numerous attmepts, never did learn.

Gaugamela 331 BCE. The struggle for the throne of the Achaemenid Empire was finally resolved through a huge battle, probably one of the largest in the history of warfare, which without exaggeration can be called, "the battle of nations." It was fought on the great plain near the village of Gaugamela, presently in northern Iraq. The Great King gathered forces recruited from across his Empire. It is estimated to be well over one hundred and fifty thousand soldiers including about thirty to forty thousand light infantry. The cavalry was a force he mustered was unprecedented on the battlefield.[121] To counter this force, Alexander could muster about forty-five thousand first class seasoned veterans. After the great losses at Issus, Darius refrained from building more heavy infantry units. A small unit of the Persian infantry took a position on the left-center of the Great King's line. As part of the cavalry in the Persian line, the Susian and Cadusian cavalry took the traditional place in the center of the formation, while Darius III was surrounded by his foot guards and the "Household Companions". In front of him were the guard cavalry, while on his left was Persian cavalry, Greek mercenary hoplites, Indian cavalry and Mardusian archers. On the right part of the line was Albanians infantry, Sakae, Bactrian, Tapurian and Hyrkansian cavalry. Both wings consisted exclusively of cavalry – in the first rank, light cavalry armed with javelins and arrows, in the second armored. The units in the center were commanded by Darius, while the left wing was under the Bactrian Satrap Besos and the right under the Babylonian Satrap Mazaeus.[122] The task of the center's troops was to absorb the impact of the enemy's attack and hold long enough to give the wings time to maneuver around the flanks. The flank units supposedly had the advantage in armored cavalry so that none of the Mace-

---
[120]P. Green, op. cit., p. 214.
[121]N.G.L.Hammond, op.cit., p. 111-112.
[122]loc. cit.

The Armies of Ancient Persia

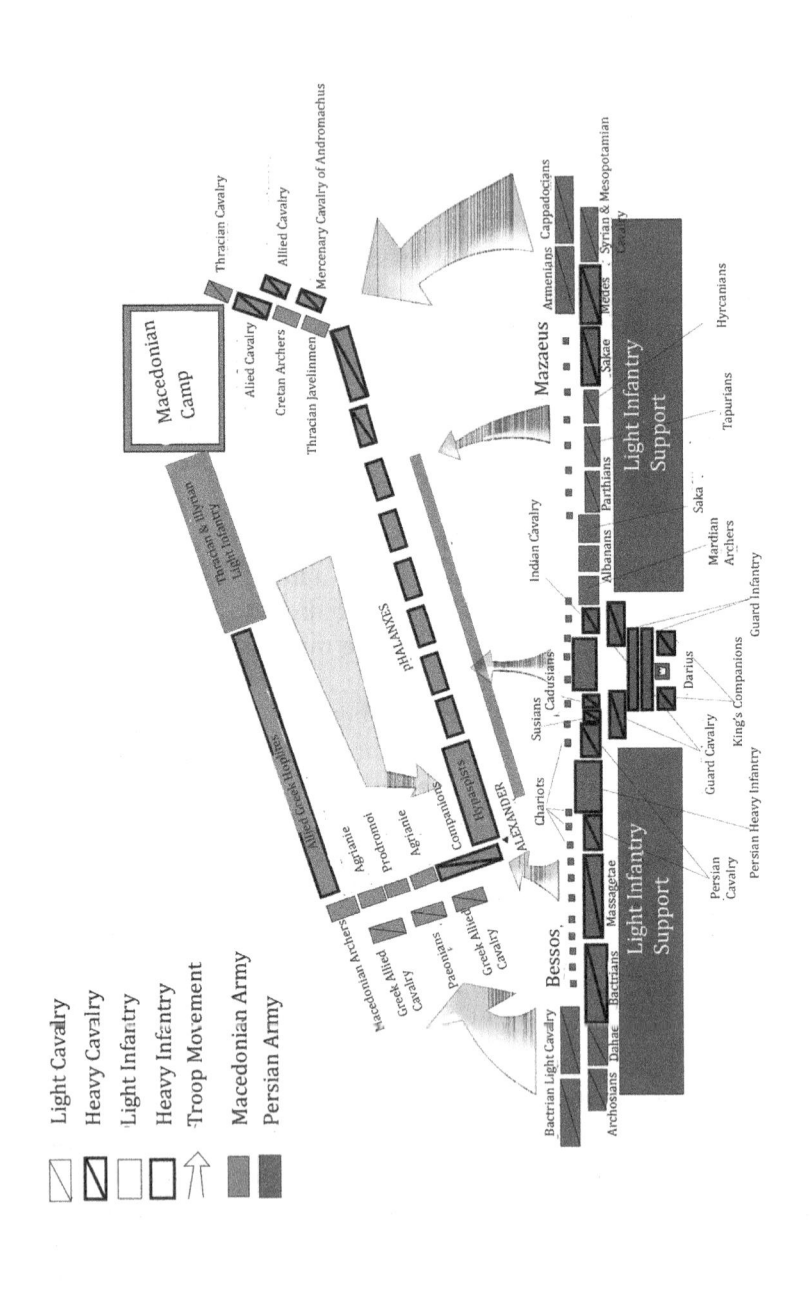

donian cavalry could halt them. Alexander had to be flanked and after a reconnaissance on 29 or 30 September 331 BCE this disposition was well known. Alexander's answer to this was the brilliant use of a mixed square formation that was never used in battle before.[123] His flanks were positioned with a combination of heavy and light infantry, reinforced by cavalry units. The strongest men would bear the brunt of the attack on the right side, inside the hollow square. The Persians tried to crush the flanks of the Macedonian lines at all costs to roll them up in order to reach the rear of the hypaspists and phalanx.

By funneling more and more new squadrons towards the wings, they weakened the center so much that one of the "corners" of the Macedonian square, typically consisting of Companions and hypaspists, broke through Darius's army, crushing the Persian infantry and cavalry. Alexander led a charge of his heavy cavalry which threatened the Great King's position, but he abandoned his chariot and fled the army. Eventually, the rest of the Persian resistance collapsed. By concentrating a charge at a select point in combination with the other units gave the Macedonians another victory. This time it was decisive. Even the Persian long spear, which was similar to the enemy's didn't help. Except for the phalanx, no other troops in this period were able to stop the massive and united strike force of three thousand hypaspists and two thousand Companions.

The Achaemenid armed forces in all the battles described, as can clearly be seen, had many common features. Let's try to extract these constants and build a uniform model for Persian troops of the period.

First, in contrast to the steppe people of central Asia, the Achaemenid troops sought out major battles. Although guerilla warfare was known to them it was thought to be cowardly and barbaric.

Secondly, when the "Royal" army was at war, the center of the battle formation was always occupied by the king along with his guards – infantry known as the "Household Companions" surrounding him. Preceding them or mixed in were squadrons of guard horse.

Thirdly, in the front rank of the guard's units were usually the "Immortals" or Greek mercenaries and with the Cardaces on both flanks. Behind the line of heavy infantry was a huge mass of light archers (Issus, Grannicus) supporting them through indirect fire. Light infantry was sometimes placed on the wings, with the lines preceded by defensive positions connected by reeds (Plataea).

Fourth, in the front line or in a mixed pattern formation, were the armored infantry (Cunaxa) or armored cavalry supported by horse archers (Gaugamela). They were most likely on the flanks (Gaugamela,

---
[123] P. Green, op.cit., pp. 264-265.

The Armies of Ancient Persia

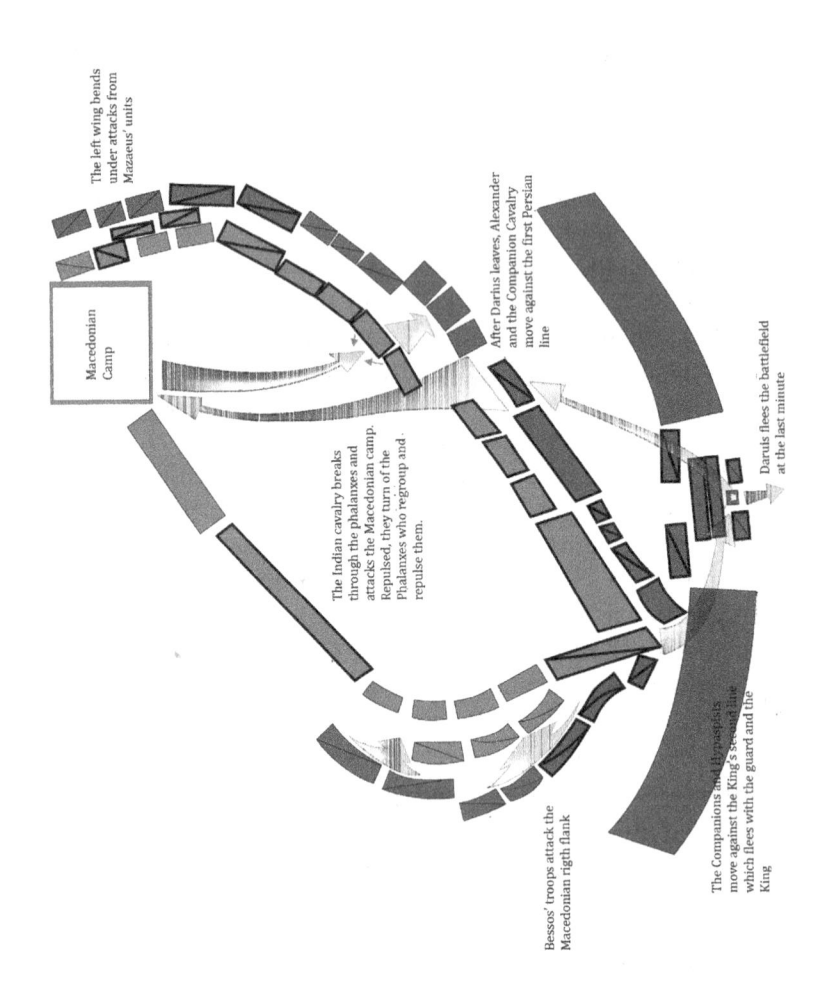

The Armies of Ancient Persia

Cunaxa) or in the center (Cunaxa). All these simple rules were consistant which did not change much over the centuries, bringing many victories to the Achaemenid Kings. Even with the fall of the first Persian Kingdom, they survived in some form for almost six centuries, returning to the army doctrine under the Sassanids.

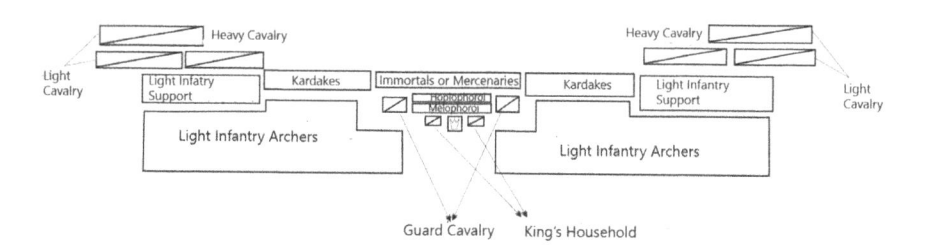

```
                Heavy Cavalry                              Heavy Cavalry
Light     Light Infantry    Kardakes  Immortals or Mercenaries  Kardakes  Light Infantry    Light
Cavalry   Support                     Hippotoxotai                        Support           Cavalry
                                      Melophoroi
          Light Infantry Archers                               Light Infantry Archers
                              Guard Cavalry   King's Household
```

After the victory of Alexander the Great over Darius III and the death of the later, a period of Macedonian dominance in weaponry and tactics began in the east. Heavy infantry armed with long spears as well as heavily armored cavalry reigned over the battlefield once again. This was mainly due to the constant fighting among the successor armies where the advantage was just the elongation of the pikes. The army whose spear in the first rank of the phalanx reached the enemy while he remained out of reach won. Unit depth of eight to ten ranks from the time of Alexander constantly increased to reached up to thirty-two ranks in the army of Antiochus III (Liwius. DZ.RZ. XXXVII, 40).[124] All this, however, led to a steady decline in the maneuverability of troop operations. It did not help to increase the numbers of phalangite light troops. Also, the cavalry, which was once strongly armored, was once again transformed into armored horse, which had been long known by the Persian and Saka. The combined operations with infantry in wedge formation was abandoned. The use of elephants to break the enemy line like today's tanks became widespread. For the next hundred years, armies outfitted and trained based on Alexander's Macedonian armies were second to none. In the east the tactics were based on massed cavalry tactics. Although mostly defensive in nature, they were mostly based on those of used by the old Iranian steppe tactics, however it was a great influenced on the use of these type units, i.e. the Selucid armies. This state of affairs remained until the middle of the 3rd century BCE, when distant events were unknown

---
[124] N.G.L. Hammond, *Starożytna Macedonia*, p. 107.

to the Hellenistic world as a new dangerous enemy emerged in the orbit of the Hellenic monarchies – they were the nomad Dahae.

Chapter II
ARSAKIDZI - RULERS from the steppe

1. Here comes the swift and light ... (Origin of horse archers)

We do not know when or where horse archers first appeared on the battlefield. The process of domesticating the horse, and the development of a highly specialized method of fighting was developed in the environment of the Great Steppe, unfortunately there is still insufficient archaeological studies in this area. To people who settled this area, hordes of highly-mobile horse archers manifested a "hellish plague" of cruel and elusive robbers who disappeared as quickly as they appeared or pillaging inhabited areas during major plundering expeditions, leaving behind only ruins and corpses. This perception of the steppe nomads was based on the cruelties they perpetrated based on their different rules of warfare. In the eyes of sedentary farmers this was a common stereotype of the invaders due to their material culture and unusual lifestyle. Without permanent homes or estates, these nomads "fused to a horse" with bows were difficult for Middle and Far Eastern farmers to understand. All these facts together contributed to the emergence of a nomads from the steppe coming from different lands, living exclusively for war, murder and robbery, blood beasts and even plagues of the gods.

The Armies of Ancient Persia

Cimmerians – people from the north. These people represented the steppe way of waging war in the ancient Middle East which began on a large scale only in the 8th century BCE. During this period, we are still not talking about formations of horse archers in a strict military sense – a specialized unit in the army. It was just a characteristic of warfare among the Great Steppe.

In the Middle East they experimented for a long time to combine efficiency of fire which characterized individual archery with the mobility of cavalry, but these first attempts were not very successful. The Assyrians were fairly quick to come up with a strange solution by transferring the solution from the cavalry to chariots, with a pair of riders, one of which directed the horses, while the was used to fire upon the enemy. Even the aristocratic Iranian people from Zagros primarily used chariots during this time period, while the basic formation used during this period was the chariots, the basic troop formation was the light infantry. Irregular cavalry (as it existed) was used exclusively in guerilla activities. As such the military organization was similar to the social organization of people living in the foothills and expanded the range of the Assyrian army's savage expeditions into Mesopotamia which strengthened the state. The situation changed somewhere in the VIII century BCE, when the Cimmerians invaded (most likely through the passes of the Caucasus). The prevailing fear of the nomadic hordes arriving from outside the boundaries of the known world is best reflected in the "Book of Isaiah" in the "Old Testament" dating from the VIII century BCE:[1] *"He lifts up a banner for the distant nations, he whistles for those at the ends of the earth. Here they come, swiftly and speedily! Not one of them grows tired or stumbles, not one slumbers or sleeps; not a belt is loosened at the waist, not a sandal strap is broken. Their arrows are sharp, all their bows are strung; their horses' hooves seem like flint, their chariot wheels like a whirlwind. Their roar is like that of the lion, they roar like young lions; they growl as they seize their prey and carry it off with no one to rescue"* (Isaiah 5: 26-29). A similar apocalyptic vision unfolded in the seventh century by the prophet Jeremiah[2]: *"Behold, I will bring a nation upon you from far ... it is a mighty nation, it is an ancient nation, a nation whose language you do not know, neither will you understand what they say. Their quiver is like an open sepulcher, they are all heroes."* (Jeremiah 5,15-16). The earliest specific mention o the Cimmerians is in Homer. Odysseus and his companions arrive near the coast of Colchis, reaching land inhabited by them:

---
[1] W. Tyloch, *Dzieje ksiąg starego testamentu Szkice z krytyki biblijnej*, Warszawa 1985. p. 158.
[2] W. Tyloch, op.cit, p. 183.

The Armies of Ancient Persia

Two depictions of horsemen recognized as Cimmerians from the Klazomenai surcophagai (J. Chochorowski, Koczownicy Ukrainy, *fig. 1)*

A Cimmerian long sword from Subotiv (J. Chochorowski, Koczownicy Ukrainy, *Tab. 1)*

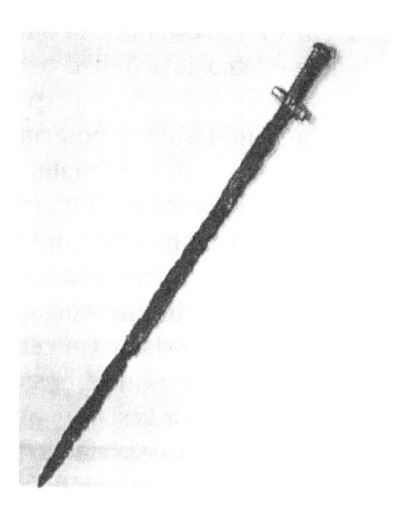

An Assyrian relief most likely showing Cimmerian cavalry from Nimrod (J. Chochorowski, Koczownicy Ukrainy, fig. 6)

> I rely on the good wind from astern of our dark-prowed ship
> with a full sail; all day long the wind blows briskly
> to the west, when all the waves grew dark
> So, having reached the extreme edge of the ocean, see land
> and the city and country of the Cimmerians,
> Who are wrapped in cloud and mist... (Homer, Odys.XI, 10-15)

The Cimmerian's mounted archers formed the mainstay of the troops, but they were not the only troop types. Warriors of high social standing used chariots pulled by a pair of horses that was like the later armored cavalry's function of "spearhead unit". The words of Isaiah testify to this but finds from Cimmerian burial mounds in Europe reveal pairs of horses and remnants of metal fittings of the chariot.[3] Images of warriors recognized by most scholars as representations of Cimmerian were placed on Greek archaic sarcophagus at Kalzomenai also provides confirmation of common use of long iron swords. A well-preserved example of this type of weapon measuring 107 cm in length comes from Subotiv in the district of Cherkasy (in central Ukraine).[4] On the same bas-relief war dogs are shown running beside the horsemen. A complete picture of Cimmerian of warrior is shown on one of the reliefs at Kalchu. It pictures him in characteristic Assyrian art of VIII century BCE showing mounted archers shooting at Assyrian horsemen. What is interesting is that he is shown firing a self-bow, and not the characteristic smaller reflexive bows used by later steppe nomads. Did the artist not capture the looking of the unknown weapon and maybe the eastern composite bow was not yet used by the Cimmerians.

We find some information on Cimmerian raids on cuneiform sources. In their expedition against Urartu and the battle in which hordes of invaders fought against the ruler of this country Rusa I (he lost ingloriously) becoming an object of a report from two Assyrian spies of Prince Sanheriba to the King Sargon II before his planned expedition to the Armenian highlands in 714 BCE. Sargon himself became familiar with the Cimmerians martial prowess in 704 BCE. Somewhere along the northern border he ws killed in a battle with these nomads.

Scythian Influences. As fast as the Cimmerians appeared, they also disappeared. While their invasions mainly affected the lands of Asia Minor and what is now Kurdistan, their military mite, however, significantly im-

---
[3] J. Chochorowski, *Koczownicy Ukrainy Katalog wystawy,* Katowice 1996. pp. 40-41, 122-123.
[4] J.Chochorowski, op. cit., p. 225.

pacted the military systems of the Middle East. In the seventies of the VII century BCE of interest to the Assyrian intelligence service, Herodotus claims that chasing the Cimmerians was an even more dangerous enemy – the Scythians. (Herodotus, IV, 12). It is only after this period that we find examples of massed horse archers and heavily armored cavalry. With its origin in these Asian nomads it was a well-executed military system. It's the origin of these tactical and technical solutions that the countries of central Asia quickly learned after coming in contact with the Scythians. For example, according to Herodotus, the Medes sent young men to the nomad camps to learn archery techniques, and consequently the means of fighting against the steppe people. The proof of contacts between the Medes and the Scythians are shown as figures carved into the façade of a tomb at Kizkapan (dated differently by various authors toward the end of the seventh century BCE, by various parties)[5] one dressed in a long coat (Kandys) from the reliefs of the Achaemenid Persepolis, while a second, in a strange long kaftan, down to the hands (which would later undermine dating) of the Scythian type. From these contacts, the Medes would emerge as excellent riders and placed them as cavalry commanders in the Achaemenid Persian armies. In the aftermath of the Scythian invasion and the rule of Cyaxares they created reforms in the Median army (transitioning from para-military to professional military – the sword)[6] and brilliant success in their battles against Assyria.

    Cavalry units are usually characterized by unprecedented mobility and a wide range of abilities. Scythian warriors moved without obstacles, even in territories captured by the enemy, avoiding larger units while ambushing smaller ones. Herodotus says that the Assyrians made an alliance with one of their chiefs, Bartatua (Partatava), that resulted in the rescue by the son of the chief Madyesa of the besieged Nineveh, the Medes were beaten back by the Scythians. The Scythians, in turn from their Middle Eastern allies and enemies learned to build and use metallic armor[7] to better protect against heavy arrows used by archers for centuries in Assyria, for example.

    According to the "father of history", the Scythian people arrived out of the east from central Asia, which has been confirmed by archaeological data at the necropolis at Pazyryk, Issyk, Tuva and many other places. The oldest evidence on the European steppes have been found in mounds in the Kuban basin. Aristocratic scale armor has been found here along with bronze helmets, beautifully decorated swords and, of course bronze arrowheads. The artifacts discovered here and later through-

---

[5]B. Kaim, op.cit., p. 163.
[6]K.Farokh, *Shadows In the Desert, Ancient Persia At War*, Londyn 2007, p. 33.
[7]Е.В.Черненко, *Voennoe delo...*, p.5.

out the Black Sea area, armor shows the progressive development and growth in the use of protective armor for chiefs and the finest warriors. The western Scythians did not completely separate armored cavalry units. It seems that they did not develop a separate military doctrine for these units. The general assumption was that during an attack, the heavy armor, like the later Persian clibanari were spear armed units, used first to breaking the center of the enemy, supported by mounted archers operating on the flanks and rear.

Because of the greater threats to their position in the line and the wealth they had, aristocrats were much better armed and equipped than regular warriors. Their armor usually consisted of scale armor of metal plates, a wide belt[8] and it is often reinforced with on the hips. Eventually they acquired metal helmets, lamellar shoulder pads and shin guards. Commercial contacts with the Greeks colonies on the northern shore of the Black Sea provided an influx of helmets and body armor from the workshops of Hellas. The Greek equipment was adjusted however, since the hoplite's needs were different from those of a mounted warrior. The inner part of the greaves was cut off, for example, so as not to interfere with controlling the horse with his legs, as there were not stirrups. The shin guards were provided with leather or felt straps to hold them onto their legs. The cheek and nose pieces[9] were also modified to make sure they were reinforced to wear as caps of the Kuban types. In the fourth century BCE, they began to produce enclosed Baszlyki type helmets covered in metal scales, cheek pieces and nasal guards. One such helmet comes from a barrow in Gladkovščina in the Ukraine.[10]

For most of the warriors there was only a shield. In the case of the western Scythians, these shields were made with organic materials – wicker woven and covered with leather, hardened hide and wood. Sometimes on the outer surface were highly stylized metal forms of panthers and deer.[11] Scythians shields were special for being elongated ellipses that were worn on their backs and shoulders. These were dried hides with the fur on the outer surface and bound with metal. Such shields were an excellent complement to armor in combat to protect the back, neck and shoulders. It was enough for a warrior to properly maneuver the shield attached to the upper part of the shoulder with their hands

---

[8]Е.В.Черненко, op.cit, p.6.
[9]Е.В.Черненко, op.cit, p.7-8.
[10]loc.cit.
[11]These types of shields came from Kelermes and Kostromski Kurgans. Perhaps other appliques for shields were the gold plate in the shape of a fish discovered prior to World War II at Witaszkow.

free.[12] In addition, there were conventional Scythian weapons – heavy spears, long swords, axes and finally great bows was the equipment that gave the nomads the ability to fight any opponent.

War Machine. To properly understand the social dynamic which gave birth to the first quasi-state formations of the steppe nomads that included the confederation of Dahi tribes, cavalry raiders and war expeditions, you should understand some of the circumstances that governed the lives of the Great Steppe peoples.

Survival in this extraordinary environment required constantly maintaining a delicate balance in which man and his resources must be completely subordinate. The violation of it as a result of human activity or as a result of even minor climate change has far-reaching consequences including starvation, bloody wars and mass migration. Hunting grounds, pastures and herds were common ancestral property. Individual clans roamed separately and when they stopped and broke out their yurts, everything centered around the headman, how he oversaw the common good, as well as being the judge and military leader.[13] The camp was shaped like a ring. As the herd grazed, they were watched over by cavalry-shepherd-warriors in a circle of yurts. The smallest animals grazed the closest to the yurts because they were the slowest and needed the least feed. On the outside of the grazing area were kept most of the horses. They were sorted by size and remoteness of the pasture before being brought into camp. In winter, the pasture that the horses had picked over were abandoned for other areas.

The migration camps were chosen, as nomads do, for example in places like Mongolia, near water sources in valleys or masked from the wind near the slopes of mountains.[14] The size of the herd and the area they covered were closely dependent on each other. Animals cannot eat all the feed from the area too quickly because then they would run out of pasture and then the herders would be forced to fight with their neighbors. The size of the herd depends in turn, on the number of people living in the camp. There can be only so many to ensure there is enough grazing area, but at the same time maintaining the stock. This brought on war, murder or exile of other nomads in order to control pastureland. It is from this background that the legend arose about cruel steppe nomads.

A rich aristocracy began to develop among these warriors which gradually subordinated the poorer layers of society. This began the de-

---
[12] Е.В.Черненко, op.cit, pp. 8-9; Shields of this type are known from finds at Nikolaevščinie, Novoj Ryzanovce, Krasnoi, Podole and Gladkovščinia.
[13] L. Podhorecki, *Tatarzy*, Warszawa 1977, p. 23.
[14] L. Podhorecki, op. cit., p. 23.

velopment of feudal relations. Private property began to develop and with it came small family encampments. Aristocrats began to surround themselves with tributaries and subjects, which included warriors who participated in war and plunder.[15] At the higher level, there were chiefs of clans or tribes that were able to develop maintain a well-trained army. Conquered tribes were given a choice: subordination, or death, and they were conscripted into the victor's army. With time, the bravest of them gained respect and property. Increasingly, larger numbers of troops were used in combat with increasingly distant neighbors. This developed into a unit that became known as an "Orda", which over time allowed the bravest of them attained positions of power and property. Increasingly they fought battles against more and more distant people for which they became known as "Hordes" which were characterized by movement and aggression.

The situation only changed when they encountered tribes with similar structure, or when their sprawling camps reached areas inhabited by sedentary population, often with a higher material culture, which was the perfect target for invasions and sometimes being incorporated into the nomad state; often providing infantry support for the cavalry troopers.[16] This allowed the warrior tribes a chance to live and get rich on plunder. Expeditions brought greater profits the further they went and the stronger and richer the enemies they attacked. The regions with plunder for the steppe raiders continued a chain reaction that in turn attracted new groups of warriors. The severity of nomadic life and its contrast with the ability to acquire property through warfare made people try to avoid that lifestyle, but often without much chance of success. The best examples of this were in history were the last years of the Greco-Bactrian kingdom or the reign of Andragoras. The richest tribal chiefs of the federations and their tribes surrounded themselves with vassals. Over time they adopted a more sedentary lifestyle by building fortresses in convenient locations, palaces and monumental tombs known today for example with Horezmu. Their governing power began to resemble the steppe frontier on the seventeenth century Commonwealth. The Dahae Confederation, however probably had a lower level of development because of their nomadic nature.

When there is contact between two such tribal societies, there is usually a long and bloody war that ends in the partial destruction, absorption or migration of one of the tribes. Such a migration provides a mass movement of people into the territories inhabited by other settled populations, or on the borders of the vast areas of states in the Great

---

[15] L. Podhorecki, op. cit., p. 24.
[16] R. Wojna, *Wielki świat nomadów, między Chinami a Europą*, Warszawa 1983, p. 69.

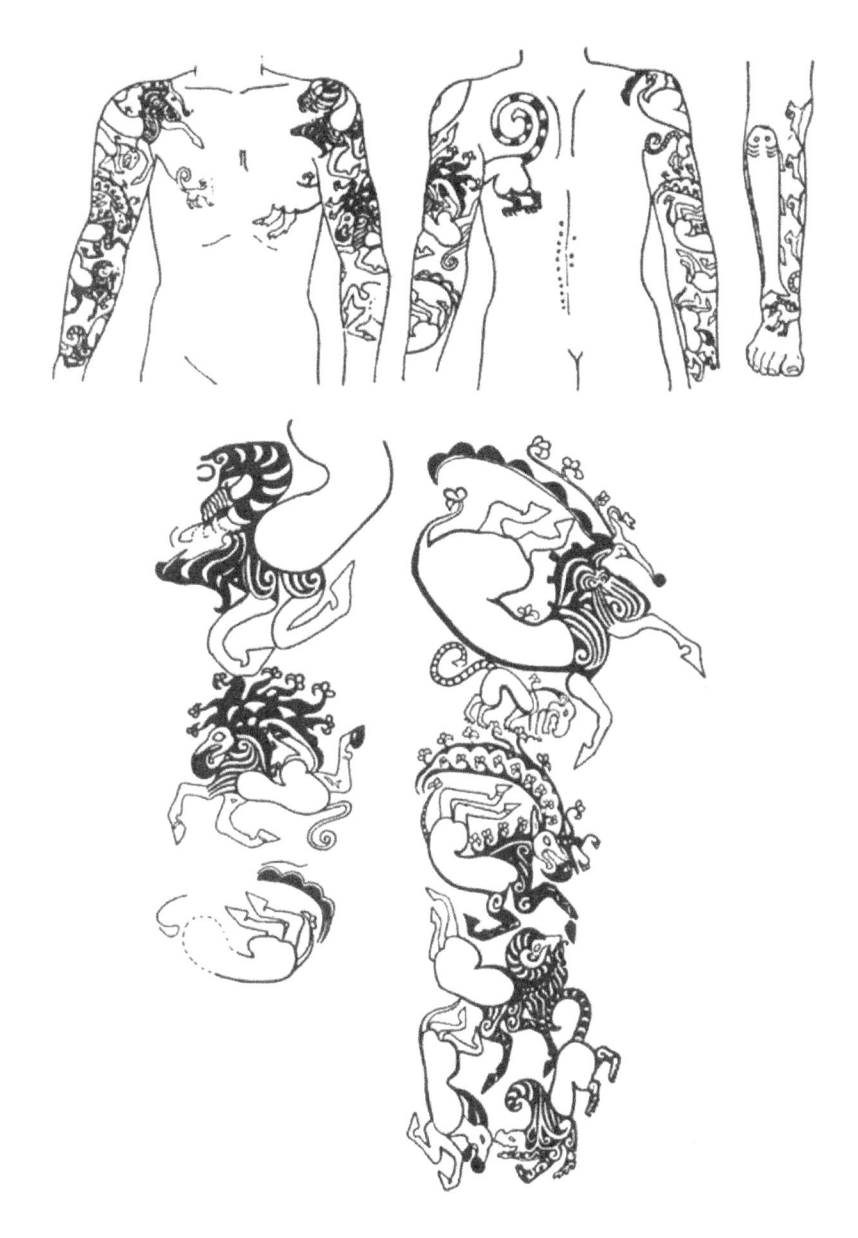

Tatoos of a Scythian commander from burial mound II at the Pazyryk necropolis (T. Talbot-Rice, The Scythians, *fig. 27, 57, 58)*

Steppe. The motive behind much migration was changing climate and severe drought in the pastures. This was them ost common cause of great wars between nomads.

Members of the aristocracy didn't just wield power through the military. In militarized societies such as the steppe tribes, you gained power by getting rich on raiding expeditions and conquests which manifested itself in the splendor of costumes and accoutrements, but more importantly in the quality and modernity of their offensive and defensive weapons.[17] Thanks to their wealth, the nomads could afford the best equipment, buying the most expensive armor, swords and helmets to provide better protection and effectiveness in a fight. Success allowed them to develop increasingly valuable and noble breeds of horses. The process for enriching the noble military class is clearly seen in the archeological finds of the Pannonian Plain in the west up to the Altai in the east, which would indicate that this was carried on in a similar way across the Great Steppe.

The wealth and fame of older and experienced warriors, who were celebrities from their tales and war trophies were celebrities, depended mainly on war for their positions in society and according to Herodotus, made hides from the head and hands of their enemies, cups from their skulls or war shirts from human skin (Herodotus, IV, 64-65) probably decorated with tattoos of the kills that powered the imagination of the young warriors who formed the core organization of the chief's army.[18] They were just poorly equipped and lightly armed horse archers, and they created havoc among the people on the edge of the steppe who fled before them.

Steppe warriors not only fought under the command of their own leaders, but often willingly, though sometimes not entirely voluntarily in the armies of powerful states that bordered the steppes – for example Persia (the Parthian Empire maintained fairly close links with the militant steppe tribes) and China. The Scythian cavalry formations appear to have remained in Achaemenid service without changing their tactic and weaponry. They were not even used in the usual manner of combining light cavalry archers with armored cavalry. After the defeat of Darius III, the victorious Alexander of Macedon also used light cavalry archers, an example of this might be the passage about the charge of one thousand Dahae on the armored troops and left flank of Rajah Porosa's army during the battle of Hydaspes. *"Once they were within range of the missiles, he released about one thousand archers on the left wing of the Indians to confuse the enemies standing there in a hail of arrows and the sudden attack*

---
[17]B. Stawiski, *Sztuka Azji Środkowej*, tłum. I. Dulewiczowa, Warszawa 1988, pp. 32-34.
[18]T. Talbot Rice, *The Scytians,* Londyn 1958, pp. 115, 165-166.

of the cavalry." (Arrian, Wypr. AI. 14) While historians do not tell us the make-up of this particular unit, it is presumed to have used the traditional fighting formation, a combination of armored units in the front rank with horse archers on the flanks and in the rear ranks, which allowed it to fire at the initial charge and then in melee. By then even the Hipparchus[19] of Alexander's cavalry which had already been made up of mixed heavy cavalry, some in the Macedonia style and some in the lighter Iranian style.

A true renaissance of the army composition consisting of heavy and light cavalry, was influenced by Hellenistic tradition though their faith to their traditional tactics only occurred during the Parthian period. Cavalry units gained the relevance and effectiveness comparable only with the Mongol cavalry during the reign of Genghis Khan and his successors. These armies did not actually need support of infantry units (which the Parthians recruited from among the hill tribes and the rural populations) at the same time gaining significant military success. The unusual importance here was the reform of tactics and weapons carried out by Arsacid between the late third and early second century BCE under the military influence of their Seleucid and Sakae enemies. To this day it is not possible to say how these people combined and influenced the military traditions of the Parthians. What is important is the fact that reflexive bows (sometimes called recursive bows) began to appear in the equipment of mounted horse archers made with layers of horn, wood and sinew (in the Arab style).[20] Although these are slightly smaller bows than the Scythian type, its construction and more powerful pull allowed the archer to shoot heavier arrows capable of piercing phalangite armor and later Roman Legionary chain mail. Such a weapon combined the old steppe tactic of the Parthians to gain sufficient military advantage to exploit the political and military weaknesses of the Seleucid monarchy to begin regular conquests of new lands, and create a powerful empire under the control of the descendants of Arsaces I of Parthia.

2.Parthians and their Army

The Parthians were one of the three tribes related to the Dahae, whose territory at the beginning of the third century BCE, was somewhere in the north and north-east of the Seleucid province of Parthia. They belonged to the larger group of Scythian peoples that inhabited the Great Steppe of the Pannonian Plain up to the foothills of the Altai.

---

[19]The title of an ancient Greek cavalry officer commanding a *hipparchia* (about 500 horsemen)
[20]Taybuga, *Saracen Archery an English Version and Exposition of a Mameluke Work on Archery* (ca. 1368), J. D. Latham et.al. (ed.) London 1970. pp. 161-162.

Their eastern neighbors of the Dahae tribes were related to the Sakae. At this time, in contrast to the Achaemenid period, when the Sakae were all called Scythians living in the north and northeast borders of the Empire. The Sakae tribes already existed as an ethnic group that occupied the area identified roughly north and east of the Okos River, now called the Ammu-Daria. They are mentioned among the people conquered by Darius I in the Behistun Inscription.[21] The eastern Sarmatians probably lived in the area north of the Dahae lands – wild and warlike, with similar bloody traditions to the Scythians. Further east of the Sakae the nomadic steppe tribes was known to the Chinese sources in the Chronicles of China (Sy-ma Cz'iena) as the Yüe. Later, when the Yüe were living around Bactria, Strabo included this tribe amongst the oldest Indo-European ethnic groups – the so-called "Tochars" related to the Yüe, but probably consisted of a variety of people of Indo-European origin as well as Altai.

The Yüe are most likely the ancestors of the Kushan who lived east and north of the border as they needed in a nomadic existence, were also known from the Chinese historical records as Hsiung-Tartar-Turkish origins, likely the ancestors of the Huns. These tribes inhabiting the northern border as "Agents of the Sakae" had long been "salt in the eye" to first the feudal lords of the Zhou Dynasty, emperors and later the united Chinese monarchy according to the Chinese chroniclers.

The reason for the mass migration south of the Dahae tribal confederation is unknown to us. Such movements are usually tied to a difficult situation within the province. In Parthia, at just about the same time as in Hellenistic Bactria, a rebellion exploded against the Seleucid government led by a local satrap named Andragoras, hoping to take advantage of the fact that the so-called Syrian wars turned attention from the East. However serious consideration should be considered that the rebellion was the result of the lack of support from the central government against invasions of nomads, which combined with the need to send troops west to fight for the Seleucids could have intensified the separatist action. [22]Both rebellious provinces were considered the "great marche" border of the Seleucid descendant's empire and as in the time of the Achaemenids, on the shoulders of the Satraps rested the heavy duty of protecting the population against raids of militant steppe tribes.

The Dahae, most likely sought the opportunity to take advantage of the unrest in the province to invade. It seemed as if military pressure from neighbors caused the movement of the tribes across the Great Steppes (similar to that which caused the migration of the Scythians in

---

[21]J. Lendring, op.cit., p. 6.
[22]A. Świderkówna, *Hellenika Wizerunek epoki od Aleksandra do Augusta*, Warszawa 1974, p. 255, J. Wolski, loc.cit.

the eight century BCE) or changing climatic conditions that led to the pastures drying up and the resulting bloody wars for aridable land. This reaction was not limited to the invasions of the Parthan-Dahae, but also the influx of the Sarmatians into the Scythian territories – into present-day Ukraine, dating from the end of the fourth or third century BCE. If you accept the possibility of the first instance, then movement of those populations corresponds to the growing power of the Yue tribes in the fourth and third centuries or later their enemies the Hsiung-nu because of the prevailing chaos in China due to the period of nearly permanent warfare known in historiography as the Waring States (Chang Kuo).

For centuries the Chinese warred amongst themselves and lost control over the steppe tribes. A broad range of new technological and military tactics were famously developed, moving north during the continuous struggle of the "Spring and Autumn" (770-463 BCE)[23] and later "Warring Kingdoms" (463-221 BCE). In the period of the "warring States" they began i.e. in the army of Cz'in developed the strategy combining massive fire power of long reflexive bows in a barrage of arrows, in combined attacks of cavalry and infantry. In the second half of the fourth century BCE, horsemen began to be recruited from the nomadic tribes as mercenaries to fill cavalry quotas in the armies of the Chinese Kingdoms.[24] This process was initiated during the rule of Wu Ling Cz'ao and its effect at what happened on the northern borders is reminiscent of the Roman Empire. The nomads were able to acquaint themselves with the latest types of weapons and ways of fighting; most importantly, at the end of the campaign they acquired weapons and loot before returning to their families in the steppes. Fighting for and with the Chinese with their bows resulted in innovations by the nomadic tribes in this technology – armor made from the best material available to nomads (processed material with superb protective value), or roasted leather. The armor they then brought with them was extensively used on the Chinese battlefield throughout the "Warring States" period and during the Han Dynasty.

Despite the doubts about the origin and dissemination of leather armor (in China and the steppes) it is most likely that due to the constant need for innovations in field of protective armor and the weapon technology developed by the Chinese (the length and tension) and the Steppe (rigid tip bone linings) of new and more powerful bows.

The steppe tribes developed armament in conjunction with the climatic changes where battles exploded for the best grazing lands for the herds around sections of the eastern steppes and nomadic tribes migrated to the fertile areas bordering the steppe. In these fights new and better

---
[23]http: // www.atarn.org/chinese/thumbrings_rings.htm.
[24]R. E. Dupy, T. N. Dupy, op.cit., p. 75.

weapons were constantly used, giving the wielders a slight advantage in early years of the battles, when even light armor increased the chances of survival against strong archery fire, while bows with great tension could be used effectively against heavily armored soldiers. Intertribal warfare consumed the eastern steppes from more or less the second half of the third century BCE, the effect of which elevated the powerful connection of the Yüe tribe, which ultimately fell area 200 BCE through a confederation by their neighbors, the Hsiung-nu[25] which caused additional movement of nomadic tribe – the last of which were the Dahae. An example of what could cause this type of an event did occur one hundred years later, leading to the destruction of the Greco-Bactrian kingdoms and the formation of the Kushite state.

Even after the Yue-or tribes collapsed after the encroachment of the quasi Hsiung-nu state, they didn't move west immediately to get out of the Chinese sphere of influence. They only shifted to the western part of Gansu Province. Approximately 176 BCE the chronicles of the Han Dynasty reported a decisive battle in the war against the Yue-or which the Yue-or lost and sealed their fate.[26] They were finally forced to emigrate, the effects of which provided the emergence of a new enemy on the borders of the Hellenistic kingdoms of Central Asia, which in turn pushed the aggressive Saki tribes south and west as were observed by Greek historians of the second century BCE as the next wave of invasions. Within decades the powerful military of the Greco-Bactrians lost territory up to the Oxus River. Even though the Yue-or that their light troops were not able to gain heavily fortified cities it did not help the inhabitants. The nomads have always been the masters of the steppes, and the inhabitants of towns on the steppe would constantly feel besieged so that they could not move freely between cities. In 128 BCE an envoy from the Emperor Chin Chang K'ien reports that the Yue-or were already in Central Asia.[27]

Without more historical and archaeological data, however, it isn't possible to get a more accurate timeline on this process. The fact is however, that the eastern neighbors of the Dahi Confederation attacked the territories bordering the steppe tribes and areas of the Scythians around 239 BCE in today's Ukraine past the Don as the Sarmatians. Interestingly, Strabo reports that Arsaces I of Parthia was at the head of the Parnia, a tribe living on Oxos (Strab. XI.9,3) far off the northern steppes of Bactria. The people living there were the first targets of the attacks from the eastern tribes, and Diodotus, the rebel Greco-Bactrian satrap-king would have been forced to repel their attacks to fit into Strabo's story.

---

[25] J. Harmatta (ed.), *History of civilizations of Central Asia*, Paris 1994. p. 174.
[26] J. Harmatta, op.cit., p. 175.
[27] M. Granet, *Cywilizacja chińska*, tłum. M. J. Kunstler, Warszawa 1995, p. 116.

The Armies of Ancient Persia

The first Dahae attacks were probably against Parthia, which Andragoras could barely contain and after his defeat, the loss of the weakened province. The rise of anti-Seleucid backlash only facilitated the invaders conquest, and rebellious satraps fell victim to wars conducted by these people, catching them by surprise. Bactria, famous for its warriors, survived and quickly moved against the frontiers of the Seleucid Kingdom to become a powerful empire.

The first clash of the Parnia-Danae troops was not so successful. The steppe tactics of war, although effective, were not strong enough to prevail against the training and discipline of the armies of the still powerful Hellenistic monarchies. During the regular battles, by turns, the rulers from Antioch hoped to reconquer the lost territories. The biggest problem the Parthians faced were the sarissa armed phalanxes and the armored cavalry. These formations had the greatest impact on the emerging military of the Arsacid state. Despite various theories the problem is we do not fully understand the emergence of the Parnia-Parthian reflexive longbow, which only first appear in Central Asian art in the first and second centuries BCE, and its appearance on monuments of the Bactrians and Sakai are not of Parthian origin. The Parnians, of course, also needed such weapons, first, to combat the phalanx, and second, to repel invasions of hostile tribes from the steppes. It was probably from them that this weapon was adopted.

The Seleucid's first expeditions east began during the reign of Seleucus II. Prolonged fighting between 237 and 227 BCE, however, did not yield results. It was not until the invasions carried out in 209-208 BCE by Antiochus III that forced the Parthian king Arsaces II to recognize the authority of the Seleucid kingdom. It appears that the effects of the wars with the Hellenistic monarchs, developed in conjunction with the ancient ways of multiple Scythian influences on Arsacid soldiers, that the Parthian army in general is organized similarly as described in Roman sources.

Compared to the typical tribal forces, the Scythians advanced the development of protective equipment between armored horsemen and their mounts. Heavy metal armor had been used on a larger scale in central Asia but was rarer at that point. Reflexive bows were also introduced from the eastern tribes. The Hellenistic army adopted those things necessary to combat Seleucid cavalry or armored infantry whose long heavy spear whose advantage is shown in the iconography starting in the end of the fourth century – beginning of the third century BCE on a ceramic dish from Koi-Krylan Kala or for the bone plate from Orlat attributed to the Sakae.[28] However, the way they used the weapon probably came from

---

[28] К. Абдульаев, *Nomadism in Central Asia*, A. Invernizzi (ed.), *In the land of the Gryphons - Papers on Central Asian Archeology in Antiquity*, Firenze 1995, pp. 158-160.

the Bactrian Greeks, unchanged in its principals of relying on the tactics of the cavalry charge.

After the changeover, which was more of a process rather than a moment in time, the Parthian warriors were able to effectively combat the enemy and begin the conquest of the areas that came to be included in their empire. It is impossible to say today how large of a force that Arsacid possessed, however, you can assume that then, as in the later days fighting against the Romans, it was not a huge army. Nor do we know whether and how they supplied the recruits provided by the steppe tribes. It is known that in his call for help against the Seleucid-Sakae, Phraates II promised payments. When he didn't fulfil his promises, they began to ravage the Parthian lands.[29] Descriptions of soldiers from a much later time, namely from the Battle of Carrhae, fighting the legions of Crassus also sheds an interesting light on the matter. Plutarch made the following comparison: "Surena himself, however, was the tallest and fairest of them all, although his effeminate beauty did not well correspond to his reputation for valor, but he was dressed more in the Median fashion, with painted face and parted hair, while the rest of the Parthians still wore their hair long and bunched over their foreheads, in Scythian fashion, to make themselves look formidable." (Plutarch. Crassus, 24) Warriors are depicted by Plutarch wearing both types of hairstyles were considered Parthians in reality they were different tribes.

The Suren clan came the northeast area of the Arsacid monarchy where they had a long and great lineage relying on a vast network of vassals. This same Suren clan were of Parthian origin, and the hairstyle their famous chieftain wore according to Plutarch, was of Parthian origin. The same hairstyle can be seen on coins of the many kings from the Arsacid dynasty, such as Phraates II, Orodes I, and Mithridates III, the rock relief of Tang-e Sarvak, etc. which is completely different from the Suren horse archers. The closest analogy for hairstyles is a military crest of one of the armored horsemen depicted in the battle scene from the Eagle plate. It was not until late in the Parthian period that the Parthian hairstyles took on the unmistakable echoes of war pennants of the steppe people, probably worn as a representation of respect for nomadic traditions – some of which were Arsacid. If the Parthians did use this hairstyle it abandoned the ancient customs of the Sakae, very early. The images of the few representations of rulers "crests" were moreover extremely decorative and transformed from the utilitarian hairstyles of the nomadic warriors and more like Sassanid combs than the armored Sakae eagle. In Parthian art there are not general examples of this type of hairstyles used in war. The light cavalry formations that inflicted such terrible losses on Crassus' le-

[29] R. E. Dupy, T.N. Dupy, op.cit., p. 113.

gionnaires was composed of native Sakae. Most of these probably belonged to the vicious and aggressive steppe tribes. They were recruited as irregular archers of private armies.[30]

Armored cavalry came from a higher social class and were appropriately, rich vassals of powerful feudal families. Surena's army was no exception. A similar system functioned well in the army of the Arsacid. According to the historian Justin, Parthian society was divided into "free" and "non-free".[31] Similarly, Plutarch provides a division into several different groups: the first may include, like Surena, representatives of the largest families, you could call them "magnates"; the second were the so-called hippeis, based on pottery shards found in old Nisa, dated from 72 BCE identifying a class of knights 'Sb'r' – i.e. *ašvaran* – with the exact meaning as the Greek *hippeis* or riders which included the most powerful feudal vassals - all in armor. The third group were the *pelatai* (clients?) which included the light armored horse archers. All these groups however, belonged to the class of free people. The term *duloi*, referred to by historians refers to the ancient word for *servi* (although perhaps it would be more appropriate as servitores) probably applied to all people dealing with the baggage trains. In the context of Plutarch's description, it appears that these troops were exclusively made up of servants. It is possible, however, that their status is similar to that of the servant, which had some troops made from prisoners of war, probably an old steppe custom, that was included in the Arsakid army. During the campaign against Sakom in the years 130-127 BC at the decisive battle, the Parthians had infantry from prisoners taken after victory over Antiochus VII Sidetens besides their own units.[32] These soldiers might not have been treated well, and in the course of battle they might go over to enemy rather than serve the Parthians. The possibility that the rebellion was an attempt at avenging honor can be rejected in advance. In the Diadoch's armies, going to the side of who paid better was the norm. A similar fate was to be met by prisoners from the Crassus army, whom the Parthians sent to the Margiana on the eastern borders of their country. If the Arsakids were acting in this way with prisoners of Western origin, they had to do the same with the nomads who had been hunted down.

Sakae warriors were well known for their combat skills and Surena[33] in particular for his combat skill during the civil war that brought King Orodes II to the throne. It is not surprising, therefore, for the mon-

---

[30]H. von Gall, *Das Reiterkampfbild in der iranischen und iranisch beeinflussten Kunst partischer und sasanidischer Zeit*, Berlin 1990. pp. 11-13.
[31]M. Mielczarek, op.cit., p. 56.
[32]P. Iwaszkiewicz, W. Łoś, M. Stępień, *Władcy i wodzowie starożytności Słownik*, Warszawa 1998. p. 147.
[33]Parthian spahbed who defeated the Romans at Carrhae, 53 BCE

arch's decision, in the face of a double threat from Arsacid Artabazes in Armenia, and the invasion of Crassus' legions in northern Mesopotamia, to set out to deal with the Armenian raid, while Surena launched his contingent of troops against the more important military opponent.

The Sakae, like true steppe warriors, continued to cultivate the old Scythian custom of taking bloody war trophies. According to Plutarch, the dead Crassus had his head and hand cut off, probably his right, because that was the ancient customs, and they took them to Orodes[34] (Florus, Zar. Dz. Rz, I, 46). All this matches the descriptions that were more than 350 years old at the time contained in the "Acts" of Herodotus (Herodotus, IV, 64-65) and was as you can see, still respected among the steppe people as was the moral norm. It should be noted that when the Parthians fought Crassus they had already been subjected to 200 years of Hellenistic culture. Although many institutions, and customs of nomadic origin were still with them, these were the bloodiest - display of macabre trophies, wearing martial shirts, or quivers made of human skin had already faded and may have even completely disappeared. The head of the slain enemy, however, was pinned down on the harness of a horse, as the Scythian "towels" described by Herodotus (a skull with the hair and the skin striped off) clearly shown on the plaque from Orlat.

Similar to Justin's take on Parthian society, Josephus divided the Arsacid army under the command of Prince Pacorus that invaded Syria and Palestine into free and not free (Josephus, The Jewish War, I. XIII. 3). In his case as with many other historians, there is a misunderstanding resulting from the feudal nature of the class divisions visible in the Parthian armed forces. Chroniclers like Josephus, just as the soldiers of Alexander the Great did, characterized the respect of the Iranian people for high born superiors to be seen as slaves to the warrior ranks of Pacorus' units. Hence, while describing the capture of Phazael the quote, *"That the thing should not seem suspicious, Pacorus left some cavlary called "free" at Herod and sent the rest as an escort for Phasael."* (Josephus, The Jewish War, I, XIII, 1) As to the type and purpose of these escorts assigned to Pacorus: *"Pacorus (...) then assigned one of the king's cupbearers about the same amount of cavalry, letting him leave for Judea to reconnoiter the enemy's position."* (Josephus, The Jewish War, I, XIII, 3) Despite the errors in assessing the status of the warriors, the above quotation makes it clear that Pacorus sent a kind of advance-guard to Judea, or rather a reconnaissance force composed mostly of light, cavalry archers. In this type of unit, the knights (hippeisaŝwara) were probably only commanders.

In the Parthian armies, the ratio of armored riders to light-armored riders is presented very differently depending on what tasks ap-

---
[34] Orodes II of Pathia

The Armies of Ancient Persia

pear to be performed, but also on he feudal requirements. During Marc Antony's invasion of Armenia, the armies involved in the battle were proportionally even 1: 125[35] while in the corps of Pacorus' cupbearer the ratio was 1:20 in favor of horse archers (Such quantitative ration are confirmed I the following quote: *"Therefore Hyrcanus and Phasael went to the embassy, and leaving Pacorus at Herod, the two hundred horsemen and ten of the so-called "free" accompanied him on their way."* (Josephus, The Jewish War, XIV, XXXIV, 2). The force of Surena at Carrhae had one armored ašvaran for every ten light troops.

The real power in the Empire and the Parthian army was exercised by a small group of powerful people belonging to several (possibly seven) powerful families and their vassals with loyalty to one's family always being higher than loyalty to the monarchy. This was similar to the system in place in medieval Japan. This was symptomatic of the approach of the great feudal families to the king. It was true that he was always chosen from the members of the ruling Arsacid family to ascend the throne, with the approval of the assembly of elders. The most senior member became the ruler, assuming the royal diadem. Plutarch says that representatives of the Surena family was also entitled (Plutarch, Parallel Lives, 21). The approval was only a partial success for the new ruler because war between the families of the various supporters was an ordinary thing in the Parthian Empire, meaning that power was far from absolute. In fact, the king could only often (and to a limited extent) count on the forces and member of his own family for support.

Members of the highest feudal aristocracy and their clients – people enriched from battle, came as armored cavalry. The chiefs and nobles were probably descended from the chiefs and nobles of the Dahae who came with the Arsacids across the steppes. As armored cavalry they fought as members of the Iranian tribes, not of the Parthian ones. It does not seem that the old Persian nobility was discriminated against by the Arsacids. This is attested to by the high positions that were still held by members of the Sassanid royal family. Very likely the Arsacid did not end the leadership in the areas with the great tradition of strong local noble government, where local magnates controlled the governments, more or less nominally (depending on the current military strength of the King of Kings) subject to their Parthian superiors.

During their early years of power, the Parthians, like the Mongols and Manchus of China certainly needed people who could administer the conquered lands on behalf of their new masters. The Greeks were also held in high opinion, but it is not without significance that the rulers and

---
[35]Wolski, *Servitia i ich funkcja i znaczenie w społeczeństwie irańskim okresu Arsacydów*, Elektrum V vol.4, Kraków 2000.

elites had in Hellenistic art, whose influences are visible, for example, in the clay sculptures of old Nisa. More likely the harassment of the local nobility and educated classes would not reap any benefits and would surely be a source of rebellion.

In summary, from approximately 1 BCE, while the descriptions are mainly from Roman historians, numerous iconographic representations and archaeological finds of reliable data on the Arsacid army, show a highly functional, well-organized armed force. This army was primarily composed of cavalry (Cassius Dio says that the Parthian infantry was poor and few). (Cassius Dio, *History of the Romans* XXXX, 15.2), divided into armored cavalry and light cavalry archers. The Parthian army specialized in conducting war in the environment of the steppe and semi-desert rolling hills of Media and Mesopotamia. The use of armored cavalry, patterned on the Hellenistic style allowed for effectively combating armored cavalry and infantry which were the main formations of the Empire's western neighbors armies, maintaining the mobility of archers in cooperation with heavy troops allowed it fight effectively with the cavalry of the Arsacid family from steppe people of the north and east. They understood how to coordinate them (and fit it into the conditions that arose) which was a mechanism one should look at for formations of the Parthian Army – their weapons, tactics, history, tactical and technical solutions, etc.

HORSE ARCHERS. As evidenced by incidents in the battles of Marc Antony in Armenia and at the Battle of Carrhae, these troops were the core of the main Parthian combat troops (Especially in the 1st Century AD). The mobility of cavalry archers was used to fighting against the Gauls or Roman Macedonians troops with surprise attacks as part of their tactics. The examples of armies of Crassus and Antonius' armies affected the later doctrines in the conduct of war which were implemented for example by Corbulo (Gnaeus Domitius), in the 60's of the first century AD.[36] Roman legions avoided being in open, flat countryside, like the plague which could be subject to fire from all sides. Their leaders tried to draw the enemy into battle in the hilly, and even mountainous land, where the use of cavalry would be hampered, and the Roman auxiliaries began to recruit large amounts of excellent archers from the eastern provinces of the Emnpire (mostly Syria). The Legionnaires armor changed as well. Chain mail did not offer enough protection to arrowheads, missiles and spears, changed to scale and segmented armor. The number of auxiliary troops were constantly increased but the Romans never succeeded in copying the success of Parthian horsed archers. Why? Because to be

---
[36] P. Iwaszkiewicz, W. Łoś, M. Stępień, op.cit., p. 232.

used effectively it must have riders, who according to Ammian Marcellinus, "were fused with the horse." (Ammian, Res Gestae II, XXXI, 2.6). Only born riders, mostly nomads, they were able to use the bow from the horse's back with skill and effectiveness, who amazed the Romans and brought victory to Surena.

CAVALRY ARCHER TACTICS. The numerous wars of the Roman Empire with its eastern neighbor – the Arsacidian Parthian monarchy - left indelible marks on ancient literature. Most of the references, however, are brief and limited to references used to calculate the years in which there were conflicts and the names of the rulers who struggled against each other. Sometimes they provide place names of the larger battles. The best source of information about enemy tactics are the few descriptions of large Roman campaigns in the lands of Armenia and Mesopotamia, left in the works of Plutarch and Cassius Dio. The source in this area is unfortunately Plutarch's, "Lives of Famous Men", parts of which are about Marcus Licinius Crassus and Marc Antoni despite the many ambiguities and blatantly moralistic tales, they convey a lot of interesting information describing tactical solutions used by the Parthian army in the first century BCE.

A closer analysis of these essays shows they are accurate in their descriptions, and they provide insightful observations made by eyewitnesses to these events, which suggests that even though Plutarch lived nearly a hundred years later, he had access to use memoirs and sources from the era. Using these sources to reconstruct the tactics of the Arsacid troops, one should take into account that the Roman army was complex and did not exist solely as infantrymen, and at that time against exotic opponents for the Parthian, tactics were temporarily applied to fight the legions that would significantly differ from one's used against the steppe people or the civil wars. These were still probably the old, but effective tactics of the Scythians.

The problem with the rivalries within the Arsacid monarchy for influence in the east since the time of Lucullus'[37] conquests weighed heavily on the minds of Roman politicians and strategists. Plutarch's generation did not ignore this problem either as the wars against the Parthians in 55-63 AD and 114-117 AD, fall into the period of the writer's life, were continually discussed and widely known in the enlightened circles of Imperial Rome.[38]

---
[37]Lucius Licinius Lucullus (118 – 57/56 BCE) Optimate politician and general who was an associate of Sulla
[38]E. Wipszycka (ed.), op.cit., pp. 99-100.

The Armies of Ancient Persia

He describes the course of the ill-fated campaign by Crassus in detail against the Arsacids of Orodes II[39] which ended in the famous battle (or rather due to its results, a massacre) at Carrhae in 53 BCE. The Romans had a force of seven legions, and four thousand cavalry when it crossed the Euphrates River by ferry at the village of Zeugma[40], moving first, along the river, and later directly across the plains, more or less along the present-day Turkish-Syrian border, in the direction of the ancient city of Harran (Carrhae) (Plutarch, Crassus 19-20). The contingent of Parthians against them were led by one of the noblemen of King Orodes II, named Surena, from the powerful feudal clan of Šūren, which consisted of ten thousand troops including one thousand armored cavalry. Orodes set of to Armenia with a much larger force to pacify the rebellious ruler Artabazes[41], a former vassal of the Arsacid's trying to go over to the Romans. It seems that after there was no assistance from Crassus, Artabazes returned quickly to Orodes and gave his sister in marriage to Orodes' son Pacorus.[42]

Surena's scouts watched the enemy as they crossed the river and ss soon as Crassus' legions moved away from it, they proceeded to attack. The Parthians encountered the Romans ready for battle after crossing a shallow gully at Balichu. Plutarch writes of this, *"The enemy, contrary to the Raman's expectations, were neither numerous, nor menacing. Surena set the main force in the rear, and they were told to cover their armor under their cloaks and skins. But, when the Romans came closer, the commander gave the Parthians a signal and the battle commenced (...) as soon as the dropped the covering from their armor it showed shimmering helmets and armor which shined like lightning of shiny steel, and their horses armored with bronze and steel."* (Plutarch, *Crassus*, 23-24). The author, though, gives many interesting details in his attempt to interpret what was described, but it shows a great ignorance of the Iranian tactics and military realities. The cloaks and skins, which he mentions have been know for a long time from the Achaemenids and in this case, it should be thought that they did not serve to hide anything from the Romans, but to shield the equipment of the men and horses from the sun. The above quotation, in addition to ethnographic trivia, also indicates that Surena, in awaiting the enemy, adopted the classic Scythian order of battle with the armored troops in the center and flanks, supported in the rear and wings by horse archers, which constituted (...) the main force (...) of the Parthian commander.

---

[39] Orodes II (95 – 37 BCE) ruled from 57-37 BCE)
[40] Location is unknown, but it was across from the Seleucid city of Samosata.
[41] Reigned 54 – 34 BCE, he was beheaded after Actium on orders of Cleopatra.
[42] P. Iwaszkiewicz, W. Łoś, M. Stępień, op.cit., p. 61.

The Armies of Ancient Persia

The initial Parthian attack was launched by the armored cavalry at the heavy infantry of Crassus' squares which shielded by his cavalry. This was aimed at probing the enemy's strength and breaking up his cavalry, in front of the Romans, as well as stopping his opponent's use of archer units around them but could not destroy the attackers. It can not be ruled out that Surena was fully familiar with the advantages and discipline of the Roman legions when he tried a frontal assault on the enemy formation. This was not a crazy attack and immediately after the Romans survived the first strike, the armored cavalry turned back and gave it over again to the light troops. They remained however in combat readiness.

Based on the words of Plutarch you can come to some interesting conclusions about the ways to transmit commands to the operating units in the field. Unfamiliar with trumpets or horns for passing some command signals the Parthians used drums instead. Their sound could be heard just before the start of the fight which could have been the signal for units grouped together, but also those watching the enemy in the field. Using war drums is confirmed, for example, in Sassanian texts reaching back to the beginning of the Parthian period (Ayyatkar and Zereran)[43] , and in Central Asia with the discovery of a ceramic body of such an instrument in the grave of a warrior in Tali Khamtuda (north of Sogdia) dating from the 3rd to 4th century AD, as well as subsequent iconographic representations from Airtam (North Bactria), Toprak Kala (Choresm), Afrasib, Punjazent, Khirman Tepe (Sogdian) etc.[44]

If the Parthians were going to break up the enemy, the first charge would give orders to all the archery units in the area to make preparations for "hunting" those who try to follow the withdrawal by the scattered remnants of the enemy troops. The attack with the armored cavalry was only designed as a "probe" and stopping the enemy, the light cavalry was probably ready to attack once the heavy cavalry withdrew. Plutarch describes the scene, *"No horns or trumpets were sounded in battle, instead they used clubs on a hollow tube with a bronze ring tightened the skin around the rim: in striking these they produce a deep and gloomy voice, menacing as a roar of the wild animals among the roar of thunder. (...) So, when the Romans heard the noise they threw their shields."* (Plutarch, *Crassus*, 24) The quote above made it clear that the Romans heard the sound of drums in the heat of battle which aimed at causing a certain psychological effect on an opponent. Most likely, when the armored cavalry retreated, the archers had in the meantime, *"secretly surrounded the Roman*

---

[43]Zoviran
[44]В. П. Никоноров, *The use of Music in Ancient Warfare: Partian and Central Asian Warfare*, 9th. International Sumposium of the "Study Group on Music Archeology", Kloster Michaelstein in Blankenburg (Germany).

squares" (Plutarch, *Crassus*, 24), at the same time firing from all sides. In addition, the complete lack of other methods of transmitting commands in the Parthian army may, apart from the messengers, have justified the assumption that this was done with the help of drums. Their sound is audible over long distances and was able to reach troops doing reconnaissance in the field, for which sending a messenger would be impossible. It is also known that the unusual methods of transmitting signals, i.e. using drums, flags or flaming arrows, were known to the steppe people up to the Mongol invasion of the Middle East and Europe.

The Parthian mounted archers used a specific technique for conducting fire, vague descriptions by Plutarch, however, does not allow for precise identification and reproduction. By analogy researchers have reconstructed these highly effective and deadly tactics using descriptions of fights from the steppes – Scythians, Turkish and Mongolian using the so-called "Parthian or Scythian circle".

In accordance with the old Scythian tactics of waging guerilla warfare, archers (in a similar manner and practice to the way the Scythians attacked Alexander's army at Jaxartes and was even used by the Mongols in the time of Genghis Khan) would suddenly surrounded by the enemy galloping at maximum speed, one after the other to the right. At the same time, they raised clouds of dust covering everything around them. They continued firing until they exhausted their stock of arrows. Plutarch writes that the legionaries of Crassus last hope clung to the idea of close combat which would have come when the Parthians arrows were exhausted. Surena had no intention of exposing his soldiers to the risks associated with such an attack. The supply of missiles, which each archer had, were placed in a long quiver which hung at the waist, enough to carry several dozen shots. After shooting all of their arrows the last line of riders returned to just behind the line of troops where camels carrying missiles were there to re-supply them, and then go back to rejoin the fight. *"While the Romans hoped that the enemy had finally exhausted their shot and cease the battle or join in hand-to-hand combat, as they had withstood for so long. But when that there were many camels loaded with arrows and those in the front rank passed near them and obtained more missles, Crassus, unable to see the end became afraid..."* (Plutarch, *Crassus.* 25)

The number of galloping riders kicked up clouds of dust that formed a kind of veil of smoke and preventing Crassus from getting a clear picture of the battlefield. This tactic is vividly described by Plutarch: *"... the riders moved about without purpose and moving into the depths of the sand dunes, they raised dust clouds from which one could not see or speak to those directly around them."* (Plutarch, *Crassus.* 25) The ring of riders whirling in the clouds of dust stretched out fluidly giving way to attacks desperately trying to break free from enemies, whose commanders were blinded by dust could not make an effective assessment of the situation to direct some of their forces against the weak link in the encircling chain of Parthian troops. Every moment of delay entailed terrible consequences as clouds of arrows falling on the surrounded enemy decimated his soldiers. In fact, except for a quick cavalry attack that might have torn through the encircled cordon of riders, there was no way to get out of the "ring of death."

Parthian horsemen galloped probably no more than 30-50m from the enemy infantry's front line, and at such a slight distance with a heavy reflexive bow as described by Plutarch, had no problem to penetrate the chain mail and legionary shield. Dust, sun and lack of water, was as beleaguering in the desert for the Romans as deadly as arrows. For every unit that somehow was able to get out of the trap there was a wall of heavy cavalry waiting to push the unfortunates back into the range of shot. The hell of fire was so horrendous as to deprive all hope of survival, so that desiring a faster death some of the poor men preferred to throw themselves on the wide spear tips than to die in torment.

The maneuver, which is known as the "Parthian shot", is fired back at the full gallop was used only in case it was necessary to withdraw before the enemy attacked and then says Plutarch, "(...) *received escape with shame.*" Their task was to delay the pursuit and they accomplished this superbly.

Any small detachment of enemy troops that broke away from the main body or chased one of the diversions to escape the Parthians or wandered in the darkness, were surrounded at night in the same way as the main body of troops and mercilessly pounded off his feet. Parthian cavalry could provoke an opponent in a very skillful way. It is due to this exact maneuver under fire that caught the son of Crassus, Publius, and his men: "*Young Crassus took, therefore, a thousand-three hundred cavalry, in addition to one thousand men from Caesar, five hundred archers and eight cohorts with large shields and set them to attack. Chasing the nearest Parthian horsemen, back to swamps, as some claim, as a strategic retreating to pull Crassus (the younger) as far as possible from his father. As his people lingered he called for the soldiers to attack and sped after them along with Censorinus and Megabocchus (...). The cavalry charged behind them, followed up by the infantry, moving with the spirit of hope that this would be a victorious pursuit of the enemy. But as they pursued they realized it was only a tactical stroke: they seemed to run away, then turn back and others even more numerous attacked them from behind.*" (Plutarch, *Crassus*. 25) This action ended in tragedy. Young Crassus and all his men were killed.

"*A lot (of people) were captured by horsemen after wandering around on the plain. At the same time four cohorts under their commander Varguntei broke out during the night only to be surrounded by the Parthians somewhere in the ravine and defended themselves only to be killed except for twenty soldiers who struggled with their bare swords. With admiration for the defenders, they were allowed to move step-by-step towards Carrom.*" (Plutarch, Crassus. 28) None of the opponents could slip out of the encirclement, the warriors of Sūren, worthy sons of the steppe rarely took prisoners, though there were also tales about those later exiled to Sogdia.

Regardless of the tactics, the firing was maintained until the opponent's formation collapsed, or gaps appeared in their lines, which the armored cavalry hit head on, crushing all that still tried to resist.

Parthian horse archers had to use a special breed of horses for the specific needs of this unit. The poor and crude iconographic representation makes it difficult to tell what they were. The horses and riders – archers shown on terracotta plaques generally resemble stocky and large ponies or steppe horses commonly used by Mongolian cavalry. For the latter, however, the Parthian horses were, it seems a slightly bit larger. In fact, widespread use of light horse in cavalry formations were better suited to the requirements of armored units than their own, it is particularly strange if it is recalled, that in the neighboring monarchy of the Arsacid's, the Sakae peoples were recruited in large numbers as Parthian mercenary units. They were excellent warriors which are confirmed from at least the second century BCE in pictorial representations, i.e. seals from Orlat, on which were shown outlined desert-steppe horses characteristic of those today of the Akhal-Teke in Trukmenistan.[45] The horses were wiry, long-legged, with a "tough" strong build resembling a greyhound. They had a large chest, and consequently the lungs, and large nasal cavities that increase the inflow of air and giving the head of the animal is easy to recognize on the representation of the "humped" shape. This amazing biological machine was able to walk long distances without fatigue, and in combat could achieve sufficiently high speeds to escape or attack, staying out of reach of the enemy cavalry. Small, though proportionally distributed muscle mass radiated a large amount of heat, though the thin and delicately covered with short, golden hair, made the animal's body immune to overheating. Such a mount was not a sprinter but a long-distance runner he was also resistant to cold and hunger.[46]

The Dahae, probably brought their own semi-wild race horses with them from the steppes. As seen from the pictorial representations

---

[45] B. Burris-Davis, *Parthian horses- Parthian archers*, http://parthia.com/pathia_horses.burris.htm.
[46] E. Hartley Edwards, *Księga koni*, tłum. M. Redlicki, Warszawa 1993. p. 42.

from the Parthian and Sassanid period they were small animals with a thick massive body and a fairly large head. Even if the horses of the Arsacid warriors interbred with them, the descendants of the steppe horses kept their amazing resistance to all weather conditions and habitats. Their small height and short gait assisted the ability to shoot. Even today, this breed of horses lives on the fertile steppes almost perfectly fitting this description. They are so-called Bashkir horses.[47] This is an old breed related to the wild, most primitive type, such as the Przewalski horses.

Just like the armies of the great steppe monarchy, the Parthian army had huge herds of horses for their troops. This made it possible to quickly trade the tired mounts for new ones. The advantages of such a procedure are shown in Cassius Dio: *"(...) in the war they run whole herds of horses behind them, which allows them to change them; they can suddenly come from afar and suddenly leave for somewhere far away."* (Cassius Dio, *Roman History* XIV 3) Justin even claimed that the Parthian horsemen were able to sleep in the saddle without interrupting the journey.

The use of the above described tactics brought Surena a total victory over the enemy with its numerical predominance. Unfortunately, it only suited itself for use in open areas, along plains or at most gentle rolling hills. It was quite a different situation, however, in the mountainous area and hence the advice given to Crassus by the King of Armenia to stick to the mountains. Marc Antony's armies fought the Parthians in this area of Armenia during the years 36 and 34 BCE, and it is probably due to the difficult conditions, that their cavalry only attacked the Romans when they descended to explore the low-laying areas. (Plutarch, *Antony*, 38-39). The fact that the Arsacid army did not actually fight in the mountains is often used by Roman commanding officers in subsequent campaigns. Plutarch presents the army of Marc Antony as a huge force, of about one hundred thousand soldiers. If this number is not exaggerated, then at the height of the struggle against the Parthians, even with reinforcements sent by King Phraata, Antony left the allied Armenian contingent of thirteen thousand armed men, which outnumbered them by double. In view of this it is quite understandable that the army of the Arsacids almost exclusively "on the run" actions, destroying only the weaker units that separated from the main body of the invaders, such as siege engines traveling on roads towards Antony besieging Phraata (Phraaspa).

During this war and other campaigns, a characteristic feature of Parthian tactics was rather to avoid clashes in general, (Carrhae was the exception because Orodes could not allow the Romans to join up with the

---
[47] E. Hartley Edwards, op.cit., p. 122.

Armenian troops of King Artabazes rebel army), and specifically to obstruct the enemy's movement to get supplies, rather than trying to stop them. The use of this tactic, dating back to the roots of strategic action of the nomadic peoples of the Great Steppe, was completely incomprehensible to the Romans. It resulted in the invaders being able to occupy large areas of Parthian land at will without a fight, which drew the unconscious enemy into the depths of a waterless wasteland suitable for handling masses of cavalry from which retreat was extremely difficult. The entire war effort of the Arsacids gave the advantage to small armies. The losses suffered in this type of fighting compared to losses incurred by an opponent were virtually negligible. *"...although his infantry chased the enemy for fifty furlongs, and the cavalry three times further, after looking at the casualties thirty were taken prisoner and only eighty-one killed, they were perplexed and unhappy, considering it unpleasant that they had beaten so few people in victory and lost so much in their defeat. The next day (...) in their march when they encountered a few of the enemy, then more, and finally they encountered the main body, as if they were not beaten and fully fresh forces, so that challenged to battle they attacked with hesitation and retreated with great difficulty back to their camp."* (Plutarch, *Antony*, 39) By keeping their losses low, the Parthians could control the march of even the most powerful enemy, and then using the appropriate terrain conditions to destroy him slowly, or force him to retreat, which at passing through barren or specially devastated areas often changed into a hell that led to the total destruction of the "victorious" enemy army.

Another feature of Arsacid strategy was a skillful combination of guerrilla warfare and diplomatic activity aimed at fomenting rebellions behind the enemy and depriving him of the support of allies. They made it difficult on Trajan during the campaign from the years 114-117 A.D. to maintained large areas in Parthian for the long-run. In 117 r. A.D. the uprising of the Jews and the people of Mesopotamia combined with a small counteroffensive of Arsacid forces led to the withdrawal of the Roman army who reached the Persian Gulf.[48] In the spirit of that same tactic In modern times, the armies of the "Arab Revolt" during World War I took place in Hijaz and areas of today's Jordan and Syria in an offensive against the Turks. These tactics famously described by the historian and orientalist T. E. Lawrence who accompanied Bedouins.[49]

A different tactical maneuver was used against Marc Antony's army, indicating to it's commander-in-chief that he could safely return with his soldiers through the Atropatene Plain, without fear of attack.

---

[48] Z. Haszczyc, *Wyprawa przeciw Partom w latach 114-117 i zwrot w polityce zagranicznej Cesarstwa Rzymskiego po objęciu władzy przez Hadriana*, Meander 1975, p. 151.
[49] T. E. Lawrence, *Siedem filarów mądrości*, tłum. J. Schwakopf, Warszawa 1971.

Antony accepted this option, since in the face of hunger, and maybe even rebellion there was salvation. He did not assume, however, that it was only intended to draw the Romans out of the mountain passes to areas best suited for the use of cavalry. As the strategist Sun-Tsu wrote in his famous treatise: *"Show the enemy a route to escape, create in his mind a vision to avoid death, and then hit this place."* (Sun-Tsu, War of War, 31) Such tricks were the norm in the conduct of steppe tactic in conducting war. According to Plutarch, Antony's army had to be rescued by a Mardin[50] guide who led the Romans to the mountains of Armenia on roads that did not lend themselves to cavalry. The witness's description of the retreat however, indicate that the man might have been in Phraata's service, because despite his assurances, the route of march, which was supposed to be safe, turned out to be hell. Antony's troops were constantly attacked (Gallus died because of his own bravado), and later they entered areas so barren the soldiers had to live on grass. Many of them died eating unknown poisonous roots – the losses were huge.

Both campaigns described by Plutarch have shown that Arsacid cavalry, operating under these conditions in the field were difficult to overcome. The main goal of this operation was to bleed the enemy, and not its total destruction. Roman chroniclers, mostly historians and not military men with understanding of field strategy, took it on face value that there was tension between soldiers and commanders about, "rebuking the cowardly Parthians." They could not understand the assumption of nomadic tactics, which the Arsacid leaders used masterful tactics to hold back a strong and numerous enemy, exposing them to big losses, but allowing them to follow the Persians deeper into enemy territory, and finally cut off their supply lines, deprive them of food and water, harass them with constant attacks, and only as a last resort to destroy the demoralize troops. The people of the steppe rarely fought large battles and then only if forced to in extreme circumstances which were then long and bloody. Skirmishes were their element. An enemy who could not effectively chase the Parthian riders were observed by them, even if forces did not fight against him, even when the invaders plundered villages and burned cities. It must be said that the success of the Romans in battles with the Arsacids were at least as a result of the efficiency of the weapons, as well as knowledge of the internal politics of their eastern neighbors and maybe possibly better intelligence. Continuous rebellions of conquered peoples, invasion of the Saki, and in addition, at the beginning of the era, behind their eastern border, a dangerous and powerful opponent in the form of the Kushan Kingdom, which emerged from the Yuezhi tribal federation meant the Roman attacks were not the only problem for

---
[50]Mardin – a town in present-day eastern Turkey

3. The Bow as a weapon of the Iranian people

Since time immemorial the primary weapon of nomadic warriors was the bow. When the Scythians reached the areas of settled populations they quickly convinced themselves about the steppe people's superiority in technical matters. It seems that the Scythians arrived out of the east, west and southern belt of the Great Steppe with a recursive bow known of and widely used in the depths of Asia, as evidence by images of the so-called "bone dragon" dating from the late Shang period of roughly the second half of the second millennium BCE.[51] It was a weapon unusual because of its size and performance. At the time it constituted the form of development in archery weapons perfectly tailored to the needs of combat and the tactics of nomadic horse archers. The excellence of this type of bow is evidenced by the fact that after the conquest of the Parthians and Hyrcania, the neighbors adopted a long reflexive bow; the Parthians still used a short Scythian type bow for a long time.[52] What is more, once this was displaced from use in the Arsacid army, it appeared in the invading force of the nomadic Turks, and experienced a renaissance during the crusades, when it was used for long-range shooting. It must also be emphasized that all bows used in Asia, except for perhaps the southeastern part and Japan, developed from this nomadic steppe weapon. For these reasons, method of producing reflexive bows, can be reconstructed based on analyzing pictographic representations, and compared with identical sized shapes and the effectiveness of the Turkish "flight bow" and the traditional Korean bows as examples.

Recursive Bow. It had a length of 80-100 cm, because it was determined that such a length was best for maneuverability and to quickly change the direction of shooting over the back of the horse – the Scythians were known to be able to ride to a place and fire, "with both hands" in any direction. Lightweight with short arms and a relatively high pull force, it guaranteed the maximum firing range.[53] The frame was made of composite technology which in addition to the wood core, included layers of tendon and horn. Some parts remained rigid like the mid-handle and the griffins end of the arms with hooks to loop the bowstring, reinforced with hardwood or antler.[54] The composite part of the bow is not an in-

---

[51] S. Zhangru, *Complete Sets of Weapons from the Yin (Shang) Site at Xiao Tun*, Annual report of the History and Language Institute of the Academia Sinica, 22, 1950, pp. 19-59.
[52] Taybuga, op.cit., pp. 17-18, 104.
[53] W. M. Moseley, An essay on archery, http://www.atarn.org/islamic/persian.htm.
[54] А. М. Хазанов, op.cit., p. 29.

vention of this period and had been practiced for a long-time prior.[55] Many bows shown on iconography are suspected of being just such a design, but with a differently shaped frame. One such bow, for example, is a small framed weapon held on the so-called, "Stele of Victory" by the ruler Akad Naram-Sina[56], another bow is shown on an even older stone plaque with Mari[57] while the oldest example of a composite bow confirmed by archeology is the well-preserved in shape and construction were discovered in the tomb of Tutankhamun, and thus dating back to the mid-XIV century BCE. The core of this is a single piece of hard, elastic wood with two side arms - one facing away from the archer, and the coming back to him capped with horn bands. The core, together with the horn strips for strengthening, gave the shape to the frame's arms, which was provided with two semi-circular cross-sections of another flexible wood. The whole of the bows arms was covered with two layers of prepared animal tendon, and finally for the protection against the effects of weather conditions, glued around with birch bark. The construction of the external frame of the bow at Tutankhamun's tombs was not reflexive. This bow, although composite in its construction belonged to a typical equatorial bow, in that the arm was not straight until the bowstring is applied.

If it can be said that the Asian steppes, Mesopotamia or Egypt were working on the invention of the composite bow concurrently, consider what might have caused this inquiry? In addition to the desire to make a more powerful wooden bow, a key cause of this process was probably the scarcity of large quantities of wood capable of producing quality bows. For all of the above areas to be out of supply must have been severe. This would have forced someone from the land of the Great Steppe to seek a better design.

The invention of the composite bow, with recursive arms collapsed without the bow string holding them in place, occurred in Central or Eastern Asia somewhere in approximately the second half of the second millennium BCE. On Chinese plates, also called, "dragon bones" dating from the second half of the reign of the Shang Dynasty, from about XII-XIII centuries BCE they appear as a logogram with the meaning of the word "bow" in which the image is depicted as the reflexive type weapon.[58] After stringing the bow, the two strongly curved arms are so characteristic as to exclude any other choice. Unfortunately, we cannot determine the length of the bow that was used to make the figures recorded on the

---
[55] I am referring to the beginning of the Iron Age, which is more or less in the Steppes of the 8th-7th century BC
[56] A. Lemaire (ed.), *Świat Biblii*, tłum. B. Panek, Wrocław 2001, p. 51.
[57] A town of ancient Syria
[58] loc.cit.

"dragon bones" man. One of the oldest preserved archaeological examples is an almost perfect condition Scythian copy dating to the VIII century BCE belonging to an officer, recently discovered by a Russian-American mission in the Scythian or Tocharian mound in the republic of Tuva, near the Russian-Mongolian border. The weapon already has all the telltale characteristics of a typical Scythian bow – a small length, reflexive construction and bow arms stiffened with horn.[59] It was perfectly suited fighting for shooting on horseback, the length of the Scythian bows is their distinguishing feature. It was probably this that influenced the necessity for shaping the "C" shape with a joint bearing the greatest amount of counter-bending, i.e. bending the arms in the opposite directions of the tension that the bow is shooting. It allows you to store in the potential energy in the strung bow, which is creating tension before the arrow is inserted in the weapon.[60] This feature allows you to use the small length of the bow to create sufficient tension to fire arrows which were effective in hurting the enemy. An extreme example is the Korean bows whose shape without the cord are bent into a circle, so that the ends of the arms touch each other, or even overlap each other in the counter-cavity.[61]

With the reflective construction, the associated composition of the Scythian bow's internal structure, differed slightly from the structure of the Egyptian bow. The Scythian bow like most bows of Asian steppe people was composed of three main layers: tendon-glued on the top side of the wooden core formed like the skeleton of a bow, but playing a much smaller role in the shaping the physical properties of the weapon then in the European variation, and the main level made of strips cut from the horn such as cattle stuck on the ventral surface of the core. When the tension layer of tendon is subjected to tensile forces stretching the stratum corneum while compressing forces are applied. Working together, they create double resistance that considerably increases the value of the force necessary to bend the entire bow.

As to the material employed to making the working (flexible) parts of the core, in different part of Asia they used different types of wood. In the Far East, the most popular woods were bamboo and mulberry; in the Middle East it was elm, maple, dogwood, etc.[62] In short bows, the core was made of layers of wood, which significantly contributed to strengthening and stiffening the entire frame. They were bonded together under

---

[59] M. Edwards, *Syberyjscy Scytowie, Kurhan pełen złota*, National Geographic nr. 6, (45) czerwiec 2003. pp. 39-55.
[60] W. Świętosławski, *Uzbrojenie koczowników wielkiego stepu w czasach ekspansji Mongołów (XII- XIV w.)*, Acta Archeologica Lodziensia nr.40, Łódź 1996, p. 39-40.
[61] *Czas łuku, Strona towarzystwa łucznictwa tradycyjnego*. http://www.bowtime.waw.pl/trad_corean.html.
[62] Łucznictwo tradycyjne, http//int/luk/archer~1/8t3.htm.

clamps of bound knots distributed across the entire length of the arms – this type of compound bonding was known and practiced in areas of the Far east today.[63] The flexible parts forming the arm's core (Arabic *duštar*) were glued on both sides of the core made of rigid wood for the static parts to prevent bending , which would create uncontrolled vibrations – "Digging" of the bow in a similar fashion to the recoil of firearms, and thus create instability and reduce the accuracy of the entire frame. [64] On the opposite ends were glued horn, bone or wooden tips called griffins or ears to attach the string. To hold everything in place in antiquity and later, only organic-bone based glue made from hide or the best from fish cartilage, skins, bladders and palates – preferably from sturgeons.[65]

All the parts of the core were glued on the so-called "Fish tail" using a large dovetail (10-15cm) connecting the riser to the arms, while the smaller (7-10 cm) composite arms with the griffins.[66] In addition to the compact dimensions of the weapons described above the design had one more advantage – they only needed about two 20-30 cm long pieces of good quality wood to produce, which you get by splitting rather than cutting, it was also possible to use an uneven, gnarled stump or branch, which was a great advantage on the forestless steppe. On the basis of iconographic remains we know that the Majdan type Scythian bows were designed to reduce vibration.[67]

The core parts were given the desired shape and counter-bend when the wood was still wet, right after cutting. This was usually done in autumn when the wood was dryer and the whole preparation process was finished before winter, which due to the low temperature was the best for gluing the individual parts together. The glue dries more slowly in such conditions, and therefore adheres better to the joined surfaces.[68] Drying and seasoning lasted several more months. Trying to do it quicker would cause the wood to crack. When the glue fully cured, the core was subjected to final mechanical testing, after which it started to put it together.

To complete the construction, it used pieces of horn, usually ordinary, long-horned cattle, but under favorable circumstances, when they managed to get one, a water buffalo. In Central Asia the horns of wild goats were often used.[69] From the interior of the horn the bone core was cut to appropriate length and width of strips, usually they are thicker at

---

[63]H.Onuma, D. i J. DeProspero, op.cit., pp. 39-40,45.
[64]Taybuga, op.cit., p. 11.
[65]http:// int/luk/archer ~ 1/8t3.htm.
[66] http:// int/luk/archer ~ 1/8t3.htm.
[67]*Gold der Skythen. Schätze aus der Staatlichen Eremitage*, St. Petersburg, 1993. fig. p. 113.
[68]Taybuga, op.cit., pp. 12-13.
[69]W. Świętosławski, op.cit., p. 40.

A bow in the grave of a Scythian or Tochar chieftain - Tuva Republic (M. Edwards, Syberyjscy Scytowie, Kurhan pełen złota, fig 46)

A traditional Korean arch with overlapping shoulder tips. (according to www.koreanarcher.org.*)*

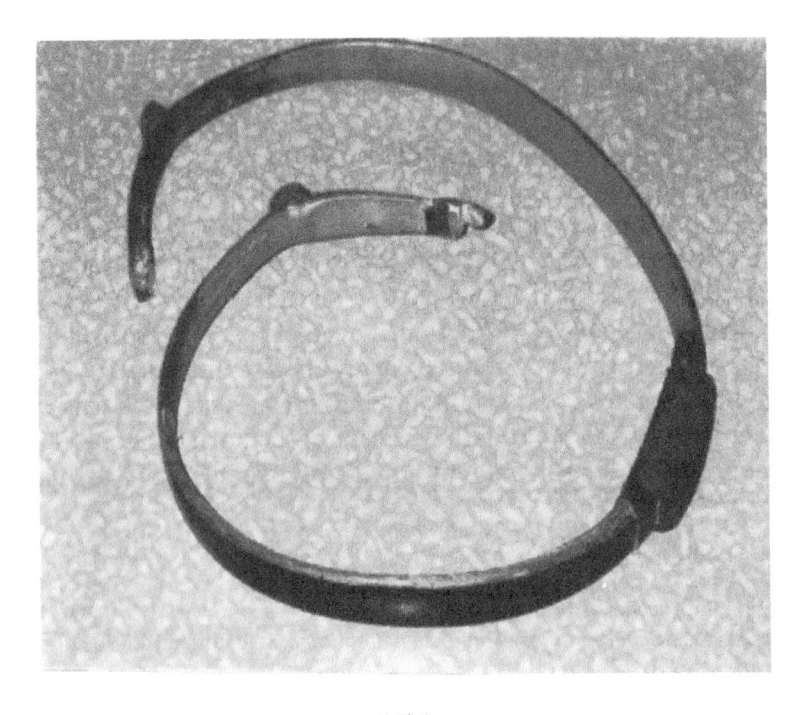

A short Scythian-type arch stuck in gorytos- openwork brick from Stara Nisa. (According to J. Wolski, *Dzieje i upadek imperium Seleucydów*, fig.13)

Achaemenid reflex bow (with rigid ones inserts at the ends of the arms and strong antiwear) in the palm of Darius III on the famous "mosaic Aleksandra" from Pompeii - probably copies of the Hellenistic painting. (according O. Dalera ed. Mocarstwa świata, *110,111)*

The Armies of Ancient Persia

The reverse of the early coin showing a Sogdian bowman with an asymmetrical, reflexive bow. (from К. Абдульаев, Armor of ancient Baktria, Fig. 3.4)

Yrzi bow from near Baghouz- (a), reconstructed from a weapons (b). (according to F. Brown, A recently discovered compound bow, fig. 2)

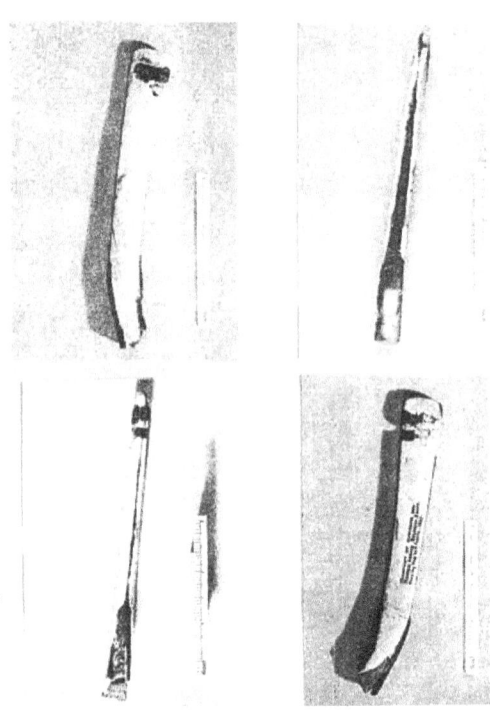

Corners of Belmes bow found in Egypt (a), fig (b) below (according to J. Coulston, Roman archery equipment, fig.3,15,16,17,18)

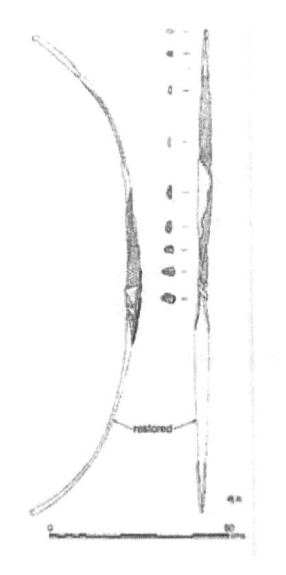

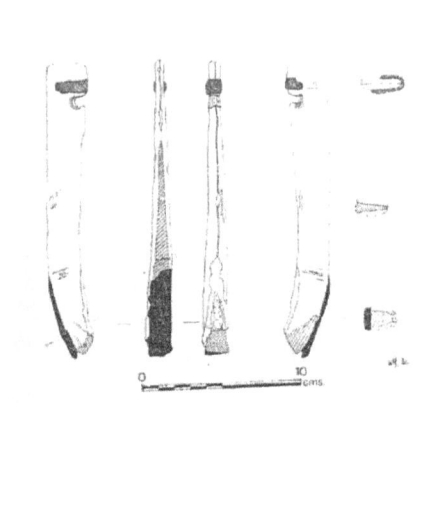

Archer shooting a symmetrical reflexive bow - Taht-e Sangin. (according to R. Takeuchi, The Parthian shot in hunting Scenes, fig. 14)

Silver Sassanid plate with a bow hunting scene (according to R. Ghirschman, Iran: Parthians and Sassanians, fig. p.249)

The bent Siyah of a reflexive bow shown in an "exaggerated" way – on graffiti from house A, block L.7 in Dura Europos (according to B. Goldman, Pictorial graffiti of Dura- Europos, *Fig.b1a, b1b)*

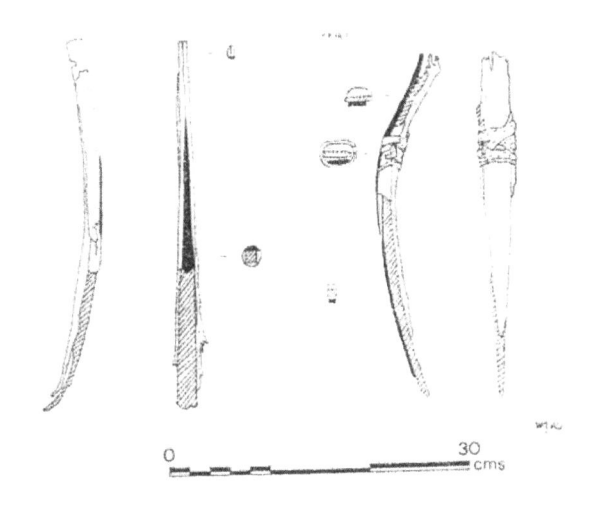

A bow from the Qum Darya find (according to J. Coulston, Roman Archery Equipment, *fig. 4)*

A representation of a warrior armed using an assimetrical bow – from a tomb painting in northern Turkistan (from А. М. Хазанов, Очерки военного дела Сарматов, *Tab.18)*

Upper Limb, Bayt al–yad

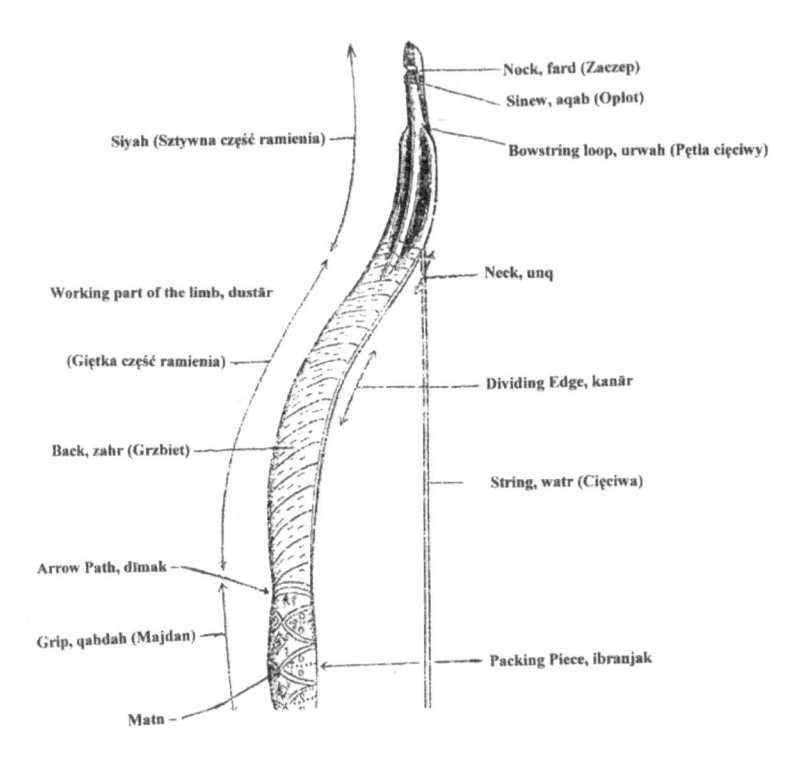

Siyah (Sztywna część ramienia)

Nock, fard (Zaczep)

Sinew, aqab (Oplot)

Bowstring loop, urwah (Pętla cięciwy)

Working part of the limb, dustār

(Giętka część ramienia)

Neck, unq

Dividing Edge, kanār

Back, zahr (Grzbiet)

String, watr (Cięciwa)

Arrow Path, dīmak

Grip, qabdah (Majdan)

Packing Piece, ibranjak

Matn

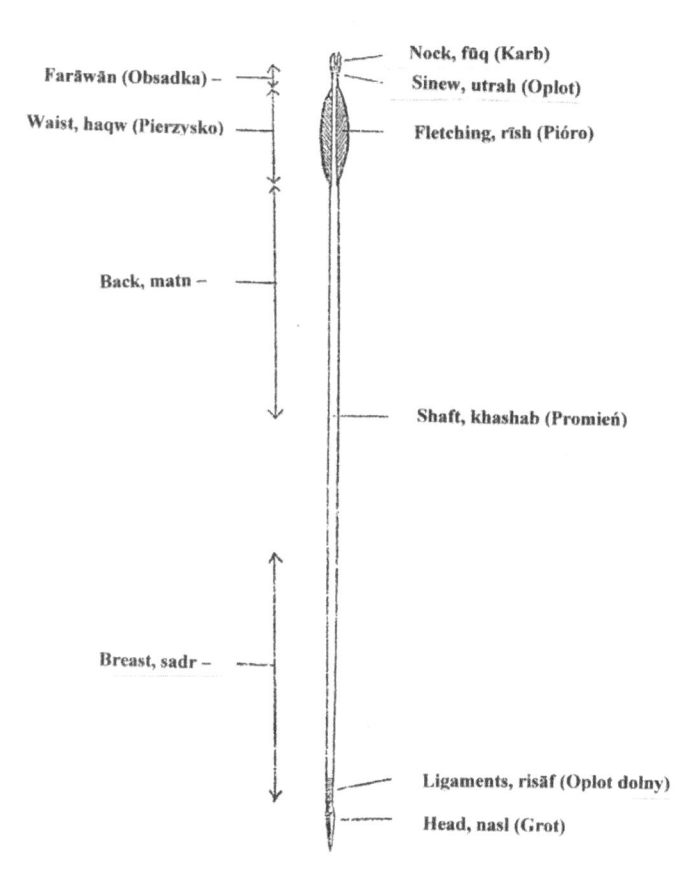

Farāwān (Obsadka) — Nock, fūq (Karb)
Sinew, utrah (Oplot)
Waist, haqw (Pierzysko) — Fletching, rīsh (Pióro)

Back, matn —

Shaft, khashab (Promień)

Breast, sadr —

Ligaments, risāf (Oplot dolny)
Head, nasl (Grot)

the base, and thinnest at the beginning of the tip. Shaped and smoothed strips of suitable thickness of approximately 3-6 mm, scratched on the inner surface to be stuck onto the core with a special serrated tool. The same tool was also used to scratch the surface of the core. The roughness protected the two layers from shifting between each other during the gluing and in use created an increased bonding surface. It is very possible (and an example of this can be seen in a well-preserved manor discovered in Yrzi)[70] that such ancient bows such as these did not have these connections between the core and the stratum corneum. They were covered with a tightly wound thick covering of sinewy. Here again, the pressure was achieved by means of string or twine tightened with a special level.

    The Saracen bows only attached the stratum corneum through counter-bending by bonding to the core, only after such an operation were the corner pieces applied. When the adhesive dries it prevents the connecting layers from moving, which preserved the shape of the binding.[71] The remaining pressure on the wood core and corner strips were used to prevent cracking during use. In the Far Eastern technology, the force is transmitted through the core by heating and bending.

    After the glue dried, the clamps were removed with the Spring being the best time for this. They then proceeded to add the tendons. These were added two to three times. The tendons came from the legs of cattle or deer, they are less greasy which is more convenient in the preparation and durable to be dried, crushed and torn into individual fibers. [72]The process of treating this material was more conducive to areas with higher temperatures, hence it was probably the reason for doing it at this time of year. Tendons were soaked in glue diluted in warm water, then laid out in flat long strips. After it dried it was removed and applied to the top area of the core and then dried. The temperature of the glue could not be too high because it would cause the collagen fibers to change and with it the loss material elasticity.

    The tendons where gradually applied with glue, after each dried, they increased the bow's ability to bend to its final shape.[73] When the layers of tendons on the back were ready (thickness of approximately 3-6mm) and well covered with another coat of glue apart from the dorsal surface of the sides of the core and the stratum corneum. After that application of the glue and drying for a short time the unfinished bow was strung and the final adjustments were made to shape of bent arms by

---

[70]J. Coulston, *Roman archery Equipment,* London 1998. pp. 239-240.
[71]Taybuga, op.cit., p. 12-13.
[72]http://int/luk/archer ~ 1/8t3.htm.
[73]Taybuga, op.cit., p. 14.

sawing the stratum corneum and the tendon layer.[74] A special template was used in order to obtain the right shape of the bent arms. At higher temperatures these actions were carried out in the summer, which helped to strengthen the form. The whole bow was then soaked once more in glue with layers reinforced by wrapping it to protect the form against splitting up. Sometimes, for example, the Sasanid bows were only wrapped at stress points, i.e. the joints of the *majdan* of the *duštar,* or *duštar* of *sijah*. The tips were left free of wrapping from the arms for the hooks of the bowstring. After the final drying, the bow reached its proper shape and tension for strength. Drying could take a few more months.

A bowstring was finally applied to the finished bow. It was usually made of twisted, dried animal guts, or in Mongolia, from dead skin, best from a starving one, because it contained little fat – horse, bull or camel are characterized by a low stretch point (less than 1 mm on the 1.6m length)[75], but it could also be from raw vegetable fibers, etc. The notch where the arrow is placed had additional wrapping to protect it from wear due to fiction. The general rule is that short reflexive bows used strong, light and thin bowstrings, and for recursive bows it was thick and heavy. During marches, the bows were worn, however, without strings, because of the tension could break it when strung.[76]

Stringing the Scythian bow, seems to be based on the shape of the already tight frame depicted on various pictorial representations, quite a lot of counter-bending requiring considerable strength and skill. This was an operation which helped to use your feet properly. Their system and method for applying the string is clearly shown on the Electrum Cup discovered in the barrow at Kil-Oba in the Crimean. Before applying the string, one of the loops was hooked on the bottom, then placed under the left thigh, resting the other on the right thigh. The left thigh pressed down on the arm and the left hand grasped the upper arm of the bow with the help of the right thigh, then the free loop of the string is hooked to the upper part with their right arm.

Strength, agility, range. As you can suppose, the tension, i.e. the force necessary to pull the length of the arrows on Scythian bows was not the same as Korean short bows or those the Saracens used until the late Islamic period, known in the nomenclature as the so-called "flight bow". These three types of weapons did not properly differ in appearance from the Majdan type which is simply a Turkish bow.[77] At best, they achieved

---
[74]loc. cit..
[75]W. Świętosławski, op.cit., pp. 40-41.
[76]W. Świętosławski, op.cit., p. 41
[77]Taybuga, op.cit., p. 11.

a pull no higher than 65 Lbs. or 30 kg, but there were some a lot stronger.

Due to short length of the arms on the Scythian bows and the light weight of the arms with a relatively high tension allowed them to fire only light arrows.[78] This was due to the short lever arm, which is the bow arm. It was not enough to overcome the inertia of a heavy arrow and give it the appropriate initial speed. From the formula $F=1/2mV2$ (where F is the arrow penetration force, V is the arrow speed, m is the mass of the projectile) we know that when the muzzle velocity decreases, it also decreases the power of the shot. In this situation, there is also a low efficiency, or ratio of energy of shots to the tension. In addition, using the cord with too heavy an arrow has a bowstring stretching effect, which causes additional loss of energy. A similar effect is obtained with arms that were too heavy, especially the ends, in relation to the pull force, the chords elasticity and the weight of the shot. Even so, with the correct arrow weight, let alone the heavy one, the force of the bow's chord with heavy arms provides little speed.

Vibrations on the end of the arms wasted considerable amount of energy,[79] which was in turn caused by too big a bow and the weight of the arms combined with the flexibility of the bowstring. Using a short bow with a light weight bowstring, the arms could be thinner, with less force, and the vibration caused at the bow ends has small amplitude and small frequency, and thus loses less energy. The use of light arrows for such a bow allows shooting them for a very long distance, because it minimizes the inertia of the bow's stretching effect, and the maximum energy is transmitted to the projectile.

Simply put, the short and light arms of a Scythian or Saracen type "flight bow" after releasing the arrows, very quickly returned to the rest position, giving the projectile a high initial speed. A light thin arrow lost little energy in flight, works perfectly for long-range shooting. Recreations with a short Turkish bow with a tension of 38.5 kg (84.88 lbs) achieved a distance of 229, 243 and 257 meters respectively (751, 797 and 843 ft) with strong range, while a long Tarter bow achieved 102 meters (334 ft).[80] This value seems to be cause by the wrong bowstring or a damp bow which diminishes it ability. For comparison, the confirmed length of the shot from a similar bow recorded at an archery competition in Mongolia is 135 bow lengths (i.e. approximately 250 meters or 820 ft).[81] An unconfirmed record shot from the Turkish "flight bow" with a

---

[78] А. М. Хазанов, op.cit., p. 30.
[79] Азятицкий лук, http://www.atarn.org/mongolian/asian_bow_r.htm.which
[80] J.Cooles, op.cit., pp. 167-170.
[81] W. Świętosławski, op.cit., p. 41.

long pull was supposedly 972 yards, or more the 800meters.[82] Scythian and Turkish short bows had a long range had one disadvantage, however, as their light weight arrows - even at high speed had insufficient penetration power.[83] They were able to beat an unarmored enemy, but they were unable to hurt armored troops over a long distance. Considering that very few nomads wore armor, a powerful shot was not needed. During the battles, the most important thing was that the enemy was within effective range before the Scythian cavalry would attack. You could maneuver to attack the enemy with a flood of arrows, and still have him out of reach. Once the fire softened the enemy, the heavy armored enemy forces led by the leaders were the first to attack the enemy front with melee weapons (i.e. spears), and light-armed archers followed them on both wings. By means of their famous riding skills, the nomads were able to regroup to strike without difficulty, "on the run". For major battles, they assumed this formation, and firing was carried out by all the warriors on horseback. Such tactics gave the steppe people victory in battle against forces in the Middle and Far East.

The relatively low force of the shot required the use of tiny, sharp bronze arrowheads with spurs, making it difficult to pull out of shallow wounds. Due to the very thin rays (the bushing tip diameters rarely exceed 6-7mm) Scythian arrows could be easily broken off at the slightest attempt to manipulate it, leaving the arrowhead in the body without the possibility of removing or pushing it through. To pull such an arrowhead out would greatly expand the wound. Leaving it, however would also have grave consequences because the bronze oxidized, giving off harmful compounds into the blood. On the battlefield, a warrior who is hit by several such projectiles, even if he were alive, would cease to be dangerous.

The length of a short reflexive bow was about 60-65% of the length of the light bow.[84] Fully strung the tension of the cord bent the arms to a horizontal position, making the force of the tension increase to the point where it could not take more without breaking the bow. It is easy to calculate the length of the Scythian bow at approximately 60 to 65 cm. The length of a pull for a shot was about 60-65 cm. This does not allow for firing from the saddle with the pull of the cord to the chin or the cheek which is required for proper targeting. Pulling the bowstring to this point is aimed with the tip, which results in two necessary points for aiming.[85] In short bows this problem is solved using so-called "tops", ie bundles tied on with string over the midpoint of the bow. The shaft and

---

[82]http://int/luk/archer ~1/8t3.htm.
[83]J. Coulston, op.cit., p. 246.
[84]http://www.atarn.org/mongolian/asian_bow_r.htm.
[85]Taybuga, op.cit., pp. 58-63.

the points created something similar to rifling, enabling fast and reliable sighting. The top was immobilized with the chord in the which increased the tension of the cord. It was only necessary to set the location with the top so that the shots hit the target at the desired distance or distances because there could have been a few tops used in battle.

All Scythians carried bows in specially combined quivers containers. In contrast to the Scythian bowcase the Achaemenid one had a pocket-quiver with a flap. Such leather bowcases made it easy to quickly pick and shoot both weapons from a gallop. The Scythian bowcase was also a protected type, although to a lesser extent than the Achaemenid and more sensitive to the weapon getting wet. Moisture protection was very important because the organic adhesives absorbed water quickly, which caused the bow to lose its properties and shape. The tendons would easily soften from the moisture and the bow would lose its tension. The covered bowcase not only protected it against moisture, but also the sensitive feathers of the arrows.

Quivers of this type are shown on the bricks that adorn the walls of Nisa, the first capital of the Parthian Empire, as well as the reserve side of Arsacid coins. The Parthians belonged to the Dahae Confederation and inherited this type of quiver from their Scythian ancestors, and as discussed, they used it for a long time until it was supplanted by the more powerful reflexive bow.[86] This should not preclude the possibility that occasionally both types were used at the same time depending on the needs of exchanging the Scythian type bows for fast firing reflexive bows against mobile, but unarmored enemy, combating armored infantry or cavalry formations at close range. In a similar way, short reflexive bows coexisted with recursive types of weapons during the Islamic period, as described in a treatise by master Taybuga acting as an archery teacher in the fourteenth century A.D. He relates, for example, a corresponding large number of archers with short reflexive bows were able to create an effective "Firewall" even at a distance of approximately 400m.[87]

Recursive Bows. The inability to penetrate the opponent's armor with the firing power of the short Scythian-type bows, and probably their poor accuracy were reasons to develop a weapon that would increase the velocity of arrows while at the same time increasing their size. We don't know when or where these attempts were first started, but the most probable was in the Middle East, when the Iranian army, still using Scythian bows faced armored soldiers from Mesopotamia and inner-Asia. During the great battles of this era Achaemenid troops hadn't adopted tactics of

---

[86]А. М. Хαзαнοв, op.cit., p. 30.
[87]Taybuga, op.cit., p. 29.

skirmish warfare. Their infantry could not retreat before an on-coming opponent while waiting for them to weaken by using light missiles. It was the strength and accuracy of the shot that counted. The Persians, as the Assyrians before them, needed a weapon that could place a salvo on a spot to stop the enemy infantry or cavalry from advancing before it could face their troops. In addition, for cavalry, it was also extremely important to have a short bow that did not touch the flanks of the horse. This factor always remained a barrier in bow size used by cavalry and was eliminated in this very unusual way.

It seems that somewhere in the second half of the VI century BCE (the first examples are shown on reliefs depicting the royal guards from the palace of Darius I in Susa, and the rock based-reliefs of the ruler from Bisoutun), the Persians began to produce long 1.2 – 1.5-meter heavy reflective bows. They probably did not differ in their design from Scythian bows, however, they were able to increase the tension of the pull for firing longer and most importantly a heavier bolt that could threaten infantry wearing laminated or quilted canvas or thick leather armor. This construction was not perfect because the long arms possessed a larger mass which subjected them to increase their inertia and elasticity. As a result, the loss of energy released from the vibrating cord after firing the arrow decreased the missile muzzle velocity. To correct the situation, they used a thicker, less flexible cord, and although losses still remain as in the Welsh "long bow" will be off-set by significantly increased the pull force. To illustrate the relationship between the size of the arrowhead and the thickness of the string, it is worth quoting the following by Taybuga[88] from his treatise:

"It is said that Tahir al Balkhi was relating the following story: 'I heard,' he said, 'about a Persian whom when he shot, no one was able to protect themselves from its penetration. I found him and worked for him for some time, but I dare not ask him questions. In the end, he went hunting one day. Then I sat with his family, so I could speak to his wife. 'There is something that you could do for me that I would be very grateful for.' 'What is it?' she asked. 'Please show me one of your husband's bows,' I said. So, she gave me one of his bows and I pulled it. To my surprise, it was as weak as one of ours. 'Good heavens!' I exclaimed, 'Can your husband pierce armor with such a weak bow?' 'Yes', she replied, 'there are two things that make this possible for him. Look at the bowstring and the arrowhead.' To my surprise, the cord was the thickness of a finger, and the tip was immensely large.' (Taibuga, Sar. Arch. V2).

---
[88] The first Khan of Sibir in the 15th century.

The Armies of Ancient Persia

The effect had to be good enough that the long reflexive bow was the crown of arms of the Achaemenid armored infantry formation for many years – the so-called Immortals and Cardaces. The Persians did not mind that it took longer to make the bow with larger pieces of good quality wood and horn. With the fabulous wealth of the empire they could afford to provide their army with the best quality weapons.

All the negative factors, however, influenced the continuation of work on the "Immortal's" bow, which was probably made by the end of the Achaemenid period. On the ends of the arms, long inserts of hard wood were added which maintained the weight of the arms to increase the velocity of exit speed so that the physical properties of the weapons approached that of recursive bows. A bow of this type is show in the hand of Darius III in the famous "Alexander Mosaic" from the so-called, "House of the Faun" in Pompeii, which is likely an excellent copy of a Hellenistic painting. The image appears to show original military weapons, not the artistic version the artist created in his imagination, which can be seen in a reasonable well-devoted shaped bent arms characteristic of the reflective bows. The arms also represent the excessive bent identical to those known images of the of the arms of a typical Scythian weapons of this type. Although most scholars agree with the theory that the mosaic from Pompeii was a copy of one that was lost, and probably the most famous Hellenistic images, there is not full agreement, however, on whether the painting the "Alexander Mosaic" was modeled on came from the beginning or the end of the Hellenistic period, though the dating of the invention of the recursive bow from the end of the period is also not certain. On closer analysis the weapon seems to have a lot of the features of the Achaemenid long bow. But it also has features like the Persian infantry bows of the Parthian period, outfitted with bone end pieces, which was based on an early version. There is much to say for the claim that it was an invention of the steppe people of Central Asia or even the Far East. If not for the "Scythian" shape of the bows from the "Alexander Mosaic", it could be considered a Yrzi-type bow known from the reign of Arsacid which merged with the traditions of the Iranian steppes.[89]

We do not know examples of bone or horn reinforced corners (siyat) on bows from the areas of Iran and Central Asia older than the second century BCE, either from archeological finds and pictorial representations. The earliest monument on which the reflexive bows are shown in a clear manner depicting bone facings are from a burial in barrow no. II at the cemetery in Orlat near Samarkand. From the barrow no. II, there is also bone lining, probably siyat along th upper part of the bow and two stiffening plates made of bone at the maidan. The shape and dimensions

---
[89] А. М. Хазанов, op.cit., p. 34.

of all the parts correspond to the weapons shown in battle and hunting scenes on the already mentioned plaques. Images of similar bows in the hands of archers are also visible on the reverse side of Sogdian coins.[90] First, however, the bone pieces and residual parts of the bow arms from Orlat can be dated stylistically, in conjunction with the place it was discovered from the period just before the Kushan invasion[91] on the basis of damaged layers in the city of Ai-Khanoum located around 145 BCE, which is only in the middle of the second century BCE, or the period immediately afterward (until about the first half of the first century BCE).[92] Secondly, the bow representations are very accurately portrayed, belong to an advanced asymmetrical type of weapon. There is no evidence that the first reflexive bows, the earliest symmetrical variety reached the Sakae and Dahae tribes earlier, or about the second half of the second century BCE. By the first century BCE, they were already standard Arsacid cavalry bow equipment as evidenced by, for example, the hunting representation of That-e-Sangin.

Although the emergence of fully-formed reflexive bows is dated late, the origins of these of these bows probably came from much older times, in the steppes of central Asia, gradually promoting the use of light armor, especially leather and bone, among the first line of warriors in the Scythian wedge formations, as well as perhaps the archers in the rear ranks, giving impetus to its creation. Two pairs of bone overlays on the ends of the bow arms dating from the fourth century BC were found Eastern Siberia, but they were still short and bent.[93]

A very interesting discovery was made from a layer dated between the third to first century BCE, from the Parthian period in Yrzi on the Euphrates near Baghouz. One arm was preserved perfectly, the mantle and two sets of cladding allowed for the reconstruction of the weapons.[94] If it is correct, apart from the dating, which is very general, we

---

[90] К. Абдульаев, *Armour of ancient Baktria,* A. Invernizzi (ed.) In the land of the Gryphons- Papers on Central Asian archeology in antiquity, a.l.a, p. 169.

[91] К. Абдульаев, op.cit., p. 172.

[92] In addition to the above facts dating can also be indicated by the unusual stylistic similarities in depicting a stylized "Roman" on the "Hunter" plate from Orlat and the plate from That-e Sangin dating back to the first century BCE. There is also a jade sword from burial no. II which shows similarities to Han Chinese swords, and dated to the middle of the first century AD – the jade sword originating in finds from inner Mongolia. Not withstanding this, it is important that the armor of the warriors shown on the Orlat plaque in battle are evidently a more primitive version of the armor known from seals Jaszczynski dated the turn of the first and second century AD and armor from Indonesia in the I-II century AD.

[93] А. М. Хазанов, op.cit., p. 31.

[94] F. Brown, *A Recently Discovered Compound Bow Seminarium Kondakovianum* 9, 1937, 1-10 i J.Coulston, op.cit., p. 300.

are dealing with the most primitive construction in the area of reflexive bows, referring to the description of one of the previously described Achaemenid "Immortal" bows.

The core of these bows was made up of several pieces of various types of wood. The two long arms touch the center of the maidan by diagonal cuts, made from an unidentified type of wood. The maidan itself was derived from the characteristic Scythian bows formed from two long rigid parts (elm and oak), which were strengthened where the arms joined. Its design and shape allowed you to hold your bow prepared to shoot. The ends of the arms were tipped with bone coverings that stiffened the bow corners which in the later Arab nomenclature were known as "siyah". Two pairs of claddings have survived, both of them slightly damaged by the so-called "loop" which is the transitional place of the siyah, for the working part of the arm, called the "duštar in Arabic. The length of the best-preserved pair is 22.5 cm, though it was probably about 25 cm, which agrees with the length of the bow lining of the reflexive bow discovered in the Roman complex at Belmes in Egypt,[95] the horn weapons at Belmes, however, was simple and acutely bent at the base of the duštar. It should, therefore, be included as another more technically advanced bow. In addition to the siyah linings, the Yrzi bow does not have any additional bone reinforcements – even the maidan.

On the arm, next to the grip small bits of the stratum corneum remained, and the slightly larger portion of the tendon layer in the middle of the arm. All the remains indicate that the construction of the arms did not really differ from the construction of the Scythian bows, as well as those used today by steppe nomads (i.e. Mongolians). The difference compared to the Scythian weapons lies, therefore in the length of the form of 148 cm, lacking a maidan and the use of bone cladding on the ends of the arms. Because of their presence, the Yrzi bow can be classified as reflexive.

The use of lining significantly improves the combat properties of bows. With stiff siyah everything is at the same speed as the arm with the trailer lining, that is, although the arm with the horn is long, and has associated advantages, when the cord is loosened, it actually works at a short speed which increases the speed of the shot. The horn also acts as a lever allowing you to tighten the stronger, harder arm of the bow with less force and thus lowering the tension, so the cord is not stretched.[96] This mechanism resembles the currently system that creates the tension for hunting bows, and requires only 2/3 of the strength to pull the bowstring to its best force, tightening it further, with only a only a small

---
[95] J.Coulston, op.cit., p. 233.
[96] http://atarn.org/mongolian/asian_bow_r.htm.

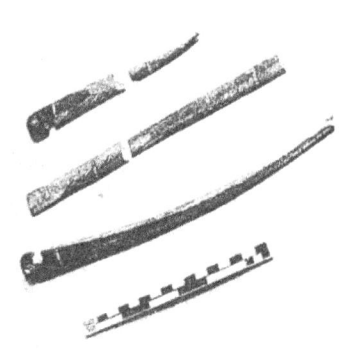

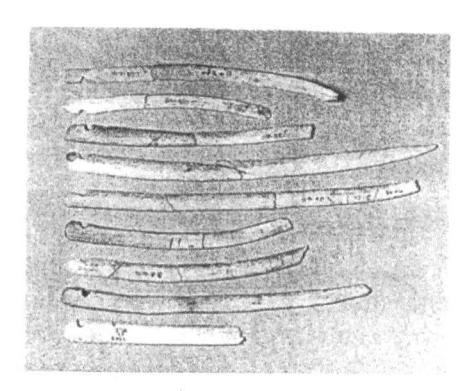

Examples of bone cladding for the ends of the arms of Roman auxilliary archer bows. (according to J. Coulston, Roman Archer Equipment, *fig. 9, 10,11,12)*

Bone reinforcements of the Roman arches of auxilliary archers. (according to J. Coulston, *Roman Archery Equipment*, fig. 13.14)

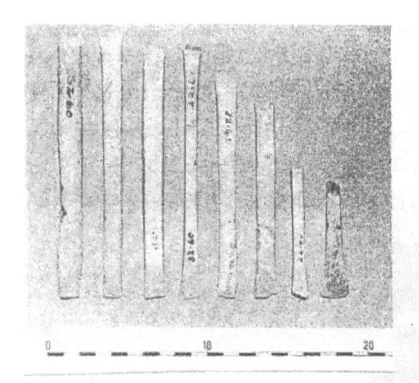

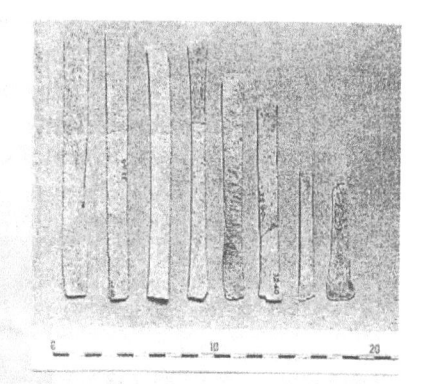

increase in the resistance so that the arms end in a similar position to reflexive bows.[97] Today, however, such support is implemented by using blocks and pulleys placed at the end of the arms. This reduces the strong vibration with the bowstring when the arrow leaves and the arms return to the ready position, as the arms are of the same length and strength as those without horn – so the efficiency of such weapons is greater. Once the bowstring is released the energy of the shot is transmitted in a more even manner.[98] All these factors positively affect the initial speed, and the energy, and thus the penetration of shots. Bone lining also displaced other material, especially wood and horn, which is the inside part of the overlay, as almost a non-working core.

 J. Coulston says that a terracotta tile from the Staatliche Museum in Berlin shows a mounted archer with his Yrzi bow pulled.[99] A simple maidan with the same length arms seems to confirm this thesis. The ends of the bow are shown at angles with respect to the arms, unlike the reconstruction presented by J. Coulston. Although due to the destruction of some critical parts of the siyah, there can be some doubt, as it can be seen on parts of the relief on Trajan's Column, where the bows used by the Syrian archers serving in the Roman auxilia, can be considered appropriate. This fact is also confirmed by numerous linings found very similar to the Yrzi type in many positions from all over the Roman Empire relating to the garrison of sagitari troops.[100]

 As one can see from Parthian iconography Yrzi bows were not the typical weapon of Arsacid archers. They seem to have used a design that was a bit more advanced based on steppe origin. This is precisely the weapon used by a warrior on the terracotta tiles from Berlin, as well as a bone plaque from e-Sangin date back to the first century BCE. The characteristic feature of this weapon is the setting of the angle of the arm. This small innovation is in effect a double-reflexive bow. On iconographic representations it can clearly be seen that when pulling the Parthian or Belmes style bows the arms are not titled back, but also curled up, and the corners bending back in the so-called "knees" take an almost horizontal position. This effect works best, although in a slightly exaggerated way, as it is shown on the silver Sassanid "plates". The king's bow is shown strained so much that the siyah became extended like a duštar. Similarly, the drawn bow is also shown on some graffiti from Dura-Europos, e.g. from building "A" or from the temple of Artemis Azanathkona.[101]

---

[97] Taybuga, op.cit., pp. 28-29.
[98] http://atarn.org/mongolian/asian_bow_r.htm.
[99] J. Coulston, op.cit., p. 240.
[100] J. Coulston, op.cit., pp. 224-233.
[101] B. Goldman, "Pictorial graffiti of Dura-Europos" in: *Parthica, Incontri di culture nel*

The Armies of Ancient Persia

In addition, the middle part of the arms received the biggest stress occurs at this moment along the "knees" and the ends of the horns. They were secured with a special thong, made of glued tendons place just above the hook. This reinforced band is visible on the well-preserved corner from Belmes dated in the first century, AD. It consisted of a wooden core that was probably in the Yrzi bow, the arm core extended to the wooden cap and covered with two bone linings in lengths of 25 cm each, touching each other without wood covering the hooks, and included an edge extending in a direction of the core on the top side. The thing has larger corners than the copy discovered in Yrzi.

After loosening the taunt chord, the arms folded back up quickly to position and he siyat can be said to add to the speed that they return to the previous angle between the them and the arms. This results in significant increase in projectile velocity of heavy shot, and hence increased the strength of the projectile penetration, on which the general design was set.

Although the Parthians used the symmetrical reflexive bows with great success, it first appeared among the steppe people in modified form around the first century BCE. Adapting to the needs of the mounted archer had to happen without losing the strength for the combat weapons, which was achieved as a result of some complicated changes in the external construction of the outer structure. First, the lower frame has been shortened along with the siyah. It seems, however, that not all asymmetrical bows were made using this technology, because of its convenience in using in the saddle. A slight increase of counterbalance in the upper arm equalizes the difference in the length, caused by the length of the riser and the sighting of the arrow along the top edge, not the middle of the bow.

Bows from Orlat or later from Niya or Qum-Darya were very visibly asymmetrical, and a significant difference in the length of the arms sometimes even making it necessary to make changes in the size of each of them and therefore the angle of them in siyat. One of the basic conditions for an accurate bow was the same movement speed for the two ends. If one of the arms is clearly shorter and the tension strength is maintained the internal structure and "faster" counter-bending is maintained. While it moves slower upon release and the upper arm is longer, the resulting pull is faster on the lower part of the chord, "breaking" the holders arrows placed in the slot, that is in effect, "beating" the projectiles, and creating dangerous vibrations which further reduces the accuracy of the weapon.

---

mondo antico, Pisa, Roma 1999, p. 35.

The way to eliminate this defect, it turns out was to release the shorter lower arm by the reduction of the counter-cavity, and lowering the force accumulated in its potential energy. Shortening the arm was carried out for the most part by shortening the length of the siyah, not the flexible part of the (duštar) which could significantly reduce the need to reduce the counter-bending force, that would contribute to the loss of the strength in the string tension. It should be remembered that the speed of the siyah equaling the speed the duštar is created from the speed of the whole arm measured from the hooks of the bowstring. Additionally, when the operation is reversed on the siyah on the upper arm, it is possible to minimize, but not exclude the need to counter-bend to achieve greater asymmetric shape, which was advantageous when using the bow from the horse and maintaining the total length of the bow to allow for long distance shots with greater strength. This is the way, for example Hunnic bows are constructed.[102]

The best know examples are two copies attributed to the Huns, or rather their Eastern predecessors. One comes from Niya in the Taklamakan desert,[103] and is dated very broadly between the first and fourth century AD, while the second is from a mass grave in Qum-Darya, near the Chinese border. They will both be described later. On medallions from Orlat we have, however, bows with very large disparity of the arm angles visible in the difference in sizes of the bend with the bow string and almost the length of the siyah. Making bows of this design indicates the start of trials for effective asymmetrical arms. Today, the difference between the arms and their counterbalanced lengths can be observed on an extreme level of asymmetrical in the Japanese Yumi bow which is used in traditional Japanese archery.[104]

From this you can complete the description of the construction and functionality of the Parthian period bows. The types presented here were probably the equipment of mounted archers in the Arsacid army. If the Parthians themselves did not use them, they were used by the enlisted troops of the Sūren clan, or mercenary, Saka contingents accepted into the Parthian service. All theoretical calculations indicate that it was a weapon of extraordinary effectiveness. Tests have confirmed this supposition. On describing the battle of Carrhae, Plutarch writes about the effects of its use:

> *"(...) they gave rise to confusion and fear. When they saw the power of the arrows and bowstrings, piercing armor, passing through both*

---
[102]J.Coulston, op.cit., p. 242.
[103]Northwest China
[104]J.Coulston, op.cit., p. 242

hard and soft cover. The Parthians, stretching the bow to the max, began firing at once from every side. This was effective shooting, because the compact and density of the Romans allowed even a sick man to hit a warrior, but powerful shot inflicted severe and critical hits from big and powerful bows that were launched from deeply bent bows with strong force. At this point the Romans stopped thinking that if the enemy were not strong, they cold close in on them in hand-to-hand combat. But the armored cavalry was opposite them and the remaining cavalry galloped around them, disappearing into the depths of the sand dunes spreading dust clouds that began to surround them so that they could neither see each other or hear their own voices. Soon, the legionnaires bumped into each other, hit by arrows and dying not an easy or quick death, but among the convulsions and torments furiously rolled and fell among their comrades of wounds from shots, trying to force them to cross blades, shot in the veins and muscles, breaking them up as they hurt themselves." (Plutarch, Crass. 25)

The Romans lost 20,000 soldiers at Carrhae, and 10,000 were taken prisoner. Among the dead were those murdered when negotiating surrender of the expedition including the expedition commander Marcus Licinius Crassus and his son Publius. (Plutarch, *Crass.* 26) Nearly all of the dead fell from the shot. The Romans, however, learned quickly. In the second century AD, and perhaps as early as the end of the first century AD reflexive type bows were prevalent not only in Syria, but even in the remote regions of the Roman Empire, where they recruited contingents of middle eastern archers. Although in other areas of the Roman Empire, climatic condition did not allow the preservation of archeological material, the bows are known to have large quantities of bone corner linings. Their characteristic shape, considerable length and their appearance in pairs – of the same length, have been found at Carleon in Wales, Bar Hill on Hadrian's Wall and many others, where we seem to have bows of the eastern Yrzi type. From known Roman locations we find bony, straight plates stiffening the central position, which indicates there were still bows with a simple grip.

SHOT. The most important part of the arche'rs equipment was the ammunition, i.e. the shot. The archaeological material commonly found in caves were well preserved examples, but we do not have the opportunity to examine the remains of rays or feather. The most common examples come from the excavations in Dura-Europos, giving us an idea about the appearance of typical arrows of the Parthian period.

According to reports by M. Rostovceva,[105] three fragments of the flights were found in Dura including a shot with two feathers and traces of painting preserved on two of them and two wooden inserts to strengthen the front part of the arrow and allowed the use of arrowheads with a sleeve.

The length of the best-preserved fragment is 27.5 cm long. It is the back end of the arrow made of hard cane with a diameter equal to 1 cm. On one end, the so-called elbow was made by filing and rounding the edges, while cutting a notch to a depth of 0.5 cm as a holder. To strengthening 2.5 cm long, the area has been soaked in glue. Near the holder, three feathers 15.5 cm long and 1.1 cm wide each were stuck. The Saracens thought that narrow and long feathers were faster than the wide ones and were therefore better combat and hunting arrows for use on short distances. The feathers were fixed to the radius with glue every 120°. Because the ailerons (the feathers) reach up to the notch, M. Rostovcev believes that the arrow was fired with the thumb or the aid of a ring overlay.[106] Practice however, indicates the opposite. Mongolian arrows, for example, have very long and protective holders that were quilted before the crease with the fingers where the notch rests with the cord deep in the "hole" between the thumb and the forefinger, which is a characteristic feature for shooting with archery rings. The radius below the feathers, toward the tip, was painted in the middle, between the feathers with a wide red ring.

The second arrow fragment is very similar to the construction described above. Its length is 21.5 cm, the diameter of the cane is 1 cm. The body is also made of cane stalks, and its notch has a depth of 8 mm. The feathers have a length of 14.3 cm but is unfortunately badly preserved. The sides of the body are painted with red circles. At the bottom of the shaft, the front is covered with painted feathers, there is a narrow black ring above the notch, between the feathers were red dots, below which were black and red rings. The third fragment of the arrow is the least preserved. It is 21 cm long with a diameter of 9.5 mm. The notch, as in the two cases above, but has a slightly deeper notch, 1.1 cm in depth. There are no feathers, but the spot to attach the feathers indicated the length of 15 cm. The sides of the notch are painted with a black and red ring on the radius with white edges. There were red dots between the feathers at their bottom.

The predominance of arrowheads with tangs for fixing the head on the shaft at Dura-Europos indicates most arrowheads were not pinned in place but driven into the reed and secured with braiding. This type

---
[105] М. И. Ростовцев, op.cit., pp. 455-456.
[106] loc. cit.,

of attachment was not the only one however. Arrowheads with sockets were also discovered. They also found two wooden shafts made of tamarisk, which strengthened the front part of the arrow, including one completely preserved. [107] It's length is 17.5 cm, the diameter at the widest point (11.8 cm from the back end) is 1.1 cm. Above is the arrowhead is driven into the reed (5.5 cm long) which tapers down to 2mm thick. Below this point it increases up to 6mm in diameter. About 2.5 cm from the back end there are visible traces of glue sticking into the tang of the arrowhead which was similar to the large triangular ones, about 4-5.5 cm long iron and bronze arrowheads from Old Nisa displayed in a museum in Ashgabat. The other one, though identical has part of the tang broken off. Such inserts not only strengthened the structure of the projectile but moved its center of gravity slightly forward to accelerate the speed of flight.

According to Rostovcev, the closest analogy to this type of arrow can be found in sites in Iran and Central Asia, arrows also show similarity from the Chinese outposts in Turkestan – the same reed shafts, with holders cut into the radius of the reed, identical to the short wooden inserts and black and red stripes.[108] Artifacts also give a good example of arrows from Roman positions and battlefields of the period, i.e. Masada, where heavy triangular heads with triangular cross-section for the shafts were discovered there.

While the pictorial representations of arrows do not leave us most information it might be possible to calculate the length of the shaft from the points to which the string was drawn. Parthian horse archers of the period usually pulled the string the length of the arm which allowed for the maximum use of the weapon's capabilities. The arrows used by them, therefore were approximately one-meter length like those currently used by the Japanses Kyudo[109] which assumes to be used similar to the Parthian draw length and techniques of archery (examples of which can be seen in some graffiti in Dura-Europas). This may prove a common root for the steppes of these techniques. The one-meter length shot also makes it possible to calculate the tension in the length of the draw. With a length of 1.5 meter the shaft is 90-95 cm, adding to the radius on the spindle and the arrowhead protruding when the cord is strung at full tension in front of the majdan, the length of the shot should also be estimated at approximately one meter.

During the Parthian period several different types of arrowheads were in use. The overwhelming technique for affixing them it seems, was

---
[107] loc. cit.
[108] М. И. Ростовцев, op.cit., pp. 455 – 456.
[109] H. Onuma, D.i J. De Prospero, op.cit., ss. 52-55.

The Armies of Ancient Persia

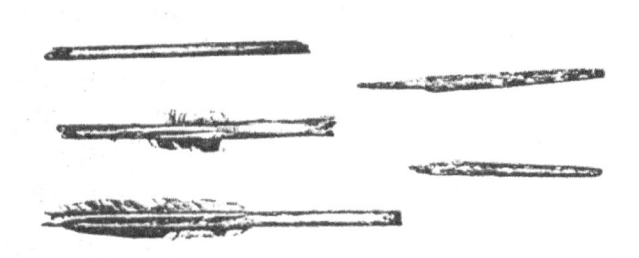

Remains of feathers and wooden inserts of arrows from Dura-Europos (according to J. Coulston, Roman Archery Equipment, *fig.45)*

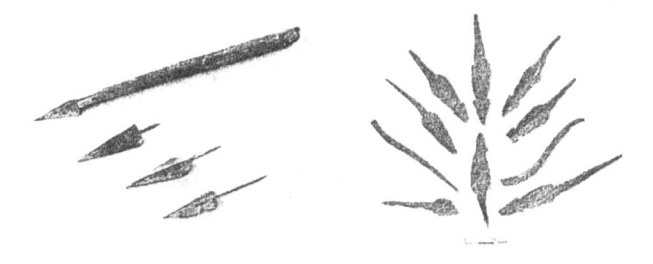

Heavy, triangular arrowheads from Masada (according to J. Coulston, Roman Archery Equipment, *fig. 46.47)*

A long stretch used by a Parthian armored archer - graffiti from Dura Europos. (according to B. Goldman, Pictorial graffiti of Dura-Europos, *Figure 13A, B)*

driving the pins into the shaft. This was the most popular because it was easy to forge. But, arrowheads with sleeves were still used. Triangular points show separate leaves, but there are also those of triangular and quadrangular shape which seem to be an anti-armor version (such points were intended to pierce all type of armor as described in the works of Taybuga). These should not be too sharp, because they risk breaking off the tip. The Saracens intentionally allowed the tip to break off, producing them very hard.[110] Large, spiked points of various types made of bone were used in central Asia and the steppe. This was most connected to the fact that metal was much rarer on the eastern, than on the western steppe as metal armor was replaced by bone or leather. The arrow points used by the Parthians, with three separate points are common for the military of Iranian-speaking people and whatever common manufacturing trends of this type of weaponry can tell us, it can only be done by examining a larger sampling. An opportunity for such research came after the excavation at Tangt-e Sangin of six-hundred sixty-six iron arrowheads by a discovery team. They all belong to the three-cornered variety and were provided with a pin to fix it to the shaft. The team dated them from the I or beginning of the II century AD, during the reign of Kushan Dynasty, roughly the second half of the Parthian period in Iran. This material was tested, with the dimensions statistically cataloged. The results are as follows:

H1- total length of the tip with the stem
H2- length of the tip of the tip (without the stem).
H3- the length of the burr.
H4 - stem length.
α - angle between the ridge of the leaf and the horizontal plane
β - the width of the tip at the widest point
Sizes: length is given in millimeters, degrees angles ..
H1 - 35 to 65 (most 45 to 60)
H2 - 25 to 57 (variation from 25 to 27-9 pieces, from 28 to 42-87 items, from 43 to 57- 20 items
H3 - 1 to 5 (most 2 to 5)
H4 - 9 to 29 (most of 15 to 23)
α - 78 to 88 (most of 85 to 87)
β - 11 to 29 (most of 14 to 19)[111]

Taking into account the possibility of errors due to the material damage, the data allows us to conclude that the large heads were proba-

---

[110] Taybuga, op.cit, p. 26
[111] М. А Итина, J. А. Рапапорт (ed.) *Культура и исскуство древнего Хорезма*, Москва 1981, p. 208.

bly used for long-distance firing. It also happens that a small sample were probably light missiles and short distance arrows. The lack of sockets on the arrowheads is worth noting.

All the points examined belong to the triangular shape with individual leaves. They all have spikes. The tip of this type is significantly more dangerous to be hit with than the spiked point, because it results in cutting a wound channel in three places, and thus causes a much greater flow of blood. By using this this type of shaft is difficult to remove, because the reed breaks off easily when you try to remove it from the wound area. Points of this type might be better suited for the injury of an unarmored or lightly armored opponent. No points examined by the team had a large barb design which were interpreted as anti-armor and is probably the result of the type of armor worn by the Kushite army. Protected by heavy armor, first line warriors could only attack at short distance, and were the object of attack by other heavy units using spears and swords.[112] The target of archers were usually unarmored, as we know from the Judean depiction,[113] or only protected in light, leather, bone or horn armor like the Sarmatians [114] which opponent archers attacks were more effectively using arrowheads with broad heads.

With the Parthians, especially in the western areas of the empire, the case was a bit different. Their enemies used mass infantry in armor forming the basis for the Seleucid or Roman armies, especially at the beginning of the of military operations of these countries against the Arsacid Monarchy. The Parthian archers were perfectly suited to fire against them up close depending on the use of flesh arrowheads also used by the Sassanids as we know from representations on their silver plates or plaques. Although the Parthian cavalry archer's equipment and tactics were not created to combat this type of enemy, they had to adapt their traditional solutions to the destruction of new types of targets. The result of this are shown in the works of Plutarch concerning the difference in the military results against the steppe people (Saki and Kushan) which was focused primarily on the old-style cavalry combat. Against these units the soldiers the Arsacids fought using traditional Scythian methods. In Summary: The typical Iranian arrow of the Parthian period was probably made of cane – glazed and painted, approximately one-meter long, and approximately 15cm oval with a cut at the end (Saki arrows had a notch on the back edge cut out) approximately 1 cm wide which were attached three set every 120° around the radius, and the notch soaked in glue, cut into the reed end. These were triangular shaped made with a

---

[112] Г. А. Пугаченкова, *Скульптура Халчаяна*, Мосcква 1971. p. 71.
[113] loc. cit..
[114] А. М. Хαзанов, op.cit., p. 58.

mandrel or brush separated by ridges or triangular sections. The radius of the shaft was reinforced with braid. Sometimes small grooves were cut in the arrows along the shaft. Arrows were distinguished by their owners with black and red rings. Hunting arrows make sense for using color coding, but it probably didn't differ much for military ones. Both types of feathers touch the notch, which would indicate traditional Iranian archery techniques.

Additional Equipment. Although the bow constituted the basic weapon of a mounted archer, it was also the most valuable piece of equipment, but it was not the only weapon for this type troop. Short swords or daggers were also commonly used. Graphic representations include examples of swords in special sheaths sewn on the gorytos style bow case, usually hung vertically, on the right side of the rider's belt, sometimes on the rear edge by the saddle. This way of wearing a sword by a mounted archer is shown in a terracotta plate in the collection of the British Museum. The same representation shows reflexive bow visible in the gorytos case, while the foot soldier has a longer reflexive bow.

The swords used by mounted archers were short for use by the rider, not exceeding 50-60 cm, or the length of the typical Scythian acinaces. The weight of the double-edged blade was compensated by a large, spherical shaped pommel. Weapons of this type were usually not given a large guard. Because on the specific fighting tactics of Parthian cavalry archer units, one can conclude that this was a typical secondary-type weapon used in regular fights in the follow-up fight. In instances where fighting was within the western borders of the Parthian Empire, these weapons were only used against similar type units after having run out of shot, when charged by a sudden attack or when withdrawal was no longer possible. Thus, the main tactics of the Arsacidian horse-archers consisted of mass firing and urgently avoiding any direct confrontation with extended melee action. In the event of clashes with the steppe people they used the old combat system which provided a general shelling of the enemy, then resulted in the use of daggers, which became extremely dangerous resulting in killing more warriors than unarmored light troops from the heavy swords of armored riders.

One of the bits of graffiti discovered at Dura-Europos, shows Arsacid horse archers beginning to wear armor in the II century AD. Although the illustration does not allow us to determine the exact type (it must be, for example, fluid in movement, which would exclude thick chain mail), with a great deal of probability we can date this from the beginning of the Sassanian period, who supported the attacks of the clibanarii with archery. This was imported into the Iranian military from the influence of the central Asian people. The Kushan, for example, only developed this in the III century AD, after the fall of the Arsacid Empire.

The strength of the Persian horse archers centered their ability to lay down a heavy carpet of fire. Maintaining this intensity required each warrior to be equipped with an adequate supply of shot and an efficient system of resupply with camels carrying extra arrows. This is reason the quiver was one of the most important pieces of equipment for the light-armed riders. It's shape, size and way it was worn changed depending on the period and area it was used. The oldest type known to the Iranian speaking peoples was the so-called gorytos pattern, which has already been described many times in this work. It was usually suspended at the waist, so it was easy to reach shots quickly. With the small length of the projectiles, they could be pulled out quickly and efficiently in one fluid movement to the bowstring. For this reason, the shape and placement of the quiver increased the maximum rate of fire, keeping going until they ran out of arrows. When these tactics were used in mixed order formations, shooting was carried out at the maximum distance, until they ran out of arrows or clashed where they fought with melee weapons. Sometimes after a short fight, one of the parties withdrew covering the enemy with arrows. This maneuver could be repeated many times. This manner of fighting was characteristic of the Scythian tribes and gorytos had been used on the vast terrain of the steppes for many centuries. They are well represented, for example, among the short bows found at Parthian Nisa dating back to the end of the II century BCE. The introduction of reflective bows, and thus longer arrows, influenced the need to modernize the quivers. Using arrows of up to a meter in length made gorytos an obstacle to rapid fire.

One battle scene is represented on a base relief from Orlat dated around the II to I century BCE clearing showing a quiver that constitutes the further development from the traditional form of the gorytos adapted for the dimensions of the reflexive bow and the arrows they used. It has two or three long circular chambers for various types of missiles including at least one with a closed decorative triangular flap with a plume over a narrow tube, which there are few cases of a better presentation showing the cord hooked in the back of the reflexive bow. It is placed so that the upper, longer arm protrudes, and the lower arm bent with the short corner with the maidan hidden by the cover. Quivers of identical shape were used for the entire Parthian period in Iran. An example of this is the extended armored "quasi-gorytos" shown in the rock relief at Tang-e Sarvak dating from the beginning of the III century AD. At the same time, however, there is an example, probably from the above described type of quiver, a long body devoid of a flap. They were mainly used by horse-archer hunters, from hunting graffiti made on the walls of the Temple of Artemis at Dura-Europos. They were worn in a similar manner to the quivers with flaps, i.e. at the waist, at the right side shown in graffiti from the "corner house" and this seems much more widespread than those at the rear edge of the saddle i.e. on the horse of the armored archer shown on graffiti from the "Christian Building" near tower 17. While the first type of quiver described were often so long that the arrows are not visible from the outside, while in the case of the second type are shallower copies that show the longer arrows. This type of quiver shows the assumed impact of the spread of the new type of reflexive bow with great counter-force, but with the bow cord removed so it cold be stored and transported, making it impossible to use wearing the elongated gorytos. A special one was used for this purpose with a crescent flap. This sort of bow, called "Sasanid" , is visible, for example, in the hand of Mithras hunting, shown in the magnificent wall mural in Dura-Europos dated to the end of the II century, BCE.[115] It is because of the functional connection of this new type of weapon, the simple tube survived without major structural changed until the late Sassanid period.

To continue to use heavy bows with massed archery for long periods of time, it was necessary, even when using advanced Parthian archery tactics, to secure the tension pad of the bowstring with the fingers. This was done with the help of metal caps or more than likely leather overlays resemble those currently used by sport archers. They protect the internal surface of the fingers and the pads by special cords and belts. The overlays were made of organic material, leaving no archeological evidence, hence we do not know their shape. The small differences in different techniques are shown in pictorial representations for example, Parthian archery techniques at Shami, as well as Sasanid techniques. They assume protective caps used by both monarchies did not differ much.

The old technique of using the index finger to pull the cord, from the middle, except that the Parthian used reflexive bows, in addition to other steppe peoples, i.e. Sakae and Sarmatians, which are confirmed by clay sculptures from Halycha and Indo-European Kushans.

The overall look of the cavalry archer would be as follows:
Most wore colorfully embroidered long-sleeved caftans. They reached a little higher than mid-thigh. They were not fastened but held in place by a decorative belt. The most characteristic part of the Arsacid's light cavalry dress were the pants. They consisted of two types of pants; ordinary Scythian, made of woolen fabric – more durable for the abrasion on the back and sides of the horse's hide which were colored narrow trousers and stretched on it was a thin bulk canvas, or

---
[115] М. И. Ростовцев, *Dura-Europos and its Art*, Oxford 1938, p. 97.

silk trouser legs fastened to the waist at the back and sloping forward in scenic folds. They were best shown on a bronze statue in Shami, depicting a standing Parthian prince.

Each rider wore long knee-length boots, made of soft leather to protect the lower part of the leg. We know from pictorial representations that the boots were often hidden under the trousers, so their task was to keep the shoes on their feet. It is possible that not everyone wore fancy trousers but the archers that did dress in this fashion and whose images appear in art belonging to the higher social classes. A well-preserved, tall rider's boot from the Parthian period was found in a salt mine in the province of Zanjan in Iran. It belonged to a man killed by a collapsed ceiling, preserved by salt, surviving in perfect condition. It was made of soft brown leather, reaching up to the knee without any shoelaces or bindings. At the time of its discovery there was stiff the stump of a leg broken off at the knee.[116]

Some cavalrymen, especially during the reign of the first Arsacids wore pointed leather or felt hats tied at the forehead, also known from Scythian relics from the Black Sea, or the Bisaun Relief. Such a hat, later called a "Bashlyk" by the Turks, was used by many people of the steppes, appears on the head of a sleeping Parthian archer in the terracotta plaque in the collection of the British Museum, and on the coins minted by the rulers of the Arsacid dynasty (up to Mithridates I). These hats were not the only headgear used by the Parthian horse archers. A rider whose image adorns the already described terracotta tile from the Staatliche Museum wears a headscarf tied around his neck with a large bow. He has a similar headscarf to a Parthian "Rulers" shown in a carved stone bust. In both, it is clear that this is not the same hairstyle described by Plutarch, also known from the statue of a standing prince at Shami or the rock relief at Tang-e Sarvak because the scarf covers all the hair without leaving them wrapped around the bottom with large bands.

Neither the Parthian, Sakae or Kushan horse archers had stirrups at this time. Up to the clashes with the Romans they probably used a Scythian type saddle somewhat like those discovered at the famous Caspian necropolis. They were made of soft materials, mainly leather, without n exoskeleton, which was produced later by Huns, Turks and Mongols out of wood. The best image of the utility saddle of the Iranian-speaking steppe people comes from the famous Parthian carpet. It shows a rider on a horse in front of a figure on a throne, holding a strangley stylized plant. An unknown artist accurately portrayed the horse's equipment, and more importantly, the image of the saddle he is sitting in. As best we

---

[116]B. Weintraub, "Violent Death in a Salt Mine", *National Geographic* vol. 2 nr.4 (7) April 2000, p. 5.

A Parthian archer equipped with two bows and a short sword carried in a pocket on the quiver - terracotta tile- British Museum (according to P. Wilcox, A. Mcbride, Rome's enemies 3, Parthians and Sassanid Persians, *fig. 18)*

can tell he is sitting on three pillows stuffed with felt, dry grass or other similar material arranged such that the rider's crotch from the withers of the horse which would be very painful to hit while riding, and in the absence of stirrups, to form a seat liner and a wedge between the back and the hips. The front cushion was so high that it covered all of the belly of the man sitting in the saddle, which makes it perfectly visible on the described image. The other two are harder to see. This type of saddle "held" the rider's body well enough and gave support as well as the "horned" ones provided by Roman saddles.

As a result of wars with their western neighbors or military contact with the mostly Alan tribes of Sarmatian nomads, the Arsacid cavalry began to use the heavier probably just Gallic or saddles of Sarmatian origin described from the characteristic shape with four holder legs called "horned saddles". They were built from wooden forms, to which were fastened the saddle straps on the animal's back – the girth, dock, etc; padded with felt, and covered with leather. The outer surfaces of the corners were reinforced to strengthen and add durability of specially molded bronze fitting or just leather.[117] The saddles provided equally good grip for the bodies like today's saddles with stirrups. They also removed the necessity of holding onto the back of the horse by embracing its sides with the legs, stiffened the seat however, which hampered the management of the mount. It's a big negative when it comes to archery in which the tactical assumption was speed and maneuverability of using these "Horned" saddles by the armored as well as the light cavalry, as confirmed by an example of a plaque from the Staatliche Museum.

Archery Techniques. In the Middle East and Iran before the appearance of the Huns at the end of the third and beginning of the fourth century AD there were several known and practiced techniques for drawing the bow, used simultaneously, depending on the tradition and preferences of a given nation. Of the two most popular and widespread of them the first, and oldest, because it was still used in ancient times before the rise of the Achaemenid Empire by the Assyrian soldiers is based on that which the archer does not pull the string with his fingers, but with the feather clip. This part of the arrow had a special flattening with a notch that caught the tension of the bow. Many eastern people, perhaps due to the small diameter of the radius in relations to the thickness of the string used a type of clamp.[118] The grip was held on the side of the index finger and the inside finger surface of the thumb. A finger ring, heart ring and middle ring to pull the cord allowed the archer to apply greater pull the bow. Never

---

[117] M. Junkelman, *Die Reiter Roms*, t. III, Mainz am Rhein 1991. pp. 34-88.
[118] Taybuga, op.cit., p. 26

the less, this grip seems uncertain and not very suitable for application using a bow with tension exceeding 30-35 kg. This archery technique is perfectly shown on the relief of the so-called "great lion hunt" led by King Ašurbanipal. The Assyrian artist provided an excellent shape of the weapon, arrows and especially the tailfeathers and the tip as well as the look and feel of the archer's equipment. Extremely interesting is, for example, the guard protecting the forearm of the ruler.

Based on pictorial remains, it is known that the Iranian people used a completely different grip. It has been determined that somewhere during the reign of the first Persian dynasty (Achaemenid) the new grip gradually displaced the older and less perfect draw. In this new system, the cord is stretched using a two-fingers and a ring or three fingers, whereby they hooked the tips and the whole hand is set vertically. This technique had been practiced by the Scythians and Achaemenid soldiers and quickly spread throughout the middle east. From Phoenicia, for example, they used two golden "thimbles" on the index and ring figure dating back from the V century BCE, forming two small holes reinforced around the edges forming a kind of archery gloves. It protected the finger ends that pull the cords.[119] Perhaps because of the Scythians, this technique had also spread to ancient Greece as well as much of Europe where it survived until the Middle Ages. They were used by the Parthians to pull their reflexive bows, and in Central Asia, the Sakae and the Kushan. On the Scythian steppes and in the Middle East, using this technique, the arrow was laid on the right side of the grip, and it was held on the outer surface of the thumb of the left hand.

The "Iranian" archery technique probably owned its popularity to the fact that it worked best when using bows angled high to launch a long shot. It is true that you can assume that due to the effect of "bouncing" to the left, risking the cord to slip from the fingers to hit them in the face and if you placed the arrow on the right side of the maidan, as did the warriors of the Iranian people, shots resulted in the so-called "phenomenon paradox" where it pulled to the right.[120] It was a proven practice of the period for Parthian and Sassanid theory, however, to avoid this through a system of finger tension on the bowstring to maintain the accuracy of the fire if it is necessary to apply the arrow as in European techniques on the left of the grip is obviously not true. You can see an example of the image of an archer from Taht-e Sangin, from Shami, or from the representations on the silver Sassanid plates which was exceptionally detailed of the Persian King using a method of pulling the bow similar to the Scythian Achaemenid or "Parthian Shot" placed on the right side of the grip. It should

---

[119]Taybuga, op.cit., p. 128
[120]Taybuga, op.cit, p. 25.

be accepted that placing the arrow on this side was the normal way to increase the rate of fire, which is always an important consideration. It must have been extremely important for all archers that if any of them took left handed shots and they needed to move quickly it would be much harder and slower to "load" it from the left side of the grip than on the right. During the course of shooting they would have to tilt the bow to the right which would surely interfere with the neck of the horse.

Methods for Aiming and Targeting When the Bow is Drawn. The technique for holding the bow and arrow is closely linked to the way you pull the bow and aim it. This ability can be implemented in several different ways depending on the type of bow, the length of the shot and other needs related to the tactical doctrine of the given people. The length of the shot is an important factor, which is significantly related to bow tension, which is a condition of the length and capabilities of the weapon. Long and heavy shot were mainly used for firing on armored opponents, which required great force, it is important to have more stability in flight so that it is less susceptible to drift from gusts of wind. Its mass, inertia and stiffness of the shaft are better than light ones for firing strong and hard. Using a long arrow, you can maximize the power of weapon tension. In order to get the best value of force, it is necessary to balance the length of the tension with the natural limits of the shooter's arm and the length of the bow arms. If we increase the latter arm, allowing the increased connection and a "Harder" bow, and increasing the force of the missiles. The sections of the arms, however, could not be lengthened indefinitely, because there is a final size where the bow is so large that the archer cannot effectively use it. It seems that the upper limit for the sensible length of the arm for reflexive bows is approximately 1.8 m along the siyah, which it reached in the Middle Ages and Chinese and Mongolian bows of modern times.[121]

Although it can be inferred from pictorial representations that shorter Parthian bows were used for these missiles was approximately 1 m. Tightening the bow of this length requires pulling the notch of the arrow to the bridge of the nose or cheek, pulling the bow using European archery techniques. Middle Eastern (Assyrians) were already using long, angular bows from the VIIIcentury BCE and later the Parthians and Sakae as well, (but perhaps under Far Eastern influences as well) pulled the bow so that the arrow notch touched the right shoulder. Their dominance through the II century BCE of this type of shooting is represented of relief images on ivory plates from Orlat and numerous "archery"

---

[121]S. Selby, *The Visible Chinese Bow*, http://www.atarn.org/chinese/visible_bow_/visible.htm.

The Armies of Ancient Persia

Part of the battle scene from the bone plate discovered in Orlat near Samarkand. (according to J. Wolski, Dzieje i upadek imperium Seleucydów, *fig.206)*

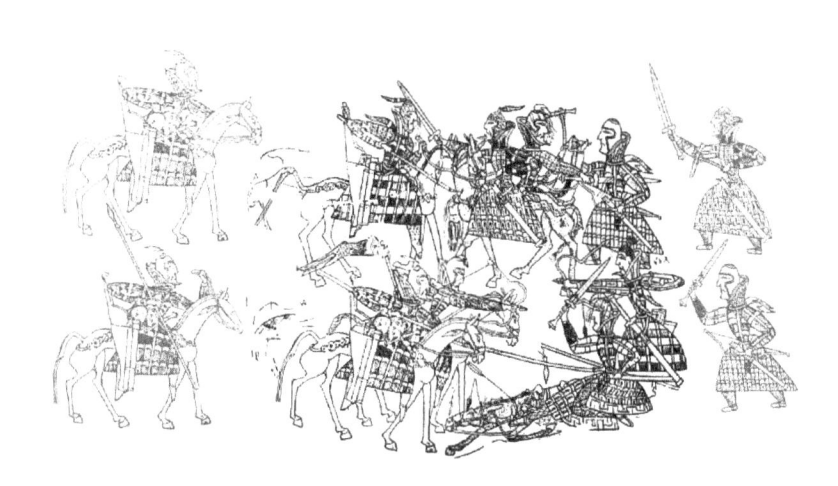

Reconstruction of the entire battle scene from the Orlat bone plate. (according to M. Mode, Heroic fights and dying heroes - The Orlat battle plaqe and the roots of Heroic fights and dying heroes ...*)*

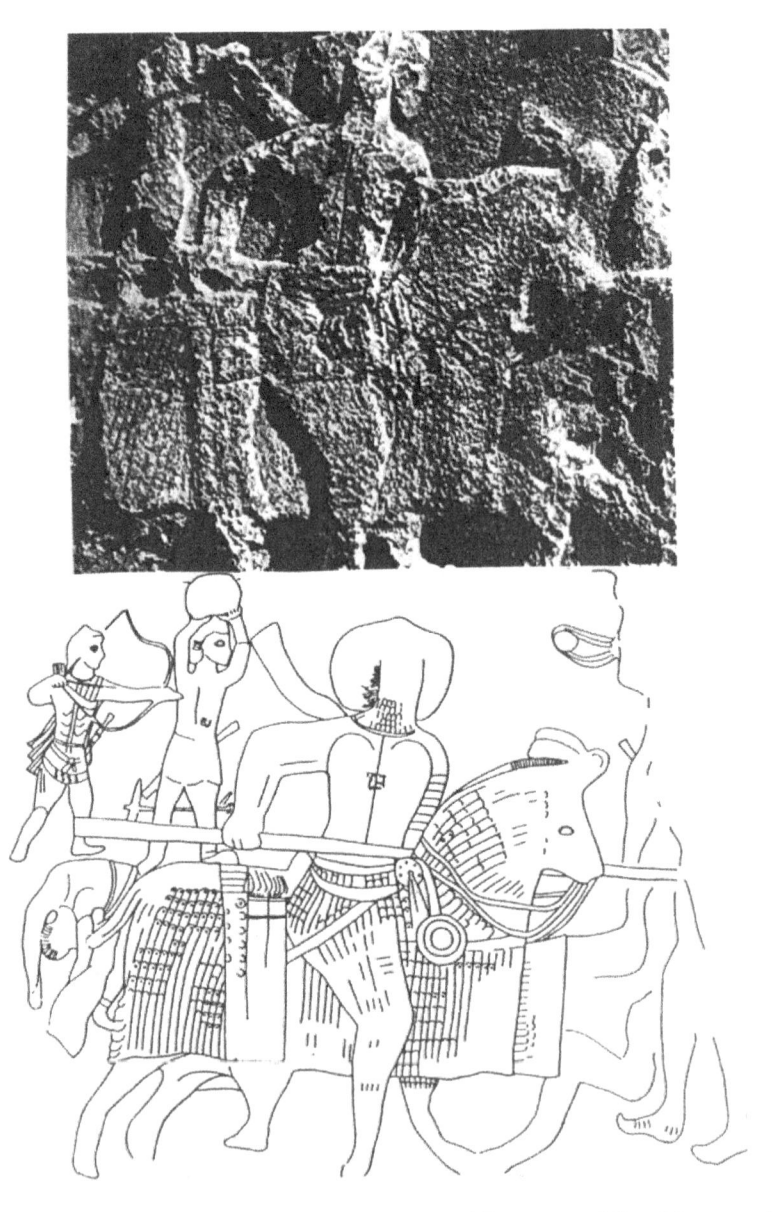

Relief from Tang – e Sarvak depicting a powerfully armored Parthian cavalryman from the 3rd century AD (a) original, (b) rendering (according to R. Ghirschman, Iran: Parthians and Sassanians, *fig. 69, B. Kaim,* Art of Ancient Iran, *fig. 134)*

Hunting scene - painting from the Mithraeum in Dura Europos (from M. Gawlikowski, Sztuka Syrii, fig. 102)

Parthian archer firing applied to tensioning the string of the index and ring fingers and middle - Shami (from R. Ghirschman, Iran. Parthians and Sassanians, fig. 125)

Kuszan archery technique - a clay sculpture fragment - Kalchandār (from G.A.Скульптура, Халчаяна, fig. 70)

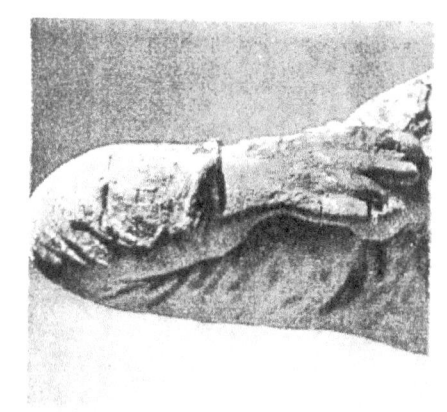

The Armies of Ancient Persia

Coin of Mitrydates I. (Parthian kings, http // www.livius.org / pan-Oct / Parthia / kings.html).

Statue of a standing Parthian prince - Shami. (from J. Harmatt (ed.), A History of Civilizations of Central Asia, fig. 11)

Reclining partisan archer – terracotta tile - British Museum (from R. Ghirschman, Iran: Parthians and Sassanians fig. 121)

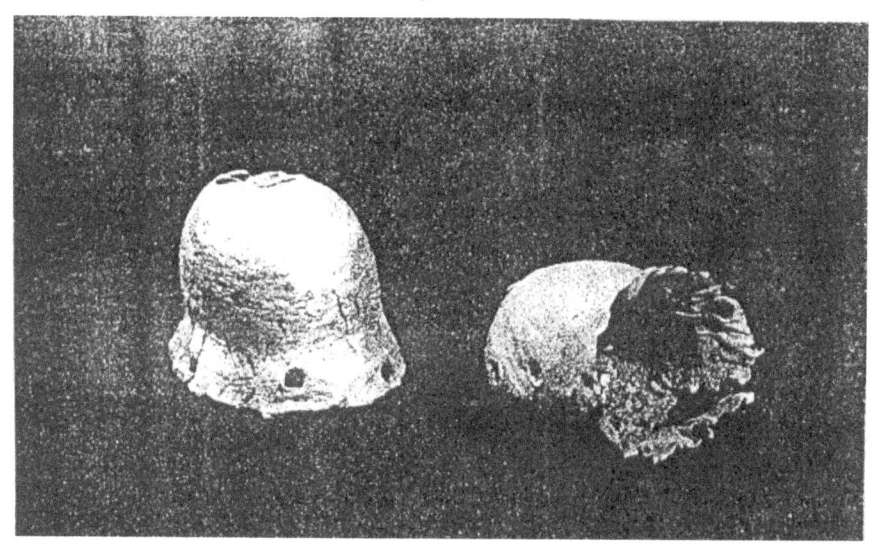

Golden caps to protect the index finger and ring finger of an archer used by Iranian archers - the Achaemenid period - Pheonicia. (from Taybug, Saracen Archery, *Fig.9a, b)*

Representations of archers shooting with long reflexive bows - from the tombs of the Han age. (from M. Granet, Chinese Civilization. *fig..320,304)*

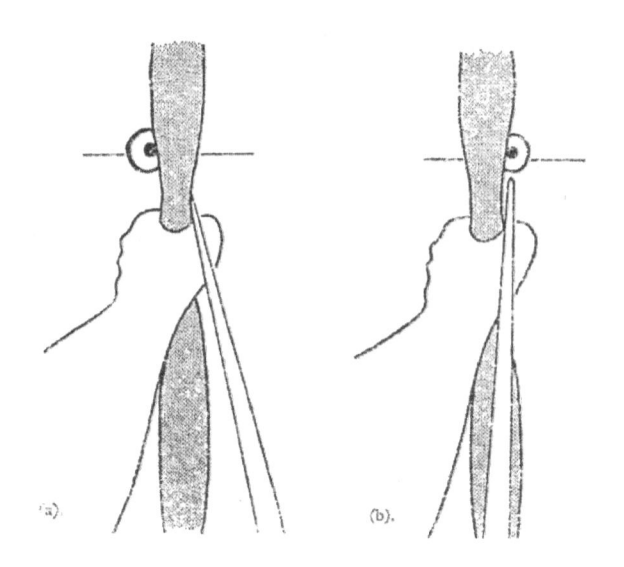

Aiming "external (a) and internal (b). (according to Taybug, Saracen Archery, *fig. 24)*

The principle of releasing the arrow. (according to Taybug, Saracen Archery, *fig. 70,133)*

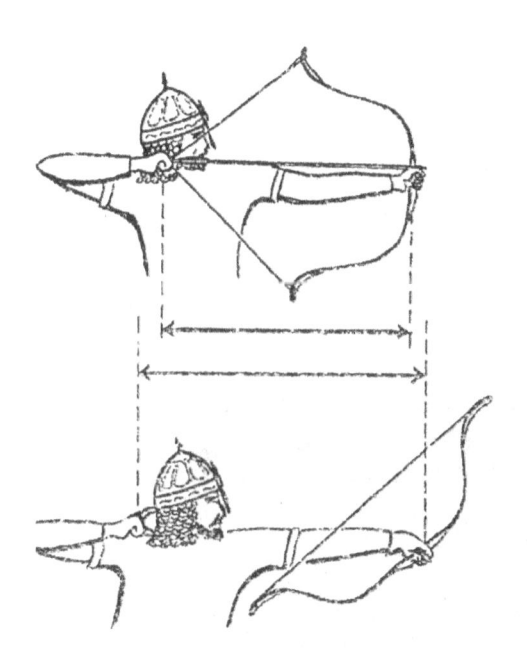

graffiti at Dura-Europos.[122] The same technique can be inferred from a variety of battlefield scenes on vessels from the late-Zhou era, as well as hunting scenes from painted tiles discovered in tombs from the Han period, showing it used in China.[123] It's use, however, is linked to this characteristic way of aiming, archer ring and the custom of setting up the shot on the right side of the grip.

Perhaps the evolutionary form of this particular technique for pulling the bow that is still in use in the Far East for holding the bow string which has only been preserved in traditional Kyudo Japanese archery, where they grabbed the cord with two or three fingers to guide the string as they did in Parthian Iran, which is confirmed by graffiti at Dura.[124] It is easy to distinguish related archery types on art by the height of the arrow pulled somewhere straight behind the ear. To get two points of targeting, first pull the arrow to the right cheek, slightly below the cheekbone.[125] The second point, something like a bowtie is at the tip the projectile. This way of "capture the moment" the best way to eliminate the error resulting from the difference in levels between the line of the eye that the arrowhead is aiming and the level of the hand at the end of the arrow. Application allows to minimize the need to measure the distance of the tip below the target, especially when shooting a strong bow, a short distance (about 50-60 m), on which shooting was carried out for the Parthian tactics for horse archery. Through this you can effectively hit exactly where it is aimed, using the eastern way of holding the grip with the finger pointing with the left hand. The archer is thus able to hit the enemy without massed fire.

Sometimes under combat conditions such targeting implementation was done in a slightly different way. In a Saracen treaty on archery it says,

> To strike the enemy who is at a distance, aim at his head, (...) because the arrow loses altitude on its way to the target. However, if you aim this way, it will reach your opponent and kill him. To in turn shoot an arrow at an opponent not too far away, you should aim at his leg because in the first phase of flight, after it leaves the bow the arrow rises (...) however, judgement and long experience are the only ways to achieve the best results. (Taybuga. 12, V)

---

[122] B. Goldman, op.cit., pp. 20-40.
[123] E. Erdberg-Consten, *Das Alte China*, Stuttgart 1958. pp. 238, 252.
[124] B. Goldman, op.cit., p. 31.
[125] H.Onuma, D. i J. DeProspero, op.cit., p. 94

Pictorial representations show how the Parthians, Sake and other people of the eastern steppes have used of the two above described techniques. These techniques show how one would apply arrows on the left side of the grip, which causes the so-called phenomena of the "paradox shots", i.e. a series of vibrations by the arrow on the horizontal plane after releasing the bowstring. In the Far East method of using bow tension with the thumb and the arrow until it bends to the left. This is due to the deflection of the cord after slipping off the thumb with a ring or leather cover slightly to the right. In the Scythian-Parthian-Sakae mode of shooting using two or three fingers to pull the bowstring, the cord "angles" left which causes the opposite effect, essentially forcing the application of arrows on the left side of the grip. The bows of these people are built to compensate for this phenomenon, which for example today is used to increase the accuracy in the Japanese yumi which slightly inclines both arms to the right. However, they also have to be slightly thicker on the right side than the left, which prevented twisting the grip on the vertical plane. Thanks to these characteristics it was possible to practice a faster way of applying arrows to the right side of the grip in conjunction with the technique of pulling the cord with the fingers in what is unquestionably an Iranian presentation.

After releasing the bowstring, the arrow deflects in one direction, then it immediately "snaps" in the opposite direction once it bypasses the grip. Once in flight, the arrow performs a few more rotations, and continues to move steady and straight.[126] Using this process it is possible to shoot accurately without using the notch on the grip, known as a "shelf" on current sports bows. According to the master Taybuga, a derivation of passing through the shaft on the vertical plane on the line using the right eye is the European method and characteristic of eastern shooting techniques for reflexive bows with a long pull, which was balanced by the fact that the target could be found on the left edge of the grip. When the so-called external targeting was used for short type bows makes use of the arrow ledge "caught of the right side of the grip" shooting method. Independent from this method was aiming using both eyes which required to set the left pupil shifted to the outer (left) corner, and the right to the inner corner requiring the head to be set obliquely to the left towards the target. This technique gives the most complete view.[127]

Japanese archery masters recommend adding slight motion to the shot, keeping both hands from the center line outside the body, done immediately after releasing the bowstring because when using a rigid arrow with a large shaft it supports improving the accuracy of the arrow's

---
[126]Taybuga, op.cit., p. 25.
[127]Taybuga, op.cit., p. 5

paradox effect. It is possible that because of the great similarities with shooting techniques between the Far and the Middle East, the Parthians had similar practices. We know also know that Saracen archers knew and used such a move, called *Katrah*. It required executing the move immediately after the release of the short, strong cord with a quick movement by both hands. It executed a line of fire whereby the left hand went forward, and the right hand moved backwards. In addition to the shooting hand, jerked as if it happened naturally, as if in response to the release of the bowstring, was performed in addition to the other arm's move of the bow. It was an integral part of the *katrah*, and the preparation for it involved gripping the center with the little finger pressed against it and pointing. Master Taybuga claimed the katrah significantly improves the power and range of the shot and if made correctly, does not affect the accuracy.

Most of the above comments concern the techniques of using long reflexive bows. Long-distance firing was associated with the application of other weapons and archery techniques. The length of the pull was associated with other weapons and archery techniques. The length of the pull used for this purpose was short Scythian-type bows of 65-70 cm which allowed for comfortable aiming through pulling the bowstring in a right vertical plane using the "perfect" eye (or both eyes) and the use of tops or fixed points on the face (depending on the length of the bow and the arms of the archer).

Measuring distance and final aiming process occurred at different times in the process of the pull. You can do it keeping the bow tight, but the eastern method consisted of pulling the bowstring by lowering the hands in advance of precluding such a possibility, or as the Mongols and Turks did. Those after a "general target" tightened the bow to almost full-length when it was in site, more or less than a fist width, and then after carefully aiming, pull the bowstring to the final position and immediately release it. This method was especially practiced by the Mamluk and Saracen horse archers.[128]

Archery on the back of a fast-moving horse was an extraordinarily difficult and demanded incredible skill and master of archery as well as horseback riding. All activity relating to the shot had to be in synch with the horse's pace, so that it would not disrupt his aim or placing the arrow in the bowstring.[129]

Pulling the bow should be carried out when the body is on the up swing and falling due to the inertia of the bow hands, in the eastern technique the weapon is pulled from above and lowered from the head, with

---
[128]Taybuga, op.cit., p. 60.
[129]Q. Zhuyong, *Horseback Archery Method, An Collection and Explanation of the Seven Military Classics*, http://www.atarn.org/chinese/horseback/Quingxi%20Zhuyong.htm.

both hands when the horse is taking a step. The shot should be taken when the body is stopped in the upper position when the animal moves to the next step. It was particularly important to perfectly combine all the activities with the horse's step as horse archers of the ancient people did not have stirrups which would have eliminated the shock caused by galloping.

It was not only necessary to shoot on the run, but to also direct the horse, doing it all provided by the assumption a maneuvering in formation. The necessary efficiency in the performance of all these volatile actions can only be possible through long-lasting exercises practiced since a child, which has always been the advantage in this area of nomadic warrior tribes. From significant disciplined forces, the Arsacids could create a "popular uprising" that was a professional force capable of fighting the invincible Roman legion.

4. The History of the Armored Cavalry

ORIGIN. The genesis of this unique military formation, like the horse archers, is poorly understood. To this day it is difficult to give a clear answer to the question of when and where armored were first used on a large scale. According to our written sources, which is mainly Herodotus, but also includes Arrian, Diodorus, Xenophon and others, large scale heavily armored cavalry was one of the foundations of Achaemenid Persian army's military power. The armored cavalry of the Massagetae are mentioned in the work of the "Father of History" (Herodotus I. 215-217), allows you to look for that formation, not in Iran, but somewhere in the steppe areas of Asia, yet before the middle of the 6th century BCE. What is very interesting about his description of the forces of Queen Tomyris fighting against the troops of Cyrus the Great, Herodotus presents details of weapons and armor of the Central Asian heavily armored warriors of nomadic people, completely ignoring the horse archers. It is not possible for the Massagetae to consist exclusively of armored cavalry. The great historian does not deal with the use of this formation, or its tactics. He does not even mention if the cavalry was divided into different types (Herodotus I. 214). The complaint in this regard should be directed more towards the sources of the Greek historian than to himself. It appears that the Persians, from whom he drew his account of the important battle tactics of the Massagetae was not unusual because they used identical tactics at the same time; to the curious foreigner they just described what the average warrior could see about the enemy standing against him in battle – the first lines of his battle order, and that the Iranian steppe people had armored cavalry.

The Armies of Ancient Persia

    Later pictorial representations from the barrows of Sakae aristocracy have been identified as Herodotus' Massagetae, which tells a lot about their tactics. In the battle scene on the ivory plate from Orlat, there are clearly at least two armored warriors in the front battle line with spears, swords or axes, shielding archers are behind them in the second line.[130] This fragment confirms the reality of events described by Herodotus 450 years later, but there are significant differences in the armored riders which can be explained that the minimal armored figures are also archers. Tactics, however, especially if they are specialized methods for specific terrain can remained unchanged for many centuries. The existence of similar fighting styles to the western Scythians seem to be confirmed in archaeological finds, i.e., "The Great Ryzhanovsky Barrow". The burial of a Scythian chief was found here with his bodyguard, who as it turns out, was a left-handed man. Thanks to that he was able to shield his master from arrows or swords, without interfering with his ability to shoot a bow or use his sword.[131] Everything indicates that Herodotus had excellent information, reflecting the military reality of the VI and V centuries BCE even to distant Hellas.

    It seems that in the Achaemenid army, but especially in the eastern units, the combination of armored cavalry and archers was common practiced, but more importance had already begun to move toward greater interaction of these formations with infantry units, which for ethnic Persians and Mede armored cavalry units already accounted for that support by their use of Sakae horse archers. The cavalry itself was already used on a large scale, for example during the battles with Alexander the Great's army, there was a large proportion of cavalry, whose numbers went to the tens of thousands of soldiers. Written sources also confirm the widespread use of cavalry by the Achaemenids who probably modeled tactics on the Scythians, wedge-shaped at the squadron level, as led by the steppe tribes.

    The heavy Persian cavalrymen remained in the same formation to fight both the opponent's infantry and cavalry with similar offensive weapons to those used by the Scythians – spears, swords, axes and short bows. Two-meter long spears were used in a similar way to those practiced by Greek hoplites depending on the need to stab from above or from below at the hip which had the advantage of being easy to repeat if you missed, even on the crowded battlefield area. This was excellent for fight-

---

[130] Until today, the identity of Orlat plates and their dating arouses great controversy. In this book as described in the text, however, it is assumed early dating of this monument in the II - I century BC.

[131] J. Chochorowski, "Scytyjski Tutanchamon", *Gazeta wyborcza, Wielki format*, nr. 5 1998, ss.16-18

ing at close quarters, but it could not match the xyston of the Companions or the sarissa of the phalanx.

The defeat of the Achaemenids in the great war against Macedonia led to the collapse of their empire and the emergence of Hellenistic monarchy in large parts of Asia under the Seleucids. The development in the field of arms, as well as the tactical use of armored cavalry fighting on both sides became indistinguishable. The advantage should have been with the military tradition of the winners.

Our main source for research on the operations of Seleucid heavy cavalry are from the numerous ancient treatises in the field of martial art and famous works by the Roman historians Livy and Polybus in which they describe thier weapons, equipment and methods of operations in examples such as: the battles of Raphia (217 BCE), Panion (200 BCE), the mission of the Syrian deputies to Aigion (192 BCE) (Livy, *The Republic* XXXV, 48), Magnesia (190 BCE) (Livy, *The Republic* XXXVII, 40), and the great review of the army at Daphne (Livy, *The Republic* 37-40). These events are supplemented by a few, albeit extremely interesting images, i.e. bas-reliefs from the balustrade of the Temple of Athena Polias in Pergamum, an armored warrior from Syria - nowadays stored in the Louvre in Paris, images from Seleucid and Greek coins, and finally archaeological finds such as the remains of armor discovered during the excavations in Ai-Khanoum. The last find is an especially interesting discovery, but also controversial because it reflects the phenomenon of mixing the construction of protective clothing that combines the influences of the Iranian steppe and the Hellenistic.

At the battles of Raphia, Panion and Magnesia, Antiochus III applied the old tactics of a right armored wing of cavalry developed by Philip II of Macedonia and used with great success by Alexander the Great during his eastern campaign.[132] The armies of the two famous conquerors decided the fate of battles, breaking the attack of heavy cavalry which was countered by an attack across the front by the right wing. The basic formation of the Companion unit was, however, unlike similar Seleucid formations, in that it was a diagonal line, which in combination with a similar inverse line formed by the foot guards represented a hollow wedge. You could easily imagine that for this type of formation to attack without breaking the cohesion of the group required amazing skills and training for both units. In such an army formation the use of armored formations required good coordination with the rest of their forces to conceal their movement, direction and movement before the point of impact in front of the eyes of the enemy commander. A wedge formed during the approach to the battlefield would make it difficult to maneuver the whole

---
[132]N. G. L. Hammond, op.cit., pp. 108-110 and 124-128.

formation. The Seleucids, most likely for practical reasons, avoided such complex formations and used a simpler line pattern. It was in fact, a simplified display of Alexander's "enclosed" army introduced as a new solution later – units of elephants, cataphracts, etc.

As a result of Antiochus III's campaign in the eastern areas of his empire, armored cavalry appeared in the Seleucid army under the name of cataphracts. To draw analogy with later solutions it is assumed that these units were much more powerful than the "mounted companions" of armored cavalry. From the archaeological finds (such as those at Czirik-Rabat or Ai Khanoum) we know that cavalry in eastern Iran from the Achaemenid times used armor for people and mounts was much more elaborate than those from the western part of the Persian Empire or in Greece. There was no mention of the cataphracts before the eastern expedition of Antiochus III also seems to confirm the eastern genesis of this unit.[133] Cataphracts were used to perform the crushing blow against the exposed flank of enemy infantry (such as during the battle at Panion)[134] as well as an important Hellenistic tactic against his camp and supplies. They probably used long, heavy spears for the fight, as well as swords or axes.

At Magnesia, six thousand of Antiochus' cataphracts were divided into two equal sized groups, both placed on the flanks of the formation created from the combined forces. The intention of command was for the decisive blow to be typically delivered by the right wing, that brought the Seleucid troops victory, for instance early in the Battle of Panion. This time, events took a different course. The charging armored cavalry smashed the units on the left wing of the army and the Romans reached their camp. Unfortunately, for the Roman generals and soldiers, the capture was not important to the Hellenistic troops and did not provoke the expected panic. What's worse, the right-wing cataphracts, unlike Panion, did not return to the battlefield. Maneuverability in attack was not and was not supposed to be the strongest suit of this unit. Their main asset was always the force of impact. By that time, the rest of Antiochus' army was defeated, though not as Livy would have it – at the hands of the Romans – but through the powerful force of Eumenes' Pergamon's armored cavalry. The battle was so typical of the so-called Hellenistic period as a "Circular" course. The Attalid dynasty had to do this after continued contact with the Seleucids, which are very reminiscent of their cataphracts.

A three thousand-man unit of armored cavalry occupying the position on the left side of King Antioch's troops fought on, despite an unfa-

---

[133] M. Mielczarek, *Cataphracts- A Parthian Element in the Seleucid Art of War*, Electrum II.
[134] The Battle of Panion will be discussed in more detail later.

vorable position and the panic surrounding these units until the end.[135] According to Appian of Alexandra, this was to the result of their inability to withdraw due to the weight of their armor, and the lack of maneuverability of the unit itself.[136] The presumption on the part of Plutarch ignores the unusually efficient retreat of the Parthian super-heavy cavalry after initially hitting the lines of Roman legionnaires under Crassus, which seems to be exaggerated , if not completely wrong (Plutarch, Crassus, p.34). The cavalry on Antiochus' left wing fought as a horse phalanx after initially slowed down the onslaught of the enemy forces, ensuring the protection of the center units.

Very similar to the above-described charge, was the movement of the right wing of King Tigranes of Armenia's army against the Romans under Lucullus during the battle near Tigrancerta in 69 BCE. Before they were broken, they were rescued by a skillful maneuver provided by the commander of the attacking units. As they retreated, they drew the Armenian cavalry into the resulting gap, attacking their flanks.[137] Unfortunately, we are not sure what type of formation Tigranes armored cavalry fought in, but it is very possible that the attack was fought in a wedge, and the cavalry fought like the Parthians against the enemy's infantry, a slightly modified version of the characteristic formation of the steppe people.

The first of these accounts gives an idea of Seleucid cataphracts way of figthing, consisting of one powerful charge in tight, but probably not too deep formation (approximately 5-8 ranks).[138] Note that unlike the infantry, increasing the number of ranks does not increase the strength of pressure. Animals can not push each other to create a continuous line, on the contrary, they would become frightened at this, adding to the confusion in the lines.[139] In addition, all the cavalrymen past the 2nd and 3rd ranks are not involved in th fight. The Steppe nomads knew this for a long time, which made the interior and the wings of one or two compact ranks of armored wedges of light archers.

The attack of the cataphracts might follow with the eastern way of attacking but could also be used to crush and break enemy infantry formations.[140] But, the Seleucid troops could also attack an exposed flank by cataphract infantry, known as "Cavalry Comrades". This is the application of the Macedonian strategy for this type of unit.

---

[135]M. Mielczarek, *Cataphracti and Clibanarii Studies on the Heavy Armored Cavalry of the Ancient World*, Łódź 1993, p. 41.
[136]M. Mielczarek, op.cit., p. 42.
[137]M. Mielczarek, op.cit., p. 42.
[138]loc. cit..
[139]J. Maroń, "Przed pierwszym starciem", *Gazeta Rycerska*, 2, 2002. s. 115.
[140]M. Mielczarek, op.cit., p. 43.

The Armies of Ancient Persia

The weapons and equipment of the heavily armed cavalry units of the Seleucids, just like their tactics, can be found in a mixed solution of Greek and Iranian solutions. Soldiers in the Seleucid Army might have been involved in the Parthian and Bactrian Kingdom independence uprisings, made up not only of Greek settlers, but also Medes as well as members of wealthy Iranian families. There was, however, no special ethnic detachment made up of Parthian, Bactrian or Hyrcanian vassals of Antioch.[141]

The armament and equipment of the Seleucid armored cavalry at the beginning of the II century BCE comes to us from the reliefs on the balustrade in Pergamum, to celebrate the victory of Attalus I over the Galatians, in the temple of Athena Polias. The sculpture represents captured weapons and armor of the opponents defeated by Pergamon. The set of armored cavalry equipment is located between them. If it belonged to the Seleucid horse and historical circumstances supported it, the soldiers wore large cuirass of metal or thick hardened leather. The breastplate was supplied with two rows of leather strips (pteruges) along the lower edges for better protection by overlapping, which covered the abdomen and thighs of the rider down to the knees, as well as one row of pteruges covering the shoulders.

The head and face were protected by a bell shaped conical helmet, made of metal with a full facial mask. The only exposed part was the eyes and the bottom of the neck below the mask. The neck could, however, even by shielded by a scale armor or a solid collar as a type discovered in early Hellenic tombs in Macedonia.

Protection for the arms were known in Central Asia during the Achaemenid period, (as evidenced by the discoveries in the burial chamber at Czirik-Rabat), part of which were armored sleeves. These guards were made of horizontal metal or cut strips of hide segmented to cover the hands and connected with to each other by overlapping vertical strips from the bottom up. It was not known exactly how the whole covering worked, as if it created some short sleeve that was tied to the shoulder as part of the breastplate or was crimped onto the arms like a hoplite greave, tied or pinned to some part of the torso. It appears that the later is possibly nearer to the truth, because there appears to be overlapping or loose strips, i.e. on the left hand of Artaban V placed on the saddle shown on the relief at Firuzabad. This is how the fragment of the Czirik Rabat sleeve was reconstructed. Such sleeves, as well as those made of leather, provide maximum protection for the arms, which has always been prone to inquires in a fight, with minimal reduction of mobility.

---

[141] M. Mielczarek, op.cit., p. 69.

Legs were equally vulnerable during attacks. During the Greek-Macedonian period they were protected by solid metal greaves, or in the east as evidenced by the findings at Ai Khanoum using the same tubular thigh protection as the sleeve.

Seleucid cataphracts from the east wore scale armor as an apron with their breastplate, which is in two-parts and clearly visible on the Pergamon relief, perhaps as used in the Achaemenid army which also covered both sides. The head of the horse was covered with a plate-like pediment covering the whole top, decorated with a stately cross-comb made of metal and feathers running all over the top surface of the cover just in front of the ears. It seems that the dense, bristle of long spears in the cataphract formation such armor was perfectly adequate.

An identical relief is shown on the Temple of Athena Polias showing a soldier in armor, which represents a small bronze statuette from Syria and now in the Louvre collection. The only difference is the fact that his breastplate is represented as a heavy muscle corset armor. This type of armor was used in the late-Hellenistic times was not only extremely popular, but also prestigious which is a representation of rulers and gods. For example, it is seen on the old Nisa terracotta figures, and even much later Kushan coins. In the east, pteruges were installed on the scale aprons.

Today, there is no doubt that all the above described parts of the uniform protective devices have their equivalent counterparts in the heavy equipment of Alexander the Great's cavalry or his Achaemenid opponents. Seleucid cataphracts, like most heavily armored cavalry of the Persians and Greek-Macedonians of the IV century BCE, did not use shields, but relied on their armor for protection.

The main weapon of the Seleucid heavy cavalry was a long spear. Presumably, the source of that weapon was Macedonia and Greece, modelled on the heavy xyston used by the royal companions. The spears the Hellenistic cataphracts used a heavy shaft that had a large lance-shaped iron tip and on the other end a second point, or iron spike. Sometimes the term "kopia" is used by the Hellenistic heavy cavalry for the word Sarissa, which is Macedonian in origin and is probably the wrong term. Professionally, it refers to the specific usage of the phalangite infantry spear. Errors like this are probably due to the poor recognition of the ancient writers of their usage of terms centuries later, referring to the field of military terminology and techniques for the use of particular types of cavalry and infantry weapons. It is possible, however, that with a specific manner of fighting the long "kopia" was used in the same way as the phalangite spears, at the end of the Hellenistic period, in an effort to increase the range of the weapons. Both of these techniques became similar that could lead to confusion. The way in which the Macedonian and Seleucid heavy infantrymen held their long spears, up to 6m long, during the fight required them to use two hands about 1m from the massive counterbalance to the extended front part of the shaft with the tip ready, for the maximum weapons capability. Based on the pictorial representation, however, not much can be said about the use of cavalry spears during the Hellenistic period. Only observing the Parthian, Sassanid and Sarmatian representations showing their technique for carrying out an attack with a spear, no matter if the enemy was infantry or cavalry, it can be said that it is actually identical to the one created by Philip II of Macedon for his heavy infantry sarissa, also the kopia spear from this period does not really differ from the old infantry sarissa.

The early Seleucid heavy cavalry companions held their spears in the middle of the shaft, or slightly beyond it (about 0.5 m) on the right side of the horse, holding the pole in his right hand, often squeezing it under the left arm while holding the reigns.[142] The tip of the spear was directed to hit the opponent in the throat, or the upper part of the chest. This technique allows the rider to use the kopia more efficiently and most importantly give the ability to deflect the opponent's blow. However, it is a technique that is best suited to use against a target that when struck, will knock the rider from the saddle.

Cataphract attacks were often supported by lighter armored cavalry "Comrades". It seems that during the attack on the line infantry formations this type of Hellenistic cavalry did not move at a full gallop (like the cataphracts), but at a fast trot or at most a slight gallop, so that it was possible to push and pull the lancehead in the opponent's before it breaks through and gets stuck. When that happened, the weapon would have to be abandoned. The same tactic was still used by the Macedonian Companion cavalry against both the opponent's infantry or cavalry as evidenced by the battle descriptions included in, for example, the "Expedition of Alexander the Great" by Flavius Arrian. According to him, the xyston was the weapon used by the armored cavalry throughout the duration of the battle, while attempting to hit the face or throat with the tip, not just as a medieval lance or Parthian spear, but also of the Sakae or Sassanid clibanarii, whose only task was the first breaking blow.[143] Arrian was a former soldier and military strategist who knew this well. The characteristic placement of Alexander's hand and body on the mosaic of the "House of the Faun" in Pompeii (the king is holding the spear high or even slightly backward on the right side), indicating an attempt to poke

---

[142] N.G.L. Hammond, op.cit., pp. 109-110.
[143] F. Arrian, *Wyprawa Aleksandra Wielkiego*, tłum. H. Gesztoft-Gasztold, Wrocław 1963, p. 22.

the spear, not thrusting it to knock the enemy from the saddle. The backrest provided adequate cushion from the strike in the absence of a saddle when the legs are wrapped around the sides of the horse, strengthened by striking force of the upper part of the body. This helped avoid losing balance from hitting the target while holding a weapon in your hands.

The secondary weapons were swords of the ordinary type, the Greek ksiphos or long, massive single-edged kopis knives in units of "cavalry comrades" (worn in the Greek manner on the left side, on a belt slung over the right shoulder) and long Iranian swords, clubs or axes fro cataphracts. The ksiphos of the Seleucid rider shown on the Pergamon relief is unusually long and narrow, almost like a fencing saber, discovered in an extremely rich grave at Prodromi in Epirus. Even here the armor of the heavy cavalry was evolving in the direction towards more powerful and better protection.

Cataphracti on the Hellenistic battlefield – the battle of Panion (Panium). During the summer 205 BCE in Seleucia, at Tigris, the eastern capital and pearl in the crown of the huge monarchy the Seleucids was in turmoil. The expedition of King Antiochus III of the Seleucids was worthy of Alexander the Great himself. However, the fame of his deeds was made possible by his troops. It was said that he was humbled by the powerful Syrian army of the barbarian ruler of the Parni, Arsaces I of Parthia, that Antiochus defeated and besieged the heavily fortified capital of Bactra-Zariaspan of the rebellious Hellenized king of Bactria, Euthydemus,[144] finally he renewed the covenant of Seleucid I Nicator with the council of the Maurya reigning over an unknown area of northern India.[145] Now the great Antiochus returned to glory with victories leading a huge army which included 150 battle elephants, real "tanks of antiquity" lent to him by the Indian ruler, bringing him spoils which no one had won since the legendary undefeated son of Philip II. At this point the young king stood at the height of his power. News of the victories of Antiochus, however, aroused concern amongst his neighbors. This was especially true at the court of Alexandria, the famous capital of the Ptolemies, where the glory of the Great King was viewed as the prophecy of an inevitable war. Everyone knew that the victor of the east wanted to claim the lands his ancestors received following the battle of Ipsos in Palestine. At this time, the Seleucid was not only a great victor, but also the leader of a seasoned army. The situation in Egypt worsened in the year 204 BCE when Ptole-

---
[144]The issue of the eastern expedition of Antioch III was discussed in an extremely interesting way by S. Kalita. (S.Kalita, *Grecy w Baktrii i w Indiach*, Kraków 2005, p. 83.
[145]A.Świderkówna, *Hellada królów*, Warszawa 1969, pp. 261-264.

my IV Philopator died leaving the throne to his successor who was still a child. The court of Alexandria was then plunged into an atmosphere of palace plots, intrigues and crime.[146] Antioch finally decided that the time for war had come.

In 202 BCE Seleucid troops marched along the Mediterranean coast, entering Ptolemy's lands in Palestine, taking the Fortress at Gaza, an important stronghold of the Egyptians in the north.[147] Egypt did not have much of a chance for an effective or quick response to these losses, however, the loss of this area from a strategic point of view were the most important lands of Alexandria. If the enemy remained there permanently, his armies would always be standing at the gates of Egypt. The excellence buffer that constituted the Ptolemies stubborn defense against opponents was inherited from the father to son.

The preparations for war were completed on the Nile in the autumn of 201 BCE. A huge Egyptian army reinforced by a significant number of excellent Aetolian mercenaries who were considered some of the best soldiers of the Hellas. They came from the hill country commanded by Gen. Scopas which went north from Rafi in the winter of 201 to 200 BCE, removing in turn, key Seleucid garrisons in Palestine, the majority of which were recently occupied by Antiochus.[148] This restored the status quo and the situation seemed to be under control, but not for long. By late spring or early summer of 200 BCE, the Ptolemaic court received news that Seleucid was already on the march south through Syria with a large army. Scopas had to act quickly. The road to Palestine led north along several roads. Antioch chose the route leading from Damascus, along the south-eastern slopes of the Anti-Lebanon Mts, south of the massif of Mount Hermon to the Panion area, where the road descends between Hermon and the Golan Heights in the Huleh Valley at the beginning of the Jordan Valley. Even in those times they were wonderful fertile areas famous for its wine-growing, and just as important safely away from the coast under the rule of the still powerful Ptolemaic fleet. It was also a road not manned by Egyptian garrisons, besides being the shortest route. Skopas' guards probably watched all the potential routes as he started a forced march to stop the enemy in the most advantageous place – while descending from the foothills of Hermon to the plains of Panion.

The course of the battle of Panion is unfortunately only known to us from one and not a very detailed source, namely the controversy

---

[146] A.Świderkówna, op.cit.
[147] B.Bar-Kohva, *The Seleucid Army (Organization and Tactics in the Great Campagns*, Cambridge, London 1976, p. 146.
[148] Loc.cit.

in its relations with Zeno of Rhodes, which mentioned in the sixteenth book of Polybius, *Histories*. That copy of Zeno has not survived, so unfortunately what remains is not a comprehensive, consistent description of the battle, but only those parts, in which Polybius does not agree with the opinion of Zeno. To make matters worse, those parts preserved and quoted by Polybius from Zeno's work are extremely vague and contradict each other. For example, it says that Antiochus placed his elephants in front of the Seleucid phalanx (Polybius, *Histories*, 18.7), while a little later he mentions a clash of the two phalanxes at a time when there is no mention of the elephants (Polybius, *Histories*, 18,9-10). In addition, Zeno also claims that the Seleucid phalanx was forced to retreat by the Aetolian troops and only the elephants in the rear stopped the attack of the Ptolemaic mercenaries (Polybius, *Histories*,19,1,4). With regards to the cavalry, Polybius writes that the Aetolian horses were terrified of the sight of the attacking elephants (Polybius, *Histories*,19,4,6), then goes on to say that supposedly the right wing of the Ptolemaic force faced fierce resistance on the left and was reportedly crushed on impact by the Seleucid cataphracts. (Polybius, *Histories*,18.8, 19, 4-6) Even stranger is the case when it comes to the escape of the Egyptian general from the battlefield. It was stated in one place that he withdrew immediately after the collapse of the Ptolemaic center, in another, he was the last fugitive (Polybius, *Histories*,19,10-11). Polybius apparently had something to criticize. If you look at the topography of the battlefield and add to the story that we have about the basic principals in the formation of a Hellenistic fighting force raises the idea that firstly: Polybius did not know the correct shape of the Panion battlefield and did not know the works of the Rhodian historian; secondly, that despite all the contradictory descriptions contained in its story in combination with the information collected in the field are sufficient to accurately reproduce the route of march of both armies, and assess where they were and what formation they used in battle.

Scopas had to depend on stopping the opponent before they arrived on the plain west of Panion (now Banias) and a rolling battle on the hilly area where it would be difficult for Antiochus III to take advantage of the heavy Syrian phalanx over the Ptolemaic phalanx who made up for their lighter Iphicratian weaponry and the tactics of the Aetolian troops. Even the uneven ground would be an advantage against the Antiochus horse, the best of all the used by the Hellenistic monarchy and composed of several corps of this elite unit that accompanied the king (continuing the traditional bodyguard cavalry of Alexander the Great) as well as a large formation of armored cataphracts, the most dangerous cavalry formation of those times. As an Aetolian, Scopas preferred to fight in a more difficult mountainous terrain with fighting skills which they have used for years in battles against the Athenians in the second half of the Vth century and the Celts in the IIIrd century BCE where he was famous among his people. However, he failed to intercept his opponents along the march by the slopes of Hermon. When he arrived on the plains of Panion he learned that the enemy's army was already camped on the north-east near the village of Panion, which in antiquity was most likely located near today's town of Banias.[149]

The town of Banias is located at the junction of the Golan Heights rising to the southeast with the southern slopes of the Hermon Massif, in the spring it still has glistening white snow caps visible in the north. West of the village was a wide flat plain about 1.5 km wide, further to the west is a very hilly descent to the Huleh Valley running south to the lake of the same name. Above this plain, which is now called the Banias Plain, it dominates the northern Tel Hamara which constitutes the southernmost part of the slopes of Hermon. Along the eastern edge of the plateau, a narrow ravine rolls its water out of the cave at the foot of Hermon, the River Nahr at Banias. Further, it turns to the southwest to fall into the Huleh Valley and combine its waters with other streams as the origin of the Jordon. This river, especially in its lower reaches, though wide enough is rather shallow and therefore completely fordable. It looks completely different, however, in the upper reaches, where there are large waterfalls and rapids that sometimes flows low as a mountain stream which cuts across the valley. At this point it is not suitable for crossing. On the east bank of the river, just south of the Banias plain rises a low hill called Tel Azzaziyat forming the lowest part of the Golan Heights and the lower peak to the south-west is today known as Tel Fakhr, separated from Tel Azzaziyat with uneven, undulating terrain. It is separated from the Banias plain by the Banias River Gorge.[150]

Polybius reports that the left flank of the battlefield was flat and separated from the Seleucids by the river, which on the left flank there was a hill or a mountain (Polybius, *Histories*,18,4,6). The description corresponds exactly to the shape of the Banias plain. The mountain rising above the battlefield on the left flank is Tel Hamra, and the river must be Nahr Banias. Additionally, the right flank of the battlefield was on the low sloped hills (Polybius, *Histories*,18.4).

In this arrangement, the hills are easily identified as Tell Azzaziyat, Tell Fakhr and the area around them. Of course, attention is drawn to the fact that the whole situation is described from the point of view of Ptolemaic forces. On the day of the battle, the main part of the Seleucid army marched in the morning from the camp and moved west. They

---

[149]B.Bar-Kohva, op.cit., pp. 149-150.
[150]Loc.cit.

crossed the river, at the source which was still shallow and possible to cross, and then on the plain in battle formation (Polybius, *Histories*,18.6). Stretched roughly from north to south, the line of the central group was made up of a heavy phalanx of the Macedonian type, cavalry of "Royal Companions" and regiments of "silver shields" guard (18.6). Among with the "companions" in accordance with the tradition begun by Alexander the third son of Philip (Arr. An. Al, III, 13, 14) probably took the place of Antioch III. Although the fragments of Zenon quoted by Polybius does not mention this, the units of the "silver shields" were usually placed on the right flank of the pikemen (Arr. An. Al, III, 11), the cavalry "companions" and usually occupied the position on the right side of the guard (Arr. An. Al, III, 11). In front of the army line, an old Indian pattern of fighting elephants was set at equal intervals (Arr. An. Al, V, 15), which were traditionally accompanied by light troops (slingers, archers, peltasts) protecting the sides of the animal from attacks. Each elephant was carrying a massive, wooden back turret, in which the "crew" occupied the space with an archer, javelin, and sometimes even a soldier equipped with a long spear. Sitting on the neck of the animal was the mahout protected only by its own armor. It is possible, that (as some evidence shows) in those times they were already also very valuable animals, after all, wore heavy metal armor protecting almost all of them body.

From the gentle rising slope of the right flank of the Seleucid army (or Ptolemaic left) were placed the heaviest cavalry of the Hellenic period, or cataphract (Polybius, *History*, 18,8). In the eastern fashion of horses and men they were covered from head to toe in heavy armor, fighting with a heavy spear in both hands.[151] Most probably, in contrast to the Greek-Macedonian cavalry contingent, "the Royal Companion" cataphracts attacked at a full gallop, using the spears like the horsemen of Central Asia, as kopia lances, after the spearpoint stuck in they fought with swords and axes. The use of such attack techniques in the absence of stirrups could cause, and is often mentioned in written sources (Livy, 37, 40, 2) difficulties relating to the force of impact. The crushing strength of a charge in this formation compensated for any defects, since it was never pushed back. The cataphracts were always set on the Seleucid flanks in units to drive in and flank the edges of the enemy's formation, making the center vulnerable to attack by other formations, especially the guard and the cavalry "companions". They also prevented troops that had been chased off from returning to the battlefield and in the right circumstances take the enemy's camp.

The choice of positioning the cataphracts on the slopes of Tel Hamra testifies to the excellent knowledge by the Seleucid commanders

---

[151] M.J.Olbrycht, op.cit., pp. 144-148, M.Mielczarek, *Cataphracti and Clibanari*..., p 72

The Armies of Ancient Persia

on the ways for using heavily armored cavalry units. An attack carried out bravely down a gentle, but high sloped gained them momentum and were virtually unstoppable against any formation of enemy troops, except perhaps a properly formed phalanx armed with sarissa. It was a perfect position to attack from, and as it follows from the later course of the battle, their position to a large extent determined the course of the battle.

The center and left of the Ptolemaic forces was opposite Antiochus' phalanx on the Banias plain. On the left flank a strong unit of Etolian cavalry under the command of Ptolemy's son Aeroposa and the center was mainly phalanx infantry (probably the heavy Macedonian type) (Polybius, *History*, 18.8). The entire center was probably preceded by the Seleucid's elephants[152] but their absence in the narrative of the battle should not give rise to hasty conclusions. The center was under the direct command of Skopas.

The right wing of the Egyptian army took position behind the Banias River, south of the Tel Fakhr plains and surrounding hills. It consisted mainly of mercenary Etolian infantry and part of the cavalry placed on the right flank of the mercenaries (Polybius, *History* 19,1.4).

The Etolians probably fought in typical hoplite phalanx formation. (Polybius, *History*, 18,4,9, 19.1), hence the reference to the clash of the phalanx later, even though such a clash dd not occur on the plain. They were probably armed a bit lighter than the typical hoplite – equipped with smaller shields, light canvas armor and long spears. The hilly terrain separated them from the northern plain, cut off by a ravine from the Banias River.

Seleucid's units on the left wing (commanded by the son of Antiochus III, also called Antiochus, called such to distinguish him from his brother, but also bearing the name of his father) which were the opposed by the Hellenic mercenaries on the southern edge of the battlefield, moved from their camp early in the morning but were not able to force a crossing of the river south to take a position to dominate the enemy (Polybius, *History*, 18.5, 19.8). The position corresponding to this description might have been as simple as Tel Azzaziyat, slightly higher than Tel Fakhr and located to the northeast of the former.[153] These forces consisted of a phalanx and cavalry. Because of the terrain, elephants were only used here as a second line and set amongst the supporting light infantrymen and cavalry behind the phalanx units (Polybius, *History*, 15, 5, 9, 19, 1.4). The Seleucids spread their lines from the northwest to the southeast blocking the way to their camp and the village of Panion.[154]

---

[152]B.Bar-Kohva, op.cit., p. 155.
[153]B.Bar-Kohva, op.cit., p. 152.
[154]Loc.cit.

The Armies of Ancient Persia

Given the above description of the arrangement of the troops and terrain, as well as Skopas' tactics it did not seem possible that he could break the Seleucid line along the northern part of the battlefield. The enemy's position was strong here and the area allowed for easier formation maneuvers. The only chance the Ptolemaic general had was stopping the attack of Antiochus' army in the north long enough for the south, on uneven, hilly terrain for his Etolian highlanders to break through the formations of the elder Antiochus and gain control of the Seleucid camp.[155] The loss of the supplies and the camp by the enemy would not have been the primary reason for the defeat of a Hellenistic army. Antiochus III was even convinced of this during his battle with the Romans at Thermopylae. To have any chance of accomplishing this plan, Skopas had to protect his left flank. He ordered (as already discussed), a large formation of excellent Etolian cavalry (reportedly the best in Greece) to stop Antiochus the youngers cataphracts on Tel Hamra (Polybius, *History*, 18, 22, 5, 18.6, 19.4). Antiochus probably assumed the collapse of the left flank of Skopas' army by a massive attack of armored cataphracts and the destruction of the Egyptian center with an elephant attack supported by the spikey rolling phalanx. The victory achieved to the north of the battlefield would allow his troops to cross the Banias River at its low point and get to the rear of the Aetolians. The elder Antiochus only had to keep them there long enough to not be pushed back into their own camp.

The whole battle was resolved by one devastating blow by the Seleucid units in the center and right wing. The Cataphracts fell on the enemy in a breakneck charge down the slope of Tel Hamra, sweeping the Aetolian cavalry away and crushing the left flank of Skopas' phalanx (Polybius, 18.8, 19.10). They joined in the attack by the slower moving "Horse Companions". The front of the Ptolemaic infantry was attacked at this point by the Seleucid elephants (9,11). These "tanks of the ancient world" broke into the compacted ranks of the terrified Egyptian soldiers, creating a terrible havoc. They were supported in the attack by lightly armored troops. Following this first line came the rolling iron of Antiochus' phalanx passing over the corpses of the enemy. Seeing the collapsing left wing, Skopas tried to stop his fleeing soldiers. He decided to place everything on one card, collecting his remaining forces he passed over the Banias River to support the Aetolians who were still fighting against the enemy.[156] On the southern edge of the battlefield the situation was in fact quite different from on the plain. Here, the Aetolian infantry boldly attacked the infantry of the elder Antiochus (It is possible that this was not the Macedonian phalanx, but mercenaries and allied infantry fighting in

---

[155] E.Dupuy, T.N.Dupuy, op.cit., p. 84.
[156] B.Bar-Kohva, op.cit., p. 156.

the hoplite style, while their formation was termed "phalanx") and supported by his cavalry in a fierce battle. However, when victory seemed certain the retreating enemy collided into a line of charging elephants under the cover of which advanced the Seleucid infantry. Even the arrival of Skopas did not help. Crazed with fear at the sight of these dangerous creatures, the Aetolian horses reared to throw their riders and increasingly led to significant confusion. The elephants broke into the ranks of the infantrymen, crushing and tearing at the poor unfortunates who got in their way. Under the weight of this strike, the Aetolians finally broke formation and rushed to escape. Now the last remnants of Skopas' horsemen lost hope. The battle was lost. Collecting the remaining troops, they managed to break away from the enemy and escape. The tired Seleucid soldiers did not pursue the escaping enemy to aggressively.

The Battle of Panion was the last great battle of the powerful Ptolemaic monarchy. Egypt was plunged into chaos. Alexandria was still to shine for many centuries of wealth and power, but the time as a great military power, however, had pass into history. Thirty-nine years later, Antiochus IV Epiphanes announced he was King of Egypt after capturing Memphis, and besieged Alexandria which only escaped its final fall under threats of Roman deputies.[157] Even earlier, however, in December 190 BCE the Seleucid state, the largest of the existing Hellenistic monarchies also suffered a devastating defeat in battle with the Rome and Pergamon at Magnesia in the Meander. The time for new powers had come.

ARMORED CAVALRY IN THE EAST. In the east, the evolution of armored cavalry formations followed a slightly different path. Before the attack on Parthia, the Dahae Confederation largely consisted of horse archers with only a small heavy contingient, evidenced by the way in which the king was shown on the first Arsacid's coins, and used a typical Scythian tactic which mixed armored and bow formations in one unit.

The formation of such elite units of heavily armored cavalry with significant armored protection for riders and their mounts,[158] started with troops of the Dahae entering Parthia, or during their battles with Andragoras' army just before the invasion. It is possible that is was the influence of their Western Hellenic enemy that they owed the formation of the Arsacid armored corps, the ability to transform the clashes with ancient armies – Greek and Romans – into a kind of equestrian phalanx,

---
[157] E.Dupuy, T.N.Dupuy, op.cit., p. 84.
[158] Then, most likely, the Dahs began supplying their heavy cavalry with metal armor on a larger scale replacing weak and other types of light armor. A very similar process was once the result of battles with the Middle Eastern armies of the Persians and Western Scythians.

the dominant eastern formation continued to be the use of the wedge formation, and the close tactical cooperation with the armored cavalry and horse archers forming both cover and support.

Despite the strong influences the Hellenistic style armies had on the Parthian army as a result of fighting, the Arsacids retained steppe tactics, i.e. the main focus was the development of protective armor, with a greater desire to shield the animals from the arrows of their nomadic enemies than the Sarissa armed infantry and the spears of the cavalry.

Today, on the basis of some vague descriptions in a passage of the ancient historians like Plutarch, for example, it would appear the Arsacid armored cavalry never abandoned their traditional way of conducting an attack, which was used in the event of a clash with an opponent using a large cavalry force, which in practice was the majority of external enemies and all rebel forces from the Dahae clans. On the eastern borders of the Parthian state cavalry never lost its lead role, so it was use in the most effective fighting method used for centuries. Thus, the development of the armored cavalry allowed for the tactical advantage of the Arsacid Army which worked with equal efficiency on all borders, against all enemies.

The Cost of the Equipment, Weapons and Mounts. On the march warriors traveled armored on one horse and on another a pack horse carrying the armor of the rider and the horse which limited them to be recruited from members of the rich, feudal lords and their followers.[159] Obviously, they were the only ones who could afford adequate equipment. In Parthian society, as already mentioned, these people occupied the highest positions, these doyens of the noble clans had the right, among other things, to approve the new rulers of the throne, and according to Pliny, ruled over the principal provinces.[160] They were referred to as "hippeis"[161] which is an exact and literal translation of the Persian term "ašvaran" (Parthian 'sb'r") corresponding to the knightly caste, e.i. the Indian class of priests. Roman sources, specifically Justin, just call them free.[162] The same applies to the references in the works of Josephus Flavius, when he writes about the contingent sent by Prince Pakorosa to Jerusalem (J. Flavius, *The Jewish War*, I.XIII.1).

At the same time in the east – the lands of Sogdiana, Kushan Bactria, and on the Sakae nations functioned and developed in a similar manner, forming a legacy back to the old Scythian system of tactics in the

---

[159] А. М. Хазанов, op.cit., p.75.
[160] Z. Haszczyc, op.cit., p. 145.
[161] M. Mielczarek, op.cit., pp. 54-56.
[162] loc. cit.

use of armored cavalry. It was undoubtedly created for mounted combat. The existence of such a method of fighting is clearly evidenced by the eagle plaques or so-called "Royal Pavillion" in Khalchayan.[163]

The Armament of Armored Horsemen of the Central Asian Peoples. With the fall of the Achaemenid Monarchy, we lose the evolutionary development of the native Iranian and Central Asia types of weaponry and protective armor. Compared to the well-known historical look, tactics and history of Hellenistic cavalry, the development of weapons originating in the steppe and intertwined to the old Persian military tradition is not well known to us. For example, during the Hellenic period they do not seem to have abandoned the use of body armor that was so popular among Persian warriors during the Achaemenid period and we only know individual examples of their outfits or finds (i.e. The armor discovered in Ai-Khanoum). At the same time this is limited to the eastern areas of the great empire of the first Seleucids. It seems reasonable to suppose that although they are presented in art only wearing Greco-Macedonian style torso armor, this trend is related to greater prestige of the wearer, not the fact that this was the only kind of armor used on the field of battle. On some Greek coins they are show for example that the rulers in helmets wear the typical Boeotian type helmet used by Alexander's companions, and the scale type eastern armor visible under the chlamys (a short cloak) fastened over the shoulder. Bactrian-Greek soldiers are shown wearing wide trousers tied at the knees and high Thracian shoes. Not much more is known about the development of protective equipment, the evolution of the long sword or war axe, were well known and used by Achaemenid heavy cavalry during the Parthian period to once again in widespread use as weapons of armored cavalry troops.

Plenty of interesting data is provided to us by monuments dated from the second and first centuries BCE, discovered in the burial mound located in the Karadara Basin near Samarkand which were referenced multiple times on bone plaques decorated with magnificent depictions of battle scenes and hunting, in an unusual style, known as the Orlat plaques.

The first shows the clash between two groups of heavily armed warriors on foot and the second showing riders on the hunt. In the eight armored fighting characters at least two different type of armor can be seen. Although they are two separate plaques, they seem characteristic of warrior groups, while some parts (especially their weapons) are shown separately, they were used equally by both bands of warriors. It presents the impression that both fighting forces belong to one closely related

---
[163] Г. А. Пугаченкова, op.cit., pp. 60-75.

group, however, they are not the same tribe.

All warriors, except for two wear helmets, which one can easily recognize as Sakae-Massagetean helmets known from finds in the vicinity of Samarkand and Kysmyči, and similar forms discovered in mounds of the Kuban River basin. The bell-shaped helmet fit snuggly around the skull, but without a nasal strip or any protection for the nose but is slightly higher than the original version of the helmet with a lower section forming cheeks guards. We don't know to what extent the helmet covered the neck, or how it is shaped, because the whole neck is part of the helmet, its design is unknown, but probably with a large armored collar. One can assume that like their predecessors, these helmets have a crescent shaped neck that is undercut to help the movement of the head safely covered by an armored collar. The top of the helmet is provided with a round reinforced plate, or additionally, an eyelet for attaching a horsehair crest to it. The edges of the helmet are bordered with a leather strip cover them. There is no trace of a wool or felt cap sticking out from under them, which was usually worn to soften the stroke of the blow to the head and separate the sun-warmed sheet metal from the scalp. In addition, the shape of the helmet is also visible on other soldiers, but probably it was made of metal scales. The helmets seem to be reproduced in metal, with a typical bell shape and characteristic cheeks. In the case of a scale we are dealing with a central ridge somewhat similar to one found in the burial mound in Gladkowščin. All that was made to allow free movement of the heads inside the collar.

The last of the warriors shown on the right side shows his hair on an uncovered head, which is collected in a knot, matching the description of Serena's horse archers who shot at the Romans at the Battle of Carrhae.

The most remarkable part of all the Orlat armor is the high, standing neck guard, made of linked, probably harden leather straps to protect the neck and collar. Each of them is wearing identical armor, cut out at the front of the chin and in the back high in the middle. The entire interior was quilted probably with a thin leather or other textile. Due to the necessity for such cover, to protect it from blows it can be assumed that these collars formed an integral part of the armor "rigidly" connected to the breastplate. Such collars protected the necks and head from sword cuts, as in the late medieval armor which extended the upper edges of the shoulder pads. It would not be able to withstand an accurately aimed spear thrust even with thick protection.

The differences in the armor is mainly the construction of the breastplate and shoulder protection. You can distinguish the following types of armor belonging to the warriors depicted on the Orlat plaques:

The Armies of Ancient Persia

The first type of breastplate design shows a highly specialized and advanced construction technology which is created from six large, leather or metal plates placed in two vertical rows. They appear to be slightly bent on vertical plane, most likely sewn with a thick thong. All the connecting strips and their rows are covered with an additional band. Such a breastplate provided strong resistance, (especially to arrow shots, but also to pole weapons that slipped through the side slots of the breastplate) while maintaining a certain amount of flexibility necessary for effectively turning away bladed weapons.

The plaque also shows the way of piercing this type of armor, and the know-how with this technique is used, observed in this presentation gives the impression that the artist was well versed in the art of war. One of the warriors looks at the other, wearing a higher type of breastplate with the sword thrust horizontally, so that its sharp point picked a covering in the plate-joint and stuck between the rows thrust into the heart before stepping back. For practical reasons, such a thrust would actually be the most effective tactic, and the use of the sword would be correct. The backplate of the first type of armor was built in the same way as the breastplate. On each arm they attached shoulder guards with long pteruges. Examples for this kind of armor is similar to the second type from the site of Chalchajan.

The second type of breastplate shown on the Orlat plaque is clearly different from the construction of the first. First, the construction makes use of much smaller plates, arranged in eight vertical rows of five. Secondly, it appears that the sides of each row are closer to the center line, running vertically through the middle of the breast, overlapping the previous one. Lastly, they are placed on the same central line, covering the edges of both sides, creating something like an ecktoskeleton. This method of joining rows of tiles does not require additional reinforcing straps. What is most interesting are the examples of the construction to cover the body as much as it did. One is the armor of late Kushan construction in the exact manner of the above, composed of only slightly larger disks, they are also known for the Chalchajan illustrations, even more similar to the armor of the so-called "Breastplate", resembling the appearance of the Eagle's breastplate armor of the Terracotta warriors of the Emperor Qin Shi Huangdi from the Chinese Qin dynasty. Their plates are arranged in the same way, with a similar size and number of plates. The number of rows is only five instead of seven. The armor of the first Emperor of China's army, discovered a little later in the tomb at Xi'an, was also composed from thick riveted leather plates.[164] These breastplates were very popular among the nomadic peoples of China living on the border areas

---

[164] P. Hessler, "Ożywić skarby", *National Geographic*, 10 (25), Październik 2001, p.90.

Coins of the Parthian rulers - Fraates II (L), Orodes I (C), Mithridates III (R). (Parthian kings, http // www.livius.org / pan-Oct / Parthia / kings.html).

Frieze with representations of the captured arms from the temple of Athena Polias in Pergamon (from E. Polito, Fulgentibus armis ..., *fig. 27)*

Images of armor on Kushan coins. (according to К. Абдульаев, Armor of ancient Bactria ..., *fig. 7,8,9,10)*

A Greek-bactrian ruler wearing a Beotian helmet and scale armor (from G.A. Пугаченкова, О панцрном вооружении ..., fig. 8)

Hellenistic armor composed of solid breastplate, helmet and covers hands bronze figurine from Syria - Louvre. (M. Mielczarek, Cataphracti and Clibanari *..., fig. 16)*

The head of the armored Kushan - clay sculpture from Halchan (Г. А. Пугаченкова, О панцрном вооружении..., fig.11)

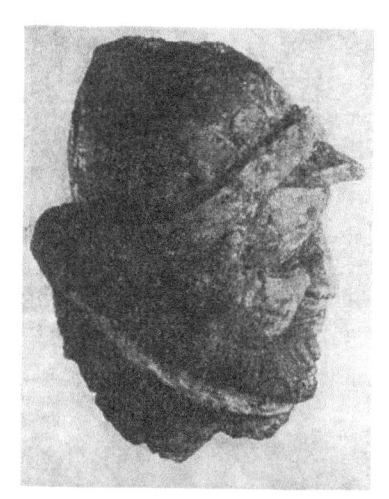

The Armies of Ancient Persia

Armor of the soldier of the "Terracotta Army" of the emperor Szy - Huang from the Ch'in dynasty - the end of the 3rd century BC (from M. Granet, Chinese Civilization.)

The Armies of Ancient Persia

The second type of armor from Halchan, described by K. Abdulaev Sakom - clay sculpture. (Г. А. Пугаченкова, О панцрном вооружении ..., fig. 10)

How to use a long spear. Images from Preslaw (a), Pantikapajon (b), Ilurat (c). (by A. D. H. Bivar, Cavalry equipment and tactics on the Euphrates frontier, fig. 3, M. Mielczarek, Cataphracti and Clibanari ..., fig. 22.19)

- 223 -

where they probably received them from the Xi'an Army. The first type of armor design seems to be characteristic of warriors attacking from the left side, the second type is only used by one of the warriors, namely cavalry warriors fighting on the front line attacking from the right.

The second of the examples shown on the Orlat plaques is of a different type of construction in terms of design part of the armor, two strips are also present. The first type used for both type of breastplates was built like laminar fashion. It consists of large plates, probably sewn on straps. In the second they were sewn on the breastplate and edged. The edging was sewn for protection on the breastplate. In both examples, they were covered from the shoulder to the hand with leather. Armor protected from the shoulder to the elbow which was liable to the greatest risk to injury. This type of protective armor resembles the type used by Chinese cavalry armor from the early "Spring and Autumn" period. On the plaque, it is not clear the way the armor is covering the elbow. In order to bend, however, as you might suppose it would have to be protected by several smaller plates to enable free movement of the arm to defend themselves during a fight. The straps or sleeves were attached to the breastplate on the arms with straps or cords and a complete cover of this type give you greater protection while maintaining maximum maneuverability.

The second type of arm guard is similar to the second type of breastplate, which seems to be a complete set, but used as body armor as the first type. Such a sleeve is composed of small overlapping plates covering from top to bottom (or visa versa), which again makes the solution a bit like the construction of Chinese armor. They are pictured with an armored sleeve with horizontal plates connected with shoulder straps like Chinese armor with vertical ropes. Like the first type, only the upper part of the arm, while the lower part is uncovered. This type of arm protection (called manica) provides better mobility; however, it is heavier than the first one.

The edges of both types of manica are like the inside of the mattress, i.e. padded with leather or fabric to avoid scaping the body, it is possible that patches are sewn into the sleeve which covered the arm. Although the arm was protected by armor to the wrist, fighting warriors do not use any other types of shields, gloves or even extensions of the sleeve, reaching to the fingers as were often found in Far Eastern armor. A very interesting part of the protective armor of the warriors shown on the Orlat plaque are the depiction of leg armor. They are made of very long pieces of armor reaching to mid-calf very similar to Achaemenid scale armor, used by the Sakae and later by the coats of Turkish nomads. In general, the "Orlat" armor coats are similar to these. Indeed, they are made similar to the slightly shorter ones shown on a ceramic vessel from Humbuz-Tepe dated from the 4th to the beginning of the 3rd century BCE, i.e. in the case of the "Orlat" armor we view this as a further development in such armor.

To protecting the legs of the rider, the lower part of the breastplate was edged by leather strips, similar to those described with the breastplate and straps that are found on type two. Some are composed of elongated plates, arranged vertically. The second type is made from larger, square plates. Both types of this protection are connected using long narrow hooks to improve flexibility of the whole structure. The difference in their design lays in the fact that, in the first type of "cuisse"[165] with horizontal stripes of narrow plates and large circles are suspended in an eastern way on thick vertically run cords while in the second case they are stitched together with narrow connecting straps that sometimes connect vertically, sometimes horizontally in rows of large plates. The plates had to overlap so that each covered the left edge of the next in the first type, and fish scales from top to bottom (or vice versa), in the second example. I contrast you can attribute this specific cuisse to the warring states. The first type is predominantly used by warriors attacking on the right side of the line, the second type on the attackers left. Some are composed on longitudinal plates, some vertically positioned. The second type is made of larger plates, so of which were square.

This rigid and durable piece of armor can be secure to protect not only the legs of the rider, but also the side of the horse from enemy attacks, which based on the relief, does not show any other type of armor on the chest or the head. In one case - a warrior trying to jump down from his mount which shows a "cuisse" visible on the embroidered trousers.

On the left thigh of the same rider, a scabbard is visible in the sheath which is a short dagger worn on a separate belt in a style used by the Sarmatians, or the tomb of a warrior recently discovered in Tilja Tepe.[166]

The protective armor of the cavalrymen shown on the Orlat plaques, despite dating from a later age (approximately the first to second centuries BCE)[167] is a representation of another development in a line of armor, which radically differs from contemporary evolution of Seleucid heavy cavalrymen.

It seems that the traditions continued from the Sake-Massagetae was strictly from the steppe character. Compared to the armor of the Syr-

---

[165]a piece of armor or padding for protecting the thigh.
[166]К. Абдулаев, "Armour of ancient Baktria", A. Invernizzi (ed.), *In the land of the Gryphons. Papers on Central Asian Archeology in Antiquity,* Firenze 1995.., p. 169.
[167]IBID, pp. 158-160.

ian armored cavalry, the armor from the Orlat Plaque shows a warrior who fights on a horse with a comparable level of protection against arrows and pole weapons, they also represent a similar state of technical advancement, but their path of development went in completely different directions conditioned by local traditions and the types of material available. Out of necessity, in this case, we have a long and uninterrupted Greek influence on the development of armor that goes beyond the influence of the Hellenistic monarchy, in the area of the steppe from Central Asia to Siberia and China.

If we have to acknowledge this influence on the evolution of the weapons of Iranian-speaking people on the far-eastern steppes, it is worth carefully looking at the example of the armor for the Sakae heavy cavalry.

The primary weapon of the warriors from the Orlat plaque was probably spears and swords. Both group of combatants use long spears, however, they are used among the fighters on the left side of the scene. We can distinguish two types of weapons, namely the old type known in Asia for centuries as a short spear with long spear points, and a long spear similar to the Greek kontos, used by the commanders of these warriors. When they used the tactics of the steppes, the primary tacics of which were discussed previously, a long spear was only used in the first and maybe the second rank whose task was to deliver the breaking blow to the line, where it shattered or drove a pocket deep into the enemy line that it would be impossible to extract they would be abandoned. When close combat started, they used short spears, drawn swords and afterward spiked axes.

As you can see from the images in this text, the Sakae armored cavalry used heavy spears, with massive, probably iron-tipped short spearheads in a diamond shaped head. At the other end of the long spear of the commander, the Greeks placed a metal spike. Unfortunately, this is very important for dating the usage, of the weapon covers the end of the "Standard era". Interestingly, among the warriors on the right side of the illustration, they do not show spears in use, and only one falling or jumping off a slain horse has one. The head of his spear is broken off and the owner is forced to use a sword. This figure, as well as his antagonist is shown with extraordinary realism and drama. The body of the warriors shown, and especially the position of the legs shows him jumping off the back of a dead horse as he is almost pinned to the ground by a powerful thrust of the enemy's spear. When you look at the presentation, you can almost hear the hiss of the arrowhead piercing the armor and feels the power of the blow that knocked the soldier off his feet. The spear was held in both hands by the attacker about 2/3 of its length from the head, strongly bend down by the weight.

In the extraordinary detail in the field of this military art shown by the artist on the Orlat plaque demonstrates the best place one should hit a rider with a spear. The blow was directed toward the stomach, more or less in the middle of the heavy cavalryman's body, making its momentum and strength to maximize the force of the spearpoint to pierce the armor. Additionally, the Scythian and Sakae armor often wore an armored belt for increased mobility as they often missing armor.[168]

Using the above technique for striking a blow, it was easy, however, to break the shaft of the weapon, which as one might expect was used almost exclusively by armored cavalry fighting in the old steppe wedge formation with the support of horse archers, in addition to the heavy cavalry of the nomadic people. The first line of those units was known in Greek as *cataphracti* and in Roman writing as *clibanarii*. If the armored units wanted to strike against the enemy (especially heavy and fast cavalry) and still protect his weapons against damage he struck the enemy on the upper part of the body, not using the full weight of the weapon and without a deep penetration of the tip. Such an attack is brilliantly shown for example in the relief of Hormuzd II in Naksh-I Rustam. The king is shown attacking the throat, not the stomach of the horsemen who are his adversaries.[169] In the same way, although with somewhat different weapons, as evidenced by Arrian,[170] spear fighting for the entire battle by Alexander the Great's Companions and the Hellenistic cavalry "Comrade" units.

Returning to the Orlat Plaque, the system positioning the warrior's spear to pierce the opponent leaping from the dead horse indicates that to increase the blow at the last minute he made an extra push with his hands, and then he put his whole weight against the shaft. This technique of wielding polearms in Central Asia has been known side the end of the IV and III century BCE (the image on the dish from Koj-Krylgan Kala) was widely practiced and is even visible on images from Preslav (now Bulgaria), Panticapaeum, Ilurat, many reliefs in Iran (Naksh-I Rustam, Tang-e Sarvak, Firuzbad) and especially when using a horse with a long spear whose prototype was (at least in Central Asia) the Macedonia xyston or Sarissa.

The technique of holding a weapon with two hands not only improves and strengthens the grip, but more importantly allows for "fencing" with polearms and deflecting your opponents spearhead before de-

---

[168] E.V.Černenko, Voennoe delo... p.6.
[169] A. D. H. Bivar, *Cavalry equipment and tactics on the Euphrates frontier*, Paper delivered at the symposium on „Byzantium and Sasanian Iran", Dumbarton Oaks 26, 1972, p. 288.
[170] F. Arrian, op.cit., p. 22.

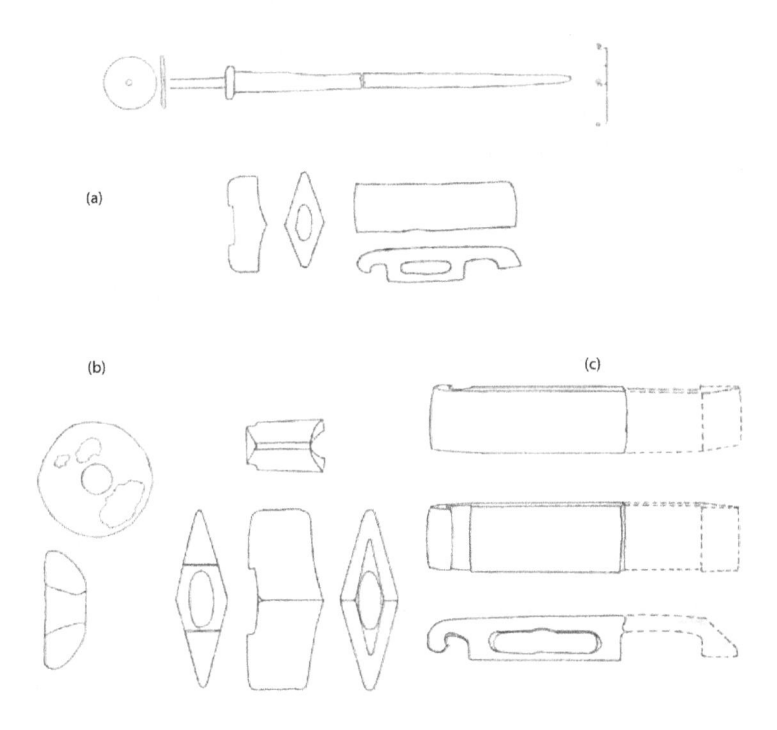

Sarmatian sword from Kalmykov (a), jade pommels and sword guards from Orlat (b), Mongolia (c) (from А.М. Хазанов, Очерки военного дела Сарматов, Tab. 9, Й. Ильясов, Русанов, A Study on the Bone Plates from Orlat, Tab. 3, 14.)

The Armies of Ancient Persia

livering your own blow. The art of war in the far east was not only fought with spears, but also with those who carried "halberds". An active style of fighting with such a weapon is presented by armored warriors depicted on the painting from the wall of the tomb of Sanshitsu-Zuka in Toung k'ou (Korea).[171] The long spear was rarely used against horses, but the handier short spear which could even be used in melees.

The secondary weapon for warriors on both sides was usually a sword with a design that included a cross between a heavy double-edged sword and a saber. There was a ratio of the size of the weapon to the size of the wielder, which was about 1 meter in length, or which was approximately 30-40 cm was made up of a long handle. It seems to have been made of wood, which has not been preserved in archeological finds. This seems to have been of considerable size in the shape of an inverted cone, which was separate from the hand guard. The pommel as can be inferred by the evidence acted as a counterweight which was a thick metal plate, or as in the case of tomb II from the Orlat of jade, which was mounted on the end of the handle. An analogy of this pommel, for example, can be seen in the construction of the Sarmatian sword from Kalmykova[172] and the heads of Chinese swords.

The construction of such a grip had a positive effect on the weight distribution of the sword, and consequently on the remarkable "acceleration" on the development of the weapon. Conditions in antiquity made a considerable shift of balance away from the bow. This is actually the only examples of Sarmatian weapons, the only remaining melee weapons from the equipment on ancient armored cavalry had such "weighted swords. The extended handle, however, had another important advantage in that it allowed the use of both hands for the heavy weapon. This immediately recalls the similar use of the fighting technique with the Japanese tachi sword.

The width of the warrior's swords shown on the Orlat Plaque show that from about 2/3's of their length it gently narrows into a thrusting point. The center of the blade had a diamond cross section running the length strengthening the structure and ending slightly before the point. Such a blade had to be made with great skill to the best performance to push its ability for use without losing its ability to cut. The strength is generated from the power of both hands, the best proof of this is the construction of large helmets and armored collars. The accuracy of the artist in the shape of the weapon is testified by the example of the handguard whose outline can easily be recognized by the sword fragment found at

---

[171] A. D. H. Bivar, op.cit., p. 286.
[172] А. М. Хαзанов, op.cit., p. 143.

the same barrow No. 2[173] as the "Orlat Plates."

Such swords were worn with a long wooden or leather scabbard with fur inside. There was a heavy metal tip and a rectangular piece on the throat as well as a scabbard mount. Similarly, jade examples were almost identical to the "Orlat" as jade fittings indicating a far eastern origins of these parts of the metal weapons. These relics, very similar to the "Orlat" original from areas of Inner Mongolia, Southern Russia, China and Korea, as well as the earliest examples of them combined with the Chinese weapons of the Han era.

Below the throat of the scabbard there was an additional ring-shaped fitting. The neck throat also has a sharp triangular cutout shape on its side, matching the grove in the upper part of the handguard, which has a pear-shaped projection. The sword was hung on a special sling attached to the main belt. This construction together with the method of placing the mount indicates the steppe origin of its design. The nearest similar example of Sarmatian scabbards and sword belts (Old Weimar – Mound No.16), Gandharian, Korean (excavations from Yeytsa) and Chinese from the period of the Han dynasty. In all of the above-mentioned cases, we are dealing with examples of spiked weapons rather than sidearms, as evidenced by the long narrow ones with strengthen ridges. If we take into account, however, that these relics are two hundred or even four hundred years younger than the Orlat presentation, we can classify them as representations of one of the two evolutionary paths of steppe melee weapons, namely those developed to pierce the heavy leather armor of cavalrymen, a classic saber shape and the others leading to the development of the Parthian-Sassanid heavy cavalry sword.

The third category of hand weapons used by the "Orlat" warriors was the war spike/war hammer such as the "nadziak". A soldier is seen equipped with one of them in the upper right corner of the scene. The fact that he does not have a sword, and at the waist hangs an empty scabbard, indicates that the spiked axe and nadziak was used as a weapon of last resort. The nadziak from the Orlat plate had a long, slightly bent down, sharp beak, and on the opposite side a round hammer. An interesting pair of iron combat nadziak were discovered in a Scythian burial mound or Tocharian in Suglug-Chem in the republic of Tuva. Five nadziak were discovered including the two (from he mounds of Suglug-Chem II) made of bronze, one of which was approximately 20cm long with the head that is reminiscent of the horseman's war spike shown on the Orlat plaque.[174] A very similar war spike comes from the Achaemenid site at Deve Hüyük

[173] Й. Ильиасоб, Д. В. Русанов, A study on the Bone Plates from Orlat, Silk Road Art and Archeology, V 1997/1998 *Journal of the Institute of Silk Road Studies,* Kamakura, tab. 14.
[174] В.А. Семенов, *Суглуг-хем и Хайыракан: могильники скифского времени в центрально-тувинскойкотловине,* p. 195.

which could indicate the spread of this weapon on the Scythian steppes and Iran during this period.

The long handle of the Orlat war spike is wrapped with a wide thong or rope to improve the grip. The strength with which you could use such a weapon is splendidly captured in the Orlat scene. You can clearly see it fatally stabs a warrior with it, but before hand the warrior is struck between the eyes while half falling out of the saddle. The hammer breaks through the helmet which was probably made of bronze. It can be assumed that iron helmets began to appear on the steppes at this time and the metal plates of Parthian could not protect from such a blow.

The most commonly used weapon of the "Orlat" warrior's equipment for long-distance was bows. This has already been described in detail in the section concerning horse archer formations, but to briefly recap: They are one of the first, if not the first examples of the asymmetric version of the reflexive bow. Based on the length of the siyat, it will provide significant force while maintaining long distance penetrating power. These bows were probably in response to the "archery" tribes of the Great Steppe whose enemy warriors spread the use of protective armor, especially leather, bone, horn or lamellar from hoofs because they were commo materials on the steppe.[175] The Orlat plaque magnificently shows the arrows used for these bows. They had large, somewhat exaggerated triangular arrowheads with barbs, (typical and well-known from Scythian graves in the Middle East and Central Asia up to the borders of China)[176] very long shafts with feathers to stabilize the ends. Although these arrows resemble similar ones found in Taht-e Sangin, they also resemble other arrows from Chinese Turkestan and the Parthians at Dura-Europos.

For the depiction of warriors on the Orlat plaque, especially those charging in the first rank the main weapons were swords and long spears, while bows were a support weapon, used before the start of the attack as fire preparation, or perhaps in retreat to deter pursuit. The image clearly shows the commanders of the warriors for both sides have their bodyguards accompanying them in the charge and shielded them with bow fire. Both (the commander and his bodyguard) do not show a difference between cavalry and infantry as they are armed with same weapons as the second row, wearing identical armor fighting on equal footing. All these facts confirm the idea, that in the case of the soldiers depicted on Orlat Plaques are a highly professional army resulting from the evolution of the Scythian military system. It is on the steppes of Central Asia that a variation of protective armor was made by Sakae and Scythian tribes on

---
[175] А. М. Хαзαнов, op.cit., p. 58.
[176] В.А. Семенов, op.cit, p.192.

The Armies of Ancient Persia

(a)

(b)

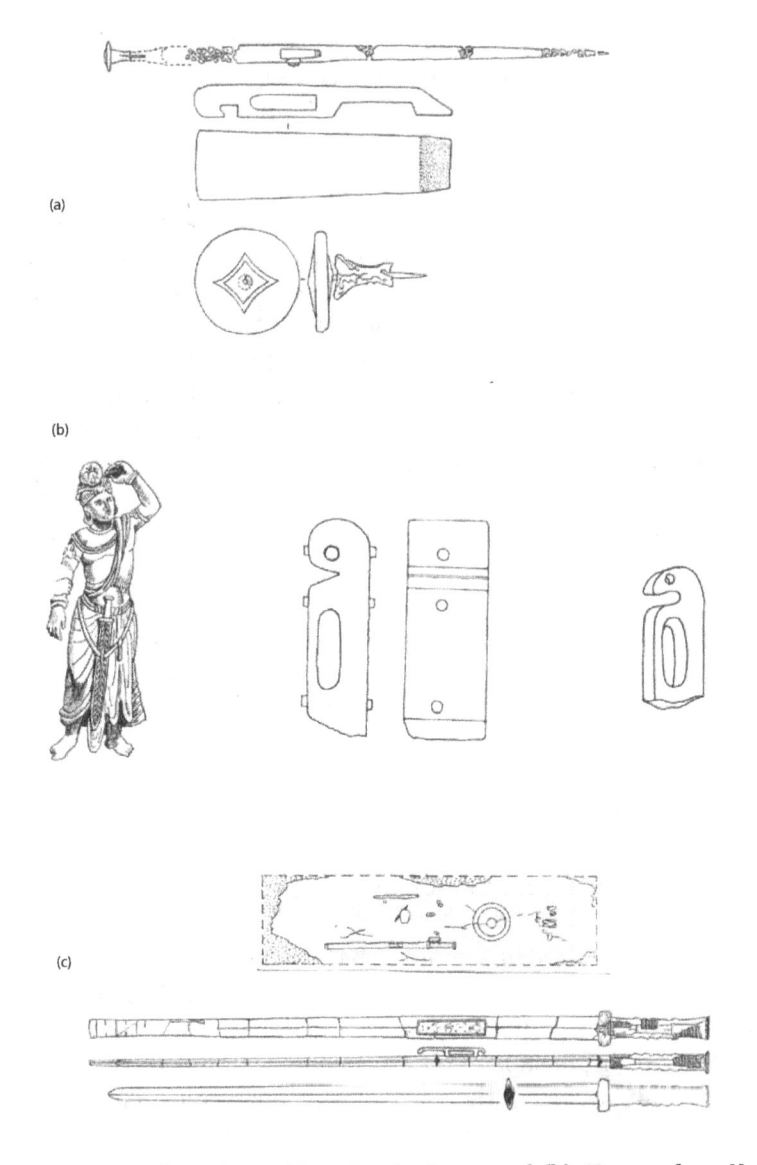

(c)

Sword guards Alt Waimar (a), a Gandarian sword (b), Korean from Yeyts excavations (C). (according to А. М. Хазанов, Очеркі военного дела Сарматов, Tab. 14, 15.7)

The Armies of Ancient Persia

their borders, and later with the Kushan.

An extremely interesting analysis and interpretation of the tactics from the Orlat Plaques is discussed in the article, "Heroic Fights and Dying Heroes – The Orlat Plaque Battles and the Roots of Sogdian Art" by M. Mode.[177]

As a result of his detailed analysis of this presentation he has stated (apart from dating it himself to a later period) that the images placed on the lining of a belt found in Barrow II at Orlat is part of a larger presentation made elsewhere and copied by craftsmen making the belt. Attention is drawn to a single warrior on foot on the upper right corner of the scene, and four horses behind a group of warriors on the left side of the scene. He identifies three of them as unattended reserve horses for the cavalrymen on the left, the one in a harness as a horse ridden by another warrior. Based on the analysis of the characters, the weapons they used and fired he reconstructed the course of the fight. After minor adjustments it can be summarized as follows: two groups of warriors are battling. Coming from the left side (let's call it the western side) there is only cavalry, coming from the right side (east) are most likely four foot soldiers led by two riders. The clash begins in typical nomadic fashion of preliminary archery. The assistant commander of the western force shoots an arrow that hits a horse in the neck of the eastern force at the bottom. The infantry commander hits the western commander in the leg. Both sides then charge. An arrow shot by an archer of the western force, hit the commander of the eastern force in the eye. The third arrow finally knocks his mount to the ground. Trying to save himself from falling he breaks his spear and draws his sword to defend himself from his opponent's blows. At the same time, both commanders meet. The leader of the southern part of the western forces with a much longer "Greek" spear wounds his opponent. Archers on both sides pull their bows. At the same time the northern wings collide. The two commanders stuck each other passing at the gallop. The horse of the northern commander of the eastern army is killed by the spear of his adversary, however, the eastern commander did not remain still and smashed his sword into the helmet of his opponent. At the same time, the northern commander of the western army clashed with the assistant commander of his opponent, who is now on foot. With a powerful blow from above on horseback he lost or breaks his sword. The he goes for the war spike hanging on his belt. The northern commander of the western wing stabs him with a thrust of the sword, but the war spike pierces his helmet and skull at the same time. The clash seems unresolved because more lines of warriors are

---

[177] M. Mode, *Heroic fights and dying heroes - The Orlat Plaque battles and the roots of Sogdian Art*, Çrân und Ançrân Webfestschrift Marshak 2003.

seen coming. The eastern army's infantry, however, seem to have less of a chance of victory in the fight against the western horsemen.

This reconstruction of the battle fits within the assumptions of Scythian tactics. Based on the appearance of the weapons we can conclude that the two warring sides were most likely Sakae or Scythians from the tribes of Sakae. The presence of a large number of infantry among the warriors of the eastern army seems to indicate, however, their origin from areas where cavalry had much less military importance, probably from the mountainous areas in eastern Bactria and Sogdiana. This could explain the large number of eastern design of their weaponry.

Heavy armor fragments have been discovered from Bactria dating from halfway through the II century BCE, although the dating is not entirely certain to be Hellenistic, was found sitting in the so-called vault in the city of Ai-Khanoum. The destruction of this great center of Hellenistic culture is dated from approximately 145 BCE. Discovered in the "vault" along with the remains of scaly horse armor, which was constructed in a similar way the Seleucid army made armor for the arms (in this case to cover their legs) which was formed from strips of metal arranged and assembled in such a way to form a reinforced sleeves and legs. In the western tradition, however, arms and legs were usually combined with a cuirass or lamellar armor, which made the body protected by a heavy armor shell.[178] The armor is further proof of Iranian influence of the Hellenistic Bactria's military techniques, which also gives an idea of the technical level of the Greek-Bactrian army from the time of its greatest glories and victories won in India. It would appear that intermingling of military traditions is a long process, with a few minor exceptions the best parts of these are dominated by its reflection in Greek art. As for the armor of Ai-Khanoum, however, the claims of Greek-Bactrian origin should be carefully considered. Although the technical features show a link with Greco-Bactrian military traditions, it was discovered in a room that contains items from the early Kushan period.[179] The armor itself appears similar to ones worn by warriors depicted on the frieze at the "Royal Pavilion" in Chalchajan, however, it was not built until the I century AD and probably show Kushan military technology which was subject to the long-term influence of Greco-Bactria and Sakae.

Although a great group of clay sculptures was discovered in the ruins belonging to the Kushans, the palace complex was built in Chalchajan, seems to have been built late in the reign of King Wimy Tatko (75-110 AD), which according to K. Abdulaev was built a little earlier in at the

---
[178] К. Абдульаев, "Armour of ancient Baktria", A. Invernizzi (ed.), *In the land of the Gryphons. Papers on Central Asian Archeology in Antiquity*, Firenze 1995., p. 169.
[179] К. Абдульаев, op.cit., p. 172.

The Armies of Ancient Persia

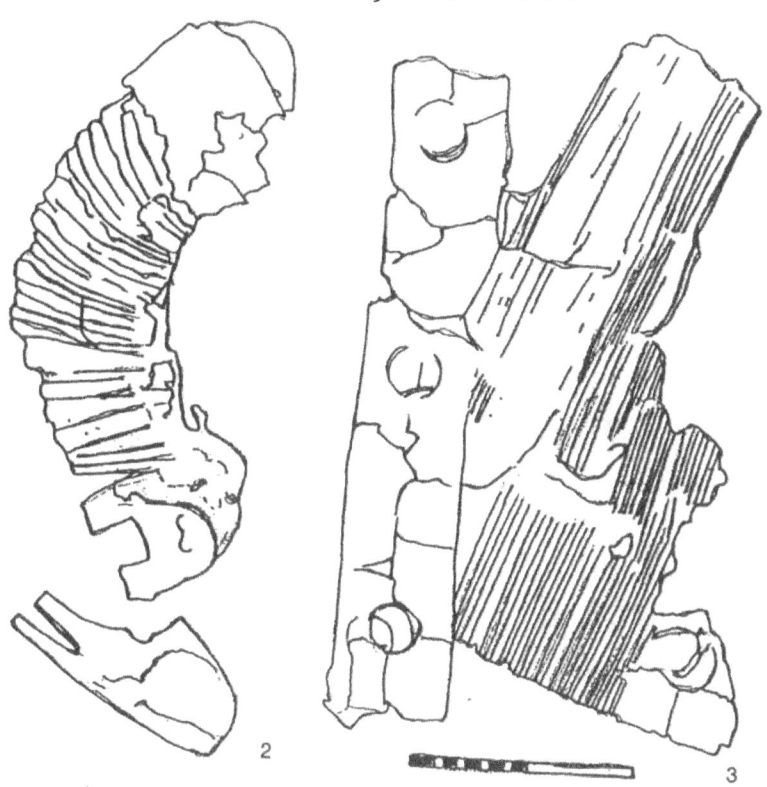

Armor from Ai - Khanoum. (from К. Абдульаев, Armor of ancient Bactria, *fig. 2)*

Armored Kushan cavalryman protected in attack by archers - clay sculptures from the so-called The Royal Pavilion in Chalkian (from M. Mielczarek, Cataphracti and Clibanari ..., *fig. 14)*

The Armies of Ancient Persia

The first type of Khusan armor - attention should be paid on the remarkable similarity of the breastplate to the construction breastplates type I from the Eagle's performance (from G. A. Pugačenkova, Sculpture of Khusan, fig. 61)

Details of breastplate type A from Khusan (from G.A.Pugachchenko, Скульптура Халчаяна, fig. 62)

Statue of the Kuszanów king- Mathura. (according to J. Harmatt (ed.),History of civilizations of Central Asia, fig 257)

A narrow sword on the king's belt Wasudeva I on the obverse of his coin (from Г. А. Пугаченкова, О панцрном вооружении ..., fig. 3)

Bust of a warrior in a collarbone and collapsed on the back of the head Solid, mattified inside a helmet resembling slightly Corinthian helmets - Old Termez III - IV CE original (a), redraw (b) (according to К. Абдульаев, Armor of ancient Bactria ..., fig. 11,5)

foundation of this powerful monarchy, when they battled the Yue tribes for lands that belonged to the Kushan of the Sakae living in Central Asia before their arrival.[180]

Analyzing the weapons and armor represented in the clay figures gives the impression that the artist intended to show some "mythical" events, or from the "heroic era", he did so in a manner commonly used, i.e. in medieval Europe, using contemporary costumes, weapons and armor. It is this "transfer of reality" that can explain the significant modernization of Chalchajan armor in such terms vs the primitive armor shown on the Orlat plaques. As has already been explained, this does not matter as much as the long-lasting influence of the Greco-Bactrian traditions. Iranian influences are reflected in the adoption of the tubular coverings of the arms and legs, and perhaps the sophisticated use of horse armor that arrived from the far-eastern steppes by the Tochar warriors.

Among the examples of the representative armor from Chalchajan are two types distinct from each other. The first belong strictly to the Kushan, wearing the armor of rulers or deities as represented on coins, which is constructed similarly to the second type of body armor shown on the Orlat Plaques. The breastplate, however, is composed of five vertical rows of large square plates. Three of these rows were most certainly placed on the chest, composed of six plates, two are located on the sides on only three examples. A cross of two rows overlap, meeting in the middle, covering a central line that runs down the chest, similar to armor type II "from Orlat" or the armor from the Terra Cotta Army of Shih Huang. The arm plates of the Chalchajan armor, however, have additional overlapping edges which aligned to the surface of the breastplate and strengthened the whole construction, being curved in the same manner as Roman roof tiles. The individual horizontal rows are not unlike the second type of Orlat armor hung on thongs. It is very difficult to say if we are dealing with an ancient form of Orlat armor or the development of this style.

The lower part of the Kushan warrior's armor below the belt was made of large square plates, similar to those on the first type of "Orlat" armor. This takes the form of a short, split skirt, reaching halfway to the thigh, an armored skirt. The loss of protection by shortening the skirt is compensated by the introduction of segmented leg armor. In addition to the long narrow strips there are also large square tiles. Manica (armored sleeve) and armored leggings was technology known from the Hellenistic era and armor discovered in Ai-Khanoum. Similarly, the appropriate parts of the later, as with the Chalchajan segments that form the limbs

---

[180]К. Абдульаев, "Nomadism in Central Asia,A. Invernizzi" (ed.), *In the land of the Gryphons- Papers on Central Asian Archeology in Antiquity*, Firenze 1995, pp. 158-160.

overlap from top to bottom, as a result of the fear that sword cuts come down from the top and not the bottom. As a result of the better properties of this type of armor, the old style manica shown in the Orlat presentation had to be abandoned.

The head and neck of the Kushan warriors are protected by a protruding, shallow collar with an identical construction to the rim of the collar of the "Orlat" armor, but maybe only slightly lower. They were well protected on the neck and shoulder from the blows of sharp weapons. This set of armor described includes simple round helmets with embosses or equipped with a reinforced strip on the edge. They were worn with a felt cap, fragments of which form a visor protruding from the forehead and along the cheeks.

The second type of armor shown on the Chalchajan frieze is strikingly reminiscent of a type of "Orlat" armor. It has been interpreted as the protective armor of the Kushan's enemy, the Sakae. There is not Sakae armor from the century BCE, but rather it is known from coins of Indo-Sakae monarchs as evidenced by the short skirt armor introduced in place of the long-coat like Orlat examples. This armor still probably had stiff armored collars, however, they have broken off as was very easy with clay sculptures.

The main figure shown at the "Royal Pavilion" at Chalchajan shows an armored rider, charging with the support of three mounted archers. From the frieze we know the main weapon was a heavy long spear that they used in a similar fighting technique as the kopia. As to the details, however, we can not say anything for certain, because the example is largely based on reconstruction. While the figures of the warriors and the representation of their clothes have survived because of the size of the figure, the copies of the weapons are entirely reconstructed and in the case of the bows, unfortunately, not in the right way.

The secondary weapons were long swords, though here too, the majority of these are known from the work of artists, for example shown on the stone statue of King Kanishka I. The sovereign is shown with a large heavy, metal bound club, and hanging at his waist with a long, narrow double-edged sword with a short handle as well as a belt that almost hangs to the ground which is about one meter in length. A very similar sword is found on coins of King Vasudeva I. The shape of the weapon does not look much like the ones used by the Parthians and Sassanids. Kanishka's weapon is more similar to swords known from excavations in Korea, and the tapering blade is pointed indicating that it was more likely used for thrusting than slashing.

The rider from Chalchajan is covered with protective armor, made in three parts, very much like Parthian horse armor. The body of the animal is protected by a kind of armor barding of sewn metal scales of equal size, with rounded lower edges. They are remarkably reminiscent of barding discovered by M. Rostovtzeff at Dura-Europos. A separate piece of armor stands, tied together with a hood covering the head and scales covering the horses neck. What is extremely interesting is that the plates are sewn inversely to the technical requirements, or the rounded edges down. This could have however, been given to a specific artistic license, you cannot see it on the scales because there is no sign of stitching, riveting, etc. that can provide a reality of such a presentation. It is clear that the construction of that armor is extremely "sensitive" to the thrust of a spear in the front, the scales would have titled backwards exposing the base to potential puncture. Last, the smallest part of the horse's armor was extensive in a completely covered head with tiny scales arranged in a similar way as a cap in reverse. It has cut-outs for eyes and ears as well as exposed nostrils. Unfortunately, not much more than that can be made about the construction of the described armor except all theories about the type of scales used an undercoat, undercoat techniques or the methods of connecting individual parts.

Combat tactics used by Kushan warriors is depicted in the central panel of the "Royal Pavilion" very reminiscent of the Sakae tactics, as known from the scene on the bone belt buckle from Orlat. Armored cavalrymen probably fought in the first line of the formation, shielded and supported by several mounted archers. The skirmishers, however, unlike Sakae warriors did not have armor, were much more exposed to potential blows for swords and arrows. Individually, they could not be the equal of armored opponents. Their combat value rapidly increased amidst the crush and confusion of the battlefield, in which the best weapons proved to be daggers and short swords. An armored or unarmored warrior could receive an unexpected thrust, which could not be protected by the heaviest armor.

The Kushan style was much more mobile than the Sakae wedges. It is also possible that they had much greater "firepower", because it consisted of several archers per armored warrior. Horse archers could also hit as a high-speed wave, known from the large-scale tactics of the Turco-Tartar people, preceding the main attack, as well easily outmaneuvering (outflank, etc) heavy and slow enemy troops. The Sakae, rather visa-versa, sought to give weight to the formation and to strengthen its impact as a force at the expense of its mobility. All these characteristics of the Kushan battle groups, symbolically illustrates the fact of placing up to three archers in armor and show armor as the most important attribute of the figures on the throne scene. The Kushan's armored men seem examples of clibanarii, as well as horse barding as with the Parthians, which probably served to protect the animals from sword blows, spears and dense formations during battles fought between nomadic horse archers.

You can easily tell that swords and armor used by Sakae and Kushan, have distinct features from the Parthians and Sarmatians. This can be explained by distinct Far Eastern influences, and more specifically the Chinese. On the basis of such clear difference and components of Far Eastern elements of their weapons, they should be separated, into a separate eastern group.

The situation with the armored units in the western areas of the western steppes, west of the Caspian Sea was occupied mostly by a number of Sarmatian tribes, and Iran under the rule of the Arsacids. In this area the armor was predominantly made of small metal scales and armor which in Sarmatian areas were usually combined with chain mail.

In the I and II centuries AD, there were no major changes taking place in Central Asia regarding armor or tactics. The apogee of its power was reached under the rule of King Kanishka I, of Kushan. The equipment and types of armor used by the armored cavalrymen is shown on the coins of the rulers of this powerful empire. They are dominated by images of figures wearing armor that is not that different from the Chalchajan figures. They consisted of a breastplate – sometimes scale, sometimes composed of three vertical rows of large plates, there were even bronze armor in the outline of a muscled torso – undoubtably with a distant echo of Greek influence. The latter type, despite the archaic appearance possessed several undeniable advantages appreciated by both Alexander III, the Great and probably the armored horsemen of the Kushan King. First of all, despite the rigidity, it protected the most vulnerable parts of the breast and stomach to blows, especially during an attack with the kopia, while the opponent is using the same weapon. In addition to the practical benefits of the cuirass, it came through contact with the legendary Javans (Mycenaean Greeks) an unflagging prestige value of particularly important figures placed on coins. At the bottom edge of the breastplate, just like those shown on the clay sculptures of Chalchajan, they wear knee length aprons made of large metal plates or scales. Under them there were the traditional tubular armored leggings mail leggings, decorated with something like rivets or beads. Likewise, the manica shield the arms without shoulder pads, coming in from just under the breastplate. A prominent collar of the older type armor was transformed into a kind of clavicle or collar (as on Vasudeva II's coins) still made of metal plates. Only some seem to be one solid part, such as the clavicle found that dates from the III – IV centuries AD, on a fragment of a sculpture from Old Termez. It is an extremely interesting position that it resembles the armor discovered in Czirik-Rabat. But, perhaps we should confirm the dating on these two objects. The figure shown on the sculpture at Termez does not have the head clearly visible, but it does have an extremely interesting type of helmet. It is very similar to the Greek Corinthian type helmet. The figure shows the hair piled up or arranged with it parted over the forehead. If we are dealing with the real helmet and not an imitation of a Greek sculpture, it must be a further development of a version of the Sakae helmets with large cheek pieces.

It is possible that the abandonment of fixed collars was associated with the gradual movement towards lighter swords designed to use more for thrusting, than a powerful stroke to "remove the head from the neck". Such a sword-saber, for example, is seen on coins on the waist of Vasudeva II.

This would be the representative image of the warriors from the III century BCE until the III century AD of the Iranian Arsacids and Sassanid Arabs in the north and est. Soon again, however, new waves of tribal steppe nomads would flood in from those areas. The glory days of mobile and aggressive horse archers were back again.

The Heavy Cavalry of the Arsacids. Although the Dahae cavalry developed along the same tactical and technical lines as those of the Scythian tribes on the Great Steppe, their short but difficult fight against the eastern tribes of the powerful Seleucid and the Sakae warriors influenced the strategy and equipment of the Arsacids. In these changes, however, the tactics of nomadic origin prevailed over those of foreign influence. Though the need to fight different types of enemy troops was known to us from descriptions in Roman sources who noted the differences between the heavy cavalry of the steppe people, i.e. the armored Sakae[181] and Parthian cavalry units – both of these units were assumed to be similar to each other.

One of the oldest examples of armor of the first Arsacid's cavalry, was the armor discovered in the so-called "Square Building" in old Nis (Mithradatkirt), not far from the current town of Ashgabad in Turkmenistan. In fact, it is impossible to reconstruct the whole suit of armor. Within this find, two complex fragments stand out of this group. In the first instance, it is 13 long, flat lamellar pieces, including 7 pieces with a length of 6.5 cm long and more than 1 cm wide. Unfortunately, only two are preserved in their entirety and 6 pieces 5 cm long and a width the same of the first. All the armor has a hole at one end for sewing a leather strap or cord. In the case of the second, the most interesting fragments of armor,

---

[181] Although it is not entirely certain, everything seems to indicate that the illustrations on the Orlat plaques reflect the reality of was among the Sakae tribes.

is composed of a plate 6 by 3 cm embossed with reinforcement along the long axis, and small identical piece overlapping by a piece of the second identical scale. Among the scale armor from the "Square Building" there are larger scales, i.e. 16 by 3.5 cm or 8 by 6 cm they probably formed a smaller more flexible version with better protection provided by large metal plates to cover the body. This is similar to the illustration of the heavy cavalryman from Dura-Europos.[182]

From the great diversity in the shapes, dimensions and systems for joining the scales found at Nis indicates we may be dealing with the remains of not one, but several suits of armor deposited in the building associated with the cult of the King's ancestors. Considering that they were left in the building by looters at the time of Nis' fall at the end of the I century BCE indicated that this armor was no longer in shape to use and therefore must have been made earlier, perhaps at the beginning of the I century BCE or earlier.[183] Similarly, on fragments of clay sculptures discovered in the room of the "deified ancestors" are shown with overlapping plates of scaled armor, which indicates the long history of this type of protective armor in the Parthian Army. Coins of the Indo-Sakae rulers, i.e. Vononesa (approximately 105 BCE), or Azes I also show mounted warriors clad in long armor of the eastern variety in the case of the second of the kings, with knee length coats.

It seems that Arsacid armored cavalry with a complete suit of protective armor emerged around the middle of the I century BCE, or even earlier, but this process is shrouded in history. Through descriptions from Roman sources we get a slightly better idea of arming and equipping the Parthian heavy cavalry, we can conclude that it was composed entirely of soldiers using long, heavy spears in combat. The evolution toward the light-weight and mostly poorly armored troops which the Dahae presented from the time of Alexander the Great was different from this kind which date from the III to II centuries BCE.

Research on the eastern military of this period is mainly based on material discovered in archeological excavations and information originated from the works of ancient authors such as Plutarch, Polybius, Livy, not to mention Arian, who as a soldier and governor of Cappadocia who had good insight into the war tactics of the eastern people as well as military theory.

In the section on Crassus in his "Lives of Famous Men" Plutarch describes, unfortunately without detail, the appearance and tactics of the armored cavalry used against the Romans by the Parthian leader Surena

---

[182] Г. А. Пугаченкова, *О панцырном вооружени парфянского и бактрийского воиинства*, В.Д.И. 2, 1966, p. 26
[183] Г. А. Пугаченкова, op.cit., p. 33.

in the Battle of Carrhae (Plutarch, Crassus, 25-26), then he mentions the campaigns of Anthony and Lucullus in Armenia, which is contained in the same bibliographical collection, one of the few sources we have about the Arsacid heavy armored cavalry.

It is hard to find any precise details in Plutarch that mention the use of metal and leather armor for men (leather was probably used to cover the rider's hands, as one might suppose in the form of a segmented, tubular manica, known at least since the beginning of the 3rd century BCE) and covering the horse armor.

It does not deal however, with the construction of any of Surena's soldiers armor. It only gives the place of origins of the warriors and their armor, because of the way this passage could be interpreted:

> "So, with this noise they immediately threatened the Romans with their armor, they dropped their shields and showed themselves in the dazzling light off the helmets and armor, shining sharply off the steel, and their horses, armored with bronze and steel shields." (Plutarch, Crassus, 24)

With respect to Surena's armored cavalry, Plutarch does not claim that they had either unprotected thigh and knee armor, which was worn by Tigranes heavily armored horsemen fighting against Lucullus (Plutarch, *Lucullus*, 28). It is possible that the Armenian cavalry used Sarmatian armor, which in the I and II centuries AD did not use any leg armor or perhaps only greaves.[184] Another possibility is that when we talk about an attack on the flank of advancing lines of heavy cavalrymen on the Roman lines, a description may concern the richest and best-equipped horses in the first line, but their poorer clients in the rear ranks.

The main weapon of the Parthian armored cavalry was similar to the Sakae or Seleucid ancestors - a long (4-6 m) spear.[185] It is possible that it was held in a similar way to Alexander the Great's companions before it was discarded, i.e. it had a leather hand loop which was placed over the wrist. Hence, it seems that Plutarch is quoted as reporting about a contingent of Gaul's fighting with Crassus' forces, *They caught the spears of their opponents and wrestling with them unhorsed their opponents who had difficulty getting off the ground because of the weight of their armor.* (Plutarch, *Crassus*, 25) There was no mention of the use of swords by Parthian cavalry. In "The Life of Lucullus" Plutarch quoting directly from a speech given by the Roman chief stated that the Parthian heavy cavalry, if they were deprived of their kopia's did not have any other means of

---

[184] А. М. Хазанов, op.cit., pp. 59-62.
[185] А. М. Хазанов, op.cit., p. 76.

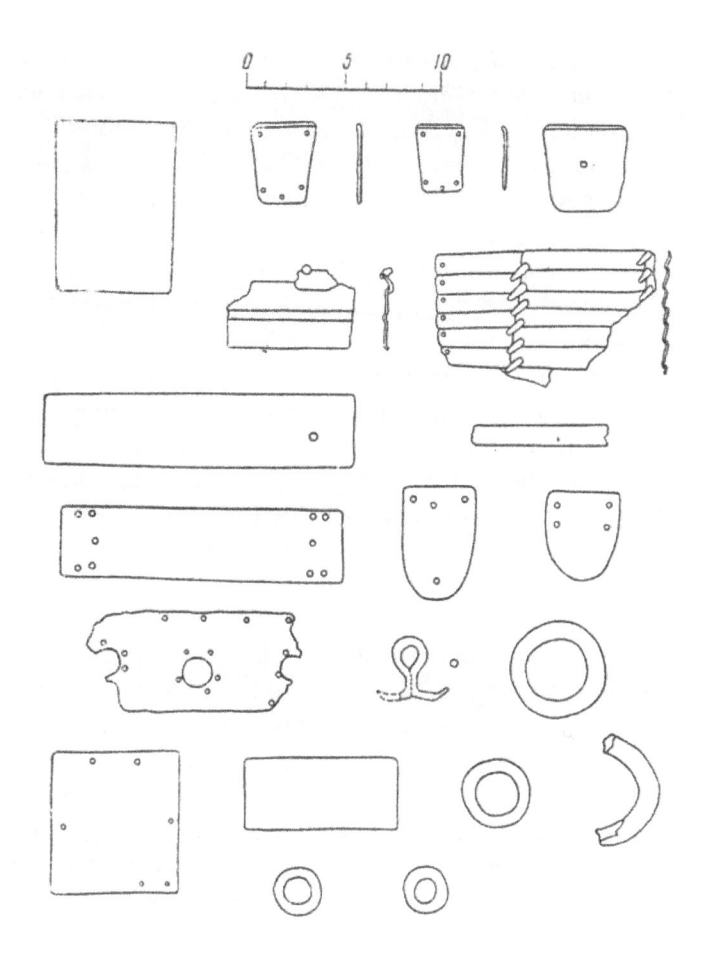

Armor tiles from "Squared building "in Old Nis (from A. Пугаченкова, О панцрном вооружении ..., fig. 2)

defense. *The were only an armored force with spears. They have nothing else they can use in self-defense against the enemy because of their weight and the stiffness of armor. They are as if petrified.* (Plutarch, *Lucullus*, 28). The author, it seems, says that the armored cavalry could not use swords efficiently because of the weight and stiffness of the armor, not the total absence of any side arms. Sidearms have been known in Iran and the steppes for a long time. It is clear that if they had some kind of secondary weapons, they used it only after breaking the spear in the second part of the fight, the characteristic way for the heavy armored Iranian cavalry since the dawn of its history.

In the face of the enemy infantry, the Parthian armored cavalry probably tried to fight as long as they could with long spears in tight formation, in the same manner as practiced by the soldiers of the Macedonian phalanx. Their weapons did not expose the riders to the dangers kopias did fighting using Clibanarian's tactics. Their specific technique involved inflicting shallow, quick thrusts to keep the weapon from getting stuck as it pierced the body. It was possible therefore to use it for the duration of the engagement. When the attack was directed at the enemy cavalry it was carried out in the eastern style of the Iranian-speaking people, meaning at full gallop. In this instance it was not possible to control the depth of the spearhead penetration and the blows entailed completely pinning the men and horses, which was described by Plutarch. It was no longer possible to pull out the shaft once the spear was driven in so deeply at great speed. The lack of a sword or axe in such a situation would mean certain death. What is almost certain therefore, although not confirmed through artistic representation, the Parthian armored units had side weapons, and from the aforementioned tactical reasons they had and were familiar these types of tactics according to finds from the I – II centuries AD. There are no references to the use of side arms by these units using the Iranian characteristic wedge formation at Carrhae only proves that after the first charge, the armored cavalry against infantry were forced to use a combat tactic used by the Hellenistic "horse companions" that is to compact the maximum formation to avoid weapons other than spears.

On the eastern borders of the state, using such tactics against an enemy that just use cavalry would be pointless and would risk the whole arm to the loss of cohesion of the line from a massive attack in wedge formation of the opponent's cavalry. It is normal, therefore, then that the practices of Hellenistic armored cavalry were quickly abandoned after the fall of the Seleucids.

As Surena and his client states came from the eastern areas, Crassus' Gallic cavalry had to adapt to the attack of the steppe tactics, which included the passage which mentions piercing both man and horses in combat.[186] The first attack in the battle of Carrhae which contains this controversial passage, shows the purpose was to cause the destruction of the Gallic Guard cavalry units in front of the Roman infantry.

First century BCE descriptions in the works of Roman historians remains our main source of information on the weapons and tactics of the Parthian heavy cavalry. They do not give a better view on this subject, while as it happens in later times monuments presenting representations of soldiers such as the relief of Gotarzes I from Bisutun – the example from Iranian art of this period showing them charging on horseback with long spears,[187] is virtually missing. Everything we know, we can say are based on the dubious analogy from the armaments of the people bordering the Arsacid monarchy in the east and north, as well as known from earlier periods based on the reconstruction of protective armor. On this basis, using parts of later finds, it is possible to reconstruct Parthian armor of this period.

Body armor was made of metal scales more of less rounded at the bottom edges and sewn on a leather base. It could have been short sleeved like the Sarmatian armor from burial mound 18 in Voronezhsk Station,[188] or more likely the tubular sleeves like those used by the Seleucid or Kushan armored cavalry. The lower part of the "vest" with the metal plates probably reached, at most to mid-thigh, for greater convenience for getting on the horse, and the legs were protected by scale armor and greaves, with the scales often made of thick hardened skin – as seen in the excavations of M. Rostovcev in Dura-Europos,[189] or like gloves, segmented leggings with overlapping leather or metal rings.

Different types of helmets were used. Because each of the armored men had to equip themselves there was no question about a unified style in this area. They were often round or conical covering the neck. A frequent element involved in their design was neck protection, most likely against arrowheads, known since the Achaemenid era, but later they widely used leather, or metal-studded collars.

An interesting incident comes from the 60's of the I century A.D. when the King of Armenia Tiridates I Arsacid came to Rome for ceremony to accept the crown at the hands of the Caesar Nero, accompanied by his wife, riding on horseback, perhaps even in armor, with his face and head covered in a golden helmet with a metal mask.[190] This would be proof

---

[186] Г. А. Пугаченкова, op.cit., p. 29.
[187] B. Kaim, op.cit., p. 164.
[188] А. М. Хазанов, op.cit., p. 59.
[189] М. И. Ростовцев, *Preliminary report,* pp. 450-451.
[190] A. Krawczuk, *Neron*, Warszawa 1988. p. 162.

A great helmet with a metal helmet shaped to imitating a face - Homs. (M. Gawlikowski, Sztuka Syrii, fig.57)

The Armies of Ancient Persia

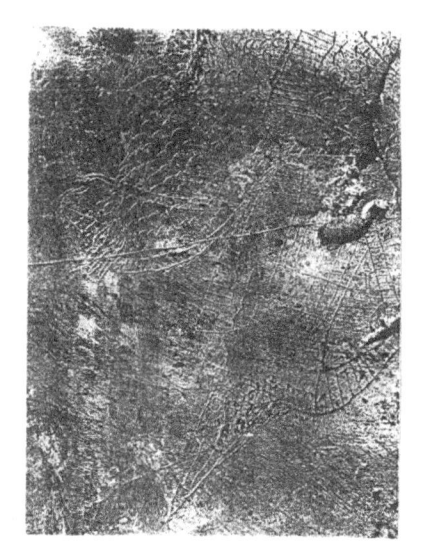

Grafito from Dura Europos showing attacking Parthian armored cavalryman original (top), redraw (bottom). (from B. Goldman, Pictorial graffiti of Dura-Europos, *fig. A14a, a14b)*

The Armies of Ancient Persia

of the continuation of the Seleucid type helmet with a protective "visor". A similar helmet from the I century AD was discovered in the cemetery in Horns (ancient Emes).[191] It should be considered that we do not see these masks on faces on late period reliefs. Roman sources do not speak about these type helmets in the I century BCE or I century AD, so they might not have been that common. Obviously, such masks for armored cavalry would immediately arouse comment from Roman soldiers.

As mentioned by Plutarch, the Parthian armored horses wore iron, steel or leather barding scales or breastplates to protect the body. Neck and head covers were worn separately, also with scales so that the body of the animal was combined into one perfectly protected suit of armor. Only its stomach and legs remained unprotected, hence the practice by the Gaul's serving under the command of Crassus of taking down the riders by piercing the horse's belly and ripping it with a sword. (Plutarch, *Crassus*, 25). This process demanded true Gallic courage and "delusion". This incident also indicates that horse armor of this period was not as long as later, in order to make this maneuver possible at all.

The main offensive weapon remained the spear. Next to that, a secondary weapon must have been swords, axes maces and clubs. The situation changed very little until the beginning of the II century AD from descriptions contained in historical sources as well as pictorial representations.

One of the earliest seems to be dated from the second century or the second half of the I century AD, i.e. a terracotta tile showing an armored spearman sitting on an unarmored horse holding his spear in a clumsy manner against a lion.

The rider wears a bell-shaped helmet, slightly extended over the neck, the edge with a reinforced strip or it seems that the riders is wearing an additional armored collar around his neck or that the helmet has an additional short leather cap. The helmet is most likely sitting on top a small textile arming cap with a small visor protruding above the forehead. The whole thing is a bit like a Kushan armored helmet from the Chalchajan illustration. The armor covering the horse's body is made of metal scales with straight, unrounded lower edges covering the body reaching probably to the middle thigh, buckled in a similar fashion to chaps, but sewn with metal scales which conform to the body. They resemble similar ones found in Dura-Europos. Feet were protected by a mantic made of metal plates. Drawings of this configuration unfortunately does not allow for more detail.

The only weapon the rider has is a short spear held in both hands along the right side of the horse. The way he holds the spear with his

---
[191]M. Gawlikowski, *Sztuka Syrii*, Warszawa 1976, p.132.

right hand shifted backwards and bent at the elbow, while the left hand is holding the front part of the weapon is the most realistic representation of the hands positioning when thrusting, using it to quickly maneuver the point, for example to charge the opponent and stab the rider. This technique also allows you to quickly change direction of the spear tip.

Another set of pictures from the II century AD were discovered in the Dura-Europos graffiti, among which perhaps the most famous shows an armored man sitting on a barded horse. Despite the detailed and crude drawing the main features of the weapon and armor are very clear and unambiguous.

The rider wears a conical shaped helmet, connected in trapezoidal segments. They are arranged in three levels, which however, seems to be an unusual construction, and completely unknown from other pictorial representations and archaeological finds. It would not make sense to "stack" segments to build a bell shape for technical reasons which would reduce the strength of the entire helmet and most importantly it was very labor intensive. Given the quality of the artistic representation and the artist's ability leaves something to be desired, but we can guess that the graffiti probably represents a conical variety of the segmented helmet called a spangenhelm which was known and used from the second century AD and perhaps earlier. In fact, the helmet was composed of four triangular iron plates that are easy to forge, slightly profiled, and joined together by riveting it to four vertical ribs. The bottom of the bell was often reinforced with a wide, riveted strip along the lower edge. The top was finished with a decorative spike or a sleeve which collected at the tips of the plates and ribs. This allowed them to place crests there and sometimes feathers. Similar helmets, however, coming from the late Parthian and early Sassanid are in the collections of the British Museum.[192] Interestingly, when you look at the whole structure, it can be clearly seen that they have three levels – a bush or spike, and reinforcing strip, just like the helmet in the picture. In order to present it properly, the graffito apparently only lacked talent.

Along the bottom edge of the armored helmet from Dura-Europos was a protective aventail falling on the shoulders, probably made of leather and trimmed with metal scales, but this could also be placed under the helmet to reinforce the lower part of the cap or a collar around the neck. Some reconstructions interpret this as a full hood covering the face, when you look at the original, the thick scales are not shown on the warrior's face, which means that it is only an ordinary armored aventail or collar. They were very popular at the end of the Parthian period as

---

[192] P. Wilcox, A. Mcbride, *Rome's enemies 3 Parthians and Sassanid Persians,* Men-at-arms series 175, London 1986, p. 34.

The Armies of Ancient Persia

seen in the example on the Fizurabad Ardashir relief.

An interesting design to protect the body combined two types of metal scales. The shoulders, upper chest and the armor apron, i.e. the part below the waist was covered with a traditional small rounded on the bottom edge scale, not mail as is sometimes insinuated.[193] The chest, abdomen and possibly the lower part of the back as well was protected by armor made with large rectangular plates, forming a breastplate that covered the most vulnerable parts of the body. Unfortunately, it is not known if they were stitched together in a "rigid" fashion or perhaps most likely with wire rings. The hands and legs of the cavalrymen, as already discussed, were protected by armored sleeves and leggings made of ringed scales. Images show that the armor apron almost reached the knee so there had to be a front and back slit.

The heavy cavalry horse at Dura was protected by strong armor made of long barding that also covers the neck and head. All the scales sewn on it were steel or bronze. In tower 19 of that city, in addition to the suits of armor, three almost complete sets of completely preserved horse armor barding were discovered. All were made using the same technology with the rounded edges of scales sewn onto a textile backing.

The first one measures 1.22 meter in length and 1.69 meter in width. The front part has a small, rounded notch of 0.7-meter width, forming a hole to assemble the armor on the horse's neck. About 12 cm from the edge of the opening on the back was an oval hole under the saddle, 37 cm long and 68 cm wide. Along the ridge runs a belt of scales, 22 cm wide in front of the saddle hole, 14 cm wide behind it, covered with a double layer of red leather. On either side of the belt is lined with barding in 30-31 horizontal rows of thin bronze scales sewn onto the double linen base. This was better than leather, because it absorbed the sweat of the animal.

The scales were 3.5 by 2.5 cm with a round bottom edge and eight holes – four on each side. Each scale ended with both sides of located on a central band with a large space available for fixing it to the foundation with a thick leather strap. Individual scales are sewn on the backing using a cross stitch of thick linen threads passing through the two upper holes on each side of the scale. Two lower ones were used to connect the scales located within one row, overlapping, which did not make use of thread, but special bronze clips. Horizontal scales overlapped so that the top covers the lower sewn group. The edges of the neck cutout for the horse, and the space for the saddle were finished off with a strip of dyed red leather, 4-5 cm wide, folded in half and sewn in place over the backing and the top of the scales. The bottom edges of the backing were reinforced with sim-

---
[193] P. Wilcox, A. Mcbride, op.cit., p. 27.

ilar strips made of red leather, 8.5 cm wide, fixed with the same thread that was used to attach the scales.

At the rear edge of the barding, on an extension running the back was a belt without regular scales in a triangular shape whose dimensions are 26 cm long and 20 cm wide at the widest part. It was covered with eleven rows of scales connected horizontally and stitched on the same backing as used for the main part of the barding, the edges are finished with the same red leather. This cover is attached to the entire leather "cover" by a sheet 5.5 cm wide, the straps of which pass through slots in the edge and are attached to the main part of the barding.

Red straps on the top edge of the armor were used to attach the armor in the front, across the animal's chest – thought they have not survived, they might have also been used in the back. Leather loops placed on the rear edge of the saddle opening were for attaching the Roman or Bosphoran saddle. The barding was connected to the saddle to serve as an additional point to secure the saddle via straps on the loops.[194]

A slightly different type of horse armor (No.2) was discovered in tower 19 in Dura-Europos. Slightly less preserved then the first, after being folded into a rectangular shape 148 cm long and 110 cm wide while the two corners were 30 cm long and 16 cm wide that was used to attach it to the front breast of the horse. The rear edge was rounded and reinforced, while its corners were as much as 18 cm further back from the central position. On the ridge it ran through the middle along the entire ridge covered with raw leather. About 28 cm from the edge there was an opening for the saddle with dimensions of 61 cm long and 38 cm wide.

Scales were an average of 6 by 4.5 cm, extremely thick (4mm) and rounded on the bottom edge. Each one was provided with eight holes – two small ones on each side, and four larger ones arranged in a square above them. Connections between the individual rows was made using forged or cut bronze rings. All the scales were forged to the same tempered thickness and completely devoid of rust. The heavy base of this foundation was a piece of canvas sewn the same way as the armor No.1 in tower 19 with overlapping rows on each side. They were sewn using a leather thong, made with a regular stich of "one on top, one underneath". All the horizontal rows of scales were attached to the base on both ends with a central belt of thick leather strapping in the same manner as the first armor. The edges of the barding and the hole for the saddle were finished with good quality red dyed leather, sewn on the scales together with the undercoat. The rear section with non-reinforced corners was sewn in a triangular shape, 18 cm wide (at the widest point) attached with raw leather. The bottom edges below the armor were fin-

[194] М. И. Ростовцев, op.cit.,p. 441.

ished off in red leather 5 cm wide and sewn with thread. The tail cover was shaped as a triangle 21.5 cm on the long side, made of raw leather in four pieces, sewn to the undercoat with the rows of scales. The edges were finished with red leather.[195]

A third set of armor has a design very similar to the two previous ones.[196] As in the previous set described scales, there were probably neck guards and head mounts, but they were unfortunately not preserved. All parts of the combined armor were attached to the animal's body by tying them with things. No eye shields are shown. At the so-called chamber – that is a point on the animal where the heart is located, there was a special strap probably for holding a metal shield, together with the reinforced barding was protection against shot and heavy infantry spears. Similar shields protected both rear sides of the groin.

All the horse armor discovered in Dura-Europos, however, only shielded the body of the horse, not the upper part of the legs like shown on the graffito.

Barding the horse, though low to the ground did not reach the hoofs however, because it made movement difficult for the animals and was very very heavy. It would seem that to effectively protect the horse against arrows and hand-weapons, armor reaching the horse's knee was sufficient and this is how it is pictured in the graffito of the heavy cavalryman in the "Christian Building" at Dura.[197] The image of the sword belt of the armored rider shown in the graffito at Dura-Europos seems to confirm the eastern technique of fighting.

Looking at the traditional descriptions of Persian cavalry, that Roman historians of the later second century AD (Inscriptions from Bithynia[198]) introduced into their works, determined that the armored cavalryman were derived from the Persians and more probably to the point that the popular term clibanarius took the place of the old one of the Greek Cataphract as probably a bit bookish or "archaic" in tone. Information on heavy armored cavalry from the eastern battlefields began to prevail over those of that maintained a Hellenistic description. The older term could have easily been replaced by a new one, first widely used by soldiers, because of the differences between the cavalrymen of the two armored formations were very small. Actually, the use of the clibanarius was limited to the group supported the horse archers. Based on some description it is possible to determine that the *clibanarii* did not cover their mounts in the early period with armor (The Sakae).[199] Later reliefs,

---
[195]М. И. Ростовцев, op.cit., p. 443.
[196]loc. cit..
[197]B. Goldman, op.cit., p. 33.
[198]M. Mielczarek, op.cit., s. 10.
[199]Depicted in the bone plaques from Orlat

The Armies of Ancient Persia

Coins of the Indo-Sakae rulers - Wonones (L), Azes I (R) (in Г. А. Пугаченкова, О панцрном вооружении..., fig. 3, A. D. H. Bivar, Cavalry equipment and tactics on the Euphrates frontier, fig. 1)

The sleeves which are artfully joined with thick leather straps, varnished leather scales (from М. И. Ростовцев, Preliminary report ..., Tab. 23)

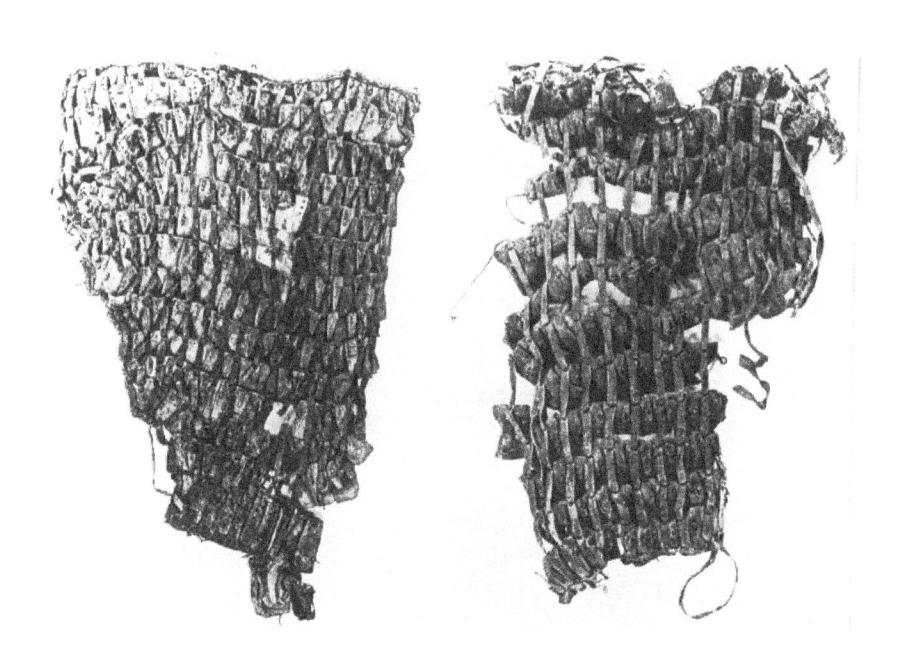

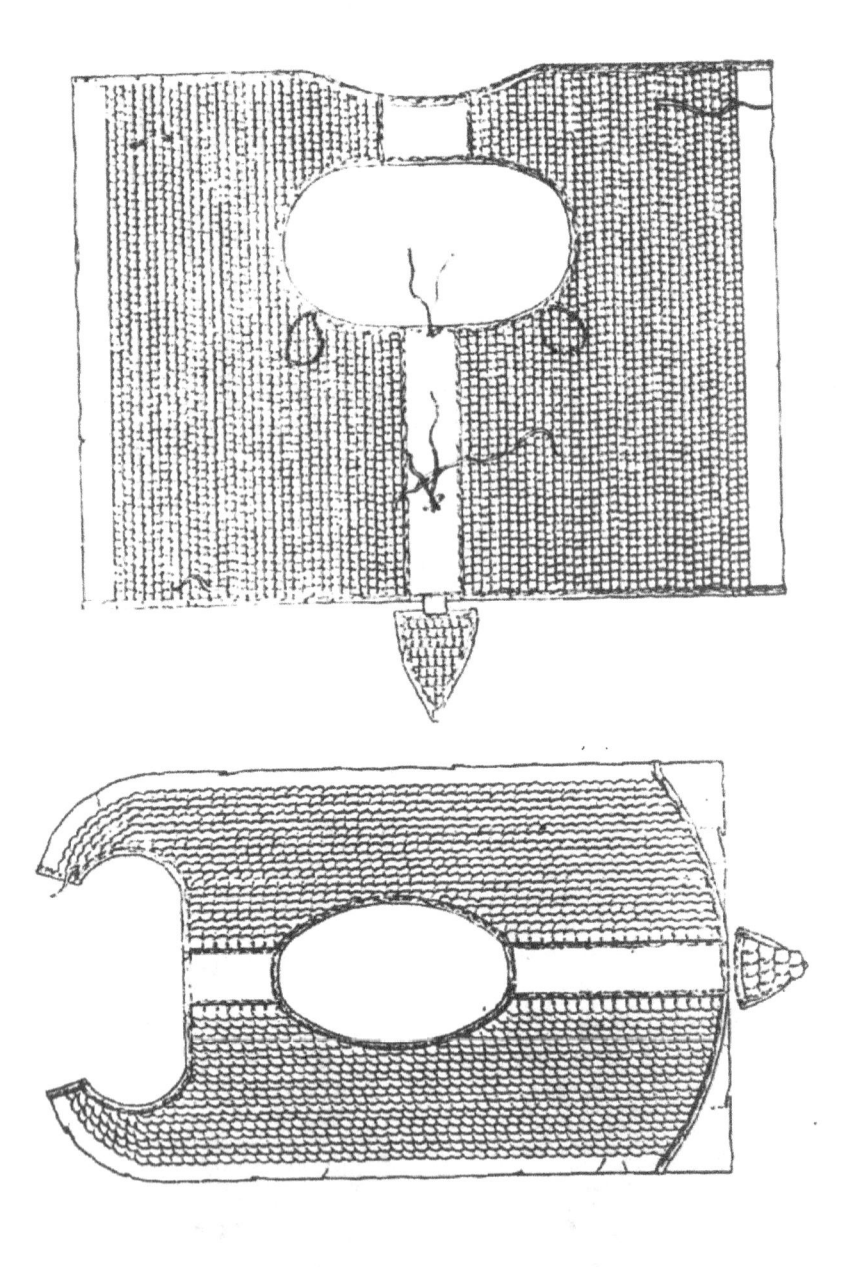

(Top - The first scale horse armor from tower 19 in Dura Europos (from М. И. Ростовцев, Preliminary report ..., Tab. 21)

(Bottom) Second scale horse armor from tower 19 in Dura Europos (from M.I. Rostovtsy, Preliminary report ..., Tab. 21)

The Armies of Ancient Persia

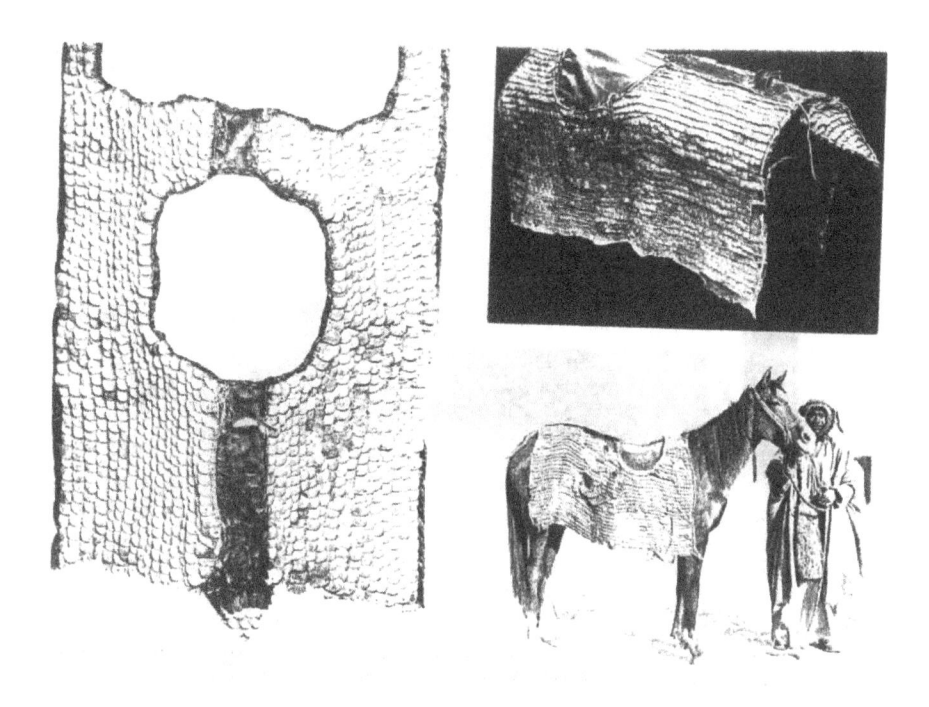

The third set of scale horse armored from tower 19 in Dura Europos and reconstruction of the method of putting on this type of armor. (in М.И. Ростовцев, Preliminary report ..., Table 22)

The Armies of Ancient Persia

(Top) An armored rider hunting a lion (Could also be an allegory of fighting the demon of Ahryman or ordinary hunting?). (from R. Ghirschman, Iran: Parthian and Sassanians, fig. 122)

(Bottom) "Spangenhelm" helmets (ribbed) from the Parthian (a) and Sassanid (b) periods. (from to P. Wilcox, A. Mcbride, Rome's enemies 3, Parhians and Sassanid Persians, fig. pp. 15.34)

however, attest to light leather or sewn metal scales (Sassanids). In the case of these representations, the coverings shown were meant for protection against the swords of other riders rather than infantry. Armored clibanarii fighting against other heavy armored cavalry under which the horses would have been doomed to death.

In Central Asia, the case was very similar. Influenced by battles against tribes using horse archers as their main force (as it pertains to this type of late-Parthian army and the late-Kushan armies which were already much smaller than the armies of the first Arsacids) the Kushan warriors wore armor comparable to the Parthian ones. An example of this horse armor belonging to a rider from the present day Jaszhan, shows similar influences to the development of horse armor for King Ardashir III or Hosroes II depicted on the relief at Tag-e Bustan and Chinese heavy armored cavalry.

The main weapon of the rider shown on the graffito at Dura is a long spear – a kopia, held along the right side of the horse. The armored horseman holds the spear in the middle of the shaft with his right hand, which is possible, but given the length of the weapon it would probably be a bit bulky. In fact, both arms were needed to hold the spear during an attack.

The image of a sword is clearly visible next to the rider. It is positioned on the waist at the left side, which may indicate the image is Parthian. The Romans wore their swords on the right side. The Persians origin of the sword are described by the Dacian in the II century BCE yet are rarely describes in Roman texts. Not much can be said about the shape and length of the blade of this weapon, however, it can be assumed that it is typical of the heavy and long swords worn by all representatives of the Arsacid noble class (i.e. Uthala the ruler of Hatry, which is shown by a magnificent full-figure sculpture of courtiers of the Sassanid kings). Graffito from Dura-Europos is the first, oldest example of an illustration of a Parthian heavy cavalryman equipped with this type of weapon.

While in the east, swords similar to a type of saber were more popular, with multiple constructional influences from Chinese swords. In Iran both the Parthians and Sassanids only used heavy weapons of this type for slashing.

The connection with the equipping of armored cavalrymen with swords is interesting in that there is another graffito from Dura-Europos, in the same armory, building and room showing an armored mounted archer shooting on the gallop with a long reflexive bow. Although from later descriptions, we know that armored cavalry also had bows and certainly did not use it at the gallop, but rather before starting the attack with "preparation fire". The rider rendered in the graffito is not, however, a clibanarius, as he does not have a long spear – a weapon characterized by this formation of heavy cavalry and his horse is not protected by armor. It should be remembered here, therefore, that *clibanarii* units were supported by the wedge ranks of the mounted archers operating behind and on the flanks, which is probably the sort of soldier we are dealing with. In the second century BCE they wore, as in the later Sassanid army, some light armor for protection against arrows, especially if fired from long distance and above all in connection with close combat fighting associated with hand weapons. The illustration is so sketchy that it does not allow us to identify the type of armor. Based on the popular conclusions in the Parthian army, scale armor, which is the best protection against arrows is quite rigid and heavy, however, one would assume that the type of armor that would require being made for mobile archer would have smaller scales than the massive heavily armored riders. It is also possible that they were made of metal and for example (as armor found in tower 19), leather or some Sarmatian armor made of bone, horn or hooves.[200] Most likely, however, is the assumption that the rider is wearing chainmail that has been sold to the Iranian military by the Sarmatians or Romans.

    This horseman does not have any other weapon except for the bow, but as a support archer he should be equipped with a sword. If we take into account, the quality and accuracy of the whole presentation we can assume that it did not deserve to the attention of the "artist". Maybe it was hidden by the body of the warrior who is shown tensing the bow at that moment and turned to the right? It is possible to see a small sword (26 to 31 cm) the size of which would not be of influence.

    The most interesting, and probably the best quality pictorial reference of this era for the Arsacid monarchy's army comes from the third century. It is based on the rock relief at Tang-e Sarvak, and it is a huge amazingly expressive low relief depicting the decisive battle between Artaban V, the last of the Arsacid rulers, and the Persian rebel Ardashir from the Sassanid family. It was placed on a rock near Firuzabad, hence it is called the Firuzabad relief.

    The relief at Tang-e Sarvak was created in the first half of the third century. The battle scene involves a heavily armed rider as well as two infantrymen. The horse is wearing heavy armor, probably made of a breastplate and apron, the application of which is not entirely clear – perhaps it is lamellar armor with long metal plates arranged so that the lower row is covered by the upper level of the horse's armor, or an ordinary barding of rectangular scales.

---

[200] А. М. Хазанов, op.cit., p. 58.

The Armies of Ancient Persia

In the case of the breastplate, which is always depicted as a quilted garment, could in fact also be a metal cuirass running vertically along a reinforced breastplate. A cuirass would be the logical development for the best way to cover the most exposed body parts of the clibanarii – the chest area. From the many pictorial representations knownto us, the aim of the long-spear in combat was primarily against the abdomen, chest and throat of the opponent. In the case of the cavalryman depicted on Tang-e Sarvak he is additionally protected by a scale armor collar that overlaps the breastplate.

The skirt of the armor reached down to the mid-thigh and the legs underneath were covered by long strips or tubular metal forms, such as mantica that protected the arms to the wrist.

The rider who is not wearing a helmet displays a typical Parthian-style hair parted with a knot on the side, in a similar way as the combing "prince" shown on the statue from Shami. It perfectly corresponds to Plutarch's description of Surena.

The main weapon was a heavy long-spear that the rider held in both hands near the end of the shaft. The spear point was not pointed up, but at the abdomen, or chest of the other horse, or down against infantry. The technique for using the spear, that the Tang-e Sarvak rider uses is combined for a specific type of target, such as an armored rider or one protected with a heavy shield and infantry armor, a strike which causes maximum impact threatening to knock the warrior from the saddle, rather than to a particular type of tactic. The above described method of holding the long-spear across the horse's neck acts as a brace for impact, using this strength to break through the thickest armor or shield, hence the portrayal on the relief of such a grip used against infantry, even though it was also used against armored cavalry. The fight against infantry may also explain the strong design of armor covering his horse.

This traditionally consists of three parts, namely: to protect the head, neck and barding, all sewn but not ordinary scales, rather they were long narrow metal lamellar mounted on a textile backing. The barding in this case is so long it reaches the horses knees. Each of the rows of scales is in contrast to the barding discovered in Dura-Europos which only goes to the tops of the legs. It also seems that the individual scales in horizontal rows slightly overlap each other so that everyone covers the right edge of the next, and the upper row was a curved surface riveted to the lower surface of the overlying plate. This way you can interpret that there is a single point located in the center of the upper part of each scale. Yet, the technique for riveting was well known by the Parthians in the III century AD and was used for example in the construction of helmets. This construction was very rigid and much more durable than the traditional armor that was only sewn. The quality of the protection was almost like plate armor. This same point however, also shows each row of scales attached by a leather thong or lace running vertically through all the rows. This technique of constructing armor had been known for centuries in the Far East and widely used in by the heavy cavalry in the Chinese states during the "Three Kingdoms" period. The barding includes the so-called "Chamber", that is where the heart of the animal is, covered by round solid metal shields. This type of armor completely protected the horse from threats of swords, spears and archery.

The horse armor depicted on the relief of Tang-e Sarvak is decorated with colorful wool tassels and bristles on the head and the tail. The edges were also trimmed similar to those at Dura-Europos - probably dyed red. It cannot be ruled out that for protection against weather the armor scales were also painted. Thigh armor found in tower 19 in Dura, for example still bears traces of varnish.

An additional weapon shown with the rider was probably a long reflexive bow. Although it cannot be directly seen anywhere, it can be deduced on the basis of the shape and length of the quiver hanging from the belt on the right side. It is characteristic for combining two or three types of bowcases for different types of arrows depending on the type of the arrowhead. Above the edge of these two "pockets" a cover and shot holder are visible. At the beginning of the III century AD Parthian armored cavalry they always used their bows to fire at the opponent's troops direct attack. In addition to the quiver, the rider did not have any other weapon, and the question arises, if this was the only weapon, or was there any other weapons? The accuracy for the presentation, though now heavily damaged, seems to speak against all these "shortcomings", the artist cannot be accused of inaccuracy – the sword is therefore obscured by the body of the rider.

The relief from Tang-e Sarvak shows the latest, heaviest and best version of protective armor of the Parthian cataphract-clibanarius which dates from the end of the second-beginning of the III century AD. Interestingly, it shows the weaponry and armor had a distinctive Far Eastern influence, perhaps Chinese, which may have resulted from trade and war between the empires. The heavy load of the horse's armor, however, had to have a negative impact on the speed of attacks and the resulting power of the long-spear which caused them to move away from this in favor of a type of cavalry shield. This is where we are for the armored units on the next great relief.

This was probably at the behest of Ardashir, the first king of the Sassanid dynasty, that it was carved on the rock wall around Firuzabad. This scene shows him in a clash between armored horsemen. The whole scene is composed of three distinct parts showing fighting between: Ardashir and Artaban V fighting in the first; his son Shapur, later King Shapur I and the Grand Vizier of the last Arsacid's fighting hand-to-hand in the second, and two senior dignitaries of the combatants in the third.[201] Everyone portrayed in the relief wears armor similar to each other, which is actually the same as the armor from Tang-e Sarvak. The only difference is that the riveting is not visible on the apron armor and the upper edges are not rounded.

The aprons reach the mid-thigh and made of long rectangular metal scales constructed in the traditional method – the right edge of each was covered by those on the left and cover from the top row. They were sewed to the base. The breastplates, as in the case of the rider at Tang-e Sarvak is in the form of a cuirass plate of a stylized muscle torso. For the clibanarii, the front of the chest and throat were made better by small plates on the armor. Such a theory confirms what seems to be a technique of stabbing thrusts, as on the relief depicting Prince Shapur piercing the Arsacid vizier. The thrust of the speartip stuck in the bottom edge of the breastplate, avoiding the strongest part of the armor, and piercing the enemy armor at the joints where the cuirass meets the apron.

The rider's legs were protected by metal leg guards composed of ring-shaped metal tubes reaching to the foot. The same type mantica covered the hands to the shoulders. The upper end was connected by straps or belts hidden under the shoulder pads to the breastplate.

The heads of the Arsacid armored troops were protected by high helmets, though in fact only the one worn by the Parthian's fighting the last pair is clearly visible, with a bell profile so that it overlaps slightly on the neck. A massive, studded rectangular metal collar on the bottom is visible on the edge to protect the neck, mainly from sword blows, and arrow heads, such as the armor collar worn by the rider from Tang-e Sarvak. At the top of the helmet there is a horsehair crest mounted on bushing sleeve. The helmet of Artaban and the vizier, who may also be the heir to the throne, are shallower hemispherical with reinforcing strips around the edges. They are equipped with shorter spikes, and in addition they are tied with decorative striped sashes whose ends flutter from behind. It seems that the type of Arsacid helmet in the last fighting pair is a similar design to the helmet of the rider shown on the plaque in the lion hunting scene dating from the second century AD. In both types we clearly see the same solutions, i.e. a bell helmet made from a single piece of metal, drawn out as a bell.

Considering the faces of all three of the Arsacid's depicted on the relief of Firuzabad in the fight against the Sassanid are very similar to

---

[201] B. Kaim, op.cit., p. 165.

each other, one can conclude that they hide them in the mask showing standardized facial features, metal masks with a helmet connected with a hinge. This very similar design interpreted as a helmet and a mask is shown in the relief of Hormazd II.[202] In the Roman parades, for example, similar visors may still appear under Persian influence, from the first century on.[203] It seems that the more popular, especially armong archers, but especially the armored, besides the spangenhelm, were triangular visors, combined with center ribs nd riveted plates.

All the Arsacids portrayed on Ardashir's relief are depicted without weapons, except for long tube quivers connected with bows and attached by straps. They are deep enough that you can see the whole over the edge of the shot's neck. None of the Parthian knights have either a personal hand weapon, nor spears, although everyone has decorative studded metal belts on their hips designed to be worn with swords by clibanarii in the second phase of fighting after contact or breaking the kopia.

Horses: The Parthian knights and their Sassanid adversaries are protected by coverings of the neck and head, but not the heavy, metal scales like those from Dura-Europos, but were light, probably made of leather or thick canvas. On the surface you can see the sophisticated shape of scales sewn up tightly in horizontal rows. This type of barding was probably to protect the animal from a shot fired by horse archers supporting the attack of the armored clibanarii. In those cases, it was used more often by the Sassanid type archers with less power, but more range than the powerful reflexive bows of the early Parthians, so the armor would be effective against them.

Scales covering the surface were protection against swords, while not affecting the horse as much as scales covering the earlier Parthian armored horses. Lightening the armor without compromising the speed of the charge, provide the basic protection of the surface. Compared to the bard-covering horse shown on Tang-e Sarvak one can say that the relief of mounts had advance a lot in several dozen years.

Saddles and Quivers. It is difficult today to determine the type of saddle the Arsacid armored cavalrymen used. Illustrated representations are not only rare, but the artists do not usually do not show the ordinary or tertiary details. One can only assume that initially they were not much different from saddles used by the Scythian cavalry and keeping them balanced required superior horsemanship skills. I can believe that these

---

[202] P. Wilcox, A. Mcbride, op. cit., p. 38.
[203] M. Junkelman, op.cit., p. 160.

horsemen, like Macedonian cavalry had to rely on sitting on skins or saddle cloths but given the nomadic origin of the Arsacid cavalry they would not have problems with this. Then the trouble of staying in the saddle once they impacted the target with the kontos was off-set by the appropriate manner of holding the spear. The style of fighting with a weapon almost exclusively using the hands affected the distribution of the thrusts by using mostly the upper part of the body.

The technique only changed as a result of continued fighting with the peoples of the northern steppes. This assumption is based on the pictorial references, for example, the terracotta plates which shows a Parthian armored horse archer around the end of the era about the first century AD with what appears to be of a saddle of Celtic or Sarmatian origin called a saddle horn. The name comes from the four horns that held the hips of the riders tightly, protruding from the saddle tree, i.e. the wooden frame of the saddle, which was attached to the saddle straps fastened to the animal's back – the example the girth, crupper, etc. A small saddle of this type was covered with leather,[204] and the outer surfaces of he horns, both front and back are in pairs, strengthen by bronze fittings, respectively. Such a saddle probably corresponds to holes in the armored cloths from Dura-Europos. As in the case of horse armor no. 1 which described about this position on the rear edge of the hole for the saddle opening, which has two leather loops that are spaced and sized to match the rear pair of saddle horns. These loops were assumed to better attach and stabilize the heavy barding on the back. The key proof of the use of the horned saddle in the Parthian Army is the display of one of them on the terracotta plaque in the collection of the Staatliche Museum from Berlin, showing a horse archer. An armored rider from the relief in Tang-e Sarvak rides a horse on the back of which is visible a horned saddle.

The strongest attack at a full gallop (which was after all the primary way the clibanarii attacked) was done in conjunction with the "horned" saddle, which was one hundred percent necessary and quite easy. The widespread use of the "rigid" technique of laying the spear across the horse's neck had a greater impact on the rider's body at the point of impact. The use of the sword in combat was greatly improved by this. It was no longer necessary to wedge the legs and body on the horse for every movement. The ability of the rider to support himself allowed them to strike harder.

The best example of how the horned saddle supported the Roman cavalryman comes from the time of the first Jewish uprising:

204　G. Sumner, Roman Army Wars of the Empire, Brassey`s History of Uniforms, London 1997. pp. 46-48.

The Armies of Ancient Persia

When the Jews were forced to flee and pushed into the valley, one of the cavalry cohorts named Pedanius hit them in the flank at full gallop and scooped up one of the fleeing enemy by the ankle, a young man strongly built and well-armed. He leaned over with his horse at full-gallop, showing considerable arm strength and the body in general, as a master horseman. (Josephus Flavius, The Jewish War, VI, 2, pp. 161-2)

All the belts fastened the saddle on the back of the horse (dock, girth, etc) were hidden under the barding through the hole that only the saddle stuck out. It was cushioned before battle and ready for the rider to mount the saddle. The practical use of the horned saddle remained the equipment of the armored cavalry for the Parthians and later Sassanids until the appearance of the Turkish people who brought the invention of stirrups.

Another key piece of equipment for the Parthian armored cavalry were the quivers. Unfortunately, because of the lack of images, we can not determine the evolution of this piece of equipment. There is no reason, however, to believe it developed separately from the quiver of foot archers.

As with the quivers in the above formation, those that remained in the equipment of the armored heavy cavalry are distinguished by two main types. The first was created in the long-known version of gorytos, shown on the Orlat plaque and the relief at Tange Sarvak. It is composed of two parts, a narrow holder and an asymmetrical flap sewn together with no quiver pocket on it. They are so deep that the shot cannot be seen protruding from it. Sometimes only their feathers can be seen above the edge of the neck.

Often, especially in the II and III centuries AD, a long stand-alone case was worn near the waist on the right hip. Examples of this can be seen in hunting equipment, which gained great popularity in the Sassanid army, when bows of greater range came into use. A quiver of this type is significantly shallower than the previous one so that the arrows can be seen above the neck. In the absence of holder, the bow could not be worn in it like in the gorytos and required a separate case. Moving away from the Orlat type quiver was probably the result of the development and spreading of the Parthian reflexive bow at the end of the period with a large counter-force known as Sasanid. Without the bowstring in place it was carried in a special half-moon holder sown on a relief of Ardaszir III (or Hosroes II) at Tag-e Bustan or later examples of the Umayyads from Qasr al-Hayr al-Gharbi on the left side of the saddle. The quiver with arrows was suspended at the waist on the right side. The Turkish people

The Armies of Ancient Persia

wore their bows with less curl, also hung them from a belt as opposed to the Persians and Arabs who wore theirs with the sword or sabre on the left hip.

5. TACTICAL PRINCIPALS

While the pictorial sources with the limited numbers of written sources available to reconstruct the type, appearance, weapons and protective armor (and in part also the methods of its use), the reproduction of the tactical principals of armored cavalry units are based almost exclusively on the numerous citations in the works of ancient historians. Unfortunately, during the reign of the Arsacid rulers, there is significantly less material than in later times, i.e. the period of existence for the Sassanid Empire. Fortunately, however, they provide a higher quality story. The main source of information in this area is based on Plutarch's "Parallel Lives", especially regarding Lucullus and Crassus, based on the works of Sallust, Strabo, Livy and Nicholas of Damascus.[205] One can also not ignore the works of Cassius Dio, however, it needs to be noted that the authors of these histories – starting in the II century BCE were important due to the military experience of the creators, has many parts missing as do Arrian's works concerning the action among others of the armored cavalry units on the battlefield. Little information, but of equal importance that does helsp fundamental research on the subject but is never the less very interesting as is the writings of other authors.

The tactical use of armored cavalry in battle depended, it seems, on the type of units the enemy brought with them in formation. Ancient historians, based on a variety of second-hand reports from various clashes, only noted the existence and operation of such tactics, which they adopted against the combat formations prevailing in the armies of the Mediterranean monarchies. For writers of the late Republic and early Roman Empire, these tactics mostly involved heavily armored cavalry fighting against heavy infantry. Only later when the Romans also began using heavily armored eastern cavalry did it lead to clashes with other cavalry of this type. Soon historians and writers improved their knowledge of the typical Iranian tactics by what is now called Persian Clibanarii.

On this basis with early Roman interactions, it was stated that Parthian cavalrymen were heavily armored rider mounted on a heavy barded scale horse armor fighting with a long spear - a type of *kontos* or even a *sarissa*. Soldiers of this specific formation approach battle in a linear formation[206] although the depth does not seem to have exceeded except in limited cases, a couple of ranks. The depth of this formation is

---

[205] M. Mielczarek, op.cit., p. 27.
[206] M. Mielczarek, op.cit., p. 105.

logical, because it was used against lines of enemy to break them, and for this purpose as they were mainly armored units, there was no reason for a huge armored cavalry block. On this basis, and primarily because of the impossibility for applying pressure from masses ranks of armored cavalry would not make sense from tactical or economic reasons. It is easy to calculate that to bring a compact formation of armored cavalry on an opponent's front with a depth of five ranks it would be difficult to equip that many heavy cavalrymen. The length of a formation formed by a thousand of Surena's armored cavalrymen in five ranks, if you calculate 1.5m for each man would be 300 m wide. Even when the attack was carried out on the weak point of the enemy formation, or his wing, trying to break the cohesion of the opponent's formation by increasing the depth of the armored cavalry block would not seem for the above-mentioned reasons, to make much sense.

The commanders of the Arsacid's armored cavalry did not adopt the tactics of the Greek-Macedonian army that placed this type of units on the wings. Preparing to fight against the overwhelming forces of Crassus, Serena followed the practices of the steppe people, which assumed the first line consisted of armored cavalry units with the winged consisting of horse archers (when you try to flank the enemy archers they extended their position to increase the "cover" his flanks); *Surena then set his main forces behind the front one's and he ordered the reflection of their arms to be hidden under their cloaks and skins.* (Plutarch, Crassus, 23). The tradition of this tactic dates back to at least the Achaemenid period and probably even earlier to the great steppe.[207]

By adopting such an order of battle, the enemy could not possibly know what to expect, and after finding that Crassus strengthened his vanguard and flanks with Gallic cavalry, he threw armored cavalry against them in the fighting style of the steppe as clibanarii. Unfortunately, Plutarch does not give any clear indication of any differences in the way the heavy cavalry attacked, during the battle of Carrhae against the cavalry and infantry, there is no mention if these attacks were supported by archers. At one point he writes, *the opponent's cavalry, circled around, shelling the sides of the Romans, and the front ranks of spears forced them to compact into a small space.* (Plutarch, Crassus, 27). That description fits perfectly with what we know about the armor and combat capabilities of units in the Hellenistic type of "comrade" warriors in a typical horse phalanx formation. Deadly attacks, interestingly, were only when the most desperate of the legionnaires as the armored lines moved away from the front lines of the Romans, while the Parthian commander could direct the attacks on an on-going basis on the opponent's troops from a

---
[207] See introduction to the cavalry and army of the Achaemenid Persians.

ring of archers. Most Legionnaires, however, in the face of such threat, hide behind large shields fell according to descriptions, victims of this attack. This suggests that after the first charge of the clibanarii against the enemy formation, the armored cavalry acted as a kind of reserve and individual support, forming a dense bristling wall of spears which frustrated all attempts to move forward against the enemy to breakthrough. The main weight of the attack was based on the formation of horse archers. It was the overwhelming number of missiles that felled the majority of Romans.

A compact formation of armored cavalry was like a line of Macedonian phalangite, highly resistant to a frontal attack. A dense "barbwire" of long spears created an unusual barrier, difficult to cross, and the armor protected them against wounds from arrows and javelins for which blocking troops would be a perfect target. The only way to defeat this type of formation would to effectively outflank it or hit it in the rear. For this reason, the flanks of the horse phalanxes were protected by light infantry, which is why the flanks of Surena's heavy cavalry was shielded by horse archers. Encumbered armored cavalryman could not fight individually.[208] They were only suitable for use in compact formation.

From the data on the size of Surena's individual formations described (Plutarch, *Crassus*, 21) it is easy to calculate the ratio of the armored cavalry to light troops, which in this case was 1:10. These proportions clearly show that heavy cavalry was not the most dominant troop type in the Parthian cavalry, only a traditional fighting style. By comparison, in the Mongol army from the reign of Genghis Khan and his successors, the armored units were 2/5 of the total number of cavalry. In addition, the equipment would probably explain the small number of these highly specialized units.

As stated by Lucan in his eulogy, part of which concerns the expedition of Lucius Verus, the armored cavalry of the Arsacids was divided into units, numbering about one thousand riders under the standard that the Romans called a dragon (Draco)[209] for smaller units, however, not much its known. The decimal system was most likely used in the Arsacid system just like in the Achaemenid Army. Dragon heads made of metal was stuck on the shaft and the torso was made of a light weight material (i.e. silk) sleeve waving in the wind was also known to be used for military purposes by he Sarmatians, and later the Romans. Similar designations for command positions were used in Central Asia, which confirms the image of the Eagle.

---

[208] А. М. Хазанов, op.cit., p. 76.
[209] M. Mielczarek, op.cit., p. 57.

The Armies of Ancient Persia

While the heavy cavalry always fought in combination with archery units, when they conducted operations against infantry, this cooperation was based on the principal of combined operations with individual archers, it seems, however, that as long as they were acting against infantry, this cooperation was based on two separate activities in support of a formation. Only when the attack destroyed the enemy cavalry, in the old Scythian model, the initial bombardment was either carried out by the horse archers, "in flight", or "standing", in formation by soldiers of either unit followed by an attack in mixed formation. Although to date, we have no actual mention of the use of wedge formations by the Parthians, considering that it was used by armored units of virtually all the eastern and northern neighbors of the Arsacid Empire, you can conclude that this way of fighting was the norm for them, as already mentioned by Roman historians. When the Imperial Roman army moved east, strategists were already deeply acquainted with the Persian method of using cavalry. Interestingly, unlike the Achaemenid cavalry, in the Parthian cavalry we do not have any mention of the use of a wedge formation at the squadron level, in many places where heavy cavalry is described. Perhaps a wedge-shaped formation for heavy cavalry was only used at the corps level, and the old, wedge-shaped squadron also had to keep in mind the greater compactness of the formation.

A characteristic feature of Parthian heavy cavalry tactics was not just clinging to the old steppe military traditions, but also, they did not create too many heavy units because of expense and the difficulty in equipping and maintaining units of armored cavalry in every area of conflict at any given time. It is theorized that a small number of heavy cavalry units, operated (apart from the "private armies" of the most powerful clans directly dealt with border incursions) as the later Roman Comitatus worked with "Imperial" troops together with those of the militia and mercenary light cavalry in threatened regions, which is confirmed by the observation that the Arsacid army struggled to fight on several fronts simultaneously. This presumption is supported by a short passage in "Roman History" by Cassius Dio, in which the noble Sylakes who ruled the territories first invaded by Crassus tried to confront him alone, then called on his subordinates fight the enemy, and only after suffering a defeat at Ichnia did he send a message to the king. (Cassius Dio, *History of the Romans*, XXX, 12.2)

On this basis, one can assume that according that the overall defensive doctrine of the Arsacid's was that until he came with relief of the Royal Army, recruited perhaps from the less vulnerable satrapies of the monarchy (but therefore made up of less experienced and hardened soldiers), so that the task of repelling the invading armies fell on the local feudal lords. These armies operated similarly to the Roman Limitanei. The feudal lords of the border provinces were just like the one-time Achaemenid satraps of the "Limes" satrapy, i.e. Asia Minor which maintained huge armies. This force, however, did not always serve to fight against external enemies, but was also used to enforce their own privileges and protect their private interests. This system was also similar to the feudal order of medieval Japan during the Sengoku period which lead to infighting that weakened the power of the central authority. The powerful feudal lords ruled the Parthian State more than the king. The King could only "divide and rule" using his own forces and the supporting nobles to suppress the ambitious wealthy nobles.

From written sources, we know that this weakness had been repeatedly taken advantage of by the Romans with the most spectacular successes during campaigns at the moment their eastern neighbors main forces were engaged, either in the suppression of numerous rebellions, or repulsing an invasion of aggressive steppe tribes. (Tacitus, *Romans*, XII, 10-11, XIII, 38). They were unable to succeed in liquidating even the Sassanid's however, who were much better at dealing with this. Indirect proof of such action regarding the main forces of the Parthian army my also be the fact that to resist Crassus' invasion, supposedly at the time when King Orodes with the core of his army was busy putting down a revolt in Armenia (Plutarch, *Crassus*, 25), necessitated the use of troops from the Šūren clan under it's own command, which was the best in the country. (Plutarch, *Crassus*, 21). Except for the fact that is was not too big, and its application of its fighting principals of steppe tactics which was still the basis of strategy of the Arsacid army, pulling the opponent into an area inconvenient for him to fight, avoiding a general clash and exposing the enemy to a "carpet" of archery fire. The noble origin of the armored riders should be considered as a masterly economic use of heavy cavalry during battle. The commander-in-chief, which was after all vying for clients as well heavy feudal cavalry, could not afford to lose the elite court in battle, people who were not only the basis to his strength, but also the support for his power. Mercenaries and the free subjects of the lower classes could die. Feudal lords had the task of command, overseeing and leading the decisive blow. Carrhae is the example of this economic use of armored cavalry.

Chapter III
The Sassanids –
The Second Persian Empire

The last century of the reign of the Arsacid dynasty was marked by rebellion and bloody rivalry for the throne. The great feudal families treated their vast possessions like almost ducal princes having not done much to help the central government, and even they did not hesitate to use it or their own purposes as a game between members of the ruling dynasty. Deposing rulers on the Arsacid throne became the norm for those who could secure the support of the most powerful magnates. Parthian rulers became dependent on the cooperation of powerful feudal families to turn a blind eye on a regular basis between their wars that were usually only their nominal vassals. The situation was even worse on the periphery of the empire. The Arsacids had been around for a long time and they had problems controlling the distant provinces which had a tradition of local power. Finally, a rebellion sparked in the south by a native local Persian ruler named Ardashir, from the powerful Sassanid against the last descendants of Arsaces I of Parthia.

Ardashir was the younger son of Papak, an aristocrat and son of the high priest of the goddess Anahity in the city of Estahr.[1] At the beginning of his rise to power, he became heir to his father, after he disposed of his older brother Shapur, who was first in line to the title of King of Persia. It is not entirely clear when he was able to do this (although it is possible that Shapur was not "removed" because he gave his brother's name to his son afterwards), the path to a great career was before he became the ruler of Persia. In a short time, he gained control of Far as well as the lands of Isfachanu and Kerman, imposing his rule over the feudal lords of those provinces. We do not know if his goal was to gain a dominant position among the great feudal families of Iran, or the final overthrown of Arsacid

---
[1] B. Kaim, *Irańska ideologia władzy królewskiej w okresie panowania Sasanidów*, Warszawa 1997, p. 15.

rule. The fact is that the growing power of the Sassanid's power finally drew the attention of the formal sovereign Artaban V, forcing him to take action. The long delay and complete lack of response to usurpation of power and battles in Persia are the best evidence of the state of the Parthian king's power. As was the old custom, Artaban gave the first order to suppress the rebellion to a local king named Ahwasz, however, when he was defeated, Artaban decided to intervene with the crown armed forces. Ardashir clashed with the Parthians in three great battles. In the last one, fought at Hormuzdegan in the area of Suzjan the army of the last of the Arsacid was destroyed and the monarch himself was killed. His head was sent to Persia and hung in the temple of Anahita in Persepolis (Estahr).[2]

Until today, there is no consensus on the exact date of this decisive clash. In truth, the text called the chronicle of Arbela gives the date of the day under the current calendar as 28 April 224 AD, but that is not entirely reliable.[3] It certainly did not happen later than the year 226. After this great victory, Ardashir began the complete conquest of the lands of the disintegrating Parthian monarchy. His armies conquered Media, Horasan and Gurgan, while his victories spread his fame far and wide. Against the growing power of the Sassanids stood a coalition of forces under Hosroesa I and the Arsacid king of Armenia, the Romans, Kushan and northern steppe people. On Ardashir's side, there was only one of the powerful Parthian families – the Karens. Armenia was defeated after a ten-year campaign. Several defeats in the field dampened the enthusiasm of the Roman troops and the steppe nomads. The Kushans also finally gave up and sent a delegation to make peace. Resistance against the Sassanid government subsided. Ardashir and his son Shapur did not forget either the Romans nor the Kushan's participation in the hostile coalition.

Just two years after the Battle of Hormuzdegan, Ardashir was crowned king in Cteiphon,[4] the capital of the defeated Arsacid, but now his victories gave powerful evidence to his opponents of his divine embrace of Hwarena and the start of a dynasty, under whose authority Iran remained until the Arab conquest in 651.

The defeat and collapse of the old dynasty brought considerable, though not drastic changes in the field of weapons and tactical doctrine. The military of the early Sassanid's in Iran we observe, continued most of the military trends from the end of the previous period. The main forces of the army remained two formations that formed the backbone of the Parthian troops. This attack force consisted of squadrons of armored cavalry supported by horse archers, which is not completely different from

---
[2] loc. cit..
[3] A. D.H. Bivar, op.cit., p. 275.
[4] B. Kaim, op.cit., p. 15.

the descriptions of Plutarch. The number and significance of infantry began to return again to its place within the battle ranks of the Sassanid army. This was part of a serious effort to improve the ability of the Persian forces to besiege and acquire fortified positions. The centralized power of the Sassanid kings also allowed, at least temporarily, to reduce the weakness of the undisciplined and autocratic feudal lords, whose influence which must have given the Great King problems but remained significant. While they were not cut down, eventually military reforms in the VI century AD carried out by Hosroesa I and Aygirvana created a professional army of lower nobility, and equipped by the ruler, led by his favored professional generals under the title of Spahbadas. In general, the entire military history of the Sassanids references the old military system of the Achaemenids, which survived in the mountainous regions of Fars in the century since the fall of the first Persian empire. The wars with the Romans, in addition, contributed to its further transformation. It can even be simplified to say that it had maintained its characteristic features, but due to the continuous bloody wars of Persia and Rome, the armies began to become more and more like each other. A new era in the history of armed conflicts began in the east.

1. The Cavalry in the Sassanid Army

Sources. Sources contributing to our knowledge of the weapons and tactics of units in the Sassanid Army are scarce compared to the rich information of the Parthian period, which does not allow us to fully recreate and study the Persian Army of this period. Thanks to the descriptions of the ancient writers, we gain a broader view of the military perspective of some, but not very long periods of history from this Persian dynasty. Although, after summing up all the information contained in them, we can roughly trace the development of the weapons and tactics, though most of the information applies only to the first centuries of the reign for the descendants of Ardashir.

Ammian Marcellinus, whose work, "The History of Rome" is one of the most important sources of research on militaria and tactics of the Sasanid Persian army focusing on the Roman's campaigns against the troops of Shapur II, in the Persian campaign led by Julian the Apostate. Interesting information by Heliodorus in turn, contained in the ninth book of his, "Ethiopia", are primarily about the mythical clash between Hydraspe, the King of Ethiopia, in whose name resonates the descriptions of Herodotus who considered the dark-skinned inhabitants of Punjab to be Eastern Ethiopians with the Persian noble Orontes. They portrayed with weapons and tactics from around the III-IV centuries AD, i.e., although the period in which the work was created was still unclear. It is difficult to see, because the information on the Persian Army from this contemporary era of the ancient writer mixes the stories from the works of the early historians, such as, Herodotus' Achaemenid army of the V-IV centuries BCE. The ancient authors fabricated portions of the information to serve as a gap filler to include colorful descriptions of imaginary battles. They should therefore be treated carefully.[5] The descriptions of the Sassanid army contained in the "Life of Alexander Severus" from the collection "History of the Augusti" is only a collection of supplemental sources previously cited that relate to events in the III Century AD.[6]

The picture captured on the basis of ancient written sources can luckily be complemented by the collected works of Arab historians such as Tabari, and the analysis of pictorial representations, which are mainly Sassanid royal rock reliefs.

Of the twenty-eight bas-reliefs of this type, four depict battle scenes. First, the most magnificent and probably the best preserved adorns the walls of the gorge near Firuzabad in the province of Fars – called the Firuzabad Relief or the Ardashir relief. Three others were placed on the rocky slope in Naksz-I Rustam, and their attribution is not entirely certain. This should of course be commonly known as a bas-relief made on the orders of Ardashir III or Hosroesa II Tag-e Bustan.[7]

Another group of pictorials representation of scenes placed on Sasanid silver plates, made with a great attention to detail and artistic value, probably as an offering of a particularly valuable gift by the king. They did not show battle scenes, only hunting, and in combination with hunting scenes from rock reliefs, and royal inscriptions such as Shapur II on the Ka'ba-ye Zardost-Stone Zoroaster in Naksz-i Rustam, and Tang-e Borag, however, which helps with the reconstruction of archery techniques and equipment used by the Sassanid soldiers.[8]

ARMORED CAVALRY. The core and main force of the Persian Army during the rule of the Sassanid Dynasty remained, as during the Parthian era, the armored cavalry. In its offensive and protective equipment is clearly seen as the continued development and improvement of the military achievements of the Arsacid Army. The earliest example of a representation of a Sassanid mounted warrior dates from the first half of the III century AD on the Firuzabad Relief. From the small details shown

---

[5] Heliodorus, *Opowieść etiopska o Theagenesie i Chariklei*, tłum. S. Dworacki, Poznań 2000. pp. 308-315.
[6] M.Mielczarek, op.cit., p. 30.
[7] B. Kaim, op.cit., p. 28, A. D. H. Bivar, op.cit., pp. 275-278.
[8] A. D. H. Bivar, op.cit., p. 278.

there, in a fight against the Arsacids, three Persian armored horsemen, including the creator of the new Iranian dynasty, Ardashir as well as his son and heir Shapur.

All the Sassanid knights wear heavy armor, but not as powerful as their Arsacid adversaries. Their bodies are protected with forged breast plates, reinforced in the edges by a border or a riveted strip. Perpendicularly through Shapur's breastplate runs a ridge to cause the points of spears aimed at the chest to slide to the side.[9] The cuirass featured two small balls or pompoms. This type of steel breastplate was worn over a long-sleeved chainmail shirt that reached down to mid-thigh, below the bottom edge of the breastplate forming a kind of apron. The elongated sleeves protected the top of hand by covering the whole area up to the fingers.

It is not possible that members of powerful families who provided the armor that would not meet all the equipment required of them. Because they were known to use Clibanarii tactics for attacks which exposed the breast and belly of the horse, the heaviest armor was logically covering these parts of the body. The use of the breastplate for this purpose was already attributed to the Parthians, but they also used stiff and heavy tubular armor for the arms and legs. With a single use kopia, the blow was derived from the use of momentum while the mass of riders on mounts in a similar manner to a medieval charge of lances, the repetition of a charge would not be possible, as no clibanarius would try to waste an attack against an opponent's hand weapons. Even if such a tactic were attempted, he could risk dying on a spear, pierced by the enemy. The risk as too great. To a heavy cavalryman, receiving a wound was only possible in a fight using edged weapons after charging the enemy first, created by a line of Sasanid cavalry that cut into the wedge of the opponent's troops. In this phase of the battle, however, having too much armor covering the hands would be more of hindrance than help. Chain mail was light, and breathable (which in the climate of Iran was a considerable advantage), non-restrictive to movements and resistant to edged weapons. At the same time, it is important advantage that it was better protection that you could combine with elements of plate,[10] for example the breastplate, as was used by the Sassanids, in the Middle Ages in Europe or in the Islamic Middle East using the so-called "Char-aina" – mirror armor.[11]

The archaeological material of preserved chain mail fragments is so low that it is impossible to create any kind of typology. Those belonging to warriors of the Iranian-speaking people are known, but it is only

---

[9]A. D. H. Bivar, op.cit., p. 278.

[10]loc. cit..

[11]Z. Żygulski jun, *Stara broń w polskich zbiorach*, Warszawa 1984, pp. 213, 210-211

The Firuzabad Relief showing the victory of Ardashir I over Artaban V, the last of the Arsacid rulers. (L. Vanden Berghe, Reliefs Rupestres de l'Iran ancien, *Table 8)*

through small fragments from excavations of Sarmatian burial mounds, i.e. the Woronżeska Stanica or barrow No. 2 at Łysoj Gore. From the Persians, such armor was found in a siege tunnel at Dura-Europos. They are also very small fragments of chain aventails preserved on helmets from the Parthian and Sassanid periods. Unfortunately, due to the small number of finds and their state of preservation not much can be said for their design. The rings were usually produced from steel, wrought or pulled wire. After they were joined, their overlapping rings were probably riveted.[12] It is possible, as in Roman mail that for strengthening the entire structure, one ring in five was solid, joined similarly to the other four but riveted.

To this day there are disputes as to where chain mail was invented, and thus the way it spread across the ancient world. The oldest example supposedly comes from a Scythian burial mound from Żurowka near Kiev dated to the fifth century BCE, however, its context requires verification. We can confirm findings associated with this type of armor to Gaul in the Le Tene and as well as Hallstatt periods.[13] It can be assumed that when the armor was invented it was not very resistant to thrusts, while retaining excellent protection against cuts, it should be attributed to people whose main type of weapon was the slashing sword, such as the Celts.[14] The arrows from short Scythian bows, could get stuck in the mesh of a well-made, riveted chainmail, which would argue in favor of its usefulness to nomadic warriors. Thus, the mail in the burial mound from Żurowka. Despite this, scale armor was better suited for this purpose, and this fact was probably the reason for the long absence of mail rings in the equipment based on the power of archery, the army of the Middle East and the steppe people. The exception was the Sarmatians, who after moving into the lands formerly occupied by the Scythians in the Ukraine and the Pannonian Plain, the use of chain mail became quite common, especially when used in combination with scale armor on the front and back.[15] The heaviest equipped Sarmatian cavalry still used complete scale armor, though chainmail was popular as well.[16]

It is possible that even the Sarmatian tribes could have used chain mail from Celtic influences, as well as Roman, but it must have been the Sassanid influence on their western neighbor. But, you can completely rule out the fact that these are the effects of the Persian's contact with this tribal army of the western steppes. The first chainmail was already in

---

[12] loc. cit.
[13] Z. Żygulski jun., *Broń starożytna, Grecja, Rzym, Galia, Germania*, p. 94,164.
[14] loc. cit..
[15] А. М. Хαзαнов, op.cit., pp. 60-61
[16] А. М. Хαзαнов, op.cit., pp. 60-62.

the army of the last Arsacids, where they were used as excellent protection for heavily armored archers which supported more and more often the steppe riders in melee, charging with the armored cavalry and replacing the old type of unarmored archer. During the Sassanid period, as we know from the scenes at the Firuzabad relief, they are already equipped as clibanarii and they appear to be the richest armor.

The Persian leg armor depicted on Ardashir's relief was still protected through tubular, segmented sections, performing the same way as the armor of the Arsacid heavy cavalry from overlapping ring-shaped segments.

Each of the Sassanid warriors whose images were carved on the Firuzabad relief is equipped with a different protective headgear. Ardashir is fighting heroically with his head exposed and hair covered in a royal tiara, decorated with two wide, striped ribbons fluttering in the wind, well-known from appearances on the so-called "Investury Relief",[17] which is a symbol of royal power. Above the tiara the hair is gathered in a high intricate bun, which sources show reached back to the ancient ways of the steppe peoples and was worn in this manner by some of the Arsacid rulers. In later pictorials it is represented as a characteristic element of royal Sassanid hairstyle.[18] Fighting bareheaded in the first line of armored cavalry, probably as commander of this type of troops at the head of the wedge formation, of course, is a kind of propaganda and artistic fiction. During the Battle of Hormozgan, Ardashir probably wore all his clibanarii armor including his helmet.

Due to the damage to the relief, not much can be said about Prince Shapur's helmet. It can be claimed, however, that he was similar to the one which protects the head of the third Sassanid, struggling to combat the Grand Vizier of the last of the Arsacids. This is a characteristic shaped head protection, probably made from one piece of metal, because there are no visible slats joining segments or riveting. Because it is shown in profile, its form can not be precisely determined. It can be assumed, however, that the helmet is either flattened or round with a slightly flattened upper portion and the bell at the rear part protects the neck. In this case, the origin of the helmet depicted on the description of the Arsacid relief could be derived from a mounted warrior on a round terracotta tile from the second century with a lion hunting scene. On the surface of the third helmet of the Sassanid cavalry is applied a symbol, perhaps of seniority, something like the Japanese Mon. The bell-shaped headpiece of Shapur's is like his father's diadem was equipped with two-striped flowing ribbons, which is how you can determine the title of Crown Prince.

---
[17] B. Kaim, op.cit., p. 28.
[18] B. Kaim, op.cit., p. 56

The Armies of Ancient Persia

The main weapon of Ardashir's Sassanid's clibanarii remained the heavy spear, which however is clear from the relief was used in a similar manner as the Macedonian infantry Sarissa. The rider holds it on both hands, with the left hand extended forward and the right one pushing the spear about 1m away from the end. With this type of technique, completely dispensed with the counterweight in favor of the spearhead. The most common way to use this type of weapon as shown by representations is placing it across the horse's neck during a charge, with the tip directed in the area of the belt to drive it under the lower edge of the breastplate, or at the throat. By attacking the lower part of the body, the cumulative momentum of the rider and his mount, supported by the inertia of the body and the protection of the opponent. The combination of the attack speed of both opponents generated enormous punching force that "stuffed" the attackers deep into the opponent's line. The point of such a lance was able to rip through mail, scale or thin plate – piercing the opponent through. (Heliodor, Et, IX, 15). For thicker breastplates and less precise aim, the frequent result was the enemy knocked out of the saddle, which the artist did not fail to portray of the Firuzabad relief. A thrust to the neck was more difficult to do yet had more deadly consequences.

The strength and speed of the attack resulting in a hit that caused the weapon to pierce the body of the enemy or breaking the shaft. In each of these cases the lance was lost after this and they had to fight with melee weapons. According to this strategy the initial opponent of the warrior should have been dead, and the fight took place with the support soldiers. The elimination of the of the enemy's troops by the clibanarii wedge went up to the second and third ranks. Due to the limit of the length of the spear it could not reach further.

The secondary weapons of the Sassanid knight (ašvaran) were swords. They were usually long (about 1m) and mainly intended for slashing and to a lesser extend for stabbing. This method can be inferred from representations on the silver Sassanid plate on which animals – mostly lions are cut almost in half with one royal sword cut. Persian swords of this period had a massive hilt and a guard to capture and block the enemy blows and significant length metal blade, although a copy in jade was found in the siege tunnel at Dura-Europos.[19] All indications points to the use of advanced fencing in combat, which unfortunately we cannot say for sure. We can say, however, that a blow from horseback, combined with the physical strength of the Persians, could cut a lightly armored opponent in half. Among the warriors on Ardashir's relief is one soldier fighting in the last couple with a side-arm, however, such weap-

---
[19] М. И. Ростовцев, op.cit., p. 194.

ons were worn near the waist on the left side. This also confirms images of swordsmen courtiers equipped with swords on later rock reliefs commemorating the great victories of Persian rulers.

Although the described images of two representatives of the Sassanid family visible do not have swords, in combat, of course they had to have sidearms, otherwise they would be defenseless in the second phase of combat. Like their companion, they would have decorative, metal studded belts, which they used to hang melee weapons on the left hip, while a quiver with arrows hung on the right.

Apart from swords, the side weapons included a wooden club with iron heads or entirely metal maces. A blow from such a weapon according to "Shaname" in the Book of Kings, "Artabanus V died in battle at Hormuzdegan". Although we don't see their appearance on the Firuzabad relief among the Persians, we have the image of a huge wooden mace in the hand of the enemy. The relief was made at the behest of King Hormizdt II. Information on the common use of maces is available from the description of the military parade of Hosroes cavalry, and where they are exchanged among the various weapons forming the equipment of armored cavalry.[20] The heads are probably metal, carefully decorated examples of such weapons broken in a clash appear on a silver plate which is most likely from Sogdiana and dated by B.I. Marszaka to the VII century AD.[21]

Two of the Persians fighting that are depicted in the Firuzabad relief have a long body quiver attached to their belt, which is probably the normal equipment for the Sassanid clibanarius. Ardashir himself probably had a similar quiver, but because of the damage to the carving, it isn't possible to confirm this. The quivers of this type were known from the Parthian period from hunting graffiti in the Temple of Artemis in Dura.[22] They are characterized by the lack of an integral cover and the length matched the length of the arrow that are just visible above the edge of the narrow throat, which was identical to those discovered by M. Rostovceva during the excavations at Dura. Despite having quivers, there is no sign of the armored Sassanid's bows. This may be due to the placement of bow on the left side, probably attached to the saddle. In the absence of this, the bow was intended to be carried in the quiver which was already typical, with the characteristic shape of the bow already called Sasanidine. This will be described in detail a little further on. Missile weapons were for obvious reason, only auxiliary weapons of the clibanarii cavalry, and it was used to carry out missile attacks before the start of the charge,

---

[20] A. D. H. Bivar, op.cit., p. 276.
[21] B. Stawiski, op.cit., p. 279.
[22] B. Goldman, op.cit., pp. 35-37.

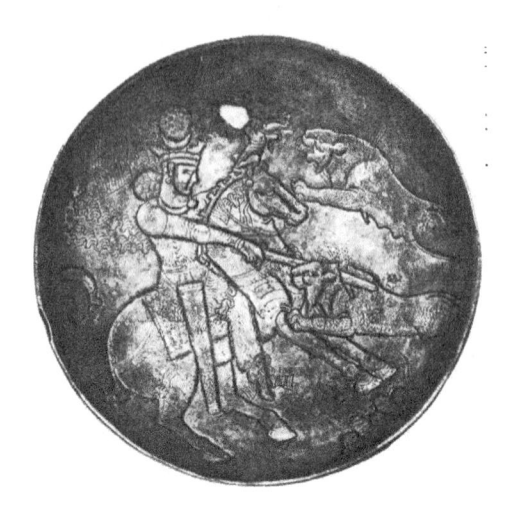

King (Perhaps Bahram II) killing lion with a sword blow - draws attention to the stroke, similar to the so-called "Italian" grip more reminiscent saber grips than sword grips (from P. Wilcox, A. Mcbride, Rome's enemies 3, Parhians and Sassanid Persians, fig. 40)

7th century Sogdian plate with a scene of a duel between two armored warriors. (from to B. Stawiski, Sztuka Central Asia, fig. 188)

Bahamas II, a Sassanid ruler receiving a delegation from one of the nomadic peoples. The sword draws attentionleading Persa delegation - simple, quite wide guards are visible. (from to L. Vanden Berghe, Reliefs Rupestresde lran ancien, *Tab. 28)*

during a retreat and other extraordinary cases. The main method of attack remained the frontal charge with a heavy spear, after which they fought with white weapons, axes, heavy wooden or metal-bound clubs, etc. in which the Persians did great.

The horses of the Sassanid clibanarii were protected by a leather or cloth barding, the use of which were mentioned from the time of Shapur II by Ammianus Marcellinus (Ammianus. History of Roman, XXIV, 8). As shown at Firuzabad they are broad animal blankets combined into armor protecting the neck and head, particularly the sides. They are different because of the shape of the reinforced studs, whose form had symbolic meaning. The barding of Ardashir's mount is studded with, for example, with metal plates cut out in the shape of a stylized royal crown with two decorative ribbons. It seems that this barding had the task of protecting the animal, not from the points of spears, which for tactical reasons were not a threat, but from the swords of the enemies. Previously, this type of blow would have been effectively shielded so that the plates did not have to be arranged into one piece of armor as was discovered in tower 19 at Dura.[23] No mention of heavy metal armor covering the horse suggests that their use gradually decreased. They only returned during the late-Sassanid period. The main combat advantage of the clibanarii units was their first strike ability through great attack speed, and heavy armored mounts would only reduce it. This fact should also be associated with a significant reduction of the weight of protective armor by relieving the exposed lower parts of the body to strikes, while reinforcing the exposed parts. This more effective protection was implemented by using solid plates instead of scale or lamellar which would have been heavier. You must not fail to appreciate the freedom of movement obtained by the introduction of chain mail. The Sassanid armored cavalry use of maneuverability and mobility in combat clearly starts from the assumption that the best defense is an attack. It appears that this gave them victory over the heavy and slow units, acting in a similar order of battle and system of the last of the Arsacid's cavalry.

Another "window" that allows us to look into the appearance and fighting techniques of the Sassanid heavy cavalry are provided by the reliefs, located on the great graves of the famous, during the reign of the second Persian dynasty, the almost legendary ruler of the Achaemenid's, on the rock wall at Nakszil Rustam. There are two bas-reliefs, including one composed of a set of two relief panels. Based on the shape of the crown identified on the main character of the double relief, A.D.H. Bivar interprets the bas-relief to have been made on orders of King Bahram II.[24]

---

[23] М. И. Ростовцев, op.cit., pp. 440-443
[24] A. D. H. Bivar, op.cit., p. 279.

The Armies of Ancient Persia

This interpretation would also explain (to be explained later) the execution of the two separate presentations. In the lower panel, the opponent of the Sassanid ruler has a helmet on his head, which can be interpreted as one of the types of Roman cavalry helmets. The similarity for this is found on the bas-relief adorning the so-called Helena sarcophagus located in the Vatican.[25] On this basis, we can say that we are dealing with the allegorical representation of the most important campaigns of Bahram II, in the later probably against the Roman Emperor Carus whose army invaded Persia in the days of Bahram II, and temporarily even occupied Ctesiphon.[26] What is strange, however, on the Sassanid relief, is the Emperor shown dying at the hands of Persian ruler, while according to written sources he died under unexplained circumstances,[27] just after the occupation of the former Arsacid capital due to the military campaign. The reason for his death is sometimes given to being struck by lightning, but it seems suspicious. It is possible that the emperor was really murdered, through a conspiracy, or by killers sent by Bahram. In either case he could claim victory over Carus with his likeness. How it happened it was no longer important. It is known that Shapur I showed the death of Emperor Gordian III under his horse in the same way, even though he was killed in the face of defeat by a mutiny of Roman officers.

The higher panel should probably be based on the comparisons by E. Herzfeld of written sources mentioning the defeat of Carus, as the great triumph of the Sassanid rulers and consider it an allegory of the victory of Bahram II by his cousin Hormizd over the Sakastanians (Sīstān).[28] This event should probably be connected to the specific relief cut into the rock at Sar Mashhad. It shows the ruler killing the lion attacking him with the thrust of the sword. The second lion is lying dead under the feet of the king. The fact that this is not one of the usual hunting reliefs as it pictures an unusual weapon used to kill the beast and the fact that the king pierces the lion with one hand, while he holds a woman in rich robes by the hand – probably the queen. Behind them there is an unknown group of nobles with the most frequently used hunting weapon – the bow. In the interpretation of E. Herzfeld, one of the lions represents the Roman Emperor, the other being the Sakastani. These are the two greatest enemies of Bahram, and his two greatest victories.[29] It is worth noticing the figure who is knocked down by the Sassanid ruler on the upper panel of the relief in Naksh-i Rustam which is not explained by any member of his family who commanded in the campaign, as he has a head-

---

[25] loc. cit..
[26] A. D. H. Bivar, op.cit., p. 280.
[27] P. Iwaszkiewicz, W. Łoś, M. Stępień, op.cit., p. 212.
[28] A. D. H. Bivar, op.cit., p. 280.
[29] loc. cit..

gear bearing an ornament in the form of a lion's head, which is known from representations on the coins of Hormizd Sakastan. In contrast to the ancient imagination or deriving from the culture of the ancient Near East, in tradition, the Zoroastrian lion is not a royal beast, but one of the helpers of Ahriman – the rulers of the darkness.[30] The message behind this presentation is not difficult to understand. The defeated Sakastan can also be associated with the figure under the hooves of the royal horse in the lower register of the relief.[31] The identity of the enemy falling under the hooves of the victor's horse of the upper register is not, unfortunately known.

It is now possible to proceed to a discussion on the armaments shown on the reliefs at Naksz-I Rustam, the characters and changes that have taken place in this area in a relatively short period, because only thirty years elapsed from the time of the battle pictured on the Firuzabad relief - these changes are surprisingly significant.

At first glance, the weight of heavy armor is evident. The chainmail is gone, while the armor is made in a style similar to the armorers of the last Arsacids. The body of the armored rider is still protected by a plate breastplate, but his apron is made of metal scales. Like the late Parthian armor, reaching to mid-thigh. The arms are covered with tubular manica composed of ring-shaped overlapping segments. Identically designed leggings protect the rider's legs against injury. The helmet of the victor on the upper part of the relief has a shape that is hard to identify. It is bell shaped round in outline, but the lack of cheek pieces and rivet marks suggests it was made from one piece of metal. The headgear worn, probably by Bahram II, is marked by placing a corymbus (topknot) on the top – characteristic of royal hairstyles, a ball of hair of other material, and the decorative wings of Bahram's crown. On the back of the helmet and breastplate are extremely fancy, fluttering wide ribbons which constitute a characteristic element of iconography for Sassanid rulers, while the arms of the breastplate show large spherical pompoms. The king's opponent as much as can be determined based on the significant damage to the relief, wears armor which based on the outline seems very similar the those of the king.

The same type armor is actually visible on the protagonist on the lower part of the scene, only the helmet is different. Its shape is also not easy to recognize, but it is clearly provided with a fastened collar from the helmet to protect the head and neck from sword cuts.

The main fighting weapon of the cavalrymen were spears that were used in a similar way to the medieval lance or the Macedonian saris-

---
[30] A. D. H. Bivar, op.cit., p. 281.
[31] loc. cit..

sa. The technique of using this heavy and extremely dangerous weapon, in comparison to the combat methods shown on the Firuzabad relief are shown with significant differences. First, the point of attack is no longer at the targeting the belt area, but the throat of the opponent. This type of thrust requires more precision and skill for the warrior, but it was also more effective and deadlier, especially when the opponent was wearing heavy armor. In extreme cases and with high efficiency in the use of the long spear, this technique allowed the riders to stab at the body without breaking the shaft and using it against the next enemy rider. Incidentally, this type of weapon used a large spearpoint capable of penetrating steel armor with a thick, stiff shaft.

The secondary weapons, most visible on the waist of the main antagonist character at the bottom of the panel of the bas-reliefs is the long sword. The weapon shown has detailed characteristics associated with the swords of Sassanid warriors and courtiers, as well as the fighting armored clibanarii depicted on other cave bas-reliefs. The weapon is characterized by considerable length, which is of course necessary when using it from the horse's back, bisected by a large guard, whose shapes can be admired on representations known from great Sassanid silver plates, with long mustaches visible on the walls of the Naksz-i Rustam gorge.

Swords were worn at the waist on the left side, while on the right side was hung a long tubular quiver of which the arrows were visible over the edge. Not visible on this presentation was the bow that was placed in a sperate case.

The horses of the cavalrymen were protected by extensive, probably leather scales combined with traditional shaped scales protecting the neck and head. No metal scales are visible on the armor which suggests a further desire to relieve the weight on the animals, especially when they increased the weight of the rider's protective armor. Thick and properly hardened by fire, it could protect horses against arrows, but could not efficiently protect them from direct thrusts of swords and spears. We can say with a high probability, however, that this was not their job. Some parts of the harness and horse armor was probably decorated with large tails, pompoms and ribbons in bright colors.

Another of the battle reliefs at Naksz-i Rustam is the so-called relief Number 3.[32] To this day, the king who ordered it has not been identified, or the events that it is linked to. So, we can not say anything about dating the relief. It presents a traditional duel scene between heavily armored cavalry. The main character does not wear a crown; however,

---

[32] Designated according to H. von Galla, *Das reiterkampfbild in der iranisher und iranish beeinflussten Kunst parthisher und sasanidisher Zeit*, Berlin 1990

The Armies of Ancient Persia

Double relief of Bahram II - Naksh-i Rustam (Top) original, (Bottom) representation (from A. D. H. Bivar, Cavalry Equipment and Tactics on the Euphrates Frontier, *fig. 11, M. Mielczarek,* Cataphracti and Clibanari *..., fig. 11)*

Relief of Bahram II at Sar Mashad. (from L. Vanden Berghe, Reliefs Rupestres de lran ancien, *Tab. 29)*

A Sassanid relief of unknown origin from a rock wall in Naksh-i Rustam (a) original, (b) representation (from A. D. H. Bivar, Cavalry equipment and tactics on the Euphrates frontier, *fig. 19)*

A stone relief of Hormizd II at Naksz-I Rustam (from R. Ghirschman, Iran: Parthians and Sassanians, *fig 220, 219)*

it can be identified by comparing it to other characters on the coins of Sassanid rulers. Its "corners" are finished with pompoms and wavy short ribbons. On the back one ribbon is longer and more fanciful. It is a king because the protagonist should be interpreted as the representation of a just ruler, wearing a plate cuirass, whose arms are decorated with two pompoms, superimposed on a long-sleeved chainmail shirt. The lower part below belt on which the quiver is hung creates a protective apron for the upper part of the legs. The whole leg was probably covered but unfortunately you can not recognize this on the heavily damaged bas-relief through segmented trousers, his arms through the sleeves of the mail shirt reaching down to the wrist. His armored antagonist is substantially the same, but the head and face are protected with a helmet that has a metal mask imitating the features of a bearded man. It is impossible to say, however, whether it is the face of the helmet's owner himself, or some imaginary face. He is not a Roman, because a characteristic Sassanid striped ribbon, fluttering at the back of the helmet, and the top of the helmet there is a small bell tassel something like a plume.

Behind the king's figure is clearly another rider holding a kind of war banner or standard in the shape of a long pole with a bar on the top of it with three balls and at the bottom with two decorative balls or pompoms. The standard bearer himself is armored just as powerfully as the warrior clibanarii. It is difficult, however, to access what type of breastplate he is wearing, his apron, however, is made of metal scales. It can be assumed that the whole armor is of similar scales as the apron or assume that the rider is wearing a plate breastplate. The arms are protected by tubular segmented manicas, but we can't tell about leg protection below the apron because they are covered by the main horses' hindquarters in the relief.

The helmet of the "standard bearer" mimics the shape of the laterally flattened high caps known from the Parthian period, for example, from the representations on Arsacid coins they were extremely popular among members of the Sassanid court. A helmet of this type made as a spangenhelm with riveted and metal sheets with ribs, dating from the IV-V century AD is in the collection of the British Museum.[33]

The main weapon of the cavalrymen is traditionally the long hard spear. The victorious ruler drives his spearhead into the throat of his opponent, whose weapon is turned as if to emphasize his defeat, it is broken just behind the sleeve of the not very large spearhead. At the waist, none of the opponents are seen to have a bladed weapon, and only the king has the typical long, tubular quiver.

---

[33] P. Wilcox, A. Mcbride, op. cit., p. 33.

The horses of all the fighting figures are protected by leather barding, probably hoods and skirts as well. Interestingly, the harness belts are visible on the top, instead of, as it used to be, hidden underneath. Perhaps, however, what we are dealing with here is some artist's specific vision, on the assumption that it covers the whole body of the horse, and the flap of the girth going down to the harder than exposing it through the corresponding hole made in it for the saddle. The ornaments of the harness and horse's armor can clearly be seen increasingly as large pompoms, ribbons and fringe.

On this basis, the style, types of armor and weapons, one can assume that this relief does not essentially differ from the previously described bas-reliefs placed on the rocks of Naqsh-i Rustam. It probably shows the fight between the ruler with a rebel, however, coming from the royal house, hence the striped ribbons present with royal diadems on his helmet, or one of the legal pretenders to the throne. Detailed attribution is not possible.

The last of the battle reliefs placed at Naqsh-i Rustam comes from the time of Hormizd II.[34] Like the previous presentation, it shows a duel between two riders. It is probably the most recent Sassanid image of this type. The main character of the scene, probably the king, knocks the opponent off his horse, stabbing him in the stomach with a lance spearpoint. Although the details of the armor are not clearly visible you can still see some interesting details. The main body shown in the reliefs seems to be protected from attack by a solid breastplate, equipped with a scaly apron extending to mid-thigh. Segmented arms are decorated with spherical pompoms. The arms are covered with segmented manica. From what we can see the legs are not protected at all, at least from the knees down the characteristic broad fancy folds of Iranian trousers are clearly visible. The King does not wear any helmet, replacing it he is wearing a head covering with small points and long striped ribbons. Prof. Hinze has identified his antagonist as a Viceroy Papak, known from his inscription on a silver dish discovered in Georgia where he is armored in a similar manner, the only difference being the legs with segmented leggings, and on the head a finely made, decorated spherical helmet, equipped with a metal mask with the features of a bearded man.[35] The style design and the individual parts of the armor suggests that he is Iranian, which speaks in favor of Hinze's thesis, but this does not confirm it.

Behind the ruler is the figure of a standard bearer. He is armored very similar to his master. He wears a breastplate, covering for the legs and arms as well as a spherical helmet which extended down the back

---

[34] A. D. H. Bivar, op.cit., p. 281.
[35] loc. cit.

and fastened under the chin with a clasp. In his hands he holds a "banner" in the form of a long pole equipped with a cross bar, which hung two decorative cones or pompoms.

The horses of both combatants are protected with leather leggings without any metal components, the horse of the king also has a headband held by a buckle. By this time, the use of leather which did not protect as well, was probably abandoned for the heads and legs. In the surface, however, barding of reinforced metal scales is visible beginning just behind the horse's ears and extending halfway down the neck. The extension of this reinforced surface covers a significant part of the sides of the neck. As you can imagine, this armor was meant to cover the horse's neck against the downward blow of a sword from an enemy cavalryman. Perhaps such a scale reinforcement is what later horse armor derives from that covers the head, neck and breast of the animal. Although they are not visible here, Heliodor says in Ethiopia that the Persian had armored cavalry from the IV century, protected against attack on the lower legs which were assumed to be metal shin guards (Heliodor, Eth. IX, 15). Please keep in mind, however, that this author was not a historian and may have mixed information from several periods.

The main weapon of the rider is a long lance held with the right hand to the rear of the shaft, without a pointed backside. The defeated antagonist, however, holds a long heavy club in his hand, probably made of wood and without any visible metal fittings. The rest of the weapons were complemented with bows but are present only in the form of quivers hung from the belts of the riders.

The last of the reliefs showing armored Sassanid cavalrymen is placed away from the previous ones from a different era. It dates from the reign of the last of the great Persian rulers, Hosroes II Parvez (according to other theories it was Ardashir III) and carved it in the rock outcrop at Tag-e Bustan. The image shows the same Hosroes as an armored cavalryman.[36] The rider is dressed in a long, unusually accurate knee length mail shirt with long-sleeves although the right arm, which could be seen, was destroyed, while the left is covered by a shield. The rider's helmet is made from a single sheet of metal, or more likely from two halves connected by ribs forming a spangenhelm. This type of helmet is visible on images of Sassanid knights depicted on the reliefs showing royal triumphs, but there are times when we see helmets that are only leather caps. The top of the bell-shaped helmet of the armored cavalryman on the relief of Hosroes II is topped with a large corymbos (comb) that holds flowing ribbons. On the bottom edge surrounding it is a long hood of chain mail covering the face with holes to see out (the top edge is reinforced with

---

[36] B. Kaim, op.cit., p. 184.

metal strips that mimic eyebrows and the lower braid of the hood). This is possibly a continuation of helmets with metal masks. Unfortunately, it is not possible to trace the progression between the two forms, due to the lack of evidence showing the development path of the Sassanid helmet. The legs of the described armored cavalryman or those not armored at all are only protected by the large skirt of the robe, or leggings made of thick, textiles or leather that covered up to the ankles. Reducing the strength of the armor was made by discarding the breastplate which is compensated by the introduction of armored cavalry shields to the equipment that resemble the crocuses of the steppes – i.e. discs made of coiled, wood braided with thread and reinforced with metal studs and or clips which does not seem to be accidental, and probably influenced by nomadic peoples. Incidentally, a quote in Amman Marcellina's "History of Rome" indicates that this part of the protective equipment was in place from the time of Shapur II. *From the first attack, the king himself was surrounded by heavily armed riders in shiny armor, towering over the others, rode around the walls of the fortress and boldly went up to the edge of the moat. Although the Ballista missiles and shot rained heavily on him, he escaped unharmed by the protection of shields arranged around him like a tortoise shell.* (Amman. History of Rome, XX, 7.2) It is possible, however, that in addition to the king's horse guard, one of the guard infantry units was equipped like all heavy infantry with large, convex, rectangular reed shields covered with leather.

The main weapon of the armored cavalryman from Tag-e Bustan was still a spear, it is much shorter and lighter than the lances used at the time of he first Sassanids. This is probably due to a change in the fighting techniques, as a light spear inflicted blows above the shoulder, as the chest was covered by a shield held in the hand, suspended on the forearm or from the shoulder. The spear attack was inflicted using the momentum of the horse and rider. Such weapons were much better suited for close combat than the old type of specialized weapon for use during battles with enemy units fighting in the same way. Its application implies there was probably a change in the overall fighting tactics. Massed charges were abandoned in favor of efficient maneuvering in combat, heavy units, not aimed at crushing an enemy formation in one frontal charge, but maneuvering around it, attacking on the flanks or in other close cooperation with light cavalry.

The heavy cavalry at Tag-e Bustan are not equipped with any side arms, perhaps the sword is not visible because it was hung by the belt on the left side, and the only secondary weapon is a bow. This time it is clearly visible as part of a crescent quiver that holds a characteristic Sassanid type reflexive bow, hanging on the saddle, on the left side. In the shape and manner of wearing the quiver, however, major changes have taken place. First, it is not in the shape of a long pipe widening at the top, but in now expands at the bottom and is suspended angled toward the front. In this shape and manner of wearing a quiver, they have clear influences of the nomadic Turkish people, and the analogy to them can also be found in the other end of the territories inhabited by the Altai people, i.e. China's T'ang Dynasty. The shape and design of saddles with tall curves instead of holding corners is probably a Turkish influence as well as most importantly stirrups. Even the casual observer can se that the rider's feet in the Hosroes II relief are positioned horizontally. This is the position for riding with stirrups when a cavalryman digs their legs in them. Positioning the feet in this manner was not known or needed before the introduction of stirrups and was never shown in the iconography of people unfamiliar with it. To this day, the outlines of the destroyed ones can be still seen, probably metal stirrups which can be dated from the beginning of the VII century.[37] In the Far East, they were completely developed in their final form where they were quite well known.[38]

The armor of the cavalryman from Tag-e Bustan shows an unusual development in the use of horse protection by the armored clibanarii cavalry. It tightly covers the head, neck, chest and forelegs of the animals that came down to the knees with heavy armor of small scales sewn together with wire or metal strips. The armor was clearly used to protect the animal from a frontal assault against dense attacks of arrows and probably spears as well. It should be remembered that the enemy posing the greatest threat came from the northern and north-eastern borders of the empire, the Turkish people employing mass cavalry archers, the large numbers of which the Sassanid Army did not use compared the Arsacids. The short and light spears o the Turkish cavalry were expertly trained to fight in close quarters and reform to fight and charge had many advantages in the face of having to fight the new style adopted by the Sassanids who armed their armored cavalry like them.

The introduction of two basic items should be considered an example of Turkish influence on Persian cavalry, the interesting and characteristic curved sabers with cross-pieces, imported from the Far East in the V-VII century AD, appearing in Persia, and approximately the VIII – IX century AD with the Turkish people to Europe. They were slightly curved in the direction of one of the towards the handle with one edge sharp and the top dull and unusual decorations on the scabbard wrapped in leather

---

[37] B. Kaim, op.cit., p. 184.

[38] Л. А. Евтюхова, *Стремия танской эпохи из уйбатского чаатаса*, Краткие Собщения о Доккладах и Полевых Исследованиях Института Археологии и Матеряльной культуры XXXIII, Москва 1948, pp. 40-44.

Relief of Hosroes II from Tag-e Bustan. (according to A. D. H. Bivar, Cavalry equipment and tactics on the Euphrates frontier, *Fig. 28)*

This and the next image are parts of a huge hunting relief from Tag-e Bustan of the VII century (according to R. Ghirschman, Iran: Parthians and Sassanians, *fig.236, s.297)*

The Armies of Ancient Persia

or skin. Images on silver plates show its use by them resembling the so-called Italian grip with four fingers supporting the bottom of the handle and the thumb pressing on it from above. This grip is reminiscent of the saber strike as it allows a much more efficient and faster use of the weapon with short quick cuts from the wrist.

It is generally known from analysis of the armed warriors of the warrior's arms shown in the battle scenes of the royal rock reliefs can be supplemented by data from written sources, i.e. battles fought by the Roman Army with the army of King Shapur II. Extensive descriptions of these events can be found in Amman's *History of Rome*. It is unfortunate that on this one occasion, a man who was an eye-witness to these fascinating events and called himself a soldier should have left such a vague description. Much better and more meaningful descriptions came from the pen of a civilian. More surprising is the almost complete lack of detailed descriptions of ranks, types of units, more detailed descriptions about their weaponry; advantages and disadvantages, and the rules of using weapons etc. In comparison with the quality of the work or Arrian, Amman appears rather a complete layman, who happened to have the opportunity participate in historical battles.

In his work, only the armored cavalry of Shapur is accurately described, its armament, however, is very different than their appearance shown on the relief (Amman, *History of Rome*, XXV, 11-13). It is possible that we are dealing with the heavy cavalry of the line units, while the reliefs represent on the kings and members of their immediate bodyguards.

Amman repeatedly mentions the development of armored cavalry from the old ways with metal plates, to the evolution of rigid plates covering the body apart from the guards which was not so far from the late-Parthian period. Amman moreover, seems to confirm the use of breastplates above all for the ruler's bodyguard when he wrote: *As soon as the day dawned you could see the gleaming armor with iron borders and shimmering breastplates. This indicated that the royal army had come.* (Amman, *History of Rome*, XXV, 1.1) The most comprehensive description of the Persian cavalry commander Merena fighting near Maranga near Ctesiphon in a battle against the Romans. "All these troops were clad in iron. Individual parts of the body completely covered with metal plates, in such a way that their rigid connections correspond to the joints in the body. Helmets had a likeness of a human face which was closely worn on the head. With metal plates completely covering the body, arrows fired at the body could only penetrate where there were small openings for the eyes which allowed limited vision or where you could barely breath through holes in the tip of the nose." (Amman, History of Rome, 1, 11-15).

The Armies of Ancient Persia

The fact that a helmet with a metal mask described by Amman has been struck in the eyes is identical to the helmet of the antagonist of King Hormizd II on the rock relief at Naqsh-i Rustam. This confirms the validity of the Roman historian. The same applies to the types of armor, spears and swords used by the Persian cavalry.

A description of the Persian heavy cavalry weapons similar to Amman's account is mentioned in *Ethiopia* by Heliodor:

Here is what their armaments looked like. The soldier must be chosen and stand out with physical strength. The helmet on his head is tight fitting, forged as a mask to look like a warrior's face. It covers the face completely from the top of the head to the neck except for the eyes so that he can see. He is armed with a spear, longer than a javelin, and the left has a free hold of the reins, while on the side hangs a sword; the whole body and not just the breast is covered with armor. It is arranged in the following way: square bronze and steel tile, wide and over-lapping on top of each other, joined together on the top forming a scale chiton that adheres to the body, but does not constrain, and although it surrounds every limb closely, it does not constrain the motion, letting it bend and strengthen. This armor has sleeves, extending from the neck to the knees, cut to the hips to allow ease in mounting the horse. This reflect the protection from wounds against missiles. He combines this armor with greaves that run from the foot to the knee. Similarly, they armor the horse. Legs are covered with greaves, they shield their head with a covering, and bard the horse with sewn dera iron covering from the back to the stomach, which at the same time the armor, thanks to the flexibility does not interfere with running." (Heliodor, *Ethiopia*, IX, 15)

If you disregard the bit of colorful style and clear reference to the description in Herodotus, *History* we have a general, but confirming description of everything he observed.

A more credible and detailed description of Hormizd's I cavalry was left in Tabari's work: "The equipment the cavalry had was brought with them: chain mail for the horse, a shirt for the soldier, a breastplate {probably plate}, plate covers the legs, a sword, a spear, a shield, a club and a rope clipped to a belt, battle axe or club together with two bows with their strings, thirty arrows and finally two braided cords that the rider would hang on his helmet. (Tabari 964) In this description, we see significant changes that have occurred in arming Sassanid cavalrymen in the two centuries since the time of Shapur II to the time of Hormizd

Relief of the victory of Szapur I, under the hooves of the ruler's horse lies the killed Emperor Gordian. (L. Vanden Berghe, Reliefs Rupestres de l'Iran ancien, *Tab. 22)*

A side-view of a Sassanid spangenhelm helmet of the IV – V centuries. (from P. Wilcox, A. McBride, Rome`s enemies 3, Parhians and Sassanid Persians, *fig. 39)*

The triumph of Shapur I in rock relief - the first group of courtiers in the lower right portion of the main scene wears helmets (probably from two solid halves joined with ribs) fitted with long, maybe leather neck covers (according to L. Vanden Berghe, Reliefs Rupestres de l'Iran ancien, *Tab. 23)*

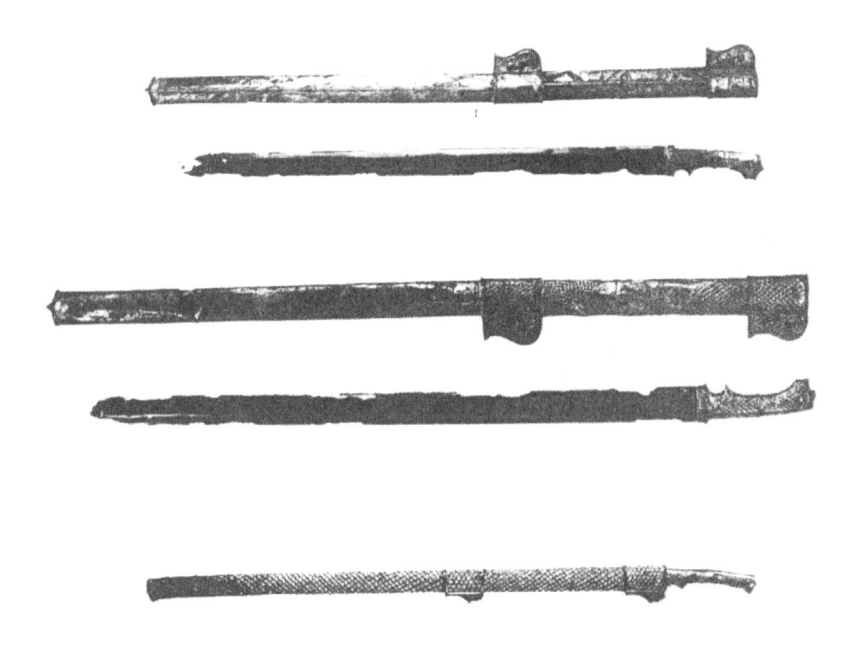

Sassanian swords with saber handles VI - VII century AD (from P. Wilcox, A. Mcbride, Rome`s enemies 3, Parthians and Sassanid Persians, *fig. 47.36)*

Khazar metal items including a single-edged sword very similar to the late Sassanid swords (from J. Chochorowski, Koczownica Ukraine, *fig. 2)*

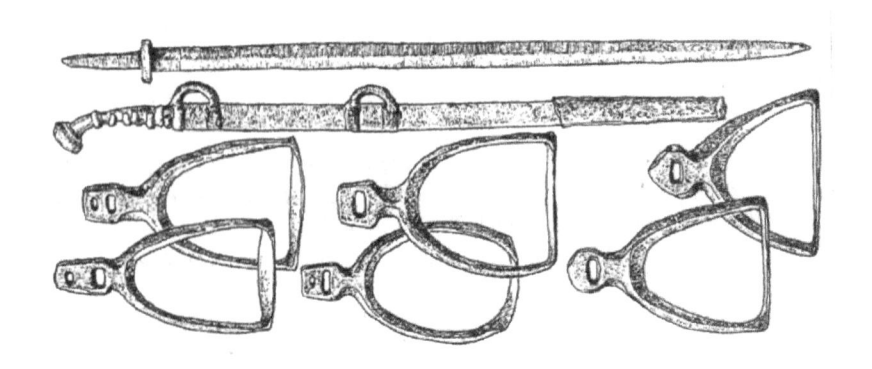

Anoshirwan. Now even the horses were protected with chain mail covers. The cavalrymen, on the other hand, wore increasingly more protective armor made up of chainmail shirts, breastplates and metal leg covers. Completing this were helmets (usually spangenhelm) often equipped with spikes for hanging, more and more complex chainmail hoods known from the relief of Hormizd Parvez or Ardashir III. In general, during the late-Sassanid period, we observe a resurgence of chain mail, which gains in popularity. Its return could be dictated by the reforms introduced by Khosrow and leading to the establishment of a professional army controlled by the Shah, and composed of lower nobility, which were the first and foremost vassals of great feudal lords and fought to defend their interests.

For this, you can complete a brief overview of the armaments of the Sassanid armored cavalry and go to the overview of weapons which were poorly documented, but extremely important formation of the Persian light cavalry.

Equipment and Armament of the Sassanid Light Cavalry. The term itself requires a bit of clarification. It seems that the Sassanid light cavalry was divided in two varieties. Cavalry supporting the actions of armored troops probably resembled similar units in the late Arsacid Army, which shows a soldier from the second century graffiti from Dura-Europos for example. The use was also similar. It was charged with supporting archery, and this function was gaining more and more importance during a fight, even attacking the heavy-duty cavalry with swords. Because of this function, the armored archers who were probably protected in chain mail from the time of the first Sassanids, got heavier and heavier armor. Over time, this formation turned into a type of cavalry support recruited from the middle-level nobility, armored and fighting in a similar way to the heaviest clibanarii. The main difference was the lack of the lance which was not needed for the soldiers in the back line of the formation, and usually, light armor (chain mail and wrought iron armor) on them (although it did happen, especially in the guards, matching the armor of the clibanarii in the first lines).

The importance of archery lost importance. On the battlefields of Iran, armored cavalry began to reign, whose numbers were constantly increased.[39]

The theory of the gradual disappearance of cavalry archers in the Sassanid Army during the reign of Shapur I is also confirmed by sources from the Islamic period describing the history of archery in the days before the invasion of the followers of the Prophet, i.e. Mardi ben Ali

---
[39] A. D. H. Bivar, op.cit., p. 275.

al-Tarsusi.[40] The Arab authors attribute the authorship of the manual of archery from Shapur I, which may in some way be related to the real military interests of this ruler.[41] After his death, archery in the Persian army declined, according to Al Mas'udi, until the time of the legendary Bahram V Gura.[42] Amman's description is blank and does not confirm this. During the campaigns against the Roman Army, Shapur II benefited from the use of large numbers of horse archers – Iranian as well as from the nomadic Hunnic tribes. (Amman, *History of Rome*, XVIII, 6.22), although there are doubts among Arab scholars about the increased use of mercenaries and allied archery units at the expense of Iranian archers. The impetus that led to the return and strength of horse archers could just be increased clashes with the Huns and other nomadic people of the Great Steppe, fighting against the armored cavalry which was not very mobile and was particularly vulnerable to attacks on the flanks. On the northern and north-eastern border of the Sassanids they always maintained garrison units of horse archers.

There is an interesting question about recruiting different types of cavalry support units in Iran. It might have been carried out in a similar manner as practiced by the Arsacids, which was among the lower classes of society, and the nomadic people. A reflection of the "Arsacid" nature of this formation is the fact that the Romans named some soldiers with Persian labels as Parthian or Spartans. (Amman, *History of Rome*, XIX, 8.11)

Units of Sassanid horse archers, like the Parthian predecessors were famous for their mobility and great range. *But from a distance we saw a broken Roman troop running, pursued by a large number of Persians. At the same time, it was not known where they came from and suddenly they attacked the marching soldiers from the rear. This example leads us to believe that these famous 'Sons of the Land' did not emerge from the womb, but it is their innate ability to move incredibly fast.* (Amman, *History of Rome*, XIX, 8, 10-11)

The main weapon of the archers in the Sassanid Army, however, were different from the bows used in the Arsacid armies, except perhaps the part of their history from around the second century AD. The Sassanid bow, which can be best seen on displayed on silver plates, had a very long and slightly curled siyah. It can be inferred from the above-mentioned description, their length ranged from half to two-thirds of the length of the duštar, which resulted in this weapon combining the advantages of a short bow for increased range and long reflexive arms – a long arm

---

[40] A. D. H. Bivar, op.cit., p. 284.
[41] loc. cit..
[42] loc. cit..

that allows the you to shoot heavy long shots. The siyah was set against the flexible part of the arm which was much smaller than the ones of the Parthian bows, i.e. Belmes type angle. The Sassanid bow was slightly shorter than the Parthian one, which can testify to the desire to improve the performance in the range at the expense of the penetration power. The most special feature of the Sassanid bow was the amount of counter-bend. The slightly asymmetrical arms (the upper one was slightly longer) was mounted at a very large angle (approx. 135°) to the long, simple maidan. The arms further benefit from a large counter pull obtained by the described duštar in the maidan and the siyah in the arms. Before applying the bowstring, the bow was shaped like the letter "V" and not "C".[43] That conforms the shape and angle of the limb connecting the duštar and the grip. Some authors interpret what is shown on the Sassanid plates, bending the tense bow as an artistic version of the weapon, not its actual shape.[44] Such a statement contradicts the presentation of the identical maidan design and bow arms on wall paintings in the Buyo-Zuka tomb at Toung K'ou (in Korea). This specimen of the bow shows an asymmetrical bow with greater distance which seems to combine Hunnic and Persian achievements in military technology. One would think it took great deal of time for the design of the Sassanid bow to reach China and Korea, but the tomb mentioned in fact only dates from the reign of the T'ang dynasty. [45]

A distinctive feature of Iranian and Sassanid archery was the unusual grip used by Persian archers. The Sassanid archers did not pull the bowstring with the pointer finger and thumb like the Scythian warriors, or the middle and thumb like the Kushan and Parthian warriors, but the ring and middle. The pointer finger in such a case was used to keep the arrow from slipping off the upper part of the thumb while the left hand held the bow, the pinkie used for tightening the bowstring. This grip is perfectly visible on the silver plates. To protect the fingertips the Sassanid archers used metal caps on the fingertips resembling thimbles or two rings. In case they broke the bowstrings and getting lost in the heat of battle they were protected by special cords passing on the outer edge of the hand and tied to the wrist. These extraordinary utensils (which could moreover hold, in addition to their rings, a leather cover similar to those used by current sports archers) are perfectly rendered on the images of kings hunting on silver plates.

With the arrival of the Huns, the Sassanids and following them the other Eastern people began to use a grip called Mongolian, in which

---
[43] J. Coulston, op.cit., p. 245.
[44] J. Coulston, op.cit., p. 245.
[45] A. D. H. Bivar, op.cit., p. 286

tension on the cord was created by the thumb. Proof is provided by the silver cidaris bowl with representations of warriors shooting bows with thumb pulls dating from the IV century AD[46] and the golden plate of Shapur II, on which an artist in a somewhat clumsy way showed the hand of the ruler pulling the bow in this manner. There is also a Byzantine treaty expressly distinguishes between the Persian and Hunnic way of shooting, the latter using the thumb to tense the bowstring.[47] It is not known whether this technique was adopted in the Sassanid army, but it reached its greatest popularity during the Islamic period thanks to Mamluk archery.

"Far Eastern" Archery Techniques – Altai warriors of the Altai in the service of Sassanid Persia. This technique of pulling the bow with your thumb is one of the oldest archeologically proven archery techniques in the world. The Steeps of the Far East should be considered the source of its origins expanding to areas of China and Central Asia. The beginning of its use in China, like the use of the reflexive bow, dates from the late Shang Period (XIII Century BCE) and is confirmed by archaeological finds of well-crafted archery rings.[48] These were prepared from characteristically highly strength jade. The earliest known specimen comes from the tomb of Princess Fu Hao, the wife of Emperor Wu Ding, reigning as the fourth Shang ruler after transferring the capital to Yin – which is currently Yinxu near Anyang. The finds were made in the midst of vast quantities (590 pieces) of jade. Apart from them, also discovered in the tomb were 210 bronze items, including 109 which were inscribed with the name of Fu Hao. There were two heavy ritual axes, which indisputably confirms the fact of assigning a grave to a specific historical figure known so far that references the so-called oracle bones – "Dragon Bones."

For the record, we know the Fu Hao took part in the administration of the state and even led the Shang Army. A massive jade ring decorated with engravings, characteristic for the art of this period show the monster or animal mask which can be identified as an archery ring, not just an unusual feminine decoration. The shape of this object also perfectly corresponds to the form used by later Chinese archer rings to protect their thumbs during shooting. It has a deep incision to catch the bowstring.[49] The construction of Chinese archery rings known from the later period, however, indicates a slightly different, though common sources of inspiration, to evolve from the Steppes. Rings No. 251 and 337 from

---
[46] IBID.
[47] loc. cit.
[48] B. Dwyer, Early Archers Rings, http: // www.atarn.org/chinese/thumbrings_rings.htm
[49] B. Dwyer, op.cit.

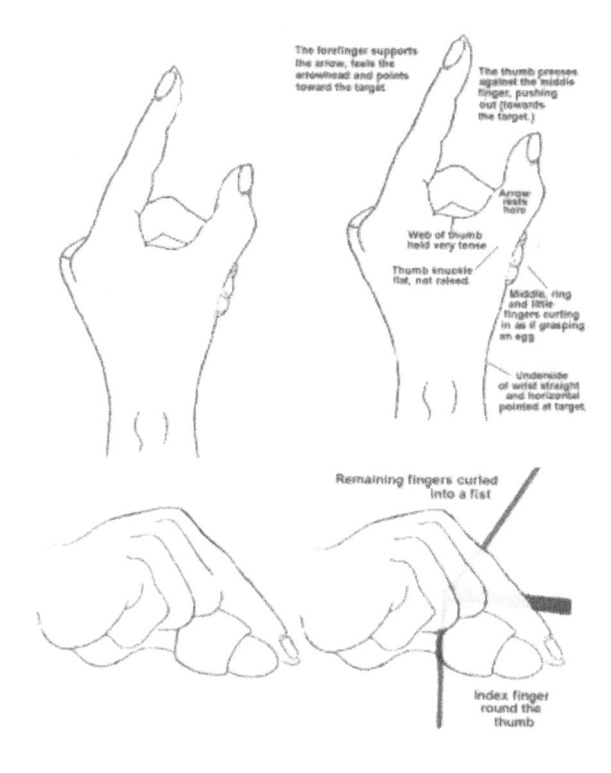

Hand holding a bowstring (a) and tensioning the bowstring equipped with a ring (b) in the assumptions of one of the oldest archery techniques so-called world "Mongolian" here in the older, Far Eastern edition. (www.atarn.org)

Chinese archery rings a) - from the tomb of Fu Hao, b and c - rings of the tomb of a feudal prince from the Autumn-Spring Period from Jinshangcün near Taiyuan. (from to B. Dwyer, Early archer's rings, Excavation of Spring and Autumn period tomb no. 251 ...)

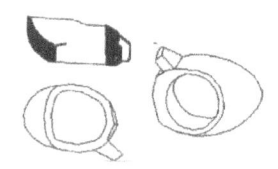

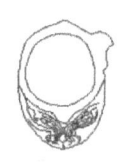

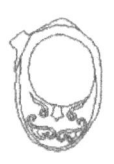

the great tomb belonging to the feudal prince of the Spring and Autumn period discovered in Jinshangcun near Taiyuan, known as the Spring and Autumn period tomb no. 251, providing a shooting surface bracket for the index finger.[50] In Chinese archery technique, tension on the string unlike the Central Asian grip, is because of the thumb pressed with the index finger placed on the back of the ring. This arrangement allows the hand to transfer the load from high tension of a forceful strike through the ring on the wrist and forearm tendons, and this allows you to fire for a much longer time without reducing its strength. To this day, this solution is used in China or Japan virtually unchanged, which provides three thousand years of tradition, with the only difference being that in the Middle Ages regular Samurai have objected to the free possession of a sword ring on a leather glove with a reinforced thumb.[51]

On the Steppe where the "Far East" technique of archery with reflexive bows was confined to the Altaic warriors – the Hsiung-nu often identified with the Huns, came to Central Asia and Iran, where it developed a slightly grip from the Far Eastern variety.

Here, at the beginning, rather than a rigid stone or metal ring, they made use of leather overlays, and they could not, in an effective way, keep the chords tight with the bent thumb supported by the index finger. The leather cover only secured the thumb pad before pulling the bow through prolonged fire but allowed for a more precise fire than with the ring through a better feel for the bowstring. Using this type of master thumb guard is confirmed from the fifteenth century AD, when they coexisted with identical ones, shape, and metal rings which were constructed similar to their ancestor's leather extension added to the surface, in the shape of a claw to enhance pulling the bow.[52]

A quiver of the Persian archer from the Sassanid period was on the right, which is confirmed by Amman's writing which said, *They pulled the bow to full height, so that the chord touched the right chest, while the kept their shot in their left hand.* (Amman, *History of Rome*, XXV, 1.13), interestingly the quote confirms the continued use of Persian bows with a straight Maidan and forming the extensions of the arms while a large Sassanid bow with a curved duštar could not be fired holding the left hand. The arrival of a new and dangerous opponent coming from the depths of the distant Asia steppes of a mixed Altaic-Iranian origin referred by the Persian as the Xionites, probably from the merging of Chyon words, hence the European "Hun", appeared on the north-eastern frontiers of

---

[50]Excavation of Spring and Autumn period tomb no. 251 and Pit of figures of Horses and ChariotsJinshangcun in Taiyuan, part 9, Wenwu, pp. 78-80.
[51]H. Onuma, D. i J. DeProspero, op.cit., p. 56.
[52]Taybuga, op.cit., p. 34.

Silver Kidarite bowl with hunting scenes from the 4th century AD where bows are clearly visible on one of them showing hand pulling the string, which is characterized by the use of a "Mongolian" grip and a ring. (according to A. D. H. Bivar, Calvary equipment and tactics on the Euphrates frontier, *fig. 20, 21)*

Sassanid silver plates with unidentified hunting scenes of (a) a king from 3rd - 4th century A.D. (and), Peroz – the second half 5th century AD (b) (from R. Ghirschman, Iran: Parthian and Sassanians, fig. 248)

Silver and gold-plated disk of Szapura II with a hunting scene (in M. Oliphant, Ancient World, fig. P. 62)

the Sassanid Empire somewhere in the beginning of the end of the III - IV centuries AD. Shapur I entered into an alliance with them and included them in his troops in an expedition against the Roman possessions in the north. In Mesopotamia there was a sizeable contingent of nomadic riders under the command of their king-general Grumates. (Amman, *History of Rome*, XVIII, 6.322)

Hunnic archers that served the Sassanids were probably equipped with bows of a different construction. First, they wee slightly longer than the Sassanid bows (about 150-160 cm in the case of the finds from Qum-Darya, they also had a somewhat asymmetrical arms and the different construction of some parts. This is the best example of the construction of the bow as complete and well preserved, but it is only discovered at the mass grave in Qum-Darya that came from the fighting in the north-eastern border of China and dated broadly from the existence of the powerful tribal federation of Hsiung-nu in this area (the first to third century BCE).[53] This bow had the typical composition of the arms, preserving three layers of a wood core, tendon and horn. The most interesting, however, is the construction of the Maidan and Siyad. The upper

---
[53] J. Coulston, op.cit., p. 242

pair were clad in bones, which survived to a length of 25.5 cm, and 1.5 cm wide, which was preserved along with part of the wooden core of the arm, with fragments of the horn on the top and tendon on the bottom. The lower portion was not preserved unfortunately, and until today all that remained was the end piece which was 7.5 cm long. Both Siyad's were slightly bent and did not curve to an additional angle with the flexible parts of the arms. The Maidan was also slightly contoured, with the central part bent towards the archer stiffened by an additional three bone sections, two of which were shaped like trapezoids. The elongated wedges end rests on the top of the bow, as is reconstructed from the maidan of the Hun bow from Jakuszowice.[54] The rear plate had the shape similar to a rectangle. Based on the length and the individual parts can be reconstructed from their recent discovery. The length of the arm was approximately 160 cm, with the upper arm a bit longer than the lower one, and hence the reasons already described it probably had a slightly larger counter-bend.[55] It's Siyad had a larger length of 30 cm on top and approximately 20 cm on the lower. Each corner was stiffened with two flat pads which short, horizontal, u-shaped hooks were cut out. The profiled maidan was also reinforced with three bone coverings. On the whole, it probably resembled the bow depicted in a later fresco discovered in one of the tombs in northern Turkestan.[56]

The second of the bows found are believed to be Hunnic from today's Niya in Tajikistan. Its arms had a similar length as the bows found at Qum-Darya. The length of the cord was 132 cm. They were constructed, of course, of composite wood, horn and sinew. The Siyad was quite asymmetrical, wherein the top was much longer than the bottom. The bone exterior lining was strengthened by a silk braid. Interestingly, a quiver was discovered along with a bow with two arms connected in the center identical to the late period ones shown on the Orlat plates. A uiver that is clearly a Hunnic design undermines the dating of the entire find, which should probably be ascribed to the Yüe nomads dating from the I century BCE to the II century AD.

Asymmetrical Hunnic type bows were adopted to the tactical requirements of the horse archer with high firepower and had an equivalent value of excellent Mongolian long bows. The equipment of the Hunnic troops was worn low on the back with a quiver on the right filled with three-cornered arrows, javelins and heavy swords with large hilts made of various material.

---

[54] А. М. Хазанов, op.cit., p. 151.
[55] See the section on asymmetrical Sakhae bows.
[56] А. М. Хазанов, op.cit., p. 150.

The Armies of Ancient Persia

From Amman's account it is know that the basic type of arrows for the cavalry and infantry was similar to those produced during the Parthian period, made of cane, *...the bowstring (...) threw reed arrows with iron points. They hit the soldiers opposite them, inflicting death from piercing their bodies.* (Amman, *History of Rome*, XXIV, 2.13). Their design had probably not changed too much. From images on the silver plates we know that the arrowheads were pyramid shaped which were imbedded in the shaft with a pin, which according to Amman was made of iron. In fact, as described in his fourteenth-century treatise on the subject of archery by Master Taybuga, of hardened steel, which was a prerequisite for the ability of arrows to pierce armor. Typical arrows for Sassanid bows, were probably not very long, but used in massed shots from the Hunnic bow. Bows of the Altaic steppe people, due to its length and most likely greater tensile strength (longer arms) much better ability to spread the tension over the long sections of the arms gives greater force and better penetration power. In short bows the stress is concentrated in a small area of the duštar which reduces the power of the pull. Because of this, both types of bows are shown in the huge hunting relief in Tag-e Bustan were used together.

As mentioned, Tabari writes about the arming of Sassanid warriors in a solemn parade arranged by Hosroes I with a large mass of weapons so that each horse was equipped with two sets of bows. This probably means a Sasanid type bow and a longer Hua-Turkish bow. The fact that it is a second supplementary bow, would ensure the continuity of fire when the first failed, which may indicate that the warriors had two spare chords, probably one of each of the examples of these weapons.[57] The bows were of different lengths and properties, particularly in tensile strength which required them to have chords of various thickness and weights which meant the use of one universal spare chord was not possible for both types of bows. Although in the IV century AD, light cavalry archers appeared on a larger scale in the Sassanid army gained greater importance and strength than the Arsacid cavalry formations. Perhaps lack of these troops caused trouble for the Persian army during the battles with the Huns, who after the death of Shapur II, abandoned the alliance of the western neighbor's border areas from invaders. The low point of the fighting was the unsuccessful expedition to the eastern by the Sassanid ruler Peroz, which resulted in a defeat for the Persians and the death of their ruler on the battlefield.[58] The Sassanids tried to remedy the dangerous situation by training and recruiting cavalry archers from amongst

---

[57] *The History of al.-Tabari*, vol. 5., The Sassanids, The Byzantines, The Lakmids, and Yemen, (ed. Yar Shater et. al.) Albany 1999.
[58] B. Składanek, *Historia Persji* t. I, Warszawa 1999. p. 222.

their subjects and entering into alliances with other nomads from the depths of the nomadic Asiatic tribes. The effect of this policy along with the help from the Turks, for example, allowed them to defeat the Hunnic kingdom of Hephthalites, which formed part of the former Kushan lands. However, the trouble did not disappear, because the Turkish nomads were not any less annoying neighbor.[59]

Sassanid Cavalry Tactics. Based on descriptions in Roman sources it is possible to only partially determine the rules governing the tactics of Sassanid cavalry operations. It is difficult to determine the precise ways light and heavy cavalry worked together. Little more is known about the operation of the entire array that became the Persian battle group.

From the mention in the speech of Julian the Apostate about the troops of Shapur II participating in the battles for Nisibis, we learned that the armored cavalry cooperated closely with large units of horse archers. From references in Eutropius, Festus[60] and Amman Marcellin regarding the armored Roman cavalry (Amman, History of Rome, XVI, 12.7), it can be concluded that the units of heavy cavalry clibanarii in this period were always accompanied by supporting units. It is repeatedly stressed by ancient historians, of the terrible consequences that resulted from being hit by the lance of a Persian heavy cavalry lancer, and the methods of attack with the use of spears shown on the Sassanid rock reliefs with a high probability we can conclude that the heavy cavalry of the Persian army in the Sassanid period principally only used clibanarii tactics.

It would be a formation similar to the Sakae-Kushan with the center ranks consisting of the heaviest armed and armored riders, with the flanks and rear supported by cavalry that primarily fought with melee weapons and armor. Often the whole unit was only made of armored cavalry, as was the case of such a group during the European Middle Ages.[61]

The main type of formation for by the attacking Persian cavalry was probably the wedge. However, they discarded this formation when fighting compact lines of cavalry. The operation of the cavalry in this formation was confirmed by Amman: "...some, violently pushed back due to the weight of their weapons became stuck...others afraid the compact went to the hills near the Taurus Mountains." (Amman, History of Rome, XXIV, 8.9). The whole group was created a one long group of riders.

The point, striking the first blow was made up of a few, probably not more than 3-5 men, a line of the choicest heavily armored caval-

---

[59] B. Składanek, op.cit., pp. 247, 250-251.
[60] M. Mielczarek, op.cit., p. 50.
[61] J. Maroń, op.cit., p. 115.

ry. When they fought personally under the ruler himself, as it happened until the time of Hormizd I, he and his bodyguard created such a core group. The cavalry bodyguard was usually given the best equipment and as armed guards were the best representatives of the court, for example, the royal sons to the heir of the throne, which can be illustrated by the example of Shapur I, who as a Prince, fought alongside his father at the battle of Hormuzdegan. The armored units remained the most compact formations, bristling with long spears. With their length up to 4m and more the first rank of charging riders they had lances of the second rank protruding as well. The remaining one to three ranks hold their spears raised, lowering the points before hitting the line when it was possible to pick out a target. Especially when the enemy riders managed to break through the spear fence of the first two ranks or managed to knock down one of the first Sassanid lines of the wedge. The riders of the back ranks formed a kind of security before the formation is disrupted by the strong concentration of an opponent's impact. The formation of armored cavalry sometimes formed such a tight grouping that, *brightness of the lamellar armor allowed free movement of the body, blinded the soldiers moving in the opposite direction.* (Amman, *History of Rome* XXIV, 6.8).

On the flanks of the armored troops and their medium support units were horse archers, who were used during the reign of the first Sassanids and again perhaps during the time of Shapur II, who remained in place and fired, while when the other cavalry charged each other they attacked on the flanks with white weapons – swords, dagger, pick axes, hatchets, etc. *One part of the troops fights with lances at the standstill so that they seemed to be chained in place with bronze bonds. The archers were next to them because from the very beginning this nation placed its greatest hopes on archery and excelled over other people in this.* (Amman, *History of Rome*, XXV, 1.13) During the charge they were bent slightly to the rear in attacking the enemy cavalry. When the armored cavalry hit the opponent's line crushing the center breaking the enemy troops and had their flanks encircled. If there was too much resistance, the whole Persian cavalry was given the sign to withdraw, showering the pursuing opponents with a hail of arrows. It seems, however, in contrast to the tactics of the steppe people, the Sassanids fighting strategy did not provide for following up a failed attack. The Persians sought to crush the enemy with one powerful blow. If this failed, the attack usually collapsed. Anticipating such a turnoff events, Persian commanders would often try to start battles in the afternoon in order to withdraw shielded by darkness if necessary.[62] This theory of "one decisive blow" influenced the used of armored cavalry, until it transformed the major force into only armored

---

[62] B. Składanek, op.cit., p. 240.

cavalry, whose lines of lower nobility had only slightly lighter equipment. It was a general assumption that charging cavalry had the support of attacking infantry and fighting elephants, however, the main blow belonged to the elite cavalry formations. In general, the use of cavalry in the Sassanid army with all the other military units is much more reminiscent of the war doctrine used by Imperial Achaemenid troops than the strategy and formations practiced by the Parthian Arsacids.

2. Infantry

The second and probably the most prevalent formations in terms of size in the Sassanid Army was the infantry. This introduction of large-scale infantry units was the fundamental difference between the armed forces of the new Persian dynasty and the Arsacid Army they defeated. The influence of the western enemies of the Sassanids on the use of infantry units is unknown – the Romans or maybe the centuries of traditions for the Farsi of the famous Achaemenid infantry. Considering the tactical solutions used by the Sassanid Persian infantry – the weapons used, their use in these formations, particularly visible in the heavy armaments reunited and reactivating the old, exceptional Achaemenid units, i.e. the Corps of Immortals,[63] though this second claim seems much less likely. Although there are differing opinions on the combat value of infantry units of the Sassanid army[64] it should be noted that, although the weight of battles fought rested with the cavalry units, during sieges and battles in fortifications, the infantry performed excellently and were simply irreplaceable. It is because of shortages of infantry in the field that the Parthians were deprived of conducting larger siege or engineering operations, which can be more vividly compared to the abilities in this area of the Roman army.

Armament of Sassanid Infantry. Just as it was in the Achaemenid army, and the Sassanid troops, there were two main formations – heavy and light armed troops. Heavy troops were composed of shield armed infantry (Amman, *History of Rome*, XXIV, 2.10), were the primary force supporting the cavalry action on the battlefield. They created a living wall, behind which it was safe for light-armed archers to overwhelm the enemy with a rain of arrows, and when they were closer a part with javelins and missiles. The heavy infantry also supported attacks of the fighting elephants, which sowed panic among the opponent's infantry and mounted units.

---

[63] P. Wilcox, A. Mcbride, op. cit., p. 33.
[64] B. Składanek, op.cit., p. 240, A. Marcellinus, *Dzieje Rzymskie* t. I, tłum. I. Lewandowski, Warszawa 2001, p. 478.

The Armies of Ancient Persia

The main body protection for the elite Sassanid infantrymen was heavy armor made from overlapping metal plates. Amman writes that, *(The Persians) loosely hang sheets of goatskins everywhere off the battlements to weaken the momentum of the projectiles and protected by shields of solid wicker and firmly adjoining with sheets of leather. They looked as if they were all iron because metal plates align with the shape of the body and covered the whole warrior giving him reliable protection.* (Amman, *History of Rome*, XXIV, 2.10). This powerful armor, however, only belonged to the soldiers of the ruler's guards, his Ten-Thousand which Amman mentions in a description of the battle of Amida (Amman, *History of Rome*, XIX, 7.8), and the infantry constituted the core of the first line of the army's infantry. The rest of the shield bearing infantry according to Amman, who saw them reminded him of equipment of the Murmillo style gladiators. They wore metal helmets, perhaps using a manica to protect the right arm, fighting with long straight swords. They used large, convex, rectangular shields made of wicker and covered with leather. (Amman, *History of Rome*, XXIV, 2.10) These shields provided enough protection against arrows; however, they could not stop missiles from catapults. Shields of this type were produced in almost the same way as the old Achaemenid *sparâ*. Similar shields were discovered at Dura-Europos, dating from the beginning of the Third century AD, at the transition from the Parthian to Sassanid period.[65] They had a single, vertical, wooden support. The edge was not covered with a metal rim, but they had a canvas cover. Commanders and the more higher-ranking officers had short chain mail shirts reaching the middle of the thigh with sleeves to the elbow[66] and helmets such as one found in the Persian siege tunnel at Dura.[67] They had a shape that resembled a thimble, but also pointed in the form of a zischägge helmet, or flattened as seen in reliefs showing the characteristic shape. They were very often supplied with chainmail aventails or hoods for additional coverings for the neck[68] which seems to be used with armored collars. The remains of a chainmail tail along the bottom edges of the helmet from the siege at Dura-Europos and a conical helmet from the British Museum collections.

The main weapon of the Persian heavy infantry was a long spear, and a large sword similar to cavalry swords but of lower quality. One surviving example comes from the Persian siege tunnel with a few corroded parts, a long sword probably belonging to a dead infantryman, the owner of a helmet and a chain mail shirt. This weapon was one meter long with

---

[65] М. И. Ростовцев, *Preliminary report*, vol.5,.il. XXVI.
[66] М. И. Ростовцев, *Preliminary report*, vol.6, pp. 192-194.
[67] loc. cit..
[68] М. И. Ростовцев, op.cit., p. 194.

a wide bisected blade, and the pommel made of jade, probably from the area of Chinese Turkestan.[69] Next to the skeleton small iron fragments were discovered, interpreted as part of the shield fittings. It is not possible to reconstruct the shape, however due to the poor state of the residue.

The first rows of compact infantry formations contained large shields covered with skins, (it is not known exactly how many lines made up the shield bearers, but we know that the Sassanid army used the decimal system) which protected large numbers of light infantry archers. The existence of this type of formation was repeatedly mentioned in written sources (Amma, *History of Rome*, XX, 7.6). These soldiers did not wear any armor, and their main offensive weapon was the heavy bow. It can be assumed that during the early days, the Sassanid infantry typically used bows called, "Sassanian", later maybe long-bows with the greatest power for shot, or of the type shown in hunting reliefs, or Hun clearly asymmetrical, with a slightly longer and more bent upper arm. The length of these weapons in relation to the height of the bow suggests that it had a total length of 1.6m.[70] Unfortunately, the relief of hunting is dated very late during the reign of Hosroes II. It is not known how thing looked prior to this, but the logical presumption is that it was not necessary to shorten the arm of the high-powered bow that didn't have to fire as quickly as the cavalry. It is also important to examine the influence of technology from the archery of the steppe people to Sassanid Iran from the time of Shapur II. Though we have to look at the what was left of the Parthian archery methods. It is symptomatic that such influences appeared when large number of Huns was aligned with the Sassanid under Shapur II, serving as auxiliary horse archers in the Persian army.

Based on the descriptions of assaults on Roman cities, and the fighting during the campaign of Shapur II and Julian the Apostate in the Mesopotamian region it can be assumed that besides archers even light infantry were armed with side-arms and joined the melee in the second phase of battle.[71]

Those who did not engage the enemy, were expected (so as not to hurt their own soldiers engaged) to continuously fire high trajectory shots into the enemy lines. Slingers and spearmen were used as a supporting force, and perhaps as was the case in many ancient armies to protect the flank of the entire army, and initially firing against the approaching opponent.

The Sassanid lord was protected on the battlefield by a large number of guard units (*pushtighban*) of unknown numbers (in the beginning

---

[69]loc.cit..
[70]Similar to one discovered in Qum Darya
[71]Ammian writes in *Roman History*..

of the early VII century AD they had a total pf six thousand men) and a personal guard, probably organized like its Achaemenid predecessor and modeled on ten thousand soldiers.[72] Very likely, along the Achaemenid example, the ruler was additionally protected by a heavy guard unit. They were the best of the best, armed with shields, spears and swords for close combat, equipped with strong metal armor and big shields. These warriors surrounded the king in a tight cordon, when he decided to fight on foot, as Shapur II did during the siege of Amida. *After burning the siege engines, they were ordered to keep fighting. The Persian king himself, was never expected to directly participate in combat, agitated by the unfortunate course of the bloody fight, he did an unprecedented thing – wading into the fight like a normal warrior. Because he was surrounded by many soldiers, he was clearly visible from a distance and frequently targeted by arrows. Consequently, many of his bodyguard was killed...* (Amman, History of Rome, 7.7-8). It can be assumed that this type of unit enjoyed special privileges, treating the mass of the ordinary infantrymen as slaves (Amma, *History of Rome*, XXIII, 6.83).

The royal archers also belonged to units of the king's personal guard, as a type of sharpshooter unit made up of the best archers in the entire army. This unit was also most likely a unit whose existence, like the Immortals, was referenced from the Achaemenid army. These archers performed tasks in today's tactical terms of being used in a wide range of activities that could be called, "Special Forces", as evidenced by Cassus from their operations during the siege of Amida. *Through the dark tunnels, poorly guarded because of the steep slope, a fugitive from the city, a supporter of the opposition government, lead seventy archers from the Persian royal guard, outstanding in their abilities and full of confidence. Protected by the silence of a secluded place suddenly in the middle of the night entered the third-floor tower and hid there. In the morning they hung a purple military coat, which was the signal to start the attack. When they saw the city was surrounded by a mass of moving troops, they emptied their quivers, put them between their legs and encouraged by a loud war-cry, released a great number of arrows with great efficiency.* (Amman, *History of Rome* XIX, 5.5) To combat the combat duty of "sharp shooter" was added the duty of "sniper" and the passage in Amman suggested that they looked for enemy commanders and were very efficient in their shooting. (Amman, History of Rome XX, 11.12) This required true marksmanship in field archery.

Sassanid Infantry Tactics. The infantry troops of the Sassanid forces were rarely used as assault units. The use of this type of formation in the

---

[72] P. Wilcox, A. Mcbride, op. cit., p. 33.

first line of attacking Persian infantry. The first line of Persian infantry used in attacks are referenced in the defensive use in sieges (mostly cities and fortresses) (Amman, *History of Rome*, XIX, 73-4; XX, 6.3; XX 7, 5.6). In such circumstances, however, it is a fact completely understandable. There was no physical possibility to use cavalry, which forced its removal from siege operations, except for those rare moments for fighting under the walls of besieged cities and combating unexpected enemy raids. Huge losses were incurred by individuals storming a fortified objective, would not be eliminated in this type of clash, which influenced the impact of attacking by peasant infantry.

During siege operations, the infantry units were protected by very large-scale engineering works – they erected high embankments which enabled artillery fire, trenchworks under the besieged walls, making use of rams, siege towers, throwing machines, etc. (Amman, *History of Rome*, XIX, 6.6; XX, 6.3; XX, 7,9,10,13).

In action during open battle, however, they were slightly different. It seems that in this case the infantry adopted a kind of two-line formation (Amman, *History of Rome*, XXIV, 6.8) (Heliodor, *Et*, 9.14). The first line was made up of shielded and medium-armed defenders forming a kind of living protective wall for unarmored companions. Soldiers of these units were kept under tight control, they maintained good discipline and were the real backbone of the Persian Army. Their discipline and training were even admired by Amman: *Thanks their military training, discipline, and constant field exercises with weapons are terrifying as we have said many times – probably among the largest armies. They place their trust in the courage of the cavalry, which are well-born, laboriously trained and well known. The infantry, because they are armed liked Murmillo style gladiators, follow orders like servants. The whole crowd moves like they were condemned slavery and does not receive support either in the form of pay, or booty. The Persians, a people so courageous and so well trained in the art of war, would take many tribes under the yoke into captivity, would have an even greater number of these soldiers if they were not constantly tormented by internal and external wars.* (Amman, *History of Rome*, XXIII, 6.83)

Between or behind units of heavily armored infantry fighting elephants were placed at regular intervals (Amman, History of Rome XXV, 1.4) which always had to be placed beyond the line of cavalry because their smell and roar scared the horses. In addition, elephants protected by armor, or only covered with textile covering with metal buckles, as mentioned in Florus[73] mentions, that they needed additional support and protection from infantry: *As for support [the heavy cavalry] they relied*

---
[73] A. Marcellinus, op.cit., *History of Rome* vol. I, p. 513 Sec. 14.

on infantry. They were protected with long, convex shields, wicker covered rawhide, and moved in tight ranks. Behind them were the elephants, huge as mountains, who with the movement of their huge bodies exterminated everything that approached them, and they brought terror as confirmed by testimony from past testimony. (Amman, *History of Rome*, XXIV, 6.8)

A mass of archers was placed between the shield bearers and the elephants in the lead, firing in a high arc over the heads of the units in the front rank. Not in sieges, but during field operations, walls were made of cane or wicker works protruding over the ranks in the center that was made up of shield bearers, while the flanks had light troops protected on the wings by cavalry units.[74]

It seems that the main target of the archers, slingers and spearman among the Sassanids were the enemy lines of troops, especially the infantry. The heavily armored riders used less carpet fire than the supporting infantry, because the task of destroying the cavalry was left to the cavalry. The infantry was moving into battle against their own kind pounding the remnants of the enemy force. The task of the Sassanid infantry became fighting an infantry opponent. Roman legions of the third century AD were no longer shield walls and steel, which a hundred years earlier crushed every opponent.

3. The Sassanid Army During Field Operations

From a military point of view, considering how long the aggressive and powerful Sassanid monarchy bordered on and led war against its western neighbor, it is extremely surprising on the sparsity of professional descriptions for operations of the Persian army from this period. We do not have a great deal of interesting references and comments on them in various historical works, and those that do lack the cold, analytical logic of the professional reasoning of a soldier in the style of Thucydides studying the history of the Peloponnesian War, Xenophon describing the fight with Persian troops of the "Ten Thousand" or the army of King Agesilaus, as well as Arrian and his research on the campaigns of Alexander the Great. Descriptions of the battles against the Sassanids are included in the works of Late Roman historians which infuse secularism with their childish admiration for the heavily armored ranks of the Persian armored cavalry with complete disregard of other units, including the spectacular units of battle elephants. Descriptions of battles are inept, vague and brief. There is no professional analysis of tactical moves, and what is most striking is the Romans were always victorious, while the defeats

---

[74] B. Składanek, op.cit., s. 240.

were neatly omitted in silence. There had to be at least as many victories since for so many centuries, unimaginable bloody and devastating wars the border in Mesopotamia and northeastern Syria basically remained the same without significant changes.

Some of the battles fought in the eastern provinces of Rome during the invasion of Shapur II as well as the campaign of Julian the Apostate against the Persians has already been described in the analysis of the equipment and armament of the Sassanid army. Now we'll look at a few short descriptions from other periods and the complimentary data obtained from them.

The first of the battles described took place in 363 A.D. on the northern Tigris. Both armies faced each other separated only by a deep current and the rushing river. Expecting the arrival of the enemy, the Persians place their archers on the bank of the shore along with slingers and spearman in large numbers to cover the ford by hitting the enemy in a hail of arrows and shot. The main forces stood some distance from the river, probably in order to prevent an unexpected attack and create opportunities for the cavalry to charge the enemy facing the shore. The tactical rules of the day in this part of the world claim that opponent at a water obstacle is essentially half the strength of the forces on the bank (Sun-Tzu, *The Art of War*, IX, 5). The main forces are composed of significant units of armored cavalry in the front formation supported by spear infantry (probably composed of heavy infantry in the frontline and medium armed in the back rank). Fighting elephants were set at regular intervals from the infantry.

The Roman commander was well aware that a prepared crossing for an opponent in a fight would end in fatal defeat. The situation could be said to be reminiscent of the situation Alexander the Great found after arriving at the shore of Granicus. The Romans used a similar trick, which according to Diodorus, the great Macedonian had used. In the middle of the night in battle formation they crossed the river and hit the unsuspecting Sassanid archers and light troops occupying the shore. They pushed them toward the rest of the Persian forces, but only arrived at dawn. The armored cavalry did not have time to arrange themselves in battle formation because they were surprised by the attack. The Roman heavy cavalry was preceded by spearman in full attack, they fell on the ranks of unprepared Persians trying to resist. The speed of the attack protected them from the discharge of arrows by Sassanid archers and cavalry, and a melee at close quarters was perfect for the Romans. The victory was total. It is reported that up to 2,500 Persians were killed with the loss of only 75 Romans. This data, however, is not too reliable.

The Armies of Ancient Persia

The next battle took place in the same year at Suma. It began with an attack on the rear of a marching column of Roman troops commanded by the Emperor Jovian, presumably by lightly armored Persian cavalry. After a long fight, this attack was repulsed by Roman light troops securing the rear. At that point, however, there was an attack carried out by a group of war elephants and led by to shock legions of the Western Persian Army. After a bloody fight, the Romans managed to stop the raging elephants and some of them were even killed, however, the armored cavalry fell onto the breaks in the line as a result of the attack with the Persians supported by heavy archers. The Roman formation broke down and the situation seemed tragic until the legions attacked supported by units in the other parts of the column. The Romans succeeded in stopping the pressure from the impetus of the elephant and cavalry attacks, crushed by ranks of heavy infantry. Additional support units attacked the Legionnaires assigned to protect the camps who showered the advancing Persians with javelins from a low hill. The Sassanid soldiers, attacked from all sides, lost momentum in their attack and began to retreat.

Another of these battles took place in the final period of the history of the Sassanid Empire. It was fought during the campaign of the Emperor Heraclius conducted from southern Armenia towards the heart of the Sassanid state. The Byzantine troops supported by Hazar nomads seized and burned one of the great sanctuaries of Persia. This was the Temple of Royal Fire in Sziz (now Taht-e Suleiman). In 627 A.D. Heraclius led an army of 70,000 entering from the north to Mesopotamia. Near the ruins of the ancient city of Nineveh he encountered a demoralized, but still powerful Sassanid army led by Razates, which Parviz (Khosrow II) personally ordered him to stop withdrawing and stand up to a decisive battle. Both armies set up camp opposite each other, however, the Sassanids continued to forage and after waiting for a day, set off at dawn in a compact formation consisting of three lines. The first two units were shock troops, probably heavy armored cavalry supported by horse archers and a large unit shield bearing heavy infantry. The Persians were forced to fight with the sun in their eyes. When the Byzantines took up their positions, Razates challenged Heraclius to one-on-one personal combat (other sources say that the battle between the two leaders occurred during the heat of battle, but taking into account the heroic duels of army commanders and heroes in Persian culture this was very important in the practice of glory, so Razates could have been tempted to such a duel). Heraclius accepted the challenge. In a long battle fought in front of both armies, Heraclius finally managed to kill the Persian general. For the Byzantines this was the signal for the attack. After a bloody, nine-hour battle during which the Persians lost 50,000 people (including a large number of officers) and 28 banners, the Sassanid army started to retreat in good order. With all his remaining troops, Heraclius pushed over the Great and Little Zab bridges, which the Persians failed to destroy. The way to Ctesiphon was wide open to the Byzantines. The quickness of the chase, however, was so great that the main forces remained far behind in poorly protected camps, in which the siege equipment was transported. Heraclius was mindful of the fate of Julian the Apostate, after a short military demonstration, he withdrew north and entered into diplomatic negotiations.

These few short reports of battle fought between the Persians and Romans give an idea about Sassanid battle tactics. Of course, reading them one should constantly bear in mind that the Roman and Byzantine sources were very happy to proclaim the glory of the victories of their own troops, with little regard for historical truth.

In these descriptions we can only see the general rules of conduct for regular battles in the field. They are in turn stepped in the chivalrous ethos of the Sassanids for destroying an opponent. The steppe tactic of pulling the enemy into the depths of unfavorable terrain, tricks and guerilla war were left to the Parthians. Again, as in the time of Achaemenids, courage was the key component and a simple way to impact heavily armed units.

Functioning of the Whole Formation. Anyone who undertakes the analysis tactical and technical terms used by the armies of ancient Persia it is striking about the many differences between the armed forces of the Arsacid monarchy and the army of the Sassanid kingdom. Of course, you cannot say that the Persians were unusual in that they have cut themselves off from the military traditions of their predecessors in a radical way. On the contrary, many of the Parthian's creative solutions were continuations, and became a source of strength for the descendants of Ardashir. In addition to continuation, the source of which clearly remained the Arsacid armed forces, however, numerous parts of it were unknown to the Parthian forces. The infantry equipment and tactics were especially reminiscent of those stored, perhaps in Farsan, of the ancient assumptions of Achaemenid military doctrine. A detailed comparison of operations of the entire array of the army of both Persian dynasties reveals far-reaching similarities.

Though attention is primarily drawn to the return of the use of large scale formations of infantry, one cannot ignore the importance that while the growth was rapid, the Arsacid neglected the engineering corps, or the common use of combat elephants, which were available again after the seizure of large areas of the defeated Kushan Empire by Shapur I in

241 A.D., and the opening of the wat to bring these animals from India. It is still true that the main shock formation was armored cavalry, the way that it was used, however, brings to mind the use of these type formations in the Achaemenid Imperial Army.

    The Sassanid battle army consisted of three types interacting with the other troops. The first type, due to the combat value and aristocratic origin, and thus the quality of the equipment, the soldiers were cavalry. This were essentially knights heavily recruited from among the Ašvaran class, the rich aristocracy, and the lightly armed, among the lower nobility and nomadic tribes. The cavalry was placed on the wings and in the center, except that its main forces, whose task was to break the enemy's formations usually occupied the place on the right flank, less frequently in the center.[75] Cavalry units took on the characteristics of the steppe people which was composed of a central group and two wings. The first line in the center was composed of armored ranks (3-5) behind which medium armed and increasingly well-equipped troops in support. At the time of the first Sassanids they were armored, as the archer shown on the II century graffito from Dura-Europos. They supported the armored units, especially in the second phase of battle when it came to hand-to-hand fighting against various white and blunt weapons. On the wings heavily armed cavalry to the place of light armed horse archers as a support and flanking force. It seems that all the cavalry was also armored and before starting a decisive charge they stood while the infantry archers were shooting. This seems to be explanation for why the heavily armored cavalry did not need bows. Long-range bows allowed them to shoot long distances (approximately 200 m) to the enemy line. It is not inconceivable that in the advance of the army they acted in a similar manner to the Mongols army units in battle, small groups of light archers.[76] There are no references in Roman sources on the application of continuous fire, however, it is believed that this system was already abandoned. In special circumstances, light-armed Sassanid made one-off charges against a retreating enemy, or smaller units to lose shot against. The use of this type of maneuvers, however, can not necessarily be composed of Persians who did not serve as light-armed cavalry, but rather more mobile units from the Iranian steppe people, for example, Saki, and Altai. The Xionites were recruited to serve in the Sassanid armed forces (Ammian, *History of Rome*, XVIII, 6.22).

    At the moment of attack the cavalry group, as with the steppe people, took the shape of a wedge, whose flanks and center were composed of armored units and horse archers. The shape of this formation is

---
[75] loc. cit..
[76] R. E. Dupy, T. N. Dupy, op.cit., p. 308.

characteristic for clibanarii, which is repeatedly mentioned many times in Roman sources.[77] It is not entirely clear whether during the charge itself the archers continued firing, or if the charge was only conducted to fight using melee weapons. It seems at the same time all three lines or center and flanks of the cavalry group would move forward. Additional support "fire" just like in the Achaemenid army was formed from massed infantry archery.

The second line in the Sassanid army's battle formation was heavy infantry providing support for the cavalry action. Their most elite troops formed part of the Guards, most likely the "Immortals" bodyguard for the King of Kings and protected the ruler when he was outside the main battle line.

The heavy infantry formed an anchor in that they interacted with all the other formations, but always remained defensive in their nature. They were protected with a reed wall, covered with raw hide shields which acted as support for the war elephants that were treated as the second line for breaking shock formations. Covered with colorful quilted covers and armor, the animals carried wooden towers on their backs to protect them using four-man crews composed of archers, slingers and spearmen (Livius, History of Rome, XXXVII, 40) (Ammian, *History of Rome*, XIX, 2.3). Treated like the tanks of today, they were extremely dangerous for infantry and enemy cavalry. Unfortunately, they were vulnerable to wounds from missiles, especially around the eyes, trunk and ears, which could cause them to go into frenzy which was as much a potential threat to their own soldiers (Ammian, History of Rome. XXV, 1.15). To protect them from attacks lightly armed troops operated with the shielded infantry. They were also probably tasked with exploiting the breaches the animals made in the enemy lines.

The mass of archers fired from beyond the walls of the infantry shields. They mostly consisted of poorly armed and trained soldiers of unusually low morale.[78] They did not try to resist the enemy if he managed to repulse the Persian cavalry and breakthrough the heavy infantry at the front. The main barrage was probably carried out in preparation for the cavalry attack, and after their withdrawal a barrier to the pursuing enemy. During the actual battle the firing stopped so as not to hurt their own light cavalry. The armored cavalry was completely immune to arrowheads.

The Sassanid cavalry sought to break the opponent's front or to encirclement. When the enemy was stronger, they received support from the heavily armored infantry and elephants, no longer working as a

---

[77] M. Mielczarek, op.cit., p. 10
[78] B. Składanek, op.cit., p. 240.

The Armies of Ancient Persia

wedge through the frontline, but more like a steamroller crushing everything in its path. The low morale of most of the non-elite infantry units, however, became the cause of this collapse for the entire army rather than giving the cavalry a chance to regroup. Instead of facing the opponent they started a panicky retreat (Ammian, *History of Rome* XXIV, 6, 12-13). The Achaemenid infantry was not much better in this respect.

From the perspective of historical events, the main weakness of the Sassanid Army, just like the troops of the Achaemenids was the limit of their ability to conduct guerrilla warfare, and their desire to only fight regular battles. Though it turned out that this is not always the case, it was effective in the case of the Romans, who practiced the same tactics and did not work well against Arab light troops. They were composed mostly of nomadic camel riders and great light cavalry who brilliantly proved themselves in combat against regular light and Persian cavalry. It should be remembered, after all that horses acted unpredictably when facing camels. Camels also allowed for quick movement in unbelievably inhospitable terrain often tasked with hitting the enemy at the least expected point. Disregarding these recurring facts, the army of Shapur I returning from Asia Minor with a large amount of loot and the prestige of a conqueror suffered several humiliating defeats at the hands of not very numerous Palmyrene troops and their Bedouin allies under the ruler of Palmyra, Odaenathus.[79] His troops were mostly made up of troops as shown on numerous Palmyrene reliefs – in addition to the armored cavalry there was also a large number of Arab camel riders well known for desert fighting. This is the lesson of, "But she went into the forest" (following small groups away from the main body). Four hundred years later, this mistake did not cost the Sassanids booty from a successful expedition, but the throne. In 691 A.D. when the Caliph Abd al-Malik completed he construction of the famous Qubbat al-Sakharah in Jerusalem, as part of the amazing decorations to the building he ordered they put evidence of the triumph over the infidel empire that ruled over the Arabs not so long ago.[80] To this day you can see in the mosaics shown there opposite the eastern and western gates crowns sent there of the last rulers of the Sassanid dynasty.[81]

---

[79] P. Iwaszkiewicz, W. Łoś, M. Stępień, op.cit., p. 292.
[80] J. Murphy-O'Connor, *Przewodnik po ziemi świętej*, tłum. M. Burdajewicz, , Warszawa 2001. p. 101
[81] loc, cit..

APPENDICES

Chronology

811- 730 BCE	Assyrian raids on Iranian Plateau areas.
727 BCE	The appearance of the first king-chief of the Medes. Deioces (Dajakku) by Sargon II deported to Syria in 715
674-653 BCE	Phraortes (Fravartiš) ruled in Media.
652-625 BCE	Invasion of Scythia (Saka Paradraya). Medes subjects Scythians, Assyrians an alliance with one of their chiefs Partatavą.
624-585 BCE	Reign of Cyaxares. Controls the tribes Iranian Plateau. Creates a modern Median army.
612 BCE	Nineveh conquered by the army of the Medes, Scythians and other Iranian peoples. Cyrus I, King of Anshan in Neo-Assyria coalition, the first attempts to introduce cavalry in Persia. Medes in coalition with Babylonia continuing war Assyria, conquering also the remnants of the state of Urartu.
584-549 BCE	Reign of Astyages (Arštivayga), the last king of the Medes.
c. 575 BCE	Birth of Cyrus II, the grandson of the king of the Medes.
559 BCE	Cyrus ascends the throne of Anshan. The remains of the ancient the kingdom of Elam turned to Persia.
550 BCE	Astyages betrayed by Median nobility and defeated by grandson. Cyrus II of Achaemenid dynasty on the throne of Medo-Persian Empire.
547 BCE	Cyrus defeats the Lydian army of Croesus at Sardis.
539 BCE	Persians gain Babylon.
530 BCE	Cyrus II dies in battle with Massagetami in Central Asia.
530-522 BCE	Reign of Cambyses II (Kambudżiya)
525 BCE	Cambyses conquers Egypt
522 BCE	Cambyses goes from Egypt to quell the rebellion of the Zoroastrians / Gaumata, hurts himself by a dagger in the thigh while mounting his horse and died.
522-486 BCE	Reign of Darius the Great (Darayavahuš). Achaemenid Empire reaches the largest territorial coverage.
522 BCE	Conspiracy against Gaumata, a wave of rebellions throughout the empire bloodily suppressed by Darius and his associates.
520-513 BCE	Dariusz conquers the north western part of India (Sind and Punjab)
519 BCE	The victorious campaign against Saka in Central Asia.
512 BCE	Unsuccessful campaign against the Scythians (Saka

	Paradraya) on the Ukrainian steppes
499-494 BCE	Uprising of the Ionian Greeks against the Achaemenid Empire.
492 BCE	Mardonius conquers the lands of the Thracians. Persians subjugate Macedonia. Amyntas king of the Macedonians is a vassal of Darius.
490 BCE	Achaemenid troops under the command of Datis and Artaphernes are defeated at Marathon.
486-465 BCE	Reign of Xerxes I (Hšayarša)
484 BCE	Revolt in Babylonia and Egypt is suppressed.
480 BCE	Xerxes invades Greece with a huge army. The Macedonians and Thracians side with the King of Kings. Victorious at Thermopylae, defeated at Salamis. In the face of the approaching winter, the Persians go back to Asia leaving Greece under the command of Mardonius with an occupying force.
479 BCE	Mardonius is defeated and killed at the Battle of Plataea. At Mycale the Greeks break the camp of the Persian forces.
464-425 BCE	The reign of Artaxerxes I. (Artahšatra)
459 BCE	Persian forces suppress the revolt in Egypt.
448/447 BCE	"Peace of Callias" between Artaxerxes I, and Delian League
431-404 BCE	The Peloponnesian War in Greece. Tissaphernes and Pharnabazus are satraps in Asia Minor continue to promote hostility between the most powerful Greek polis to gain for Persia
404-359 BCE	Reign of Artaxerxes II
401/400 BCE	Rebellion of Cyrus the Younger against the authority of his brother Artaxerxes II. Battle of Cunaxa in which Cyrus dies. The return march the Greek contingent of its army to the north, on the Black Sea coast (Anabasis).
400-387 BCE	War with Sparta. Expedition of King Agesilaus to Asia Minor.
359-336 BCE	Reign of Philip II of Macedon.
373 BCE	Revolt in Egypt.
368-367 BCE	Rebellion satraps in Asia Minor.
359-338 BCE	Reign of Artaxerxes III Ochus.
342 BCE	Reconquest of the rebellious Egypt.
338 BCE	Artaxerxes III murdered by the eunuch Bagoas. He ascends to the throne, but soon dies.
336-330 BCE	Reign of Darius III

The Armies of Ancient Persia

334 BCE Alexander the Macedonian crosses the Hellespont and defeats the satrap armies at Granicus.

333 BCE Alexander defeats an army commanded by Darius III at Issus.

332 BCE Alexander of Macedon lays siege to Tyre and Gaza taking the cities.

331 BCE 30 September or 1 October- Battle of Gaugamela.

330 BCE Alexander takes and burning Persepolis. Darius III dies while escaping in Hyrcania.

329 BCE Bessus, the assassin of Darius and usurper who took the title Artaxerxes IV is captured and executed (328).

323 BCE Alexander the Great – to the Persians, Alexander Cursed dies in Babylon.

322-301 BCE Diadochi war. Seleucus Nicator is the master of the whole of the East.

261-246 BCE Rule of Antiochus II Theos.

Prior 250 BCE First signs of independence of the satrap of Bactria, Diodotus.

ca.250 BCE Successor State ruled by Seleucid satrap Andragoras. Satrap of Bactria Diodotus accepts the title of king.

247 BCE Beginning of the era Arsacid. Arsaces I of Parthia (Aršak) is the leader Parni.

246-226 BCE Reign of Seleucus II Kalinikos.

239 BCE "Wars of the Diadochi" makes it impossible to recover Seleucid control of the Party and Bactria.

After 239 BCE Parnów invasion under the leadership of the Party of Arsaces I of Parthia. Death Andragoras.

209-206 BCE Antiochus III travels to the east forcing Arsaces to recognize his power, defeats the Bactrian Euthydemus with whom he makes peace, renews the treaty with the Raja Punjab.

191 BCE Antiochus III is defeated in a battle with the Romans in the gorge at Thermopylae.

190 BCE Antiochus III is defeated at the Battle of Magnesia.

171-138 BCE Mithridates I (Mehrdat I) the king of the Parthians.

170-168 BCE Mithridates I conquers the Elymais, Media, Persia, and Bactria.

146-141 BCE Parthians occupy Seleucia and defeat troops of Seleucids. Demetrius II gets into captivity

138-127 BCE Reign of Phraates II (Farhad II).

129 BCE Phraates II asks the defeat of the armies of Antiochus VII Sidetes. Antioch killed on the battlefield of Ecbatana.

124/123 BCE	Phraates II dies on the battlefield of the Sakami.
123-88 BCE	Reign of Mithridates II (Mehrdat II).
ca.120 BCE	Establishment Ctesiphon.
ca.100 BCE	Migration of Sakae from Central Asia to the south, then to north-west India.
ca.100 BCE	Creation of the state Kushan in Central Asia.
95 BCE	Parthians regain control over eastern Iran. Some of the tribes Sakae become subjects of Parthian Feudal clan Surena).
64 BCE	Land Western Asia from Pontus to the borders of Egypt come under the authority of Rome, as provinces or client kingdom.
53 BCE	Defeat of the forces of Crassus at Carrhae.
51-39 BCE	Pacorus' raid on Syria and Palestine. Pacorus is killed in battle troops against Labienus at 40/39 r. BC
38-2 BCE	Reign of Phraates IV.
36 BCE	Mark Antony's invasion of Armenia and the Araratcy Kingdom ends in disaster.
20 BCE	Phraates IV (Farad IV) is negotiating with Octavian Augustus room. Parthians return standards legion gained under Carrhae.
51-80 AD	Reign of Vologeses I (Walagash I)
53 AD	Parthian-Roman war with Armenia.
63 AD	Vologeses I and Emperor Nero include room after a long war of Armenia.
75 AD	Sarmatian Alans invaded the north-western Iran.
114 AD	Trajan invasion troops to Armenia and Mesopotamia.
117 AD	Hadrian includes Parthian territory.
147-191 AD	Reign of Vologeses IV.
162 AD	Vologeses IV invades Armenia and Roman Mesopotamia.
164 AD	Counterattack against the troops Lucius Verus ends occupation Ctesiphon by the Romans
191-208 AD	The reign of Vologeses V.
198 AD	Anti-Roman action by Vologeses V provoke Roman reply. Army Septimius Severus takes Ctesiphon for the third time.
217 AD	Another Roman attack on the Parthia is stopped after an inconclusive Battle of Nisibis.
224 AD	Ardashir I defeats and kills the last Parthian Shah of Shah's Artabanus V at Hormozdgan
233 AD	Alexander Severus begins a campaign to destroy the Sassanid but is defeated by Ardashir around the

The Armies of Ancient Persia

	Ctesiphon.
241-272 AD	Reign of Shapur I.
244 AD	According to Persian sources Shapur I defeated the army of the Emperor Gordian III at Misiche, were he is killed on the battlefield.
ca.256 AD	Shapur I defeated the armies of Philip the Arab, especially at the battle of Barbalissos.
ca.258 AD	Shapur I defeated a huge army under Emperor Valerian at Edessa. Valerian along with 70 thousand prisoners of the army and the people of Syria deported to Persia. Shapur captures Syria and Cappadocia.
260/261 AD	The army of the King of Palmyra, Odenathus attacks suddenly and forced the Persians to retreat. Odenathus tries to take Ctesiphon, but is repulsed, and then returns to Syria. (The first demonstration of the strength of the Arab peoples in the desert).
293-301 AD	The reign of Narseh.
296 AD	Narseh defeats the armies of the Emperor Galerius in Armenia.
309-379 AD	Reign of Shapur II.
320 AD	Shapur II repulses the Arab invasion.
337-350 AD	Army Shapur II invades Mesopotamia and lays siege to the Roman city of Nisibis. Chionites forces invade but the king returns from an expedition to Central Asia.
357 AD	Army of Shapur II inflicts a defeat the Chionites. Their ruler Grumbates is forced to provide troops to support the Persians against the Romans.
359 AD	The second expedition against Roman Mesopotamia and Syria. Shapur receives Pali Nisibis and Amida.
363 AD	Emperor Julian the Apostate invades Persia. Achieves a victory at Maranga but dies in battle. He may have been killed by one of his Christian soldiers.
420-431 AD	Reign of the Bahram V.
421 AD	Bahram V inflicts crushing defeat on the Hephthalites at the Battle of Merv.
438-457 AD	Reign of Yazdegerd II.
449 AD	Yazdegerd II issues an edict prohibiting Armenia profess Christianity which produces a great rebellion there.
451 AD	Army of Yazdegerd II inflicts a defeat on the rebel Armenian forces at the battle Avarayr
459-484 AD	The reign of Peroz I (Firuz I)
484 AD	Peroz I slain in battle with Hephthalites.

The Armies of Ancient Persia

484-488 AD	Reign Balász
484 AD	Balasz I grant Armenia the right to profess Christianity.
488-496 AD	The first reign of Kavadh I. The Khazars came through the Caucasus passes invading north-western Iran.
496-498 AD	Usurpation Zamasp and the rise of Mazdak.
498-531 AD	The second reign of Kavadh I. Persecution of Mazdakism.
502-504 AD	Kavadh's first war with Byzantium.
527-531 AD	Kavadh's second war with Byzantium.
531-579 AD	Reign of Chosroes I (Khosrow) also known as Anushirawan the Just.
540 AD	Chosroes War with the Byzantines, Persians occupied Antioch and a large part of Syria.
553 AD	Sassanids and Turks destroy the Hephthalites Kingdom.
579-590 AD	Reign of Hormizd IV.
588 AD	Turkish-Hephthalite Army invades Sassanid lands Central Asia. Bahram Chobin to defeat them and destroys the Turkish Army to the east and west.
590 AD	Bahram Chobin takes the throne from Hormizd IV.
591-628 AD	Reign of Chosroes II Aparvez (son Hormizd IV).
591 AD	With the help of the Byzantine Emperor Maurice, Aparvez ascends the throne.
602 AD	Emperor Maurice is murdered, Aparvez departs on a destructive expedition to the Byzantine East.
602-621 AD	Sassanid armies occupied Mesopotamia, Palestine, Egypt and Anatolia. Constantinople under siege.
619 AD	Turkish and Hephthalites Empires invade the eastern Sassanid area, however, they are defeat and are repulsed.
623 AD	The Byzantines under the command of Emperor Heraclius with the Hazaras marching through Lazica and Georgia on strike north-western Iran.
628 AD	Battle of Nineveh. Sassanids suffer defeat. Chosroes murdered by the nobles advocating the adoption of peaceful conditions Heraclius.
632-651 AD	Reign of Yazdegerd III.
637 AD	Sassanid forces are destroyed by the Arab armies under Qadisiya.
638 AD	Arabs occupied Ctesiphon.
642 AD	Army of Yazdegerd III is defeated at Nahāvand. The fall of the Sassanid Empire.
651 AD	Yazdegerd III murdered in the vicinity of Merv.
651-838 AD	Fighting in north-Islamic Persia and Azerbaijan.

Glossary

Achaemenid Empire - the first Persian dynasty ruling from approximately 550 BCE when Cyrus the Great defeated the last of the Mede rulers - Astyages, until 331 BCE, or the death of Darius III at the hands of conspirators led by Bessus satrap of Bactria. Bessus declared himself King of Kings as Artaxerxes IV but was sentenced to death for regicide by Alexander the Great in 330 BCE.

Acinaces - short sword commonly used by Iranian warriors, with a small, flat, shaped or molded Two animal heads, heart-shaped, square or other shape the guard, in the scabbard is a bulbous extended sectional pad. It was worn at the waist, on the the specific belt attached to the leaf-shaped extension of the scabbard, usually with the handle facing rearwardly.

Apadana - Columned reception hall, usually built on a square plan, with massive towers at the corners, porticoes for each corner, or at least on one side. It is a characteristic of Achaemenid Palace architecture. Greatest examples of this type of construction is called. "Apadana of Darius I" in Persepo, "Hall of hundred columns" in Persepolis " and the Apadana Palace of Darius I in Susa.

Argead Dynasty - Macedonian royal dynasty derives its legendary origins Greek Argos. They were the ruling dynasty from at least the sixth century BCE till death Alexander IV, son of Alexander the Great in 309 BCE murdered by Kassandra.

Armor - metal, bone, horn, or made from horse hooves as plates in multi shaped sewn on a backing or with other similar to the construction of lorica squamata or lamelar. This way manufacture of body armor belonged to the oldest and most effective process. By making them rigid plates in the areas where high mobility was not needed, or placed there in overlap occurred until somewhere in the end of the second half of the second century AD when the Parthian invented the first plate armor.

Arsacid - The longest reigning royal dynasty of ancient Persia. Claiming his descent from the Scythian chiefs of the nomadic Parni tribe from the steppes extending to the east of the Caspian Sea, ruling over the majority land of ancient Persia and Mesopotamia from 141 BCE, starting with a victory over Mithridates the Great. Its history as a dynasty adopted, however, the first time the tribal confederation of the Dahae invaded Parthia from approximatley 239 BCE. The name of the dynasty derives its name from the first ruler, Arsaces I of Parthia and the chief of the tribe Parni, which led the invasion of Scythian tribes, and defeated the Selucid satrap of Antiochus to began building the Arsacid Empire. The last ruler Arsacid ruler Artabanus V died on the battlefield of Hormozgan in 224 AD trying to suppress the rebellion in the Sassanid Persians.

Aspis - heavy, round, shield made of wood, with the outer surface of the forged sheet metal used by heavy infantryman. The Greek word meaning "Assist", used with the heavy infantry weapons of the infantryman called Hoplite. It was worn on the left forearm mounted using a wide metal grip (Porpax), while the second, soft (argive) held the soldiers left arm. Aspis shields appeared with the equipment of the Hellenic polis soldiers from the Greek dark ages, which is probably about VIII BCE. By the VII-VI BCE it replaced all other types of shields. Gradually it fell into disuse during the Roman period somewhere approximatley the end of the II. BCE. During the reign of the last Achaemenid they became part of the integral equipment of Persian armored infantryman.

Asymmetric Reflective Bow - dating back more or less I c. BCE - III. A.D. centuries. It arms were positioned at opposite directions at rest, with the lining covered in bone, curling toward siyat and reinforced with three bony plates at the maidan. The arms were approximatley 160 cm in lengh, the upper frame was slightly longer than the lower. The Qum-Darya bow is an excellent example of this which is typical for hunnic bows. Bows of this type were probably designed to shoot a long arrow with power for a long distance (Approx. 250 m).

Ašvaran - the Persian term corresponding to the Greek hippeis - "riders" - the class feudal knights in ancient Persia, whose existence is confirmed during the reign of the Arsacid Dynasty. They belonged to the top of the social class, among others, the most powerful feudal lords of the seven major clans Parthian, and all their clients. The Ašvaran came to battle as armored knights, or lightly armed and armored horsemen to support the heavy cavalry attacks. Clients of the most powerful clans were formed into their own private armies, which they owed their allegiance, even allowing for who inherited the crown within the king's family.

Backplate - Part of armor to protect the shoulders and back of a warrior. Sometimes it covers the neck for protection against cuts swords.

Battle Axe - a kind of lightweight axe with equal sized blades on the opposite sides. Some were equipped with a small hammer or beak on one side instead of a blade. It was mounted on long wooden or metal haft that provided a high impact force. Widely used from the Bronze Age until the eighteenth-century AD.

Barding - type of covering that protected a horse's back during the Parthian period. They were often of metal scales for the armored cavalry. During the Sassanid period it covered the rest of the body. It was worn in conjunction with a guard neck and hood on his head so that the barding created a complete horse armor. The best-preserved examples of armored barding from the Parthian period come from the tower 19 in Dura-Europos.

Bell helmet – A round helmet covering the head, made since the bronze age made of leather reinforced with metal, bone, etc. or iron. It was often forged from a single, two or more metal pieces riveted together. Protective element that came with the bell helmet could include a neck, cheekguards, and other pieces of protection.

Belmesa Bow - bow belonging to the group of retroreflective bows, with the siyah of the same length. Known from findings in the Egyptian town of Belmesa dating from the Roman period. In general terms it is a composite bow arms of the type used by the Parthian and Roman army which were reminiscent of medieval Mongolian bows, which had small arms, had an angle of approximately 100-110 ° and reinforced with bone covered siyat. Length of the arms was probably approximately 150 cm. This is similar to the bow of Qum-Darya - known for a bow discovered in a mass grave near the north Chinese border. There was discovered perfectly preserved, complete in the composite pose.

Bittern - a bunch thread tied on the bowstring of a bow forming kind of sighting instrument - the equivalent of the rear sight of a gun. Looped or grip for fast aiming without pulling a chord to a fixed point on the face or arm of the archer, which it not needed for short bows, eg. Turkish flight bow.

Blade - the proper weapon, used for combat against its opponent blade, part of an edged weapon, sword, saber etc. Made depending on the era in different lengths, different shapes and types, usually the most durable materials. Equipped for stiffening and reduction weight in one or more ways. There are several parts on the blade - closest to the handguard

guard, at the end of the engraving, two or one blade, in the case of sabers also blunt back.

Boeotian Kettle Hat - a specific type of helmet commonly used in the Greek and Macedonian cavalry - shaped hats with dangling pleated ruff. It was made of metal - usually iron or bronze, of an unusual shape, which could be sometimes be made of the hardened leather. The helmet of this type did not limited visibility, while maintaining maximum protection.

Boeotian Shield - a kind of shield elliptical in shape, with a semi-circular cut-out on the sides, probably made in the technique similar to those used by aspides. Its distinctive shape was derived from similarly shaped shields from the Mycenaean period and the so-called, "Dark ages". "Boeotian" shields were gradually replaced in popularity by round aspis shields.

Bow - Any flight weapon where all the parts except for the chord o are glued together to form completely functioning weapon.

Bowcase - flat leather case for the bow, usually separate, but in Iran the bowcase is often connected to quiver. The bowcase was usually worn on the back, belt or attached to the saddle. Often richly decorated.

Breastplate – Is composed of either plate or assembled from smaller components of armor that protects chest and abdomen warrior. Combined with a collar protector it created complete armor for the torso.

Cardaces - The Achaemendid heavy infantry, probably recruited of the sons of military settlers, but from people who did not belong to wealthy noble families. According to Strabo they were youths who underwent a kind of national service military. Armed with bows, short six-foot spears, scaly armor, small reed shields, acinaces swords or other edged weapons. Fighting in a linear pattern similar to hoplites, but probably looser. Gradually, their way of fighting and weapons came closer to the Hellenistic style. It is possible that "new" Immortals were recruited from the Cardaces.

Cataphract - heavily armored Hellenistic cavalryman, who fought with a long spear in a compact linear formation. Cataphract or Cataphracti were a heavy formation of the ancient cavalry used to attack the enemy in mass. The charge was carried out at a gallop to the set one powerful thrust of a two-handed lance. In addition to the spear their equipment included heavy clothing or lamilar armor, a sword, cutlass or xiphos were carried, the helmet often had visor-shaped with features of a face. The term "Cataphract" comes from the Greek was used for a very long time by Hellenic historiographers and their Roman successors. About II century A.D. it was replaced by the commonly used the term "clibanarius" coming probably from the Persian term.

Chafron - stylized metal plate - mostly bronze or iron fixed on top of the horse's head, which is a kind of "helmet" to protect the animals head from the blows of edged weapons and spears. Chafrons were already used by Scythian warriors to protect the valuable armored cavalry mounts in the Hellenistic period and the part of the horse's armor was expanded, so that has covered the entire top of the skull. Generally it was equipped with a combs, etc.. The armored cavalry Parthian chafrons were replaced by mail hoods covering the entire horse's head. After discarding their use by the cavalry early Sassanid of approximatley the early fourth century AD a return to the use of chafrons, by the time of the last Sassanid they returned to use complete horse armor fully protecting the front half of the animal's body.

Chawchan - palace complex of the Kushanera located in Bactria, dating back to the early period of Kushan Dynasty, probably at times Vimy-Tak-to. Is famous for its so-called relics. The "Royal Pavilion" with its group of great clay sculptures depicts the ruler and his aides in a scene at the throne, attacking riders, etc.

Clibanarius – heavy cavalry; armored rider in the Iranian armies and later also of Rome. Their characteristic fighting technique was performed at full speed charge and use a long spear to strike the blow. At times the impact drove through two opponents at once. After striking the body of the opponent with his spear the clibanarius abandoned it and proceeded to fight with melee weapons - a sword, ax, or blunt weapon - mace. Most likely, the differences between kataphrakti and clibanari were only language not their make-up. The first term was older and stemmed from the Greek, the second, was probably of Persian origin, however, both describe the same soldier. They were heavily armored spear armed cavalry in plates – the type of armor used in the medieval Middle East, which protects the chest and back from mostly thrusts weapons – especially spears. In India and Persia until the eighteenth-century AD, it consists of four Solid metal plates, usually of steel, arranged so that the two most protected chest and back, two smaller sides. All the plates had bolted leather straps. This type armor usually worn over thin, dense protective chainmail to protect the rest of the body from weapon blows weapon.

Companion cavalry - an ensemble of heavily armored cavalry of the Macedonia Guard's. They were "Companions" of the king - that is, the rich landowners of the whole of Macedonia. Initially, they might have been formed into the branches that corresponded to the functions of the Achaemenid bodyguard cavalry unit, the so-called "relatives and friends Royal "later - at the time of Philip II transformed into a powerful shock formation shock. The body of Companion cavalry numbered four hundred strong (Squadron), which is the equivalent of a royal unit among the adjutants of the Persian ruler - the so-called. "Accompanying of the table."

Composite Bow - A composite bow whose core is made of wood but also from the stratum corneum on the ventral and on the dorsal surface of bow also made of tendons. The ends of the arms called horns or Arabic siyat (singular. Syah) in ancient bows it included the bone facing stiffened with hardwood.

Copia - heavy, long spear cavalry, relying on the momentum of one decisive impact, after which rammed deep in the opponent's body, or a broken copia is abandoned. Gripping the copia was usually done half halfway up the shaft from the tip. Spears in ancient Iran usually held with both hands.

Crater - In the Hellenistic and Roman world was a large open ceramic dish. It was often gorgeously made and decorated for mixing wine with water in Greek-style.

Cuirass - part of the armor, made as a plate, forged metal jacket protecting the body of a soldier. Composed of two parts - a breastplate and backplate held by leather straps. Used in Greece already since at least the eighth century. BC as hoplite body armor. In Iran, it was used by the cavalrymen during Achaemenid and Hellenistic periods, and after several centuries of breaks, heavy cavalry of the Arsacids and Sassanids.

Dagger - a short, curved knife worn by warriors of Arab and Turkish tucked into his belt. Often richly decorated, which used to benchmark the status of an adult male. Used as a personal weapon.

Dahae - probably part of the Scythian tribal confederation, whose encampments stretched east from the coast of the Caspian Sea. They were already mentioned from sources of the Achaemenid era. It was composed of three major tribes, one of which was the Parni tribe. In approximatley 239 BCE an invasion of warriors from the Dahae Confederation swept away the rebel satrap of Seleucid province of Parthia giving birth to the reign of the Arsacid Dynasty in the territories of ancient Persia.

Dehqan - lower nobility in Persian during the Sassanid era. They probably emerged within the caste of Ašvaran knights or created from the ennobled population. A free class - from the Greek polis - from records of the period Parthian. The Dehqan usually formed the core of the client army of the great feudal lords, after the reform Hosroesa and were given armor by the King. They were subjected to the control of his commanders.

Draco / Dragon - a kind of standard made in the shape of a dragon with a stick on a metal pole at the head and fluttering in the wind the body in the form of long sleeve of lightweight material. Known to the Iranian military peoples - Eg. The Persians and Sarmatians which was adopted by the Roman cavalry.

Dragon bones - bones from the shoulder of cattle or turle shell (plastron) used in Chinese Divination late Shang period (1,200 BC), covered with signs the oldest known type of Chinese writings. The bone was burned in certain places, or how it is done today in Mongolia over the flame fire opal. With the cracks read the answer to the question, then recorded It, along with the question on the bone folding in the archive.

Duštar (from Arabic.) - flexible, the working part of the arm of the eastern bow, below siyah, made of wood core and the horn layer and sinewy, with a length dependent on the type of bow.

Edged weapons - the lower part of the blade for melee weapons. Formed very differently depending on the specifics of a particular type of weapon. Generally, the arms for thrusting shaped in a long, narrow and sharp points for simultaneously cuts and thrusts engravings were made strong, broad, but still sharp, often just before the end of the pommel widened to form a so-called "feather". In the case of specialized weapons exclusively, or almost exclusively for cutting engraving it was very massive and short, sometimes rounded or, in extreme cases, such as certain Celtic sword was completely sharpened perpendicular to the cutting edges.

Fletching - Part of the arrow used to stabilize its flight. Feathers at the rear of the arrow actually slows the flight of shots, otherwise give the arrow a stabilizing spin. The feathers from birds of prey such as eagles or falcons were thought to be the best for this purpose. The arrows used by Iranian tribes usually had three feathers.

Flight bow - short Saracen composite bow used for shooting light arrows for long distances. Flight bows have a length of 1m, traditionally made of layers of turned and prepared tendons on the wooden core. Arms folded onto the duštar with a small built-in, not tufted siyah of bone.

Galata - An immigrant population of Celtic origin settled in the III century BCE into the area of central Anatolia which from then was called Galatia. The Gallic tribes were famous as great warriors often recruited as mercenaries in the Hellenistic armies. The most famous examples are sculptures of Gallic warriors from the so-called Pergamon altar dedicated to Zeus in gratitude for military victory over the combined forces of Pergamum Galatians and Seleucids during the time of wars for the inheritance of Alexander the Great's lands, known as "The War of the Diadochi."

Gerron - reed-leather shield Persian imperial infantryman. It was made of raw cowhide around thick cane stalks after which it was dried to give the strength. Sime shields as high as 1.5m was used by infantrymen in the first line of shielded lines Persian infantrymen from an opponent's arrows.

Gorytos - leather quiver, worn on the belt of Iranian peoples, called the pocket-quiver. In the Achaemenid gorytos the flap protects the bow and arrows against moisture and the quiver covered the two parts, in Scythian pockets there were only arrows. Gorytos of warriors were richly decorated with golden plate, bony studs, probably also embroidered, embossed etc.

Greave - Part of armor to protect the leg from the ankle to the knee. Typically made from one piece of sheet metal or brown iron, respectively profiled to the shape of your legs. Armored greaves were especially prevelant in Hellenic Macedonian infantry and which they borrowed from the Iranian peoples - Mostly Scythians, Persians, the Carthaginians, and the Romans during republic, et al. The most commonly occur of two ways to put on greaves - Sliding them over their legs and clamping and fastening with the leather strips.

Greek-Bactria - Hellenistic state created approx. 250 r. BCE by Seleucid satrap Diodotus in the area of his satrapy of Bactria, formerly one

The Armies of Ancient Persia

the farthest northeastern most province of the Achaemenid Empire. The monarchy Greek -Bactria fell under the influence of Kushan invasion of the Tochar in the second half of the II century BCE.

Guard - The collectedt personal military usually constituting the backbone of the army, sometimes a type guard for the ruler. Best equipped and armed, composed of the best-trained soldiers, usually with high morale.

Hilt - Grip portion of melee weapons protection against "sliding off" of blade weapons of the enemy to the hand of a person holding the weapon, and the gri[the hand from the handle to the blade. It was made in a variety of shapes, simple in the shape of flat bars or discs.

Horseman's Pick - blunt weapon to be fighting for a short distance, reminiscent ax, except that instead of the blade-like ax nadziaki had a long, penetrating beak. On the opposite side was typically a small blunt side like a hammer. The force focused on the tip of the ax was so great that it was enough to break through helmet, or armor opponent without much problem. It was constantly used in warfare from the Bronze Age to Eighteenth century AD.

Hypaspist - The name comes from the Greek word aspis meaning round, heavy, wooden, often bruised bronze shield - hypaspistai would open translation of "covering up the hard disk" or "hidden under the heavy shield" - Companions. Composed of three units of a thousand soldiers it became formation of Guards infantry in the Macedonian army. Probably founded by Alexander I, it was the elite infantry consisted of the strongest, best trained and equipped soldiers. A bodyguard of the King of Mecedonia was recruited as hypaspis. Equipment of the Hypaspist in the time of Philip II was a long spear, approximately 4m in length, sword, shield aspis in the type of metal or cloth and reinforced armor. Soldiers of this formation were like the Persian "Immortals" - not only the backbone of infantry, but also the second line of the royal guard.

Imacz - handle shield. It can be a single, centrally placed, or in pairs. Made of wood, wood, cord or metal.

Immortals - elite, professional, Guard formation of armored bow-armed Persian infantry. Its heyday was in the period Early Achaemenid's, when it was the inner circle of bodyguards for the King of Kings. The name was first given by Herodotus is derived from custom of restocking members of that unit to a permanent state of ten thousand soldiers. Recruitment was probably carried out from among the best of the Cardaces. The best known representation of the Achaemendid Immortals comes from the platform of Darius' Apadana in Persepolis. After the fall of the Achaemendid monarchy the formation of Immortals seems to hae disappeared from the arena of history only to appear again in the service of Sassanid Shahs.

Javelin - a type of polearm designed for throwing. usually very light, with no great tip. The spearpoint has a bur to hinder removing it from the wound. Javelins did not have tooling, but versions used in the Greek world, had a leather strap which was wrapped around the shaft. At the time it was thrown the swirling javelin stabilized its flight. Apart from the usual spears in ancient times, there are several known examples of them, such as the Roman pilum, small, loaded with a lead weight which stabilized the light weight.

Kalkan - round, light shield of the nomadic peoples of Turkic-Tatar. Made of twisted and braided thread switches fig or willow, center fitted with a metal boss and four staps covering hooks of double handles. Generally does not exceed 1 m in diameter.

Katana - a kind of a long Japanese sword with a length of more than 2 shaku (30,3cm), with a blade bent slightly, smaller than the tachi sword, worn tucked into his belt, blade blade facing upwards. Often during the Azuchi-Momomyama (1574 -1602) and Edo (1603 -1867) katana worn as a long sword in called Dai-sho.

Khatrah - characteristic movement of archery Saracen executed after releasing a shot which added to its momentum and increasing coverage. Khatrah makes appropriate discharge reaction forces arising after the release of the chord, also forces proper handling of arms and hands in the last phase of shooting, which positively affects on the accuracy of shot. It consists of throwing a hand holding a bow to the front, after releasing the arrow.

Korymbos - the type of ornamental headgear, hairstyles for Persian rulers also known during the Parthian, but also widely used by the Sassanids. He derived probably from the slicked-up and the jutting tufts of hair of Scythian warriors. Hairstyles of rulers were placed into this shape on top of the head, above the crown where the hair was covered with some sort of material. This very characteristic element of hairstyles for Sassanid rulers. It is known quite well from representations on the reliefs and images of beaten on coins.

Ksyston/Kontos - long spear of Macedonian cavalry of up to 4 m in length, with one or double-sided points, one at each end of the shaft. Kontos may consist of two identical parts connected to a metal sleeve. Grip placed in the middle of the shaft, or slightly beyond was created by wrapping a rope or strap. A leather loop was attached to the grip to wear on the wrist, to prevent dropping the weapons, and allowing pulling the tip from the body after it struck the enemy.

Kšatria - in India the caste of princes and knights descended from the caste of Aryan Knights. The main occupation of the Kšatria was a war and preparing their whole life training to handle weapons, melee combat and riding horses or fighting in chariots. This is the same order of chivalry that Prince Sidharta Gautama, known as Buddha, belonged to.

"Kuban" type helmet - characteristic type of helmet known early-Scythian from findings in the area of the river Kuban, found in Central Asia. Its bell was made of bronze, it was supplied in small cut above the eyes and very short Nosal. Helmets of this type may be a form of reinforced Scythian cap, whose long cheeks and neck guard are made from the metal.

Kulah - a high cap, rounded at the top, flattened laterally, especially popular in the late Parthian and Sassanid periods. The kulah were often richly decorated and even their design was copied during Sassanid period on some helmets.

Kushan - A tribe of Indo-European origin from Tocharian tribe of steppe nomads from China along with the other four tribes Tochia They are known perhaps as the people of Yuezhi. The Nomads were living in lands initially north of the Chinese border but were defeated, however, by the Altai people called Xionnu to help the Chinese moved to Central Asia and approximately the second half of second century BCE. They caused the collapse of the Greek-Bactrian state. Finally, in the first centruy A.D. they established under the rule of King Vima Taktku of the Kuei-Shang tribe. This powerful country in the Bactria reached up to the valley of Kabul.

Lamellar - type of armor using a metal plate, which built as the so-called flap armor. Lamellar appears in different sizes. With the scale length varying between 3 to 1 inches.

Length of the arrow - the main, wooden part of the arrow, the shaft. In ancient times arrows were made of different materials - mainly wood, cane, bamboo, and combinations thereof. The length of the shot could be approximatley 60-65 cm, some more than 1 m.

Linothorax - type canvas armor Greek and Hellenistic used with several layers of laminated canvas.

Lochagos - The commander of a lochosu in the armies of the Greek classical era, the Macedonian army and troops Hellenistic - that is, at the bhead of one of the columns of infantry, as well as perhaps a larger unit. In the armies of the Macedonians this type of soldier was the most experienced, best trained and armored, commanding his subordinates.

Long bow - long medieval bow commonly used in the English archery units. Probably derives from the Welsh longbows, as it is known as a the bow Welsh used. The best created from Spanish yew, as their tension strength reached up to 70-75 kg.

Maidan - the grip which is the rigid part bow with curved arms placed equally centrally in composite curves slightly shifted toward the lower arm arcs with a large asymmetry for example. Japanese Yumi arms are placed even at 1/3 the length of the entire arms of the bottom chord hook. Maidan is usually covered with materials providing good grip and protects the arms against the ravages of sweat from his hands. In the simplest version wrapped with just a thin strap or cord.

Machaira - the type single eged sword or combat knife, with a heavy blade with a wide point designed primarily for cutting. Commonly used in Macedonian and Hellenic infantry and cavalry, originating perhaps from the Middle East, possibly Thrace, where he used it quite commonly tribal warriors, it was used by Hellenic infantry.

Manica - Part of armor, used as an arm guard, known from the period Achaemenid or early Hellenistic period (around the third century BCE) it was mostly made in segments, and secured with cords alternating the connection, it is a ring-shaped metal, sealed with along the inside with narrow leather belts. Some parts were made of hardened skin, and then, probably from the middle period of the Parthian metal. In time typical armored maniki was replaced by long-sleeved chainmail.

Masada - a powerful fortress overlooking the Dead Sea fortified first used by the Hasmonaan kings of Judea, later by Herod the Great located at the flat top of a huge rock plateau. It fell in the Jewish uprising in 70 AD after besieged by the Romans and finally occupied after the collective suicide of the defenders.

Massagetae - Iranian nomadic tribes inhabiting the steppes and semi-deserts Central Asia over the river Oxos - today Ammu-Daria. The founder of the first Persian Empire - Cyrus the Great - died fighting with them. They passed gradually to a semi-nomdic lifestyle Massagetae. Sources from the Seleucid and Parthian period called them Saka, creating a state called Chorasmia. Their army remained however, a steppe style army, mostly composed of armored cavalry fighting with clibanari tactics. The military prowess of the people is most likely shown in the so-called, "Orlat Plates." The Saka were pushed to the south and west by invasion of people Yuehzhi creating a new state called, Indo-Saka in Punjab and then occupied the so-called Sakastan to the north - on the eastern fringe of the Arsacid Empire.

Mattresses - padding on the inside surface of the helmet or metal armor pieces, glued or fastened with rivets, which acted as protection against sunburn heated by the sun, it absorbed weapons hitting the armored surface. The mattresses edge also protected the wearer's body against the edges of the plates.

Neck Guard - part of the helmet, solid, lamellar, chain mail, or in the form of a flap of skin bare or armored scales attached to the back of the bell helmet protects the neck and sides of the neck, sometimes strapped under the chin and forming a protective hood.

Nesan Horse - race of extremely noble horses bred on the plains Nesa of the Medes, used as mounts by combat commanders and powerful Persian knights. The best were trained to kill with their hooves against warriors opposite them as well as fighting or biting an opponent's horses. Nesan horses were highly valued as mentioned in Herodotus' "Acts". White horses of this breed pulled the chariot of Ahurmazda.

Nisa - the first capital of the Parthian empire founded by Arsacid after the occupation Parthia in the Seleucid province situated in the foothills of Kopet Daghu in the current Turkmenistan, 19 km from the capital city of Ashgabat. Italian excavations uncovered Numerous wonderful monuments of early Parthian architecture, including two buildings interpreted as a dynastic temple which worshiped the dead kings and their families.

Notch - a place on the shot at the end of the radius (the shaft) and to place back braid, covering the string. Often, arrows of the steppe peoples included a bone cap. Usually having a diameter slightly larger the arrow diameter.

Parthian Shot - archery technique used by archers of the nomadic steppe peoples, reported after using it against the Romans by Parthian mounted archers, which involved shooting back at the pursuing enemy. Shot this was done to escape, turning in the saddle. Regardless, for most of the Parthian period it had already been in use to rankle the enemy when such a situation was available. Arrows were kept in the left hand with a bow.

Pavaise - a tall shield used in the Middle Ages to shield crossbowmen, in ancient times such high rectangular shields were made of thick, hard cane stalks covered with untreated hide. They were used to build barriers in front of rows of light-armed infantry archers, barriers to field camps, and finally large, combat infantry formation. Finds of fragments of type cane pavaise comes from Dura-Europos and barrow of Akbeit. A lot their use is known from Greek vase paintings of the Classical period.

Peltast - a type of light armed infantry armies in the ancient city-states Greece, Macedonia and Persia, composed of unarmored spearmen. In the period of the Peloponnesian War it consisted of mostly Thracians, and later other nationalities. Typical Peltast was equipped with several spears, a shield made of wicker plaits covered with hardened skin with preserved hairs, sometimes they had a heavy combat knife or dagger. The soldiers of this type of fight in loose formation were thrown at attacking infantry or cavalry with a barrage of javelins. They rarely joined the melee. The effectiveness of peltast troops led to service of the Ateń Union during the Peloponnesian War, in the early fourth century BC. The prevalence of this type of troops, eventually changed to the tactics and weaponry heavily armored infantry.

Pendet - rope or strap fastened to hilt of melee weapons as well as holding polearms to protect them from dropping by the cavalry during the battle.

Peytral - the type of leather or metal sewn on armor apron expected around the breast of the saddle in battle. Peytral was used to protect the animal from the blows, especially as it seems by the Arsacids against infantry. This sort of the horse armor was used by Massagetae warriors mentioned in Herodotus.

Phalanx - military formation in the Macedonian infantry fighting in a compact group with a long from 5.5 to more than 6m, spears called sarissa. Introduced for use by Philip II as the backbone of infantry in the army, and later the armies of Alexander the Great, the Seleucids and Ptolemies of Antigonides. The phalanx epitomized the typical linear array of Greek hoplites and similar weapons to the Macedonian royal guards.

Pike - a long, heavy infantry spear held by both hands on the shaft shifted far to the rear, up to the middle. The torque of the pikes were usually the heaviest, which balanced the weight of the front tip of weapons along spear. No ancient sources not mention the practiced of driving the back spears into the ground to protect themselves from attacking cavalry as was done in the Middle Ages. Most likely this type of weapon fought actively and they blunt the back so not to accidentally hurt another soldier in formation. The first spears introduced it seems to be in the phalangites in his army Philip II of Macedon, which were called sarissa, and the soldiers sarissoforoi. This type of weapon was 5.5 to 6m was in length used in the armies diadochi.

Pin handle - an extension of the blade for melee weapons, placed inside of the handle and connecting to the pommel. They often do not sit entirely hidden inside hilt, but mounted on it only two riveted or glued, organic cladding. The handle is usually done with the least hardened steel, which obtained the flexibility to protect the blade from breaking. The Japanese swords were never cleaned the handle printed with the signature of the blacksmith who created the weapons, as well as any information on tests carried out.

Pommel - part of a sword or dagger often presented as a very fancy ending the back of the handle, and a counterweight to the blade. The heads helped the warrior to pull the weapon out, eg. due to its sinking too far into the body of an opponent. Throughout history, they developed dozens of shapes and types of heads in the areas of ancient Iran the most popular were spherical, a bar and rarely mushroom

Pteruges - leather or made of laminated canvas belts fastened on the lower edge of the carapace of the Greek type, to protect against injuries from the thigh down to the knees and groin. Widely used in hoplite armor of VI century BCE. Typically, two layers of pteruges were fixed, positioned so that the upper often overlaps the lower belts. In the Hellenistic armor, often each row overlap so that it covered the left edge of the previous. In Roman officer armor was attached a long row of utilitarian straps, reaching just over the knee, and on the other edge of the carapace holding a very short ornamental belt. Pteruges of armor were used even early by the Celts.

Recursive bow - a bow which before stringing the chord is bent in the shape of the letter "C" or "V" with the arms facing the archer who is holding the maidan to shoot, or having any, even a minimal counterweight.

Reflexive bow - a bow whose entire limbs curve away from the archer when unstrung. The curves are opposite to the direction in which the bow flexes while drawn.

Ryton - a horn shaped drinking vessel, sometimes beautifully decorated, finished as fantastic or real animal. It was especially popular in the circle of the ancient culture of Iran.

Saddle - part chord designed to help the archer aim shots. Saddles chords are usually secured with additional string.

Sakae - Iranian nomadic people living in the steppes to the Northeast the borders of ancient Persia, until the arrival of Yuezhi, and later the Huns. In the inscriptions Achaemenid thy were called all Scythians, later the name was applied only began to the people identified with Herodotus as the Massagetae.

Somatophylakes - the seven men who were the personal guards of the Macedonian kings. They were probably recruited from hypastis chosen because of their blind loyalty to the ruler, along with their military strength and efficiency. These people lived with the king every day, dressed like him, addressed him by name, they had the right to carry weapons at his palace.

Sarissa - long pike infantry Macedonian and Hellenistic with the shaft made from dogwood or ash, heavy, dull course of and not too great, spear tip. Its invention is attributed to the Macedonian king, Philip II.

Sarissoforo - heavily armored infantry soldier of the Macedonian and Hellenistic with the main weapon used being the so-called long pike. Sarissoforo, was also equipped with a small wooden shield worn on a belt running over his shoulder, with one handle on the long forearm. Sarissophoroi were named from the weapons they used. Fighting in tight formation, the branch called syntagmami, 8-10 composed of the 16 in rows of 16 soldiers. At the time of Philip of Macedon and his son Alexander sarissoforowie usually used quilted vests as armor, only the first ranks of the troops have any armor, eg. the type linothorax, subsequently the phalanx began to use increased armor.

Sassanids - Persian, originally from Parsi ruling dynasty, who ruled the ancient Persian Empire after defeating Arsacid from 224-226 BCE. The Sassanids fought major battles with Rome for centuries to master northern Mesopotamia and Syria, to the east they conquered a large part of the Kushan state, the south they occupied, and later conquered a large portion of the Arabian Peninsula. The Sassanid Dynasty finally collapsed as a result of the Arab conquest in the seventh century BCE. The last sSassanid Shah Yezdegerd III died in exile in 651 A.D.

Sassanid Bow - a bow belonging to the recursive bow of Iran used of the late Parthian period to the end of the Sassanid. Without chord the arms curved in the shape of the letter "V" of the straight or nearly straight legs attached to the grip angle of approx. 120-135 °, and long, slightly collapsed siyat to set to the arms at an angle of approx. 140 °.

Scythian bow - short, reflex bow of large composite collapsed arms formed in the shape of the letter "C" on a very large scale, and not great power for light short shot. Used in areas of the Great Steppe, from at least IX - VIII BCE. In Iran from the invasion of Scythian in VII century BCE.

Segmented armor - armor type that originated in ancient classical Greece, made of hardened leather, canvas or laminated technology linothorax. This type of armor is characteristic for the army of Greek and Hellenistic (sometimes it was worn by officers in the Roman army) whose name comes from the protecting back flaps -shoulder straps, which protected the shoulders and tied to special rings on the chest. Since the III century BCE a chainmail armor flap began to be used by the Celts, after their clashes with the Romans, they made chain armor - durable, breathable and flexible movements becoming the basic type of armor Roman legionnaires.

Seleucid - originating from the end of the Macedonian dynasty reigned after the death of Alexander Great over the eastern lands of his empire. They derived their origin from one of the generals of Alexander's army - Seleucus Nicator. The Seleucids fought constant battles with the reigning Ptolemys in Egypt for control southern Syria and Palestine called the Syrian Wars. These lands were eventually won after the victory in the great battle of Panion. In the north Seleucid armies clashed with the troops Attalides, and later the Romans. Gradually the disintegrating Seleucid monarchy lost all lands east of Euphrates to the Parthians, the rest was eventually occupied by the legions of Pompey the Great.

Shoe - metal fitting the lower end of the scabbard.

Siyat - a reinforced handle that facilitates tension of even very strong bows and increase arms length without reducing the force of their "release".

Siyah (horn) - rigid arm of the bow constituting the type of reflexive bow easing the tension of the bow, improving release of the chord and allowing for greater speed of the arm with its greater length allowing for greater distance of heavier shot. In ancient times siyat were stiffened using linings made from the bone, in the Middle Ages they were made from a hard, lightweight wood.

Spangenhelm - the so-called ribbed helmet made with several triangular or trapezoidal iron plates combined iron ribs and riveted. This type of helmet especially popular in the late Parthian and Sassanid periods probably due to the low manufacturing cost and production rate at a relatively high strength structure.

Spear - type polearms fitted at one end of the shaft with a spearpoint, the other side with sharp, ornate elemental figure or having it plain and devoid of any additional elements.

Suren (actually Surena) - the most powerful feudal families of the Arsacid Empire. Surena even had the right to place the official ceremony royal diadem on the head of the new ruler. Dominion over lands at the north-eastern border of the Parthian monarchy, including the so-called areas of Sakastan. They maintained a powerful army of the great contingent of armored cavalry contributed by their vassals and huge masses of excellent horse archers recruited probably in large part to the warriors of "wild" steppe tribes. Support by Surena ensured the Arsacid Orodes II victory in the battle for the throne, the whole army he led coming from this clan, the commander according to unnamed sources of Roman known Suren, or Surena. It was he who probably led his own warriors in a massacre of Mark Licinius Crassus' legions at the Battle of Carrhae. Suren's clan even held his enormous influence among the Sassanid in exchange for support Ardashir I in his battle for the throne.

Syntagma - basic infantry of the Macedonian file during the Hellenistic period of two hundred fifty-six people - for sixteen men in sixteen ranks. Syntagm infantry in the army of Alexander Grand may be somewhat fewer approximately eight to ten people in one column. The infantry of this type consists of phalangites or sarissoforoi that fought in three basic arrays - open, loose and compact - with an average density and disciplined - the strictest, which was formed at the moment of greatest danger, for example. They adopted battalion formation in the phalanx of Alexander III during the attack on-protected war elephants and infantry of Raja Porosa during the battle of the Hydaspes. The circular pattern was built by introducing the rear halves of lochos into the front linr (resulting in a longer, but thinner line), or closing columns in normal setting (which shortened the line length, while maintaining its thickness).

Szysz - the peak part of the onion-shaped helmet called Szyszak. Szysz for helmets rib collected peaks plates and reinforcing ribs design, it is also often decorative function taking the form of high-bush which was deposited with the bristles cements, etc. plumes. Frequently in Iranian helmets from the era achaemendid shape more or less sharp pointed.

Tachi - a kind of long single edged Japanese sword, its most "militant" and the oldest type. Typically, more than 90 cm length of tachi have quite strongly curved blade, was worn in contrast to the katana type swords when not under his belt hung on a special swordblet. If the blade was signed the signature was conventionally struck so as to be positioned on the outer the stem surface grip, so you know who made the sword that they were wearing. In the period 1530-1867 Shinto century AD tachi swords lost their popularity to katana swords.

Tasset - Part of armor to protect the leg. During Achaemenid's thigh armor was used by the armored cavalry eg. of an elite troop adjutant of Cyrus the Younger, and the Scythian heavy horsemen. The Scythians thigh armor was in the form separate strips mounted on leg leather leggings across the entire outer surface with metal scales or strips. In the Hellenistic period appeared of the thighs of the riders made like a manica with chain mail, leather or metal strips. This type for maximum protection with good mobility survived heavy cavalry of Iran until the late Sassanid period. In parallel with it, however, they coexisted with legg armor of scaly armored, roasted leather, bone plates or plate.

The Armies of Ancient Persia

Terlica - wooden skeleton saddle to which was attached straps to hold it on back of the animal. Skeletons have such used by the Persians, the Sarmatians, Celts and Romans distinctive horned saddle, saddle and Drug Administration of Turkic peoples - Huns, Avars, etc.. To this day, the saddle with heavy wooden skeletons are used eg. in Mongolia.

Tiara - distinctive headdress Achaemendid infantry described in the "Acts" of Herodotus, and shown on the reliefs of the royal complex palace in Persepolis. The tiara probably had a pointed shape, but it was made of soft felt, the pleated caps had a very long tail that was used wrapping face for protection against dust and sand. It is possible that such caps of Persian type tiaras wrapped long strips of fabric into the shape of a turban.

Tok - butt spike fitted to the lower end of the shaft polearms - mainly spear. In the Persian army they were used with Hellenist types of weapons. Butt spikes were used to fight when spear tip was lost, cavalry put the spear into the ground when troops had halted, and perhaps most importantly tapping the wounded enemies lying under the feet of the attacker's hoplites.

Tocharian tribes - nomadic steppe tribes of Indo-European origin living in the lands north of the borders of China, known in the annals as the Yue people. After the defeats suffered at the hands of the Altai nomadic Hsiung -nu, this powerful tribal federation moved in the mid-II century BCE to Central Asia where it has created a powerful state, led by the kings belonging to the Kuei-Schang tribe. The country has been conquered at the beginning III century A.D. by the Sassanids under Shapur I, and fell during the invasion of the Huns. Tocharians belonged to one of the oldest migration waves of Indo-European peoples, and the oldest Indo-European language group called hetisco-tocharian.

Tuw - old Polish type of tubular quiver.

Umbo - A boss mounted generally in the center of the shield, to protect the hand wielding underneath it. The umbo of ancient shields took on various shapes - from bars and circles through cones stretched long, sharp or blunt spike designed for active combat with the enemy. Germanic examples are typical of bosses of the ancient era

Wakizashi - type short (less than 2 shaku - that is 30.3 cm.) Japanese sword forged and "dressed" in the same way as katana sword, often representing a set called of the two weapons called Daisho. The wakizashi was used for personal defense, collecting trophies of war, and committing ritual of honor seppuku suicide.

Xiphos or ksiphos - a short, double-edged Greek sword, with flared blade and quite prominent the guard, with a short handle and a heavy cylindrical head. Commonly used by hoplites, and Macedonian guards. It seems to have been designed equally for cutting and thrusting. Its shape is derived perhaps from the shape of bronze swords from the Archaic period. One of the most famous examples of the Xiphos comes from the so-called. Philip's tomb in Vergina - former Macedonian Aigai.

Yrzi - bow belonging to the recursive bows, which was the most primitive in the group structure. It has a long, straight arms, and almost equal in length, reinforced by bone core, but not not a curved siyat from the plane of the arms. Light curve in the horns of the arms. This type of bow shape incomplete letter "C". Length arms was about 150 cm.

Yue-or - see "tocharians"

Yumi - long, asymmetrical Japanese bow, were made of laminated bamboo strips and wood Azusa, coated with lacquer which was slightly reflective. The majdan this bow is about one third of the entire length of the arm from the end of the lower arm. It is probably related to the way it was used to shoot from the horse, or a not exactly known tradition of constructing Yumi. These curves designed for the practice of traditional archery kyudo with a pull force for approximately two-meter the length of arms is approx. 30 kg., and the length of the shot is approx. 1,05-1,10 m.

The Armies of Ancient Persia

Rulers of Persia

Median Kings
Cyaxares	624–585 BCE
Astyages	585–549 BCE

Achaemenid dynasty
Achaemenes	about 705 BCE

First ruler of the Achaemenid kingdom

Teispes	~640 BCE
Cyrus I	~580 BCE
Cambyses I	~550 BCE

Achaemenid Empire
Cyrus the Great	559 - 530 BCE

The Great King, King of Kings, King of Anshan, King of Media, King of Babylon, King of Sumer and Akkad, King of the Four Corners of the World, King of Anshan and Mandana.

Cambyses II	530 - 522 BCE
Bardiya Gaumata	522 - 522 BCE
Darius I	522 - 486 BCE
Xerxes I	485 - 465 BCE
Artaxerxes I	465 - 424 BCE
Xerxes II	424 - 424 BCE
Sogdianus	424 - 423 BCE
Darius II	424 - 404 BCE
Artaxerxes II	404 - 358 BCE
Artaxerxes III	358 - 338 BCE
Artaxerxes IV	338 - 336 BCE
Darius III	336 - 330 BCE
Artaxerxes V	330 - 329 BCE

Killed by Alexander III ending the Achaemenid dynasty.

Argead dynasty
Alexander III of Macedon	336 - 323 BCE
Philip III	323 - 317 BCE
Alexander IV	323 - 309 BCE

Seleucid Empire

Seleucus I Nicator	311 - 281 BCE
Antiochus I Soter	281 - 261 BCE
Antiochus II Theos	261 - 246 BCE
Seleucus II Callinicus	246 - 225 BCE
Seleucus III Ceraunus	225 - 223 BCE
Antiochus III the Great	223 - 187 BCE
Seleucus IV Philopator	187 - 175 BCE
Antiochus IV Mithridates	175 - 163 BCE
Antiochus V Eupator	163 - 161 BCE
Demetrius I Soter	161 - 150 BCE
Alexander Balas	150 - 146 BCE
Demetrius II Nicator	146 - 139 BCE
Antiochus VI Dionysus	145 - 142 BCE
Antiochus VII Sidetes	139 - 129 BCE

Parthian Empire

Arsaces I	247 - 211 BCE
Arsaces II	211 - 185 BCE
Arsaces III	185 - 170 BCE
Phraates I	170 - 167 BCE
Mithridates I	167 - 132 BCE
Arsaces VI	132 - 127 BCE
Arsaces VII	127 - 126 BCE
Arsaces VIII Vologases	126 - 122 BCE
Arsaces IX	122 - 121 BCE
Arsaces X Mithridates II	121 - 91 BCE
Arsaces XI Gotarzes I	91 - 87 BCE
Arsaces XII	91 - 77 BCE
Arsaces XIII	88 - 67 BCE
Arsaces XIV Orodes I	80 - 75 BCE
Arsaces XV	77 - 70 BCE
Arsaces XVI	77 - 66 BCE
Arsaces XVII Phraates III	70 - 57 BCE
Arsaces XVIII	66 - 63 BCE
Arsaces XIX Mithridates III	65 - 54 BCE
Arsaces XX Orodes II	57 - 38 BCE
Arsaces XXI Pacorus I	50 - 38 BCE
Arsaces XXII Phraates IV	38 - 2 BCE
Arsaces XXIII Tiridates II	30 - 25 BCE
Arsaces XXIV Mithridates	12 - 9 BCE
Arsaces XXV Phraates V	2 BCE - 4 CE

Arsaces XXVI Orodes III	4 - 6
Arsaces XXVII Vonones I	8 - 12
Arsaces XXVIII Artabanus III	10 - 40
Arsaces XXIX Tiridates III	35 - 36
Arsaces XXX Cinnamus	37 - 40
Arsaces XXXI Gotarzes II	40 - 51
Arsaces XXXII Vardanes I	40 - 46
Arsaces XXXIII Vonones II	45 - 51
Arsaces XXXIV Mithridates	49 - 50
Arsaces XXXV Vologases I	51 - 77
Arsaces XXXVI Vardanes II	55 - 58
Arsaces XXXVII Vologases II	77 - 89/90
Arsaces XXXVIII Pacorus II	77 - 115
Arsaces XXXIX Artabanus IV	80 - 81
Arsaces XL Osroes I	89/90 - 130
Arsaces XLI Vologases III	89 - 109
Arsaces XLII Parthamaspates	116 - 117
Arsaces XLIII Mithridates IV	130 - 145
Arsaces XLIV	140 - 140
Arsaces XLV Vologases IV	148 - 191
Arsaces XLVI Vologases V	191 - 208
Arsaces XLVII Osroes II	190 - 195
Arsaces XLVIII Vologases VI	208 - 228
Arsaces XLIX Artabanus V	213 - 226
Arsaces L Tiridates IV	217 - 222

Sassanid Empire

Ardashir I	224 - 242
Shapur I	240 - 270
Hormizd I	270 - 271
Bahram I	271 - 274
Bahram II	274 - 293
Bahram III	293 - 293
Narseh I	293 - 302
Hormizd II	302 - 309
Adhur Narseh	309 - 309
Shapur II	309 - 379
Ardashir II	379 - 383
Shapur III	383 - 388
Bahram IV	388 - 399
Yazdegerd I	399 - 420
Bahram V	420 - 438

The Armies of Ancient Persia

Yazdegerd II	438 - 457
Hormizd III	457 - 459
Peroz I	457 - 484
Balash	484 - 488
Kavadh I	488 - 496
Djamasp	496 - 498
Kavadh I	498 - 531
Anushiravan, Khosrau I	531 - 579
Hormizd IV	579 - 590
Aparviz Khosrau II	590 - 628

House of Mihran
Chubineh Bahram VI — 590 - 591

House of Ispahbudhan
Vistahm — 591 - 596 or 600

House of Sasan
Kavadh II — 628 - 628
Ardashir III — 628 - 629

House of Mihran
Shahrbaraz — 629 - 629

House of Sasan
Khosrau III — 630 - 630
Shahbanu Borandukht — 629 - 630 (First reign)
631 - 632 (Second reign)
Peroz II Gushnasp-Bandeh — 630 - 630
Khosrau IV — 631 - 631

House of Ispahbudhan
Farrokh Hormizd — 630 - 631

House of Sasan
Hormizd VI — 630 - 631
Yazdegerd III — 632 - 651

The Armies of Ancient Persia

BIBLIOGRAPHY

Historians and Ancient Writers

Flawiusz Arrian, *Wyprawa Aleksandra Wielkiego*, tłum, H. Gesztoft-Gasztold, Wrocław 1963.
Gajusz Juliusz Cezar, *Wojna galijska*, tłum. E. Konik, Wrocław 1978.
Kasjusz Dion Kokcejanus, *Historia Rzymska* t. 1, tłum. W. Madyda, Wrocław 1967.
Diodor sycylijski, *Bibliotheke*, C. B. Welles (ed.) London 1963.
Józef Flawiusz, *Dawne Dzieje Izraela*, tłum. Z. Kubiak, J. Radożycki, Warszawa 1993.
Józef Flawiusz, *Wojna Żydowska*, tłum. J. Radożycki. Warszawa 2001.
Lucjusz Annejusz Florus, *Zarys Dziejów Rzymskich*, tłum. I. Lewandowski, Wrocław 1973.
Heliodorus, *Opowieść etiopska o Theagenesie i Chariklei*, tłum. S. Dworacki, Poznań 2000.
Herakleides z Kyme in.*Die Fragmente der griechischen Historiker*, F. Jacoby (ed.)Berlin 1923.
Herodoti, *Historiae*, editio tertia, t. I/II, Oxonii, 1943.
Herodot, *Dzieje, przeł.* S. Hammer, Warszawa 2002.
The History of al.-Tabari, vol.5., The Sassanids, The Byzantines, The Lakmids, and Yemen, (ed. Yar-Shater et. al.), Albany, 1999.
Homer, *Iliada*, tłum. K. Jeżewska, Warszawa 1999.
Ksenofont, *Wyprawa Cyrusa*, tłum. W. Madyda, Warszawa 2003.
Tytus Liwiusz, *Dzieje Rzymu od założenia miasta ks. XXXV-XL*, tłum. M. Brożek, Wrocław 1981.
Ammian Marcellinus, *Dzieje Rzymskie*, t. I, tłum. I. Lewandowski, Warszawa 2001.
Ammian Marcellinus, *Dzieje Rzymskie*, t. II, tłum. I. Lewandowski, Warszawa 2002.
Pismo Święte Starego i Nowego Testamentu, Pallottinum 1973.
Plutarch, *Antoniusz, in. Żywoty sławnych mężów*,(z żywotów równoległych), tłum. M. Brożek, Warszawa 1997.
Plutarch, Krassus in. *Żywoty sławnych mężów (z żywotów równoległych)*,tłum. M. Brożek, Warszawa 1996.
Plutarch, Lukullus in. *Żywoty sławnych mężów (z żywotów równoległych)*, tłum. M. Brożek, Warszawa 1997.
Sun-Tsu, *Sztuka Wojny*, Warszawa 1994.
Sy-Ma Ts`ien, *Syn Smoka, Fragmenty zapisków historyka*, tłum. M. J. Künstler, Warszawa 2000.

Korneliusz Tacyt, *Germania, in. Dzieła*, tłum.S. Hammer, t. II, Warszawa 1957.
Korneliusz Tacyt, *Roczniki*, tłum. S. Hammer, Wrocław 1956. Prace współczesne
К. Абдульаев, "Armour of ancient Baktria", A. Invernizzi (ed.), *In the land of the Gryphons- Papers on Central Asian Archeology in Antiquity*, Firenze 1995.
К. Абдульаев, "Nomadism in Central Asia", A. Inwernizzi (ed.), *In the Land of the Gryphons, Papers on Central Asian Archeology in Antiquity*, Firenze 1995.
F. E. Adcoc, *The Greek and Macedonian Art of War*, Berkeley 1957.
M. Andronikos, *Vergina: The Royal Tombs and the Ancient City*, Athens 1984 (wyd. II 1993)
B.Bar-Kohva, *The Seleucid Army (Organization and Tactics in the Great Campagns*, Cambridge, London 1976.
S. Bittner, *Tracht und Bewaffung des persischen Heeres zur Zeit der Achaimeniden*, München 1987.
A. D. H. Bivar, *Cavalry equipment and tactics on the Euphrates frontier*, Papers delivered at the symposium on „Byzantium and Sasanian Iran", Dumbarton Oaks 26 1972. ss. 271-301.
M. Brosius, *The Persians, An introduction*, New York 2006.
C.G.Brown, "Xenophon's Cyropedia and Military Reform in Sparta", *Journal of Hellenic Studies* 126 (2006) ss.47-65.
F. Brown, "A recently Discovered Compound Bow", *Seminarium Kondakovianum* 9, 1937. ss. 1-10.
J. Chochorowski, *Koczownicy Ukrainy Katalog wystawy*, Katowice 1996.
J. Cooles, *Archeologia doświadczalna*, tłum. M. Mickiewicz, Warszawa 1977.
J. Coulston, *Roman archery eqipment*, ala.
Е. В. Черненко, *Скифо-персидская войиа*, Киев 1984.
Е. В. Черненко, *Скифский доспех*, Киев 1968.
Е. В. Черненко, *Скифские лучники*, Киев 1981.
Е. В. Черненко, *Военное дело Скифов*, Никоолаев 1997.
O. Dalera (ed)., *Mocarstwa świata*, tłum.B. Kruk, Warszawa 1994.
R. E. Dupy, T. N. Dupy, *Historia wojskowości*, Starożytność-średniowiecze, tłum. M. Urbański Warszawa 1999.
M. Edwards, "Syberyjscy Scytowie, Kurhan pełen złota", *National Geographic* Nr 6, (45) czerwiec 2003. ss. 39-55.
Л. А. Евтюхова, *Стремия танской эпохи из уйбатского чаатаса*, Краткие Собщения о Доккладах и Полевых Исследованиях Института Археологии и Матеряльной культуры

XXXIII, Москва 1948, сс. 40-44.

"Excavation of Spring and Autumn period tomb no. 251 and Pit of figures of Horses and Chariots Jinshangcun in Taiyuan", part 9, Wenwu, ss. 78-80.

E. Erdberg-Consten, Das Alte China, Stuttgart 1958.

K. Erdman, *Die Kunst Irans*, Berlin 1953.

K.Farokh, *Shadows In the Desert, Ancien Persia At War,* Londyn 2007

M. Gawlikowski, *Sztuka Syrii*, Warszawa 1976.

R. Ghirschman, *Iran: Parthians and Sassanians*, London 1962.

R. Ghirschman, *Perse. Proto-Iraniens, Medes, Achemenides*, Paris 1963.

Gold der Skythen. Schätze aus der Staatlichen Eremitage St. Petersburg, 1993.

B. Goldman, *Pictorial graffiti of Dura-Europos, Parthica*, Incontri di culture nel mondo antico, Pisa, Roma 1 1999, ss. 19-107.

М. В. Горельик, *Сакийский доспех*, Б. Б. Бернгард, Г. М. Льевин, (ед.), Центральная Азия Новые памятники писсменности и исскуства,Сборик статей, Москва 1987 с. 118

M. Granet, *Cywilizacja chińska*, (tłum.) M. J. Kunstler, Warszawa 1995.

P. Green, *Aleksander Wielki*, (tłum.) A. Konarek, Warszawa 1978.

N. G. L. Hammond, *Alexander the Great: King Commander and the Statesman*, Park Ridge (NJ) 1980.

N. G. L. Hammond, *Filip Macedoński*, tłum. J. Lang, Poznań 2002.

N. G. L. Hammond, *Geniusz Aleksandra Wielkiego*, tłum. J. Lang, Poznań 2000.

N. G. L. Hammond, *Starożytna Macedonia*, tłum. A. Chankowski, Warszawa 1999.

J. Harmatta (ed.), *History of civilizations of Central Asia*, Paris 1994.

E. Hartley Edwards, *Księga koni*, tłum. M. Redlicki, Warszawa 1993.

Z. Haszczyc, *Wyprawa przeciw Partom w latach 114-117 i zwrot w polityce zagranicznej Cesarstwa Rzymskiego po objęciu władzy przez Hadriana*, Meander 1975, ss. 143-156.

А. М. Хазанов, *Очерки военного дела Сарматов*, Москба 1971.

А. Хазунов, *Катафрактарии и их роль б истори военного искуса*, В.Д.И, 1968, нр.1, сс. 180-191.

D. Head, *The Achemenid Persian Army*, Kingswood Grove 1992.

P. Hessler, "Ożywić skarby", *National Geographic*, nr. 10 (25), Październik 2001. ss. 71-91.

Й. Ильиасоб, Д. В. Русанов, "A study on the Bone Plates from Orlat", "Silk Road Art and Archeology", V 1997/1998 *Journal of the Institute of Silk Road Studies*, Kamakura.

М. А Итина, J. А. Рапапорт (ed.) *Культура и исскуство древнего Хорезма*, Москва 1981.

P. Iwaszkiewicz, W. Łoś, M. Stępień, *Władcy i wodzowie starożytności*

Słownik, Warszawa 1998.

M. Junkelman, *Die Reiter Roms*, t. III, Mainz am Rhein 1991.

B. Kaim, *Irańska ideologia władzy królewskiej w okresie panowania Sasanidów*, Warszawa 1997.

B. Kaim, *Sztuka starożytnego Iranu*, Warszawa 1996.

J. K. Kozłowski (ed.), *Encyklopedia historyczna świata*, Kraków 1999.

A. Krawczuk, *Maraton*, Warszawa 1989.

A. Krawczuk, *Neron*, Warszawa 1988.

G. Lach, "Sztuka wojenna starożytnej Grecji; Od zakończenia wojen perskich do wojny korynckiej", *Zabrze* 2008, ss. 99-100.

J. Laesse, *Ludy Asyrii*, (tłum.) G. Krasicka-Meuszyńska, a. l. a.

T. E. Lawrence, *Siedem filarów mądrości*, (tłum.) J. Schwakopf, Warszawa 1971.

J. Maroń, "Przed pierwszym starciem", *Gazeta rycerska*, 2, 2002. ss.113-116.

M. Mielczarek, *Cataphracti and Clibanari Studies on the Heavy Armoured Cavalry of the Ancient World*, Łódź 1993.

M. Mielczarek, *Cataphracts- A Parthian Element in the Seleucid Art of War*, Electrum II.

J. Murphy-O'Connor, *Przewodnik po Ziemi Świętej*, (tłum.) M. Burdajewicz, Warszawa 2001.

M. J. Olbrycht, *Aleksander Wielki i świat irański*, Rzeszów 2004.

A. T. Olmstead, *Dzieje Imperium Perskiego*, (tłum.) K. Wolicki, Warszawa 1974.

H. Onuma, D.i J. DeProspero, *Kyudo, Japońska sztuka łucznictwa*, tłum. W. Nowakowski, Bydgoszcz 2001.

L. Podhorecki, *Tatarzy*, Warszawa 1975.

E. Polito, *Fulgentibus armis, introduzione allo studio dei fregi d'armi antichi*, Roma 1998.

Г. А. Пугаченкова, *О панцырном вооружени парфянского и бактрийского воиинства*, В.Д.И. 2, 1966, сс. 27-43.

Г. А. Пугаченкова, *Скульптура Халчаяна*, Моссква 1971.

А. А. Пузикова, "Новые курганы скифского времини Белгородской Области", *Краткие Собщения о Докклладах и Полевых Исследованиях Института Археологии и Матеряльной культуры*, 107, Москва 1966, сс. 80-91.

M. Roaf, *Mezopotamia. Wielkie kultury świata*, tłum. H. Turczyn Zalewska, Warszawa 1998.

G. Roux, *Mezopotamia*, Warszawa 1998.

М. И. Ростовцев, *The excavations at Dura-Europos conducted by Yale University and the French Academy of inscriptions and Letters*, Preliminary Report of Sixth Season of Work, New Haven 1936.

М. И. Ростовцев, *Dura-Europos and its Art*, Oxford 1938.
В.А. Семенов, *Суглуг-хем и Хайыракан: могильники скифского времини в центрально-тувинской котловине*,
E. Schmidt, *Persepolis*, vol. 2, Chicago 1953.
B. Składanek, *Historia Persji* t. I, Warszawa 1999.
С. А. Скоры, "Скифски довги мечи", *Археология* 1980, 37. cc. 24-25.
B. Stawiski, *Sztuka Azji Środkowej*, tłum. I. Dulewiczowa, Warszawa 1988.
D. Stronach, "Pasargadae"; *A Report on the Excavations Conducted by the British Institute of Persian Studies from 1961 to 1963*, Oxford 1978.
G. Sumner, *Roman Army Wars of the Empire, Brassey's History of Uniforms*, London 1997.
A. Świderkówna, *Hellenika Wizerunek epoki od Aleksandra do Augusta*, Warszawa1974.
W. Świętosławski, "Uzbrojenie koczowników wielkiego stepu w czasach ekspansji Mongołów (XII- XIV w.)", *Acta Archaeologica Lodziensia* nr 40, Łódź 1996, s. 39-40.
R. Takeuchi, "The Parthian Shot in Hunting Scenes", *Bulletin of the Ancient Orient Museum*, vol. XXII, 2001/2 Tokyo.
T. Talbot Rice, *The Scytians*, London 1958.
Taybuga, *Saracen Archery an English Version and Exposition of a Mameluke Work on Archery (ca. 1368)*, J. D. Latham et. al. ed. London 1970.
W. Tyloch, *Dzieje ksiąg Starego Testamentu Szkice z krytyki biblijnej*, Warszawa1985.
L. Vanden Berghe, *Reliefs Rupestres de l'Iran ancien*, Bruxelles 1984.
H. von Gall, *Das Reiterkampfbild in der iranischen und iranisch beeinflussten Kunst partischer und sasanidischer Zeit*, Berlin 1992.
J. Warry, *Armie świata antycznego*, Warszawa 1995.
B. Weintraub, "Gwałtowna śmierć w solnej żupie", *National Geographic* vol. 2 nr.4 (7) kwiecień 2000.
P. Wilcox, A. Mcbride, *Rome's enemies 3, Parhians and Sassanid Persians*, Men-at-arms series 175, London 1986.
E. Wipszycka (ed.) *Vademecum Historyka Starożytnej Grecji i Rzymu*, Warszawa 2001.
R. Wojna, *Wielki świat nomadów, między Chinami a Europą*, Warszawa 1983.
J. Wolski, *Dzieje i upadek imperium Seleucydów*, Kraków 1999.
J. Wolski, "Servitia i ich funkcja i znaczenie w społeczeństwie irańskim okresu Arsacydów", *Elektrum V* vol.4, Kraków 2000;
S. Zhangru, "Complete Sets of Weapons from the Yin (Shang) Site at Xiao Tun", *Annual report of the History and Language Institute of the Academia Sinica*, 22, 1950.

S. Żygulski jr. *Broń starożytna Grecja, Rzym, Galia, Germania*, Warszawa 1998.

S. Żygulski jr., *Stara broń w polskich zbiorach*, Warszawa 1984.

Artykuły i strony w Internecie Азятитцкий лук, http://www.atarn.org/mongolian/asian_bow_r.htm.

B. Burris-Davis, *Parthian horses*, http://parthia.com/pathia_horses.burris.htm.

Czas łuku, Strona towarzystwa łucznictwa tradycyjnego. http://www.bowtime.waw.pl/trad_corean.html.

B. Dwyer, *Early Archers Rings*, http://www.atarn.org/chinese/thumbrings_rings.htm.

J. Lendring, *The behistun inscription*, www.livius.org/be-bm/behistun/behistun01.html.

Parthian Kings, http//www.livius.org/pan-paz/parthia/kings.html.

Łucznictwo tradycyjne, http//int/luk/archer~1/8t3.htm.

M. Mode, *Heroic fights and dying heroes- The Orlat battle plaqe and the roots of Sogdian art*, Çrân ud Ançrân Webfestschrift Marshak 2003;

W. M. Moseley, *An essay on archery*, http://www.atarn.org/islamic/persian.htm.

В. П. Никоноров, *The use of Music in Ancient Warfare: Partian and Central Asian Warfare* in: 9th. International Sumposium of the "Study Group on Music Archeology", Kloster Michaelstein in Blankenburg (Germany), mailto@harpa.com?subiect=Music Archeology.

S.Selby,*The Visible Chinese Bow*, http://www.atarn.org/chinese/visible_bow_/visible.htm.

Q. Zhuyong, *Horsback Archery Method, in. An Collection and Explanation of the Seven MilitaryClassics*, http://www.atarn.org/chinese/horseback/Quingxi-%20Zhuyong.htm.

Wykaz skrótów Anab. – Ksenofont, *Wyprawa Cyrusa*, tłum. W. Madyda, Warszawa 2003.

Ant, – Plutarch, "Antoniusz", in. *Żywoty sławnych mężów,*(z żywotów równoległych), tłum. M. Brożek, Warszawa 1997.

Daw.Dz.Iz. – Józef Flawiusz, *Dawne Dzieje Izraela*, tłum. Z. Kubiak, J. Radożycki, Warszawa 1993.

Dz.Rz, – Tytus Liwiusz, *Dzieje Rzymu od założenia miasta ks. XXXV-XL*, tłum. M. Brożek, Wrocław 1981.

Dz.Rz. – Ammian Marcellinus, *Dzieje Rzymskie*, t. I-II, tłum. I. Lewandowski, Warszawa 2001/02.

Et. – Heliodorus, *Opowieść etiopska o Theagenesie i Chariklei*, tłum. S. Dworacki, Poznań 2000.

Ger. – Korneliusz Tacyt, *Germania, in. Dzieła*, tłum.S. Hammer, t. II, Warszawa 1957.

His.Rz. – Kasjusz Dion Kokcejanus, *Historia Rzymska* t. 1, tłum. W. Madyda, Wrocław 1967.
Il. – Homer, *Iliada*, tłum. K. Jeżewska, Warszawa 1999.
Krass. – Plutarch, *Krassus in. Żywoty sławnych mężów* (z żywotów równoległych), tłum. M. Brożek, Warszawa 1996.
Luc. – Plutarch, *Lukullus in. Żywoty sławnych mężów* (z żywotów równoległych), tłum. M. Brożek, Warszawa 1997.
Odys. – Homer, *Odyseja.* per. – z perskiego.

Index

INDEX OF PLACES

Ai-Khanoum 171, 202, 217, 234, 238
Alans 188, 334
Albanian 117
Alexandria 12, 208, 209, 215
Aleksandrovka 36
Altai 132, 133, 134, 296, 308, 310, 315, 327, 347, 356
Amida 319, 320, 321, 335
Anatolia 4, 14, 18, 34, 37, 38, 39, 98, 336, 344
Antioch 12, 14, 17, 137, 139, 202, 203, 204, 205, 208, 209, 336
Arachosia 25
Aria 25, 89, 90
Armenia 3, 4, 10, 11, 12, 14, 15, 16, 17, 18, 25, 41, 44, 90, 126, 140, 141, 142, 143, 144, 149, 151, 204, 243, 244, 247, 271, 273, 325, 334, 335, 336
Ashgabat 20, 179, 349
Asia Minor 4, 6, 7, 8, 14, 18, 29, 36, 41, 45, 59, 88, 89, 90, 99, 107, 126, 270, 329, 332
Assyria 3, 4, 25, 26, 27, 30, 41, 60, 64, 67, 74, 90, 95, 124, 125, 126, 127, 169, 188, 190, 332
Atropatene 11, 150
Attica 7
Azerbaijan 3, 4, 336
Babylonia 3, 4, 10, 25, 26, 27, 30, 83, 117, 331, 332
Bactria 9, 10, 13, 19, 25, 59, 89, 97, 108, 117, 130, 134, 136, 137, 138, 145, 204, 205, 208, 216, 217, 220, 221, 234, 235, 237, 238, 333, 337, 341, 344, 345, 347
Bar Hill 177
Belmesa 339
Bisotun 32
Biszapur 14
Bithynia 254
Black Sea 8, 17, 41, 60, 128, 186, 332
Byzantine 16, 17, 18, 19, 307, 315, 325, 326, 336
Cadusii 104, 117
Cappadocia 14, 25, 243, 335
Carleon 177
Carrhae (Carrae, Harran) 10, 138, 139, 141, 142, 144, 149, 176, 177, 218, 243, 246, 268, 271, 334, 355
Caspian Sea 3, 9, 47, 241, 337, 342
Caucasus 3, 15, 17, 18, 124, 336
Celts 3, 210, 278, 352, 353, 356,
Čertomlyk 48
China 13, 19, 22, 86, 130, 132, 134, 135, 141, 176, 197, 219, 226, 230, 231, 296, 301, 308, 310, 313, 347, 356
Chaeronea 103, 112
Chorezm 35
Chorsabad (Dur-Szarukin) 75
Cimmerians 26, 124, 125, 126, 127
Colchis 90, 124
Constantinople 18, 336
Ctesiphon 13, 14, 16, 18, 19, 285, 300, 325, 334, 335, 336
Cunaxa 8, 25, 31, 74, 83, 89, 94, 96, 98, 111, 112, 121, 122, 332
Cyprus 6, 18, 26, 61, 91
Cz'ao 135
Cz'in 135
Dahae 9, 22, 62, 122, 130, 132, 133, 134, 135, 136, 137, 141, 148, 168, 171, 215, 216, 242, 243, 338, 342, 345
Dara 18
Dura-Europos 20, 14, 83, 174, 177, 178, 180, 183, 184, 185, 190, 231, 239, 243, 247, 249, 250, 251, 253, 254, 259, 261, 262, 264, 276, 280, 305, 319, 327, 339, 350
Edessa 14, 18, 335
Egypt 4, 5, 6, 8, 24, 25, 45, 38, 39, 88, 89, 94, 99, 104, 107, 153, 154, 158, 172, 208, 209, 210, 213, 214, 215, 331, 332, 334, 336, 339, 354
Elam 4, 26, 64, 98, 116, 331

Elephantine 24, 89
Erebuni (Erevan) 54
Eretria 7
Estahr 272, 273
Ethiopia 5, 87, 89, 274, 294, 301
Euboea 7
Euphrates 3, 20, 98, 99, 103, 144, 171, 227, 354
Faleron 41
Fars (Parsua, Persyda) 4, 9, 13, 20, 274, 275, 318, 326
Firuzabad 205, 260, 262, 263, 275, 277, 278, 279, 280, 284, 286
Fraaspa (Fraaty) 11
Gandara 26
Gansu 136
Gaugamela 8, 46, 63, 71, 94, 104, 105, 112, 117, 121, 333
Ghassanids 16
Granicus (Granic) 8, 60, 63, 96, 105, 107, 111, 112, 324, 333
Greco-Bactria 9, 130, 136, 234, 238
Halys 4, 185
Hamadan (Ekbatana) 4
Han (dynasty) 4, 135, 136, 171, 190, 230
Hatra 13
Hellada 208
Hellespont (Sea Marmara) 8, 49, 105, 107, 333
Homs (Emesa) 248
Hormuzdegan 273, 281, 316
Hsiung-nu 135, 136, 310, 313
Hulajgorod 31
Humbuz-Tepe 36, 38, 45, 224
Huns 16, 134, 176, 186, 188, 306, 307, 310, 315, 320, 352, 356
Hydaspes (Dżhelam) 111
Hyrkania 10, 71, 116
Ilurat 223, 227
Imgur-Enlil (Balawat) 26
Indus (Hinduš) 24, 25
Indo-sakae 239, 243, 255
Ionia 6, 24, 25, 88, 89, 94, 95, 107, 332
Iraq 3, 117
Iran 3, 4, 11, 15, 20, 21, 22, 24, 25, 27, 28, 32, 35, 36, 38, 41, 42, 43, 45, 47, 48, 49, 50, 52, 53, 54, 56, 57, 59, 60, 63, 65, 68, 69, 70, 73, 81, 82, 85, 87, 89, 90, 91, 95, 98, 99, 111, 112, 122, 124, 133, 139, 140, 141, 144, 152, 168, 170, 179, 181, 182, 183, 184, 186, 188, 189, 192, 193, 194, 197, 198, 200, 202, 203, 204, 205, 208, 217, 226, 227, 230, 234, 238, 241, 242, 244, 246, 247, 258, 259, 260, 267, 272, 273, 275, 276, 277, 287, 291, 293, 298, 302, 303, 305, 306, 307, 310, 312, 314, 320, 327, 331, 334, 336, 337, 340, 341, 342, 343, 344, 349, 351, 352, 353, 355, 356,
Jaksartes (Syr-Daria) 62
Jerusalem 11, 19, 216, 329
Jewish people 10, 11, 12, 89, 140, 141, 150, 216, 265, 266, 349
Kalmykova 228, 229
Kizkapan 127
Koi Krylgam Kala 48, 137
Kurdistan 4, 11, 126
Kushan 11, 13, 14, 15, 134, 151, 171, 181, 182, 183, 185, 186, 189, 206, 216, 219, 220, 221, 231, 234, 235, 238, 239, 240, 241, 247, 250, 259, 273, 307, 315, 316, 326, 334, 341, 345, 347, 353,
Kysmyči 40, 41, 217
Lakhmid 16
Levant 18
Lydia 4, 36, 80, 88, 89, 96, 97, 98, 331
Macedonia 3, 7, 8, 22, 24, 25, 27, 30, 32, 44, 48, 58, 60, 61, 62, 63, 67, 70, 71, 88, 91, 94, 95, 96, 98, 103, 105, 107, 110, 111, 112, 114, 115, 116, 117, 119, 121, 133, 142, 201, 202, 204, 205, 206, 207, 211, 212, 213, 214, 217, 227, 246, 264, 268, 269, 279, 286, 324, 332, 333, 337, 340, 342, 344, 345, 347, 348, 350, 351, 352, 353, 354, 357
Magnesia 202, 203, 215, 333
Maka 25, 176
Maranga 300, 335

Marathon 7, 24, 40, 41, 42, 47, 87, 94, 332
Margiana 139
Massagetae 5, 16, 28, 29, 45, 59, 112, 350, 351, 352
Mede 3, 4, 6, 18, 26, 27, 37, 38, 41, 42, 46, 50, 52, 53, 56, 59, 64, 65, 68, 69, 70, 71, 73, 74, 75, 81, 93, 94, 97, 116, 127, 201, 204, 331, 337, 349
Memphis 31, 38, 40, 75, 215
Mesopotamia 8, 9, 10, 12, 13, 14, 15, 16, 18, 26, 27, 36, 41, 60, 90, 95, 96, 98, 124, 141, 142, 143, 150, 153, 168, 310, 320, 323, 325, 334, 335, 336, 337, 353
Mongols 129, 133, 141, 146, 148, 154, 165, 166, 167, 171, 172, 174, 178, 186, 190, 199, 228, 230, 269, 307, 309, 311, 314, 327, 339, 343, 356,
Mycale 8, 332
Nabatea 12
Naqsh-e Rustam 293, 300
Nehawend 19
Nisibis 16, 316, 334, 335
Novaya Ryžanovka 75
Olympia 38, 40
Orlat 38, 45, 137, 140, 148, 170, 171, 175, 176, 184, 190, 191, 200, 201, 217, 218, 219, 224, 225, 226, 227, 229, 230, 231, 233, 238, 239, 240, 242, 254, 266, 314, 349,
Palestine 6, 13, 18, 140, 208, 209, 334, 337, 354
Palmyra 14, 329, 335
Panion 110
Panticapaeum 88, 227
Parthia 132, 133, 134, 136, 137, 138, 139, 140, 141, 142, 143, 144, 145, 146, 147, 148, 149, 150, 151, 153, 168, 170, 171, 174, 175, 176, 177, 179, 181, 182, 183, 185, 186, 187, 188, 189, 190, 197, 198, 203, 204, 205, 207, 209, 215, 216, 217, 230, 231, 239, 240, 242, 243, 244, 246, 247, 250, 251, 259. 260, 261, 262, 263, 264, 265, 266, 267, 268, 269, 270, 271
Pasargadae 5, 20, 47
Pazyryk 44, 127, 131
Pergamon 120, 203, 205, 206, 209, 215, 344
Persepolis (Parsa, Parsua) 6, 20, 30, 31, 33, 42, 43, 45, 47, 49, 50, 52, 53, 54, 55, 56, 57, 64, 65, 68, 69, 70, 72, 73, 75, 77, 83, 85, 86, 87, 89, 127, 273, 333, 346, 356, 337,
Persia 3, 4, 5, 6, 7, 8, 9, 12, 13, 14, 15, 16, 17, 18, 19, 20, 21, 22, 24, 25, 26, 27, 28, 29, 30, 31, 32, 34, 36, 37, 38, 39, 40, 41, 43, 44, 45, 46, 47, 48, 54, 59, 60, 61, 62, 63, 64, 65, 66, 67, 68, 69, 70, 71, 74, 75, 76, 77, 81, 83, 84, 85, 87, 88, 89, 90, 92, 94, 95, 96, 97, 98, 99, 101, 103, 105, 107, 108, 110, 111, 112, 114, 115, 116, 117, 119, 121, 127, 128, 132, 141, 150, 152, 168, 169, 171, 183, 187, 189, 201, 203, 206, 213, 216, 251, 254, 258, 259, 260, 264, 267, 268, 270, 272, 273, 274, 275, 276, 277, 278, 279, 280, 281, 282, 284, 285, 294, 296, 300, 301, 302, 305, 306, 307, 308, 310, 315, 317, 318, 319, 320, 321, 322, 323, 324, 325, 327, 328, 329, 331, 333, 335, 336, 337, 338, 341, 342, 343, 344, 345, 346, 349, 350, 352, 353, 356,
Petra 12
Phoenicia 189
Pinaros 112, 114
Plataea 119, 62, 84, 91, 94, 99, 119, 333
Plataeans 7
Qadisiya 19
Qasr-al Hayr al Gharbi 266
Qum-Darya 161, 175, 176, 313, 314, 320, 338, 339
Ram Hormuz 19
Rhodes 18, 209
Sagartians 62
Sakae 6, 10, 28, 29, 31, 38, 41, 44, 49, 51, 59, 62, 90, 111, 117, 121, 133, 134, 137, 138, 139, 140, 148, 171, 176, 185, 186, 189, 190, 198, 200, 201, 207, 216, 217, 224, 226, 231, 233, 234, 239, 240,

242, 243, 244, 254, 285, 286, 331, 334, 349, 352, 354, 355
Salamis 7, 61, 332
Samarkand 41, 170, 191, 217
Sar Mashhad 285
Sarmatians 134, 135, 136, 182, 185, 225, 240, 260, 269, 278, 343, 356
Sattagydia 25
Scythia 5, 6, 8, 16, 25, 26, 27, 28, 29, 30, 31, 33, 35, 36, 37, 39, 41, 44, 45, 46, 47, 48, 54, 55, 57, 58, 59, 60, 62, 63, 75, 77, 78, 81, 83, 91, 92, 126, 127, 128, 129, 131, 132, 133, 134, 135, 136, 137, 138, 140, 143, 144, 146, 152, 154, 155, 156, 165, 166, 167, 168, 169, 170, 171, 172, 182, 184, 185, 186, 189, 198, 201, 215, 216, 226, 230, 231, 233, 247, 264, 270, 278, 307, 331, 337, 338, 341, 342, 344, 346, 347, 352, 353, 355,
Seleucia 3, 8, 9, 10, 14, 63, 133, 134, 137, 138, 144, 157, 187, 191, 201, 202, 203, 204, 205, 206, 207, 208, 209, 210, 211, 212, 213, 214, 215, 217, 225, 234, 242, 244, 246, 247, 333, 343, 344, 349, 351, 354,
Shami 185, 186, 189, 193, 194, 261
Shang 152, 153, 308, 309, 343, 347, 365
Sogdia 25, 31, 145, 148, 158, 171, 216, 231, 234, 281, 282
Sparta 7, 8, 84, 306, 332
Old Nisa (Nisa, Mitrdatkert) 179, 206
Mogila 43
Subotiv 125, 126
Tag-e Bustan 259, 266, 275, 294, 295, 296, 297, 298, 315
Taht-e Sangin 53, 159, 189, 231
Taht-e Suleiman 325
Tang-e Sarvak 138, 184, 186, 227, 260, 261, 262, 263, 264, 265
Taurus 316
Termez 231, 241
Thermopylae 94, 214, 332, 333
Tochar 134, 154, 156, 230, 238, 345, 347, 356, 357
Toung K'ou 227, 307
Thrace 6, 24, 25, 81, 91, 348
Turks 17, 18, 150, 152, 186, 199, 315, 336
Turkmenistan 3, 20, 242, 349
Yemen 18, 315
Yin (Yinxu) 152, 308
Yrzi 158, 164, 170, 171, 172, 174, 175, 177, 357
Yüe 134, 136, 314
Zagros 3, 124
Zanjan 186
Ždanovo 36
Zeugma 144

INDEX OF NAMES

Abd al-Malik 329
Abdalonymus 58
Abdulaev, K. 223, 234
Achaemenid 3, 4, 5, 6, 7, 8, 17, 24, 25, 26, 27, 28, 29, 34, 36, 37, 38, 39, 41, 42, 44, 46, 48, 49, 54, 55, 59, 60, 61, 62, 63, 64, 70, 71, 75, 76, 78, 80, 82, 83, 85, 87, 88, 89, 90, 91, 92, 93, 94, 95, 96, 97, 98, 99, 104, 105, 107, 111, 112, 116, 117, 119, 121, 127, 132, 134, 144, 157, 168, 169, 170, 177, 188, 189, 195, 200, 201, 203, 205, 206, 216, 217, 224, 230, 247, 268, 269, 270, 274, 284, 317, 318, 319, 320, 321, 326, 327, 328, 331, 332, 337, 338, 342, 344, 345, 348, 352, 355,
Alexander the Great 3, 8, 13, 27, 30, 32, 35, 37, 48, 54, 57, 58, 59, 60, 61, 62, 65, 69, 70, 75, 77, 82, 83, 89, 90, 91, 94, 95, 96, 98, 101, 103, 105, 107, 108, 110, 111, 112, 114, 116, 117, 119, 121, 132, 133, 140, 146, 170, 201, 202, 206, 207, 208, 210, 211, 217, 227, 241, 243, 275, 294, 323, 324, 333, 334, 337, 344, 351, 353, 354, 355
Anahita 273
Andragoras 9, 130, 134, 137, 215, 333
Antioch III 208, 212
Antony (Marc) 141, 142, 149, 150, 151, 334

Appian of Alexandria 203
Ardashir I 277, 334, 355
Ardashir III 259, 275, 279, 294, 301
Arrian 27, 46, 47, 48, 54, 59, 61, 65, 67, 71, 94, 95, 96, 103, 104, 107, 110, 114, 116, 133, 200, 207, 227, 267, 300, 323
Arsaces I 9, 133, 136, 208, 272, 333, 338
Arsaces II 9, 137
Arsacids 9, 11, 14, 22, 141, 144, 149, 150, 151, 182, 186, 200, 215, 241, 242, 259, 264, 269, 272, 275, 278, 279, 286, 296, 306, 317, 342, 351
Arsites 60, 105, 107, 108, 110, 111, 112
Artaban V 205, 260, 262, 272, 277
Artabazes 140, 144, 149
Artaphernes 7, 332
Artaxerxes II 8, 74, 83, 89, 101, 104, 332
Artaxerxes III 8, 89, 94, 103, 332
Artybios 61
Aspatines 49, 50, 55
Aššurnasirapli II 26
Astyages 4, 331, 337
Azes 243, 255
Bahram Czobin 15, 18, 336
Bahram II 15, 282, 284, 285, 286, 288, 289,
Bahram V Gur 16, 306, 335
Bessos 117, 333, 337
Cambyses I 4, 5, 6, 27, 55, 89
Cambyses II 55
Cardaces 66, 77, 92, 93, 94, 104, 114, 116, 117, 119, 170, 340, 346
Cassius Dio 142, 143, 149, 267, 270
Corbulo, Gnaeus Domitius 11, 142
Crassus, Marcus Lucinius 143, 144, 145, 146, 147, 148, 149, 177, 204, 243, 244, 246, 250, 267, 269, 270, 271,
Cyrus the Younger 8, 31, 36, 47, 48, 59, 71, 74, 89, 91, 98, 99, 101, 103, 104, 332, 335
Cyrus II, the Great 4, 5, 22, 27, 28, 29, 45, 89, 96, 97, 98, 200, 331, 337, 349
Dariusz I the Great 5, 6, 7, 13, 14, 18, 24, 25, 26, 27, 31, 32, 50, 55, 56, 60, 61, 65, 66, 67, 68, 70, 77, 79, 83, 84, 85, 91, 98, 134, 169, 331, 332, 337, 346
Dariusz III 8, 10, 11, 37, 44, 48, 49, 59, 67, 81, 89, 105, 114, 116, 117, 119, 121, 132, 138, 139, 140, 142, 157, 170, 332, 333, 334, 337, 355
Datys 7
Diodorus 27, 47, 70, 71, 200, 324
Eutropius 316
Festus 316
Florus 140, 322
Fu Hao 308, 309
Gordian III 14, 285, 335
Gotarzes I 247
Grumbates 335
Hadrian 12, 150, 177, 335
Heliodorus 274, 275
Heraclius 18, 19, 325, 336
Herodotus 4, 5, 27, 28, 29, 30, 31, 41, 45, 46, 47, 48, 49, 54, 59, 60, 61, 62, 64, 65, 66, 67, 71, 74, 75, 77, 83, 84, 85, 86, 87, 89, 90, 91, 93, 94, 96, 97, 99, 104, 116, 127, 132, 140, 200, 201, 274, 301, 345, 349, 351, 352, 356,
Hormuzd I 225
Hormuzd II 227
Hydarnes 71, 94
Josephus 140, 141, 216, 266
Julian the Apostate 16, 274, 316, 320, 323, 325, 335
Justin 27, 139, 140, 149, 216
Kanishka 239, 241
Kartir 15
Khosrow I 17, 336
Khosrow II 18, 19, 305, 325, 336
Leonidas 7
Livy 202, 203, 212, 243, 267
Lucan 269
Mardi ben Ali al-Tarsusi 305
Mardonius 6, 7, 59, 61, 94
Masistius 30, 31, 48
Maurice 18, 336
Megapanos 71

Merena 300
Mihran 18
Mithridates I 9, 61, 186, 333
Mithridates II 10, 334
Mithridates III 10, 138, 220, 337
Naram-Sin 153
Narseh 15, 335
Nero 11, 247, 334
Odenathus 335
Onesilus 61
Orodes I 138, 220
Orodes II 11, 139, 140, 144, 149, 271, 355
Otanes 60, 71, 74
Pakorosa 216
Papak 13, 15, 272, 293
Partamasir 13
Peroz 16, 17, 315, 335, 312
Philip the Arab 14, 335
Philip of Macedonia 27, 103, 105, 110, 202, 207, 208, 332, 342, 345, 351, 352, 353, 357,
Phraates II 10, 138, 333, 334
Plutarch 67, 138, 139, 140, 143, 144, 145, 146, 147, 148, 149, 150, 151, 176, 177, 182, 186, 204, 216, 243, 244, 246, 250, 261, 267, 268, 269, 271, 273
Polybius 209, 210, 211, 212, 213, 214, 243
Pompey, Gnaeus 3, 10, 354
Procopius 16
Ptolemy 8, 9, 96, 117
Ptolemy IV 208, 209, 213, 354
Rhadamistas 11
Shalmaneser III 26, 64
Sargon 26, 126, 331
Sassanids 13, 19, 63, 121, 182, 239, 254, 259, 266, 272, 273, 274, 276, 295, 296, 305, 306, 307, 313, 315, 317, 318, 323, 325, 326, 329, 336, 342, 346, 353, 356
Seleucids 9, 10, 63, 134, 201, 202, 203, 204, 208, 211, 213, 217, 246, 333, 344, 351, 354
Seleucus Nikator 8, 137, 333, 354
Shapur I 14, 15, 262, 263, 272, 285, 303, 305, 310, 316, 326, 329, 335, 356
Shapur II the Great 16, 273, 274, 275, 276, 279, 284, 295, 300, 301, 306, 307, 315, 316, 317, 320, 323, 335
Strabo 9, 66, 134, 267, 340
Sun-Tsu 25, 151
Šūren 144, 271
Surena 10, 138, 139, 140, 141, 143, 144, 145, 146, 149, 243, 244, 246, 261, 268, 269, 334, 354
Sy-ma Cz'ien 134
Szy-Huang 222
Taybuga 133, 152, 155, 164, 165, 167, 168, 169, 172, 181, 188, 189, 197, 198, 199, 310, 315
Theodosius II 16
Tigranes 71, 204, 244
Tiridates I 247
Tiridates 11
Tomyris 28, 200
Trajan 12, 150, 174, 334
Tutankhamun 153
Tyssafernes 74, 99, 101
Uthal 259
Valerian 14, 355
Vasudeva I 239
Vasudeva II 241, 242
Verus, Lucius 12, 269, 334
Wima Takto 341
Vologeses I 11, 334
Vonones 243
Xenophon 8, 27, 30, 31, 36, 38, 47, 48, 64, 67, 71, 74, 83, 89, 90, 93, 94, 95, 98, 99, 101, 103, 104, 200, 323
Xerxes 7, 8, 29, 30, 31, 48, 49, 50, 59, 60, 65, 66, 67, 71, 77, 83, 84, 85, 87, 88, 89, 91, 94, 97, 104, 116, 332
Yazdegerd II 16, 335
Yazdegerd III 19, 336

About the Author

Marek Adam Wozniak was born in Radom, Poland in 1976. He received his doctorate in archeology from Nicholas Copernicus University in Warsaw. He has participated in digs at locations in Egypt and Cyprus as well as in the near east. He specializes in the military and technical aspects of society

Look for more books from Winged Hussar Publishing, LLC – E-books, paperbacks and Limited Edition hardcovers. The best in history, science fiction and fantasy at:

>https://www. wingedhussarpublishing.com
>or follow us on Facebook at:
>Winged Hussar Publishing LLC
>Or on twitter at:
>WingHusPubLLC
>For information and upcoming publications

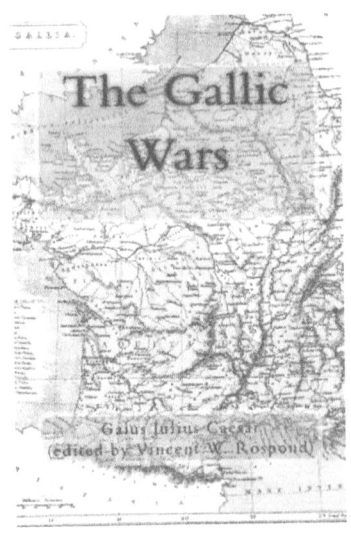

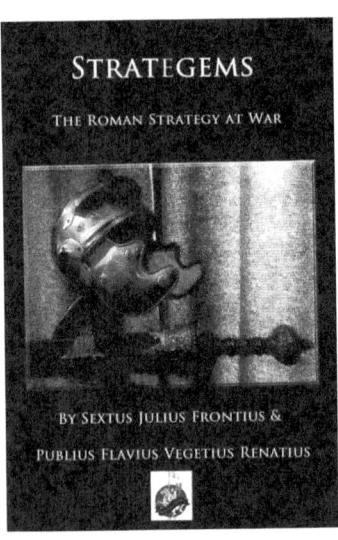